Master Beloved, who hast committed to
us the swift and solemn trust of life, since we
know not what a day may bring, but only that the
hour for serving Thee is always present, teach us
how to be constantly alert to the claims of Thy
will and the call to service.

Lay to rest, by the persuasion of Thy Spirit,
our doubts and fears. Consecrate with Thy
presence the way our feet should go ... that
our humblest work may radiate. Lift us above
unrighteous anger and mistrust into faith sublime.
May we be modest in our times of wealth, patient
in the hours of our adversity, serene in our
disappointments, and humble in our moments of
shining achievements.

In all things, draw us toward Thy perfection
that all the world may see in us Thy radiant
reflection. And keep us ever mindful that we
shine for Thee.

~ Earlyne

Astara

This book is part of a series of eight books. Altogether they cover a large and comprehensive body of esoteric material gleaned from sacred texts, timeless philosophies and teachings of Great Masters as channeled through Astara's founders, Robert and Earlyne Chaney.

Each Degree book contains 22 Lessons covering some of the most important aspects of achieving spiritual understanding, oneness with self, raising self-awareness and initiating collective, universal and even cosmic consciousness.

For more information about the content of each Degree, about other books written by Robert and Earlyne Chaney, and about Astara as a metaphysical non-profit since its beginning in 1951, visit our website - www.astara.org

Prologue

HAIL! DISCIPLE OF THE SECOND DEGREE!

The fact that you now have these pages in your possession is indicative that you have found some measure of truth in the First Degree. You have gained a higher level of spiritual understanding — thus we salute you.

We offer now the Lessons of the Second Degree with the prayer in our hearts that they will again provide new impetus to your soul-searching. In these Lessons we teach further concerning humankind on all levels of being. And through the study of the Second Degree we hope you will gain a further understanding of YOURSELF.

To know oneself is to know God — to know the Divine Being in a limited fashion, true, since the finite mind can not wholly grasp the concept of Infinity. We firmly believe the true study of humankind is to look within. We concur wholeheartedly with the immortal Socrates who said in 468 B.C.: *KNOW THYSELF!* These same words were found carved above many a gateway leading to the temples of the Mysteries. To us today they still point the way toward Mastership.

Through the Astarian Degrees, the Astarian learns that earth life is but a reflection of higher plane reality. You are taught that within each soul lies the domain of spirit through which it will become a Master. You must not cease to strive until attainment is reached. The ultimate goal is to find God and enthrone the Divine Spirit in the Holy Temple within, which every Astarian must construct, as only you can do. In order to find God you first must find yourself.

THE IMMORTAL SOCRATES

The primary requisite is *light* which makes all things visible to the disciple. So the soul, seeing the light of truth, will behold also its fellow beings and the unity of work which must be performed with them.

You learn to walk unfettered, having the listening ear which discerns the still, small inner voice that whispers deep within. You learn to keep silent that you may make no error in giving knowledge which you yourself as yet have scarcely begun to fathom. In your faithful heart you carry the devotion to Astarian principles which will cause you to live a life of truth, united in harmony and universal love. Before you, the disciple, can take your place with the initiates you must become familiar with the requirements for each successive step in unfoldment, and you find that those who instruct you can do no more than direct ... for it is *through one's own efforts* that one will become proficient.

MYSTIC ASTARIANRY

From youth to old age human beings find themselves on a path which, if properly followed, brings ever greater progress and new experiences. These awaken one's soul and develop one's spiritual qualities.

Astarianry, with the study of its Degrees, embodies the entire gamut of a life on Earth. When you understand its esoteric meaning and apply its teachings to your daily living, you gain a degree of wisdom which will enable you to make your life one of true spiritual usefulness to yourself and humanity.

From the moment you become an Astarian, life takes on new meaning. Each Degree carries you forward in soul progression. You are guided in understanding the first principles of life. You are persuaded that you are an important disciple in the ancient Order of Melchizedek — to which Astara is linked — and, as such, have a duty to fulfill in that relation.

You learn first to assume your duties as a being of the material world. Gradually you are able to withstand every test given you. You see that the temple of life must be built upon a sound foundation. As you gain in understanding you perceive that Astarianry is in itself a symbol of human life, which in turn is a reflection of reality through spiritual life.

You see in the visible universe an immense Temple built by the Grand Master Architect, the Creator of all manifested life. The temple of Astarianry is patterned after the plan of the Great Temple in that the light of wisdom shines upon it, and upon those in it who strive to learn the truth.

As a disciple you discern that you should divide your time in such a manner that there is opportunity to serve and worship the Builder of the Universe — time to search your inner space and prepare for still greater responsibilities in the future — and time to render willing service to all humanity while still being an integral and important part of your family unit in everyday living and experience. You should add to your faith in God the hope for results which will inspire further efforts. You should have that charity of soul which will prove of assistance to all. You should work in freedom and with fervent zeal, forming your character with that strength and beauty which alone comes to one of wisdom.

As you progress from one Degree to the next, you learn more of yourself as a moral citizen who has an influence of which you must make proper use. You grow to know that although you should consider all souls as your kin in a universal familyhood, you must be loyal always to truth. Insofar as you are able, you must establish conditions for peace and spiritual growth for everyone and help them gain that liberty which comes from a knowledge of truth.

Later you grasp the reality of a community upon a higher plane of life, where familial duty has grown into a definite state of spiritual love where the one great law is that of Love itself. You learn how to create an inner temple within where you may worship in truth and holiness your Father-Mother God. Having grown to a state of perpetual loving-kindness and compassion for all souls, you devote your whole energy to teaching and helping your "family" live their lives to the best of their ability and, by your example, lead them to wisdom and attainment.

Spiritual truths have always been given to the world through different types of expressions and embodiments to be acceptable to different types of minds. They are preserved through the ages, and withstand the natural changes of time and culture. These Lessons have as their purpose the illumining of truths taught in the Mystery Schools of ancient days and lands. The evolutionary changes of time now make it possible for the esoteric and symbolic teachings to be acceptable to seekers in the Aquarian Age. It is hoped they will serve the seeker of truth under the banner of Astara.

Wear your Degree title with both pride and humility, disciple of the Second Degree. You have gained the first rung of the Ladder — that which leads upward to the heart of God. Anchor your feet confidently upon that Ladder and turn your thoughts toward the second rung — the study of Astara's Second Degree.

Here we propose to probe more deeply into the mystery of humankind — the inner spiritual soul and the outer physical being ... the YOU with whom you spend every moment of your life ... the YOU with whom you are destined to spend the remainder of eternity.

What is man, that thou art mindful of him? For thou hast made him a little lower than the angels, and hast crowned him with glory and honor.
(Psalm 8:4-5)

Each soul is seemingly a separated and individualized particle of God. As a drop of water may be separated from the ocean and, regardless of its many transformations, in its final analysis remains water ... so the soul, particularized, remains a unit separate in the eternal cycles of progress, yet ever in and part of *GOD*. The soul is a divine spark cast from the Unquenchable Flame. It must, because of its inherent nature, eventually reach again its first estate as a ray of light receiving its essence from the Ineffable Light, and shine once more in harmony with God, its Father-Mother.

This spark of light, THE HUMAN BEING, has been precipitated into many wrappings of ever-coarser grades of matter until each soul is completely buried in the encompassing physical web known as earth life. The search for satisfaction is the effort of the hidden soul to answer the admonition, *KNOW THYSELF!* This effort results in evolution — the gradual refinement of the wrappings, until it is able to use them as they are intended, as vehicles through which the soul progresses.

The Supreme Being, in order to make it possible for unawakened souls to comprehend the plan of evolution, has formulated, created appropriate rites, ceremonies, and teachings to be used on Earth as symbols of the reality of higher planes. Consonant with the development and expression of these ceremonies and teachings on Earth, is produced a similar activity upon higher planes with corresponding increase of power. Infinite Wisdom, mindful of the darkness in which Earth disciples grope, has given seekers a key to all this splendor in the immutable law, *AS ABOVE, SO BELOW!*

Thus saith the voice of the Teacher:

Child of light, thou hast done well.

Thou hast walked in the path laid out for thee. Thou hast been obedient under command, faithful in thy efforts, cheerful in thy service. Thou hast indeed sown better than thou knowest, and thou shalt reap the harvest. The Master of Ceremonies will attend thee, and the hand of the Keeper of the Door will lead thee in.

Thou shalt be seated upon the throne of that kingdom which is in every disciple. Thou wilt start at the foot of the physical Ladder of Jacob, but thou wilt reach into invisibility with the power of thy spirit.

Even as the angels attended Jacob in his dream, so shall they attend thee in thy dream of Earth. Thou wilt be awakened and the morning sun shall give thee light, and thou wilt be a leader among humankind for thou hast proved thy worth.

Humbleness of thought, willingness to serve, kindly charity for all, and the light of the spirit have made thee worthy to enter thy Kingdom.

So mote it be!

* * * * * * * * * * * * *

READ NOT TO CONTRADICT AND REFUTE ... NOR TO BELIEVE AND TAKE FOR GRANTED ... NOR TO FIND TALK AND DISCOURSE — BUT TO WEIGH AND CONSIDER.

— Sir Francis Bacon

"Gnothi Seauthon" -- Know Thyself

Second Degree — Lesson One

GREAT CAVALCADE OF THE LONELY ONES

In the days of antiquity, when the Mystery Schools were in their glory, many of the ceremonies of initiation differed in the details of their teachings, but there were four basic precepts in all their dramas, all their symbols, all their secret rituals, all their teachings:

1. KNOW THYSELF!

2. THE PROPER STUDY OF HUMANKIND IS TO LOOK WITHIN.

3. HUMANS ARE MADE IN THE IMAGE AND LIKENESS OF GOD. THEREFORE WE ARE ETERNAL.

4. THAT WHICH IS ABOVE IS LIKE UNTO THAT WHICH IS BELOW, AND THAT WHICH IS BELOW IS LIKE UNTO THAT WHICH IS ABOVE, FOR THE FULFILLMENT OF THE GREAT WORK.

All of which sums up the admonition that each soul is a miniature of Something Infinite, and to know this undefinable Something we must study and understand OURSELVES.

This fundamental truth will, in the fullness of time, permeate the mass consciousness of humanity and humankind will ultimately come to know that each person is a god — albeit, in the majority, a god in ruins. Yet even now, even in the completely material person, there echoes the faint message that each is a ruler of one's own domain ... though the profane cannot find their kingdom.

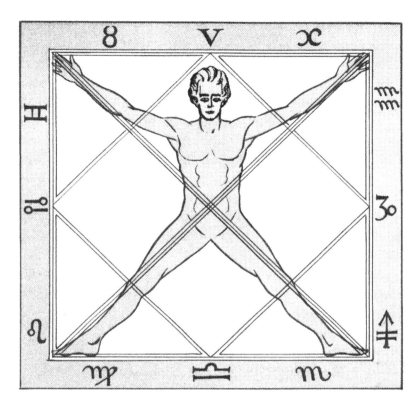

But for the truth seeker, your searching feet unceasingly travel through your daily rounds; your strained but eager eyes, opaque with distant memories, strive ever to pierce the mists of materialism that swirl before the star of your hopes; your vigilant hands grope endlessly for the star only to embrace the vacuous stardust; and your longing, lonely heart keeps an eternal quest for the key to the power which surges around you — untapped, unperceived, mysteriously elusive.

It is little wonder that many of the initiates of the Mysteries of earlier times became theurgists in the latter days. They were taught well in the temples of Mu and Atlantis — in that ancient Order of Melchizedek — the perennial truths that even as the human body consists of bone structure, blood, nerves, cells, heart, brain, glands — each initiate is only imaging or reflecting the Heavenly Being, and the finite human is only a cell in the Immense Body of the Infinite or Heavenly Being.

The planets and stars are force centers or chakras in the body of the Solar Deity, just as the glands are the physical counterparts of the force centers or chakras in humans. The Heavenly Being was, and is, called the *Macrocosm*, and the human being was, and is, called the *microcosm* — the *Great Being* and the *little being*, the *Great Face* and the *little face*.

The maxim, *Humans are made in the image of God*, was taught in a most unique manner in the Mystery Schools of Mu, Atlantis — yes, even in ancient Egypt and Greece. The hierophants, or Masters of the Lodge of Melchizedek, caused to be built a statue of the Grand Man of the Universe and placed it in the temples of Astara in Mu and Atlantis and in the temple of Asta-Ra (Astara) in Egypt. These sages computed the measurements of the Grand Being according to their estimation of the proportions and boundaries of our solar system, and built their statue to scale. It was not of solid substance but was hinged together so that the opening "windows" in the body revealed the glands, chakras, kanda, the Tree of Life and the Tree of Knowledge as they corresponded to the planets and stars of our heavens ... not as a physical body from a physical standpoint, but from an esoteric standpoint.

The statue was not an object of worship, but served as a textbook for many of the lessons taught to the neophytes in the temples. This magnificent figure was also used as an oracle for the gods. Through the head of this unique "statue" the voices of the planets spoke to those divine Children of the Mysteries.

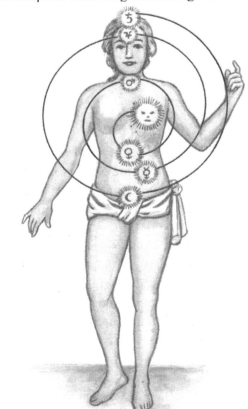

Perhaps the initiate *ALBERTUS MAGNUS* was remembering the glory of this Grand Being of the Mysteries when he, in more recent times, built a facsimile — his unfathomably inscrutable *Android*, his man of brass. The various constellations of the heavens were clearly marked upon the feet, limbs and organs of this mysterious brass figure. Supposedly, the figure could "talk," but Magnus never claimed it to be an oracle in any way.

But the statue-being of the Mysteries most surely was. The hierophants and Ptahs used the figure to reveal many mysteries to the neophyte seeking initiation. By understanding

INNER BEING *— as depicted in* Gechtel's Theosophia Practica

the inner workings of the "divine" human being, the neophyte gained a better self understanding. And in reverse, by dissecting a smaller wooden figure of a human, the mystery was no longer such. In the temples of the Mysteries the seeker was taught by means of the hinged statue, even as we strive in our Lessons and with our charts to teach the same to you. Would that we, too, possessed such a means today! The brain of the figure acted as a receiving station through which spiritual beings of higher dimensions could communicate with the Earthean disciples and initiates.

MAGNUS
Man of magic, astrology and medicine

Among the writings of the Egyptian demigod *HERMES* are found these immortal and highly significant words penned to his principal disciple, Tatian:

EGYPTIAN DEMI-GOD, HERMES

If thou wouldst contemplate the Creator even in perishable things, in things which are on the earth, or in the deep, reflect, O my son, on the formation of man in his mother's womb; contemplate the skill of the Workman. Learn to know Him according to the divine beauty of the Work. Who formed the orb of the eye? Who pierced the openings of the nostrils and the ears? Who made the mouth to open? Who traced out the channels of the veins? Who made the bones hard? Who covered the flesh with skin? Who separated the fingers and the toes? Who spread out the spleen? Who formed the heart like a pyramid? Who formed the caverns of the lungs? Who made the honorable parts of the body conspicuous and concealed the others? Who is the mother, who is the father, if it be not the only and invisible God who has created all things by His will?

In the early 17th century *JAN BAPTISTA VAN HELMONT*, that learned disciple of the teacher Paracelsus, wrote: *Man is the mirror of the universe.* The doctrine of the reflection of the Heavenly Being the Macrocosm, in the physical and spiritual bodies of each human the microcosm, was taught among the wise of the Hindus, the Egyptians, the Lemurians, the Atlanteans, the Tibetans, the Chinese, the

JAN BAPTISTA VAN HELMONT

Chaldeans, the Hebrews, the Greeks, the Polynesians. The form of the Grand Being of the Heavens is composed of the myriad suns, moons, stars and planets of the universe. The human body reflects this glory.

The Qabbalistic Scriptures of the Jewish tradition, the *ZOHAR*, teaches: *The different parts of the body conform to the secrets of the supreme wisdom. The skin represents the firmament which extends everywhere and which covers everything, like a cloak. The flesh, the bones, the veins, represent the celestial chariot, the forces which exist within the servants of God. However, all this is but a cloak; for the deep mystery of the Celestial Being is within. The mystery of the terrestrial being is according to the mystery of the Celestial Adam. Yet as we see in the all-covering firmament stars and planets which form different figures that contain hidden things and profound mysteries, so there are on the skin that covers our body certain figures and lines which are the planets and stars of our body.*

When first you enrolled in the study of Astara's Degrees, one of the initial requests was for you to sit before a mirror and gaze deep into your eyes, seeking to find YOU. That was some time ago. You are not now the same person you were when you sat so silently and earnestly striving to penetrate your own unknown. Since that half-forgotten time you have experienced certain tests, certain victories, perhaps some failures — definitely some spiritual progress and unfoldment, else you would not now be holding teachings of the Second Degree in your hands.

HIEROPHANT, PRESENTING CRUX ANSATA

You, then, have experienced an initiation since that time. Perhaps it was a minor one — perhaps a major. Do you remember? Can you recall it? It was on the astral, in the Temple of Astral Astara. All First Degree disciples were guided through the mystic ceremony and presented with their Crux Ansata, which is their "spiritual diploma" of graduation from the First Degree.

Your image in the Hall of Images has now a vital change in it. Around your neck hangs a silver Crux Ansata suspended from a white cord — the symbol of the Disciple of the First Degree.

During the months of First Degree study you have been daily enveloped with rays of light, directed to you from Astral Astara. Every cell in your body has been vitally charged and changed, and you should be in every way a different person than you were before — unless you have created new karma of so drastic a nature it has counteracted the blessings of the daily downpouring of celestial dews. Another initiation and a change in the symbol around your neck await you when you complete the Second Degree.

Since that momentous time of self-analysis, you have been given many facets of truth; many gems of light. An incomparable Formula has been placed in your hands, offered by those much wiser than we, and utilized for countless ages wherever and whenever people sought to know God. And so we ask again that you contemplate yourself in the light of all you have learned since you began your walk on the Astarian path. Analyze yourself often during these coming days as you progress in the Second Degree.

As stated, the initiates understood the importance of seeking god-dom through the study of the human being. This pathway is a lonely one. But it is well marked by the plodding feet of pilgrims who trod the path in yesteryears. The multitudes who scoffed at these alchemists, philosophers and mystics have long since passed over the hill of time and left no record of even having passed this way at all. But the lamps the great ones lit gleam brilliantly all along the way ... lights that can never be obliterated, or even dimmed.

APOLLONIUS OF TYANA

Yonder is a mystic of forgotten fame who walked the way before you in the 1st century A.D. Above the babble of distant, long-ago voices you can hear his name called if you listen well — *APOLLONIUS ... the miracle man of Tyana*, the man who was more god than man. The world has yet to know the true works of this mighty one, for every effort has been made to destroy his writings; even all records of his life, and all his wondrous deeds. But one day the world will know, for the records will be found...and when they are, what an awakening is due the world of orthodoxy!

PYTHAGORAS

And there is another who lived almost 2,600 years ago who the savants of our modern world have called a deluded quack. We call him *PYTHAGORAS* — the light of whose genius still radiates in today's dark caverns of organized ignorance and bigotry.

This footprint here on the path was made by a mystic alchemist, astrologer, philosopher and magician called *ALBERTUS MAGNUS of Ratisbon* (1193-1280 A.D.). His contribution to the world of science, which we have already mentioned, is even yet ignored — or ridiculed as being quite impossible. But his achievements have yet even to be attempted by the wisest of wise. His magic is termed "medieval" by our scholars, thus they have never even attempted to lift the veil of his wisdom.

PARACELSUS

And here is a footprint imprinted in more recent times, engraved by the passing feet of *PARACELSUS* in the early 16th century, who dared to heal through nature's way; who stood his ground in the face of all opposition and healed while his accusers objected. Those who even now scoff at his system of "superstitions" would do well to learn of his "witches' brew" which restored sight to the blind, cleansed the leper, mended the broken limb, and healed those given up by his unhappy colleagues.

This flagrant "fraud" had the audacity to invoke the aid of "spirits" in bringing about his healings! — and how could such an unholy practice be tolerated! He learned well the secrets of the dervishes of Persia who could touch a wound and cause it to vanish; he taught at length that each man and woman was an immortal soul encased in a human form. Those who called him "Fraud!" are now unremembered and their handiwork has left no sign of their once-presence among the peoples of the earth plane.

That shadow there on the path is *ROBERT FLUDD*, (1574-1637) true son of the Mysteries, who brought the ancient Masonic Order to rebirth in the dawn of the new age. *HIPPOCRATES*, too, belongs among the immortal mystics, the alchemists, the philosophers and metaphysicians, for he taught of a microcosm and a Macrocosm — a human made in the image of God, and a god within the human being.

But now we pause to contemplate the record of one certain philosopher and scientist whose courageous search into the realms of mysticism lifts his memory out of obscurity and places his page in Time's Book of Unforgettables. The world called him *DEMOCRITUS of Abdera.*

In the middle of the 4th century, B.C., from his school and laboratory in Greece, this master alchemist informed a startled world that the entire solar system was composed of atoms which he called the "bricks" of the universe. His was not a popular theory. It was born amid a world of myth and superstition; a world which was indoctrinated in fear of gods and demons, around whose capricious will and whims the events of the Earth revolved — the rising of the sun, the phases of the moon, the flow of tides, the raging of storms. His world dared not laugh at Democritus, for he was honored among his colleagues — but because his pronouncement was not understood, it was feared. It was Democritus who laughed — not at other's ignorance but at his fears and follies and foibles. He became known as "the laughing philosopher of Abdera."

He was reluctant to credit himself for his discoveries of the atom, declaring he was only enlarging upon the wisdom of his own teacher, the learned *LEUCIPPUS*, who first pointed out to him that nature was not to be feared but rather to be understood. Events in nature transpired according to natural law and were not instigated by the gods or demons. There must be some unseen cause at work, Democritus declared, from which the effects of the forces of nature derived their source. He persisted in his theory of the universal "building blocks" of incredibly small and indestructible masses called atoms. *"Sweetness and bitterness, warmth, cold and color are only appearances; in truth, nothing exists but atoms and the void ..."* are his words now remembered by our modern world.

He further confounded his fellow scientists by stating that miracles were scientific and workable by a not-understood law of nature. He was a champion of supernatural phenomena, declaring it also to be in harmony with divine law. And he declared that each person had a soul composed of some sort of atomic fire! — this from the brave lips of a lonely Master, 2,500 years ago. No, his world did not laugh at this strange one — they simply ignored his "ludicrous fantasies."

Only one man echoed his teachings — a man called *EPICURUS*. From his school in Greece, called *The Garden*, he aligned himself with the Unforgettables by promulgating the theory that the universe was composed of atoms. He also taught that the supernatural was not supernatural at all ... but natural ... as were all things in nature. His teachings about the atom were soon forgotten ... but he will long be remembered as the man who reasoned that since pleasure is the only good perceived by the senses, pleasure must demonstrate a perfect harmony of body and mind. His ideal, however, was a refined and fastidious pleasure — not the ribald, raucous pleasure popularly applied to his teachings. Although he made a gallant effort to entrench his atomic theory in his world of philosophy, it nevertheless died with him. It lay in its grave of silence for five centuries, undisturbed and unsought ... while a world waited, and the darkness was deep.

Then rose the star of the Roman poet, *TITUS LUCRETIUS CARUS*, in 96 - 55 B.C. He expanded the atomic theory in a poem, *On the Nature of Things*. In his voluminous work he explained in detail the atomic structure of the universe. He taught that orthodox religion created superstitions, fear and ignorance and caused people to fear death as the doorway either to oblivion or torment in the life after death. He sought in vain to interest science in his imponderable, visionary ideas of the laws of nature.

"Water dripping from the eaves hollows a stone; the best plough-share of iron imperceptibly decreases in the fields ... the brass statues at the gates show their right hands to be wasted by the touch of the numerous passersby who greet them. These things we see are lessened ... but what bodies depart at any given time the nature of vision has jealously shut out of our seeing ... nature therefore works by unseen bodies." His remembered words of long ago.

He pleaded his cause futilely at the door of science, but he only grasped at shadows for the door did not open to him. For who, indeed, among the scientists could possibly endorse such unscientific fallacies. How could one measure a miracle? How weigh a soul? His pleas appeared only to seal the door more firmly against truth — and the atom and the soul breathed silently on in their world of shadows for another 1,600 years.

Even then there were only glimmers of light. In the Renaissance, experiments by astronomers caused a renewal of interest in the atomic theory and the structure of the universe. *GALILEO* came along, and *ROBERT BOYLE*, and *SIR ISAAC NEWTON*, and *LAVOISIER* ... but the world paused only a moment to listen, then hurried to forget. No one paused long and no one listened long until the early 19th century, when JOHN DALTON, an English chemist, astonished a complacent world by his "discovery" of the atom.

Why do we make so much concerning the awakening of the world to the atom? Because the light now being thrown upon it in our modern laboratories will sooner or later prove a truth mystics have attempted to tell the world since time began ... that we live in more worlds than one ... in more bodies than one; that there are many planes of energy and life; that we each possess a body conforming to each of these planes; that the atom is not "matter" but a concentration of energy and that since there are many differing forms of the atom, there must be many differing levels of energy ... thus many differing planes of life existing throughout the universe; that since we are a miniature universe we too must possess many differing bodies of energy.

No longer are these teachings taught furtively in the halls of the Mystery Schools. No longer do we mystics need to cover our truths with symbols and allegories. We now stand able to convince a world of the new age that science itself has lifted the veil of Isis and has found truth standing there in all her glory.

Yes, the way is lonely, but has been well marked, and honored are we to follow the lead of these lonely ones. Better is it to be numbered among the disparaged than to be among the forgotten conformists.

These children of the light who fought their battles for truth are reborn initiates of the Mysteries. Long ago and far away, in some other life and in some other clime they learned of the human being and God, the universe and the enigma of the human soul. These learnings they remembered when they returned to Earth again as Plato, Pythagoras, Magnus, Democritus and all the rest. And deep in the dark recesses of your mind, beloved Astarian, so do you remember. You learned many things before ... and we shall help to bring all these things again to your remembrance!

SELAH!

THE TEMPLE OF THE LIVING GOD

In preceding Lessons we have made steady progress toward establishing a solid foundation upon which to build a better understanding of YOURSELF. Because we paused to outline a survey of the planes, the bodies, the sutratma, the permanent seed atoms, the science of birth and other detailed subjects, we are now better prepared to pursue our studies.

In a previous Lesson we discussed several bodies:

1. the physical body, consisting of the dense and the etheric;

2. the astral body, consisting of the body of carnal desires called the *kama rupa*, and the body of aspirations called the astral;

3. the mental body which registers concrete thoughts;

4. the spiritual sheaths, which includes the higher mental or causal body.

In succeeding Lessons we shall consider each of these bodies. In this Lesson we shall begin study of the dense physical form from an esoteric viewpoint.

THE DENSE PHYSICAL FORM

Some disciples hold the physical form in utter contempt, and in their wisdom-searching, disregard this most majestic temple of the divine god-self within. They seek to discover a wider knowledge of the celestial planes and do not pause to reflect upon the book of life which is as near to them as breath ... their human form.

These disciples would do well to contemplate the marvel of their physical form, for truly it is wrought with wonders. The mechanism of it, the operations involved which enables the High Self to work through this intricate instrument, behooves us to pause and contemplate its creation. We will stand mute before the immeasurable wisdom of the Creator, once we realize the eons of time it has required the Divine Being to build this temple.

Let the seeker who despises the physical form realize that it represents, at this present stage of evolution, one's most precious possession. This knowledge will come into full fruition when they enter the astral world at the time of transition. Having lost the physical form, they will then realize the supremely significant part it plays in their progression. For it has evolved from meager and wretched beginnings in the dim and faraway past to the refined instrument of today, only by walking the dark and tragic road of personal experience.

Even so, one must never forget that each person is NOT only the physical body, but a spiritual being inhabiting it. It is the failure to discriminate between the form and the being within that has caused the interminable war between science and religion.

A more complete understanding of the first two chapters of the Book of Genesis in the Holy Bible would clarify the proposition most thoroughly, if only both science and religion would pause in their battles to contemplate the mysteries. The first chapter of Genesis tells us: *And God said, Let us make man in our image, after our likeness ... So God created man in His image, in the image of God created He him: male and female created He them.*

This refers to the inner being and *not* to the physical form. It refers to that spark of divinity which has dipped into matter to inhabit a physical form, breathed there by the divine Monad above it.

The formation of the *physical body* is described in the second chapter of Genesis, and is completely differentiated from the description in the first chapter: *And the Lord God formed man of the dust of the ground, and breathed into his nostrils the breath of life, and man became a living soul.*

This body formed of the "dust of the ground" refers to the physical body, composed of solids, liquids, gases and ethers of the physical plane of life. This physical form has evolved through long evolutionary periods of time and has progressed from an animal like form to the refined, upright form inhabited by the soul today.

Since that momentous time of our initial birth into human form, when God "breathed into man the breath of life" and the inner being entered into the physical form, evolutionary progress has been marked by a continual expansion of consciousness, and before us still stretch the vast untrodden pathway of eternal soul progression. In the brain, the instrument of the mind, there lie millions of unawakened cells, holding their precious unsprouted seeds of expanded consciousness — seeds which will one day give birth to fruit from both the Tree of Knowledge and the Tree of Everlasting Life.

The perfect physical form toward which we are all evolving in this coming sixth root race will be sustained not by a single spinal column as of now, but with a double spinal column, formed by the ganglia of a chain of nerves which will be linked together. This will unite the cerebrospinal nerve and the sympathetic nerve, and their union will consummate the ultimately perfect, regenerated physical form.

In our present day studies concerning the dense physical form, we must outline the component parts which make up the whole, and each part must be analyzed completely if we are to arrive at satisfactory knowledge. We shall list the parts now in our outline, and consider each in future Lessons:

1. The bony structure and spinal column

2. The nervous systems

   A. The sympathetic system

   B. The cerebrospinal system

   C. The vagus nerve

3. The endocrine system

4. The heart

5. The blood

6. The eyes

7. The brain

Using this outline as our basic "platform," we shall begin our study of the bony structure and the spinal column and progress, through the Second Degree, to an ever-expanding quest for self-knowledge and, hopefully, attainment of some measure of wisdom.

THE STRAIGHT AND NARROW WAY

In the early days of our evolution the bony structure was not solidified as it is today; the upright structure of the body represents millenniums of evolutionary progress and development. The straightening of the spinal column required many eons. Our upright posture of today signals most significantly that we are reaching Godward.

When the human being was in its infancy the bony structure had not crystallized and was more as cartilage. Crystallization began during the Lemurian Age. Until the process of solidification was completed, human beings were able, without being aware of anything unusual, to enter into and become a part of the etheric realms surrounding the body. With the physical senses of taste, sight, hearing, feeling and smelling as yet undeveloped, each person was involuntarily psychic. The etheric surroundings were, in those early days, a natural part of life.

Even some glimpse of the astral world was a natural function, which is an indication that the Third Eye was more prominent than the two physical eyes, which were as yet only partially developed. The bony structure of the skull had not yet crystallized, and the etheric webs of protection which later wove themselves about the chakras were not yet so dense a veil between the two worlds.

As the bony structure straightened and solidified through the incredibly slow cycles of evolution, several natural events occurred:

1. The bones of the skull knitted increasingly closer, closing off the "window to heaven" at the top of the head, until today we have only the "soft spot" found in infancy and another opening near the medulla oblongata at the base of the skull.

2. Around each spinal chakra was woven an ever-thickening etheric web, composed of the four physical ethers which closed away the higher realms and barred the human body from their vibrations. The web was woven particularly dense in the Third Eye and around the crown chakra, until at last the veil was completed and the Holy of Holies of the temple in the head was hidden away from the developing physical senses.

3. The appearance of the backbone, the vertebral structure, signaled the birth of the optic thalamus, a part of the Third Eye in the brain, and the coming of this important optic nerve marked the approaching birth of the superconscious contact. For not only did the optic thalamus give impetus to the developing sense of physical eyesight but provided a forcefield for the inflow of higher spiritual forces which could not enter the aura until the spine was straight, because ...

4. Human beings' approach to divinity is signaled by the upright spine. The animal kingdom with its horizontal backbone is controlled, as you know, by a

group soul. An animal does not possess an individualized soul, as do humans, nor does it possess a divine spark of God. A group soul is a celestial being or Deva who ensouls different species of animals with an extension of itself, until an animal-soul in the influential area of a group soul is ready to be born into the human kingdom. It is at that time only that the individual divine Monad expresses through three things which distinguish humans from the animal: the upright spine, the upright larynx, and a warm human-type bloodstream.

The influence of the currents of the group souls sweeping around the Earth can enter only the horizontal backbones of the animal kingdom, and not the upright spine of humans. It is through these currents that the group souls maintain their contact with their animal species. These group soul currents cannot affect the human kingdom for we are connected through our upright spines to our individualized Oversoul.

5. Only through the bloodstream is the Oversoul able to operate through the dense physical form. Before the bony structure became ossified, it was not possible for the marrow, in its state of imperfection, to manufacture the type of red corpuscles so necessary to one's evolutionary progress Godward. For it is only through human blood — the "river of life" — that the Oversoul is able to infuse itself in the personality aspect. Thus we could not reach toward the superconscious until our bony structure became crystallized, and the marrow of the bones began to issue a type of blood through which the Oversoul could finally become operative.

With the development of human blood — which differs radically from that of the animal kingdom — came also the development of the nervous systems and, through the nervous systems, the sense organs became sensitized to the physical plane.

In days of long ago before human beings actually stood upright, the skeleton was laid along the outer layer of the flesh with only a hardened skin covering. Human beings had attained a human consciousness, but had no contact with the Oversoul or superconsciousness whatever. Through the interminable process of evolution the skeleton form shifted inward, and the nervous systems developed on the outside of the bony structure, thus exposing the inner nature to development through impulses reaching the senses through the nervous systems.

With the skeleton frame developing further within the human form and the nervous systems developing on the outside of the bony structure, the lethargic consciousness became increasingly stimulated into higher degrees of consciousness as the physical senses gained prominence.

One goal now facing the human kingdom is to etherealize both the inner skeleton and the dense physical form through the medium of the blood. As we learn of the karmic energies and the vibrations of the picture images flowing in the bloodstream and how to dissipate them by and through higher living habits, the bony structure will become increasingly refined until we attain our ultimate goal. An etherealized bony structure will indicate also the transmutation of the human form out of the solids, liquids and gases of our dense material plane into the four physical ethers of the etheric realm.

The question may arise as to why, if once we lived in this etheric state during our days in our faraway Garden of Eden — why should we have had to dip into the ocean of matter to put on a coat of skin and pass through eons of time awaiting the ossification of the bony structure, in order simply to attain again that desired etheric state in some distant future?

And the answer is that when we existed previously in that etheric Garden in our etheric forms, we possessed only that — a form. We had developed no degree of consciousness which would mark us as individual, thinking beings, but were as puppets under the control and protection of "gods" whose very protection and control would not have allowed our individual progression toward our own godhood, which could only be attained by entering the world of matter and learning through our personal experiences.

For during these eons of time, not alone did the bony structure develop and become upright but the causal forcefield of each individual gained impetus and power as each person, responsible solely for his or her own actions, learned life's lessons on the hard road of human experience. Not only will the bony structure become etherealized, but the "coat of skin" will be so refined it shall become a body of light.

The hierophants of the Mystery Schools in ancient days were highly skilled in the art of physical transmutation, and understood well the mystery of the alchemical formula of salt, sulphur, mercury and azoth as it applied to the human form. Working with the blood and the mysterious marrow of the bone, they were able to transmute the solids, liquids and gases of the physical form into the four ethers, thus lifting our entire physical form out of dense matter into etheric matter, causing it to disappear completely from sight.

As we proceed in our evolutionary path we will, in the endless course of time, come to know and understand this intricate arcane secret of the marrow of the bone — and when we do, the Lost Word of the Mysteries will be recovered and we will have overcome death. We will be able, through the power of our own minds, to transmute the atoms of our dense form into the higher vibrational structure of etheric matter and, so far as your physical form is concerned, pass from mortality into immortality.

In our next Lesson we shall research the Tree of Life and the Tree of Knowledge. We shall consider the science of initiation and at-one-ment with the High Self by transmuting the energies and powers of the sympathetic nervous system by utilizing the power of the mysterious subconscious mind to perform miracles.

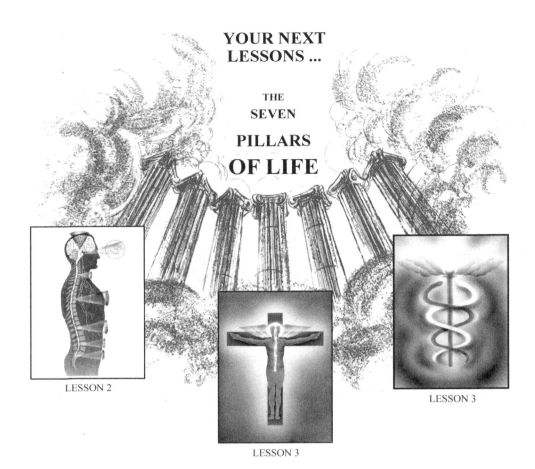

YOUR NEXT LESSONS ...

THE
SEVEN
PILLARS
OF LIFE

LESSON 2

LESSON 3

LESSON 3

Imagine an imposing temple ... the temple of your Self ... the temple of Life, not made with hands, eternal in the heavens.

What are the Seven Pillars that not only make this temple a thing of beauty but which also add the qualities of usefulness and permanence?

The Seven Pillars of the temple of your Self are: (1) Self-improvement, (2) Stability, (3) Self-expression, (4) Security, (5) Understanding, (6) Love, (7) Unity.

The materials of which these pillars are constructed are available in the teachings of Astara, coupled with your own life experiences. Each Lesson of *Astara's Book of Life* is a temple builder in the truest sense.

For example, in **Lesson 2, Human Being — Animal or Child-God?** ... you learn many symbolic mysteries concerning the potent forces flowing along the spinal causeway and the nervous systems, the astral Self, how the conscious mind impresses the subconscious, the reservoir of memories.

And in **Lesson 3, Roots of the Tree of Knowledge** ... you gain more enlightenment to enhance the Seven Pillars through teachings concerning your "built-in communication system," the person of tomorrow, the mystic marriage of the nervous systems, the cosmic caduceus of the Mystery dramas, the transcendental power of love.

As you study these Lessons you will add to the beauty, usefulness and permanence of the Temple of your Self.

OUTER POSSESSIONS ARE TEMPORARY.
INNER POSSESSIONS ARE YOURS FOREVER.

WHEN THE STARS COME OUT

We are such little men when the stars come out,
So small under the open maw of the night,
That we must shout and pound the table and drive wild
And gather dollars and madly dance and drink deep,
And send the great birds flying, and drop death.
When the stars come out we are such little men
That we must arm ourselves in glare and thunder,
Or cave in on our own dry littleness.

We are such little men when the stars come out!
Ah, God behind the stars, touch with your finger
This mite of meaningless dust and give it substance.
We are so little, under the frown of the night!
Be You our bodies, You our eyes, our lips,

Our hands, our feet, our heartbeat and our hunger,
That we may face the infinite spaces, and live ...
And stand in quietness, when the stars come out.

So Great Is the Work

They say
That with the passing years
The fire of visions burns dim;
And embers of our yearnings
And our goals
Smoke with the scent
Of dying dreams.
And they say
That often,
When the end approaches,
The door swings wide
To bade the Reaper come.
"Welcome, Death ...
Come and take me
And give me rest ..."

But not for me ...
I find
That with the passing years,
My visions stretch
The length and breadth
Of shining uncharted seas.
The words of my pen
Flow like a river
Wild with wine and honey.
And my soul ~
Straining against the
Slow turning limitations of Earth's ways ~
Grows only tired
Of bending to the
Frustrations of slow accomplishments.

The teachings
Pour in like a torrent ~
But the finished page
Grinds out pace by pace
Like slow-passing eternity.
And as the years go by
My dreams burn so high and deep
I think my little me
Cannot contain the strain
Of joy, of agony ~
So great is The Work
So small am I!

~ Earlyne

Human Being -- Animal or Child-God?

Second Degree — Lesson Two

THE FORMATION OF THE PHYSICAL FRAME

Before we begin our quest into the nervous systems (the Tree of Life and the Tree of Knowledge), let us first complete our studies of the bony structure, the spinal column, and the arcane mysteries involved.

The first evidence of the dense physical form in the embryonic stage in the womb is a pulpy jellylike substance, which resembles the albumin or white of an egg. In this substance there appear tiny particles of solid matter. These minute particles gradually drift toward each other, until they aggregate into different points of contact. These points of contact are slowly enlarged into the joints of the skeleton, and from these joints the minute particles of solidified matter extend themselves from one joint to the other until a distinct framework is formed.

This process of crystallization continues during fetal life, and does not cease at birth. It continues throughout the entire lifetime. Though ossification of the body should cease around the fourteenth year, actually one of the principal causes of death is its continuing process, affecting not only the bony structure but the arteries as well.

As one reaches adulthood the synovial fluids which keep the organs and arteries plastic become too stagnant and congealed to keep the ethers flowing throughout the body. Lack of these ethers causes the bones to become brittle and to shrink as one enters one's latter years, so that the person remains no longer upright and tall but often bent and somewhat dwarfed. The important arteries also lose their elasticity as do many of the muscles. Calcium deposits often form around the skeletal joints. Thus the ossification process continues, eventually resulting in rigidity not only of the bones but of the entire body.

The bones of the young are composed of three parts gelatinous substance to one part solid earthy particles. In the elderly, the formula is reversed to three parts of very solidified earthy matter to one part gelatin substance. The cause of this drying out, congealing process can be attributed to our habitual indifference to purification not only concerning our bodies and the intake of our food and drink, but also the purification of our minds. But the manner and means of keeping the physical body in a more plastic state is not under discussion in this particular Lesson.

When the infant form begins to crystallize in the womb of the mother, the marrow of the bone holds much mystery, for out of its substance flows the fluid which later becomes the blood of the incoming entity. The blood, rising from the bone marrow, carries the vital "life" throughout the body, since it is the vehicle for the four ethers which make life possible in a dense form.

When the personality image enters the physical form at the moment of birth, it also enters the bone marrow, and from there permeates the entire form through the bloodstream. Thus it is not the skeleton itself which is the foundation of the soul-in-man, but the marrow in the bones.

THE SPINAL CAUSEWAY

The *Royal Way*, the *King's Way*, the straight and narrow way, is that closely guarded and barricaded highway which serves your own High Self — the spinal column. Perhaps you have never realized its importance in the eternal scheme of your evolutionary life, or perhaps you *have* entertained subtle intimations that it *is* a channel of preeminence in the great plan of your becoming.

The *columna spinalis*, when viewed separately and apart from the physical body, resembles a serpent standing upright, balanced on its tail. Here we discern one of the many reasons for the adoption, in ancient times, of the serpent as a symbol of wisdom — not that the bony structure of the spinal column itself was the object of reverence. Rather it was the upraised kundalini serpent fires that make their home in the spinal column.

Descending its entire length is the vital spinal cord. A wise Creator has seen fit to surround and protect well this "river of light," for it is indeed the straight and narrow way which will carry the race out of the wilderness of Earth into the paradise of heaven.

The spinal cord carries the brain fluids unimpeded down the entire length of the spinal column for the first seven years of life. It is only after the age of seven that a substance called the terminal filament begins to fill the lower end of the spinal cord. It forms in the vicinity of the twelfth dorsal vertebra and moves downward. Finally, in most adults, the terminal filament usually impedes the flow of the spinal fluids to the lower end of the spinal cord.

It is an accepted fact among medical scientists that the seat of consciousness, located in the brain, extends down the spinal column via the spinal cord and its fluids. They have termed the spinal cord "an elongated brain." The mind substance pierces the terminal filament to reach the tip of the spinal cord at the base of the spine, there to form what we term "the third brain," or the "root brain." It is this fragmentary extension of consciousness, working in conjunction with the generative organs, which constitutes the most powerful seat of mental activity in some people today. This root brain dominates the lives of those who have never raised the kundalini fires of the spinal column out of the generative organs.

A major endeavor of the new age person will be to clear away the accumulated filamentary debris at the lower extremity of the spinal cord to create an unimpeded channel to the brain.

The seat of consciousness at the base of the spine possesses far more power than ordinarily suspected, related to both physical and mental activities. Medical scientists would do well to examine their mentally ill for spinal injuries. For many mental patients are suffering from nothing more than an injury at the base of the spine, reflected in the head glands, the treatment of which might once again bring mental clarity.

The spinal cord carries a precious cargo: the brain dews from the head downward, and the Chrism Golden Oil from the generative organs upward. Every nerve trunk is attached to this spinal cord, and extends into the body through the openings in the spinal column itself. The vital fluids flowing through this straight and narrow way are more precious even than the blood. Their substance is not of the earth or earthy — they are mysterious gaseous fluids, influenced in no way by what we eat or drink.

These etheric fluids — the Chrism Oil and the brain dews — are highly vulnerable, however, to mental influences, to soul power, to pranic energies.

THE SPINAL COLUMN IN THE MYSTERY DRAMAS

A careful study of most of the ancient religions and the Mysteries reveals that the spinal column played a tremendously important role in their revered dramas and teachings. It was symbolized by various objects, depending upon the particular drama or teaching:

1. a winding road;

2. the upraised serpent;

3. a winding stairway;

4. the seven-knotted wand;

5. the three-knotted wand;

6. the thirty-three doors of the mystic hallway;

7. Jacob's ladder;

8. the straight and narrow way;

9. a long-stemmed unfolded lotus.

The brain dews were termed "manna from heaven" in certain of the Mystery dramas. They descended from the brain down the spinal cord to feed the "children of Israel in the wilderness" at the base of the spine. These mysterious *waters* or *dews*, still termed the "sacred river in man," flow downward from the Holy Mount in the skull, descend the entire length of the spinal column, and ascend again to that upper region. To the ancient Egyptians, the River Nile symbolized this sacred inner purifying stream, and the River Ganges represented it to the Hindus.

In the Christian Mysteries it was known as the River Jordan. The medulla oblongata at the upper end of the spinal cord contained the Flaming Sword, guarded by the Cherubim who stood at the gate of the Garden of Eden to prevent degenerate humankind from reentering its paradise until the race attained regeneration, becoming pure and perfect once more.

The center of this Garden was found in the high and Holy Mount in the skull where, in its midst, grew the Tree of Knowledge of Good and Evil, the cerebrospinal nervous system. The medulla oblongata also represented Golgotha. It was here that "man of matter" was transformed into the Christ, through crucifixion upon the double cross created by the currents of ida, pingala, and the vagus nerve as they intersect in this center.

Pingala, the channel for positive force, leaves the base of the spine to travel upward and connect with the pineal gland in the head, and also opens into the right nostril. Ida, the negative channel, travels upward to connect with the pituitary, and opens into the left nostril. These two currents intersect the spinal cord at the base of the skull in the medulla, forming there a double cross with the vagus nerve.

They intersect again in the solar plexus where we find the abdominal brain. Here ida and pingala cross with the current in the solar plexus, which we call the Holy Breath. The combination of these three currents forms another double cross, giving birth to a mysterious fluid which comes into full power every twenty-nine and a half days. The cycle of this alchemical formula in the laboratory of the solar plexus is judged by the time of the month when the moon is in the sign which the sun occupied at the time of the individual's birth.

The yogis of India often carry a seven-knotted staff which symbolizes the spinal column and the seven chakras. The three-knotted wand symbolizes the ida, pingala and sushumna.

Prominent in the Egyptian Mysteries was a most important and significant pillar called Tap. This pillar represented the backbone of the god Osiris. The pillar Tap was most peculiar in that it featured two spinal columns in one, joined together and "doubled in amenta." This ancient pillar symbolized the double spinal column of future humanity, when the two nervous systems will be joined together in the spine. All this relates to a mystery which we will later pursue when we teach of the human of tomorrow — the Master-Being, the regenerated god.

The initiate in the Mysteries was taught much concerning this straight and narrow way. For this spinal pathway is a principal means of your future regeneration, your paramount hope of attaining mastery over self, over life, over eternity. The objective is to remove the impediments in the spinal cord, making it a clear channel for the alchemical mixture of the brain fluids and the fluids from the generative organs; destroying all the barriers which prevent the brain dews from reaching kundalini and which prohibit the Chrism Oil from ascending with the kundalini fires to reach the Holy Mount in the head.

BONES OF ANTIQUITY

The ancients understood the significant properties in the bones far better than we today. The teaching that a vital spiritual essence permeated the bone marrow became distorted among the common tribes, and eventually the bones themselves became the object of ancestral worship, of magical ceremonies.

We include these teachings concerning the bones because we feel Astarians should be familiar with the important place they occupy in the lore, legends and religious rites of antiquity. The ancients knew that the bones were permeated by a nutritive fluid and that the processes transpiring in the tissues of the bones were necessary to physical life. We concur with this knowledge and belief.

They believed, however, that the vital force in the skeletal structure was infused with some degree of consciousness. It was customary — and still is among aboriginal tribes in many lands — in cremating their leaders and chieftains, to preserve their bones. It was believed that some life essence still remained in them and acted as a direct channel through which the departed ones could speak or make their beneficent influence felt and known. The idea of the spirit in the bones was a prominent part of the religious life of all ancient peoples and tribes, though many of their ceremonies differed.

AMONG THE EGYPTIANS

The bones were of exceptional interest to the ancient Egyptians. They knew the marrow to possess extremely vital force. The bone marrow of animals was frequently used in concocting salves which wrought many of their healing miracles. It was from the Egyptians that the Greeks learned their healing arts and sciences, one of the greatest of these being knowledge of the bone marrow. This accounts for the sacredness attributed to the dead form by the ancient Egyptians. The entire skeleton of their great kings, queens, initiates and priests was preserved through mummification. This process was to preserve the forces in the bone marrow rather than the physical form itself. They did not employ mummification to insure some future resurrection of the body, as is the popular belief.

The Egyptians were well aware of the doctrine of reincarnation and were also familiar with the soul-science of birth as we have taught it. They were acquainted with the auric egg, which we have called the personality image; and they were aware of the structure of the etheric and the physical form in the womb. They believed that

THE SPINAL CAUSEWAY

1. *Cerebrum* — the Father, embracing the " Pia Mater" or Blessed Mother.

2. *The optic thalamus* — a part of the third eye. Receiver of contacts from the superconscious through the brain stem and the fourth ventricle.

3. *Cerebellum* — the chauffeur of the human automobile, or the controller-manipulator of the body.

4. *The medulla oblongata* — the holy altar sheltering the unquenchable flame, the flame which never perishes, which emits the sound of the soul note and plays your own individual symphony of the spheres.

5. *The vagus nerve* — channel of the Holy Breath, or the inner breath of the yogi. The passageway of the permanent heart seed atom and the life cord in the sutratma.

6. *The twelve dorsal vertebrae* — the entrance place of the Ark of the Covenant of the Most High God, where the "twelve stones" are set up " which are there to this day."

7. *The spinal cord* — the baptismal font of the regenerated soul. The Royal Way upon which kundalini travels on her journey toward the Holy Mount, the Brahmarandra. The pathway of the holy fire.

8. *The root chakra* — the basic chakra for lifeforce.

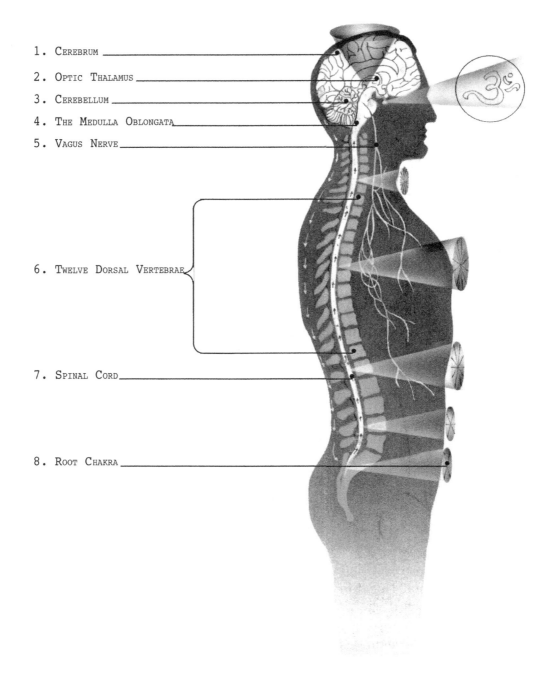

1. CEREBRUM
2. OPTIC THALAMUS
3. CEREBELLUM
4. THE MEDULLA OBLONGATA
5. VAGUS NERVE
6. TWELVE DORSAL VERTEBRAE
7. SPINAL CORD
8. ROOT CHAKRA

THE SPINAL CAUSEWAY

"Jacob's Ladder," the "Raised Serpent" and the "Thirty-three Steps of Mystic Initiation," represent the thirty-three vertebrae of the spinal column.

the soul, at the time of rebirth, could further its evolutionary processes by drawing power from the mummified form and the divine properties built into it during the previous incarnation, and endowing the new form with them. Their ultimate purpose in preserving the bones of their great ones was to insure preservation of some of the vital powers intact in the bone marrow. Not all Egyptians were mummified ... only those who had attained some stature of leadership, usually a king or queen, or a priest or an initiate-healer from one of their Mystery Schools.

The mummifying process was a most intricate one, attended by powerful rites and ceremonies which, in truth, caused a tremendous occult power to be generated in the mummies themselves. Through this power the departed soul could maintain a spiritual contact during its sojourn on the astral planes, and *could* indeed draw the power into its new skeleton and bone marrow in its next incarnation. They believed their great Ptahs and kings never lingered in the upper worlds for long, but returned quickly to Earth to lead their people. Their plan was to transfer continuously the power attained by the Great One to each new body and increase it with each incarnation. Thus they helped their priest-kings more rapidly attain their ultimate perfection.

Their ideas concerning this perpetual preservation of the bodies were based upon knowledge and not superstition. Understood in this light, the ancient Egyptians were not steeped in confused, primitive superstitions. Rather, they possessed a knowledge as yet remote even to our greatest modern thinkers.

In addition to the portion of spiritual qualities of the initiates remaining in the skeleton form, the rituals and ceremonies engaged in during the mummification process endowed the mummies with a tremendous power, because of the intense mental force generated. This powerful thoughtform held in the mummy was also expected to be of great benefit to the reincarnating god-initiate.

Since only masters of the art could engage in mummifying the great ones, and only those who revered the departed one were selected to perform this auspicious function, only thoughts of love and power were created to become a part of the mummy, thus insuring a blessed and powerfully beneficent thoughtform.

The mummy was believed to possess some degree of consciousness, in that if molested in any way after the burial ceremonies were completed, it could cause a curse to fall upon its tormentors for disturbing its peaceful period of waiting. Otherwise, it was simply a powerful force for good, waiting to be absorbed by the great soul as it again came into earthly incarnation. (The powerful genie guarding the tomb of the Great One was also a part of the "curse" of the Pharaoh, but this idea must wait a later time.)

AMONG HINDUS

It is of interest to note Hindu rites and ceremonies concerning disposal of the dead, not only in ancient times but even today. The death ritual is most involved and complex, but the portion which concerns us in this Lesson is that which related to the bones of the departed, and the esteem with which they were and are regarded.

The usual Hindu death ceremony includes cremation of the body which leaves the bones exposed, at which time they enter into a ceremony called the *Sanchayana. Yana* is an Indian word meaning "bones." "Sanchayana" refers to "the collecting of the bones." The time selected for the Sanchayana is most important. An uneven numbered day must be chosen, falling during the dark of the moon. Certain star constellations are also desirable for this particular ceremony. Great care is used in selecting the gatherer, who is usually a woman. The process of collecting the bones involves ritual. The bones are to be placed in an urn during the ceremony. A plain urn, if the departed is a male; an urn adorned with the design of a bosom, if a female.

Among some Hindus the Sanchayana involves elaborate preparations. The fruit of the Brhati plant must be attached by a red and blue thread to the left hand of the woman selected as the gatherer. A certain type of stone upon which the gatherer is to stand is then placed beside the cremation site near the bones. She must then cleanse her hands carefully with leaves from the Apamarga plant. Stepping upon the stone, she is to close her eyes and, maintaining a calm, tranquil state, lift the bones one by one using only the thumb and ring finger of the left hand, and place them silently and gently in the urn.

The urn is then sealed, usually during chanting, and transported to a specially prepared and carefully selected trench which no water except rainwater can reach. Sometimes the trench is dug under the roots of certain trees. Some Hindus prefer not to place the bones in an urn, but to carry them directly to the trench site where a yellow cloth, containing herbs and grasses is spread, upon which the bones are placed.

Others put the bones in miniature barrels or upon open rafts which are then floated on rivers to the accompaniment of chants and mantrums. If flowing water is not available, the bones are carried to some remote location and buried.

Other Hindus prefer not to save the bones, and engage in a second ceremony. The bones are pulverized, mixed with butter, and tied in a silken cloth. A second crematory fire then consumes them. Or the pulverized bones are strewn upon flowing water — a river or a stream.

BONES AND IMMORTALITY

Since time immemorial bones have been used in ceremonial magic and medicine. Most ideas behind these ceremonies are completely distorted, but they tend to demonstrate the ancient teaching that the bone marrow possesses a quality and a power unattainable by any other part of the human form. Most of the early teachings have degenerated into tribal superstitions.

It *is* true that the bones of the departed can be caused to carry the power of a curse or a healing. Intense mental energy has gone into the thoughtform permeating them through the voice vibrations of the magical chant. The skull of a great chieftain *can* be used as a point of contact with him in the upper worlds but only because it has been imbued with power through chanting and thoughts of the participants as they engage in violent, emotional ceremonies, directing all their mental powers toward this particular object.

It is important to remember that no spiritual power permeated the human skeleton until the human race had gained its upright stature, its human bloodstream, and its upright larynx. The essence in the bones via the bone marrow bespeaks the human's divinity, and will play an important role in our future evolutionary development.

THE MAKINGS OF A HUMAN BEING

In previous Lessons we presented brief references to the nervous systems. We must now add to those studies, because these with which we are presently concerned would be most incomplete unless we pursued our teachings and enlarged upon the important place the nervous system occupies in esoteric anatomy.

The sympathetic and cerebrospinal nervous systems are, in truth, one intricate network of nerves which ultimately work together in performing their various operations. We shall consider them separately in these writings, however, for on the surface their functions are seemingly separate. Thus will we arrive at a better understanding of them. Actually, there are three principal divisions:

1. the sympathetic nervous system;

2. the cerebrospinal system;

3. the vagus nervous system.

THE SYMPATHETIC NERVOUS SYSTEM

In the long ago past when the race was expressing in its early forms, the sympathetic nervous system began its first real operations and development. I say *first*, even though the physical form of the animal possesses a sympathetic system, and it is not peculiar to humans alone. But even though humans share the sympathetic system in common with the animal kingdom, the system rising into birth in humankind in our early beginnings was a *part of one's own individual nature* and not under the subjection of the group soul as is true of animals.

The sympathetic system was the only obvious nervous system throughout the first eons of the soul's physical development, although the cerebrospinal was there in embryo. The sympathetic first expressed simply as currents of desire. It required many millenniums before it became crystallized enough to be called a nervous system, and to become definite organized lines of force in the human form.

The sympathetic system consists of a double chain of nerve ganglia originating in the cerebellum, passing downward through the medulla oblongata at the back of the head, and extending down the entire length of the spine on either side of the spinal column — one chain of ganglia on the left and one on the right.

The two cords are united by concentrated nerve centers or plexuses located in the head, in the heart, the solar plexus and in the stomach. The cords converge in the pelvic area and again in the brain where they originated.

INSTRUMENT OF THE ASTRAL BODY

We have said that the sympathetic system expressed first as currents of desire, which crystallized through incredibly slow evolutionary processes into an instrument for the astral body ... or better should we say the astral body developed simultaneously with the sympathetic system, and now uses the system for expressing today. Through this system our desires well up, and are activated in the abdominal brain of the solar plexus. It is of interest to note that the sympathetic system has its most prominent seat of activity in the gigantic network of nerves which forms a force center at the solar plexus, which ties it intricately to the astral form. You already know that the astral form has its contact in the solar plexus. It is via the sympathetic system concentrated there that it makes its most powerful connection.

During the interminable expanse of time while the human form was developing both physically and astrally, the sympathetic system was gaining its tremendous power, until it arrived at the place it occupies today ... which is to carry on all the automatic functions of the physical form. For instance, you do not need to *think* when you breathe ... you breathe automatically. You do not need to be aware of your heart for it to perpetually beat. And all the other automatic functions in your body — the elimination processes, the surging of the blood through the veins, the metabolism, the chemical compounding, the structure, the growth, the pressure of the blood, the activity of the lungs — all these proceed by impulses supplied through the automatic command of this giant of power.

This power has come to the sympathetic system through the long process of evolution as the subconscious mind, operating through it, gradually made the operations of the bodily functions a part of itself. A child learning to walk requires the initial use of the mind, working as the supervisor of the cerebrospinal system. But soon walking becomes an automatic procedure and slips into the realm and under the dominion of the sympathetic system. When first learning the multiplication table, the mind must labor to make the knowledge an integral part of itself. Once accomplished, the knowledge slips into the kingdom of the subconscious and one automatically *knows* one's figures. Habits of life — driving a car, typing a computer keyboard — the knowledge of these things, once possessed, becomes in part a function of the automatic operation of the sympathetic system controlled by the subconscious.

Now let us approach more subtle functions of this automatic nervous system, which concern its connection with the subconscious mind. Each time you seek rebirth in a new physical body, *you* inherit a sympathetic nervous system which you have built during preceding incarnations. You also inherit a storehouse of mental substance very closely aligned with this nervous system — the subconscious mind — which *you* also have built. This subconscious mind has its indwelling seat of contact in the pituitary gland in the brain. The magnificent queen of the body, the pituitary, holds under her control the complete third dimension of the human being. She supervises her kingdom through four channels:

1. the sympathetic system;

2. the glandular system;

3. the bloodstream; these performing their functions under the power of

4. the subconscious mind.

We are dealing at present only with the sympathetic system as it operates through the subconscious mind. This system is negative-feminine in polarity. The pituitary gland is negative-feminine in polarity. The subconscious mind is negative-feminine in polarity. It is well to keep this in mind for better understanding the mysteries of the inner soul.

HOW THE CONSCIOUS MIND IMPRESSES THE SUBCONSCIOUS

The nervous systems are the vehicles of your developing consciousness. Their development in early humanity was actually the means by which you evolved into you. For without your nervous systems you would be reduced to a senseless, soundless, sightless, immobile mass of multiplying protoplasm.

The nervous systems organize and control the complete mechanism of consciousness, in that the senses operate through them.

The elaborate nerve network consists of uncountable numbers of cells, constantly changing and multiplying under the impact of thought. With the development of your mind, used strenuously or meditatively, thought vibrations cause activity and expansion in the cells of the nervous system. When a mental activity passes below the "threshold" of consciousness, this process can be said to have come under the domination of the subconscious, and since the subconscious operates through the sympathetic system, that particular activity of consciousness will have passed under the automatic operation of the sympathetic nervous system.

To clarify with an example, let us say that your waking conscious mind has been busily engaged creating a negative thoughtform of illness. Somewhere along the way a fear has entered that perhaps you may be harboring some dread disease, and the thought fastens itself in your mind. You dwell upon it, and you *believe* it to be true. This is akin to giving an order of illness to the subconscious mind. Even though this negative activity may pass out of the waking mind, it will have slipped under the threshold of

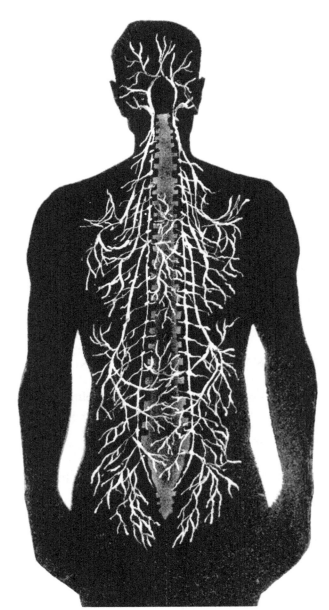

THE SYMPATHETIC NERVOUS SYSTEM

The sympathetic nervous system consists of a double chain of nerve ganglia, rising out of the cerebellum in the brain, passing downward through the neck and medulla oblongata in the back of the head and extending down the entire length of the spine on either side of the spinal column — one chain of ganglia on the left and one on the right. The two cords converge in the brain, the heart, the solar plexus, the abdomen and the pelvic area.

consciousness into the realm of the subconscious as a command to bring the thought into actual manifestation as a form of illness. Thus, from conscious through subconscious, your inner state of mind becomes "externalized" in the outer condition of your body.

The subconscious is all powerful in its workings. Anything you *believe* with extreme intensity takes on the quality of a command to the subconscious, operating through the automatic functions of the sympathetic system. Giant that it is in power, the subconscious has limited reasoning ability, and is hardly capable of logic. It only acts to carry out the directives of the waking conscious mind. The cells of the sympathetic system, imbued with the negative polarity of your fear, will actually begin to produce that which is feared.

The negative thoughtform becomes integrated into the subconscious mind, and it will operate automatically through the sympathetic nervous system to bring the feared disease into manifestation *unless* a more powerful positive suggestion is given to counteract the original command. The subconscious will obey *the more powerful of the two commands!*

If the command to let go of the fear of disease is more powerful than the thought of disease, the negative thought is erased and will become devoid of power. The power of the new thoughtform — that of bodily perfection — begins to take action and you experience a healing and a restoration of health.

As we have previously mentioned, this is one of the methods of our Astarian healings. We speak to the subconscious mind of the Astarian who has asked our help, and command it to set to work to bring about a healing. *If* we are successful in convincing the subconscious of the worthiness of our command, we have an instantaneous healing. Usually it requires longer.

Sometimes we must repeat our commands and affirmations over and over, until the subconscious mind *must* let go of the negative thoughtform and allow our suggestions of perfection and healing to operate.

Although our healing work has no direct connection with this particular Lesson, it does relate to the workings of the sympathetic nervous system, so we felt it pertinent to mention it again (see *Lessons Two* and *Three, First Degree*) to give you an insight into the incredible power of the subconscious, as it functions through the automatic operations of the sympathetic system.

THE RESERVOIR OF MEMORIES

In the superconscious mind storehouse lie the memories of long past lives and events. The human brain does *not* store memories. It is only a mass of cells *through* which the levels of the mind function. *Memories can come into consciousness only as they proceed from the superconscious mind.*

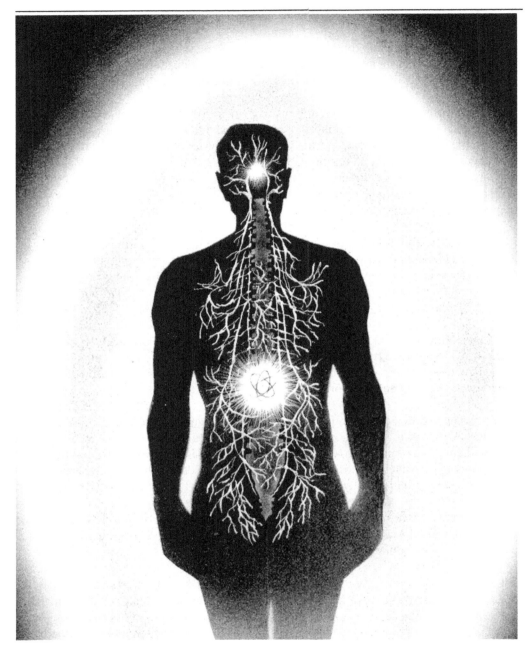

THE SYMPATHETIC SYSTEM AND THE SOLAR PLEXUS BRAIN

The sympathetic system is the instrument of the astral body. Through the sympathetic, desires well up within and are activated in the abdominal solar plexus brain, the home of the emotional seed atom, the contact point of the astral body.

Some advanced souls are able to contact the superconscious and receive a flow of inspiration directly into the waking consciousness. But at the lifewave's present level of mind evolution, most memories filter from the superconscious through the forcefield of the subconscious and into the waking consciousness.

The subconscious is *not in itself* the reservoir of memories. It is true that memories do come *through* the subconscious, but only as they are released into it from the superconscious. It is important that you remember this. Most medical scientists and psychologists proclaim the subconscious to be the channel of past memories. With this we partially agree, except we declare the *true* home of memories to lie in the superconscious storehouse from which they find their way into the subconscious forcefield.

However, to keep the discussion simple, we shall join the psychologists in teaching concerning subconscious mind memories. But you must keep in mind what we have just said ... that they were placed in the subconscious *through, by* and *from* the superconscious.

So, let us say: through the subconscious mind-sympathetic system storehouse pour the memories of long-past incarnations ... many loves, many hates, many temptations, many upsurgings of anger and revenge, deep chasms of grief and sorrows, gleaming heights of aspiration and achievement. These half-remembered occasions and vaporous memories, winging their way from the storehouse of the past, infiltrate the subconscious and the automatic workings of the sympathetic system.

PHOBIAS, COMPLEXES AND INHIBITIONS

What releases these hidden darknesses? Several things. First, we must remind you of the permanent seed atom in the heart which holds in itself the *akashic record of all your past lives, feelings, incidents, actions, progressions and talents.*

Out of this seed atom pours a constant flow of picture images. These infinitesimal bits of akashic recordings are swirling centers of energy, colored, conditioned, qualified and created by the nature of your past as well as by your present actions and thoughts. They flow steadily and constantly through the bloodstream, bringing bad karma or good, health or disease, misery or happiness, as the bloodstream deposits them in the glands and sympathetic nervous system.

Unless the negative picture images are counteracted by powerful thoughts of health, happiness, success and perfection, the sympathetic system will automatically react to bring undesired effects into your body ... which is simply a reaping of past-planted seeds. The undesirable karma *can* be overpowered, unless it is of a nature which belongs in the realm of a much higher cosmic scheme than are the operations of the sympathetic nervous system, a realm about which we spoke in describing the science of rebirth.

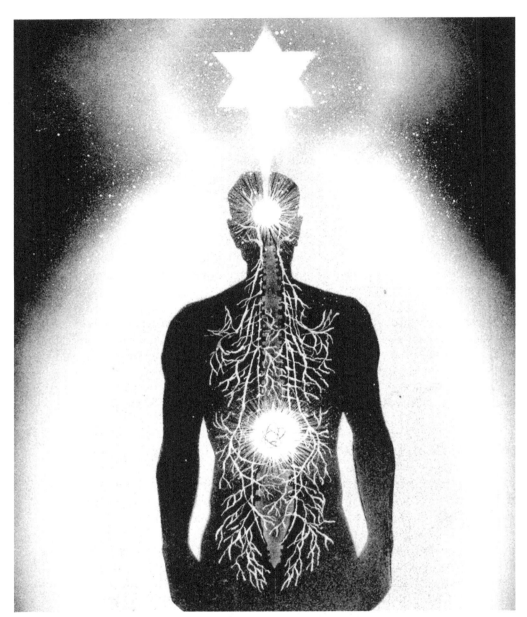

THE SYMPATHETIC SYSTEM, THE ABDOMINAL BRAIN
AND THE PITUITARY GLAND

The subconscious mind, operating through the sympathetic system, has gradually made the operations of the automatic bodily functions a part of itself. The pituitary gland holds complete dominion over the third dimension of one's being through the sympathetic nervous system, the glandular system, and the bloodstream. All of these perform their functions under the power of the subconscious mind, operating through the pituitary.

The ordinary individual, then, is victim or beneficiary of his or her past. The heart seed atom can well be called a mill of the gods.

> *The mills of the gods grind slowly,*
> *but they grind exceeding fine.*

This heart seed atom slowly "grinds out" these energy records, and the soul reaps its harvest. Many misunderstood fears within us have been placed there in the long-dead past, and well up again to haunt us through the mysterious operations of the sympathetic system. Most illnesses can be explained by, and traced to, laws broken in this present life — wrong thinking, wrong living in general. But many of those deeply hidden complexes — unexplainable hates and loves, unusual temptations, overwhelming fears, mysterious neuroses — these belong to the world of the subconscious as it externalizes through the sympathetic system. And the sympathetic system, in turn, is only the instrument of the karmic akashic record carried in the heart seed atom.

We meet an apparent stranger, and strong vibrations are set into action that strike us with a turbulent impact, either attracting or repelling. We wonder why. Some outwardly innocent occasion produces circumstances that begin the churnings of violent vibrations that arouse within us either fears or angers, loves or hates ... unexplained. We wonder why. It is the sympathetic nervous system in action, bringing into manifestation all the harvests of your past sowings. We call it karma. *As ye sow, so shall ye reap!*

Negative eruptions of innate emotion, dark hatreds, destructive fears — can all these be removed and overcome as they are released by the heart atom? Can they be neutralized before the sympathetic system can make them a *reality* in your life? Is it truly possible to overcome one's karma?

It is indeed possible to dissipate most types of karma before the seeds can take root and flower into manifestation. How?

1. One way is simply by being an Astarian. One who becomes an Astarian immediately comes under the benevolent watch of the Order of Melchizedek, which indicates that you are daily bathed in glorious radiations of the mystic White Light. To become an Astarian implies that *one means to attempt to walk in the light henceforth, and the one who so tries will be given every assistance by unseen hands every step of the way.*

Those who do not follow through with this noble intention are not aided and abetted in their misdeeds, to be sure. But those who TRY to walk the Astarian way will be constantly assisted. This does not imply that they shall have no more karma. It does mean that when the seeds of bad karma are evident, if you, the Astarian, will bend your own efforts to erase them by *right thinking, right doing, right service,* the Teachers will take ten steps toward you to help for every one step you take for yourself. Blessings from unexpected sources will fill your life in spite of your hardships.

2. Holding the Astarian affirmation constantly in mind will cause the power in destructive karmic seeds to become weakened:

I AM SURROUNDED BY THE PURE WHITE LIGHT
OF THE CHRIST.
ONLY GOOD CAN COME TO ME.
ONLY GOOD SHALL GO FROM ME.

3. Instead of prevailing upon the Father/Mother to *Please, God, heal me of my afflictions!* learn to say: *Today I shall send a note of encouragement to Mrs. Smith who just lost her husband. I shall send some flowers to Sally Jones who is ill. I shall find time to pray for Joe Brown who has arthritis so badly. And, dear God, won't you please help that little child who was hurt down the street yesterday? And, then, while I am doing these things for others, God, if there is some healing somewhere in Your universe for me, may I be so favored as to be worthy of receiving it.*

Keep eternally busy thinking of and doing for others if you would be healed yourself, if you would dissipate the seeds of unpleasant karma in your own life. *It is the most powerful healing magic in the whole wide world ... serving others either with thoughts, prayers or actions.*

4. Take your Astarian studies seriously. Absorb the Teachings. Truly become a sincere seeker and sharer of the White Light.

BE CAUTIOUS OF HYPNOSIS

A harmful manner in which dormant inhibitions might be released in your waking conscious mind is through uneducated hypnotists. For instance, let us say that even though there may be unpleasant karmic recordings hidden in the recesses of your being, they have been released by the seed atom only gradually so that you have been able to cope with them. An unschooled hypnotist, using you as a subject, could trigger these undesirable emotions into increased action. Beware of *any* hypnotist who is not a devoted student of the esoteric sciences, for such a one neither knows the dangers involved nor understands the various levels of the human mind.

In the hands of a trained esoteric hypnotist who knows how to dissipate the power of these negative aspects, hypnotism is a wonderful and remarkable tool. But under the control of a neophyte-hypnotist, you can become a victim of your own reactivated weaknesses. The same is true of dabbling with drugs such as LSD, mescaline, etc.

THE SYMPATHETIC SYSTEM AND THE CHAKRAS

In our study of the First Degree we linked the plexuses of the sympathetic nervous system with the spinal chakras. Now that we are entering deeper mysticism, it remains for us to amplify this teaching.

We must qualify the teaching that the chakras are a part of the sympathetic nervous system. The chakras are not only etheric counterparts of the glandular system, they are connected etherically with the sympathetic system, and both they and the glands use the sympathetic as their instrument of expression. In this sense they are indeed a part of the sympathetic system. However:

It must be remembered that the sympathetic system is very tangible and can be discerned by medical scientists — whereas the chakras are composed of etheric substance and cannot be perceived, nor is orthodox science aware of them.

The etheric body has its own nervous system, a counterpart of the sympathetic and cerebrospinal systems in the physical. The chakras of the etheric body are the negative plexuses of that body, just as the sympathetic nervous system is the negative system in our physical form. The chakras, operating through the etheric nervous system which we call the nadis, perform for the etheric body what the glands do for our physical. They link together the sympathetic nervous system of the physical body and the etheric nervous system of the etheric body. In this sense they, the chakras, are indeed linked to the sympathetic system of our physical form ... but in an etheric sense only.

There is much more to be said concerning this, but it is out of place until we have pursued our studies of the cerebrospinal nervous system. We shall return to the subject again when we have had an opportunity to clarify much concerning the cerebrospinal.

Keep this in mind:

The subconscious-sympathetic system belongs to your past.

The waking conscious-cerebrospinal system belongs to your present.

The superconscious-double spinal cord belongs to your future.

The double spinal cord is representative of the future time when the sympathetic nervous system will have "married" with the cerebrospinal system, and the superconscious will have at last come to dwell within, to pour its wisdom and its perfection into and upon the glorious you of tomorrow.

Roots of the Tree of Knowledge

Second Degree — Lesson Three

YOUR BUILT-IN COMMUNICATION SYSTEM

Raise your foot an inch and lower it again. To accomplish this simple act you have sent the equivalent of thousands of "telegrams" along hundreds of "wires" to scores of "stations" where the messages were delivered and acted upon by an army of cells, tissues, ligaments and muscles. Imagine what happens when you walk or run or talk or do housework or drive a car! The "wires" which carry these important messages comprise the cerebrospinal nervous system. We turn to it now, not merely in its physical aspect but as a vital segment of the esoteric anatomy of the Tree of Knowledge.

The cerebrospinal system encompasses the brain and extends down the spinal cord to be buried in a mass of gray matter at the base of the spine. It is called the voluntary nervous system in that it operates under the conscious functions of your mind, whereas the sympathetic operates automatically without the thinking processes involved.

The sympathetic has been operating for eons and has become the instrument of the developing astral form. The cerebrospinal is, comparatively speaking, still in the process of birth. This system is the child of the mental body, the product of your mental growth and the instrument through which the conscious mind operates. It is the instrument of the senses, the channel for the functions of volition, sensation and consciousness. Through this system you see, hear, taste, smell and feel. It is indeed the roots of the Tree of Knowledge of Good and Evil in the individual, the channel of consciousness through which you will eventually evolve into godhood.

This incredibly intricate system of nerves could well be compared to a telegraphic system, with the brain the central station. The spinal cord and the network of nerves represent the connecting "telegraph wires" over which the messages are conveyed.

The cerebrospinal is the instrument of the Oversoul, and through this instrumentality the soul is able to progress and develop. Through the cerebrospinal the Oversoul communicates with the outside world by means of the ever-expanding consciousness of the soul.

We have told you the sympathetic system was the first to manifest in the early days of our beginning, although the cerebrospinal was there in embryo. Until the

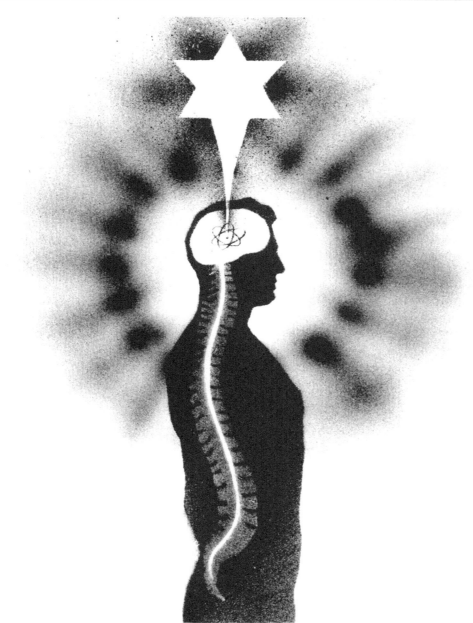

THE CEREBROSPINAL NERVOUS SYSTEM

The cerebrospinal nervous system encompasses the brain, and extends downward through the spinal cord to be buried in a mass of gray matter at the base of the spine. Physically it consists of the brain, the spinal cord, the peripheral cerebral, the spinal nerves, and the sense organs. Metaphysically, it is the instrument of the Oversoul and through it the soul is enabled to evolve. Through the mental seed atom in the pineal gland, it is connected with the mental body.

cerebrospinal began to flower, you were under the domination of the instinctive sympathetic system and, with your undeveloped consciousness, unable to attain a high degree of evolution. The cerebrospinal manifests only that portion of perfection which you have been able to build in more recent incarnations, since the mind is only now arriving at a point worthy to be called "mind."

The cerebrospinal develops through the impact of outer experiences upon its sensory terminals. Impulses of the physical world react upon the nerve ends, causing sensation and waves of nervous energy to be transmitted to the fibers of the brain. From the brain the impulses are carried to the inner vehicles of consciousness such as the astral, mental and causal "brains."

Let us say you experience an injury to the brain serious enough to prevent the mind from functioning through it. Nevertheless, the heart will continue to beat, the wastes of the body will be eliminated, the blood will continue to surge through the veins, breathing will proceed even though there is no conscious mind operating in the form. The automatic functions will continue under the direction of the sympathetic system while the volitional functions of the cerebrospinal are in abeyance. In this sense they are two independent systems.

On the other hand, under more normal conditions they operate as a unit. Let us say that for some reason you find yourself unable to eat food for awhile. The unfed stomach, the functions of which lie under the direction of the sympathetic system, will soon become prominently noticeable to the mind through the cerebrospinal system.

Music, bringing a pleasurable sensation to the mind through the cerebrospinal system, will reflect soothingly upon the organs dominated by the sympathetic, and can even help to heal disturbed conditions in them. In this cooperative esthetic sense, they operate as a unit.

The cerebrospinal experienced its primary functions during the latter years of the Lemurian epoch and has gradually been developing since that time under the impacts from the simultaneously developing human will. Since your will power is yet in its infancy, the cerebrospinal has developed very slowly, but as the will evolves its higher potentialities, so will the cerebrospinal increase in power.

In earlier days humankind was exposed to visions and the influence of the etheric and astral worlds which, to the lifewave, were a natural part of its existence. Our psychic faculties were involuntarily operative because of three things: (1) an active pineal gland; (2) a dominating sympathetic nervous system; (3) a skeleton of softer cartilage. (See *Lesson Two, Second Degree*.)

THE BEING OF TOMORROW

As the brain developed, bringing the cerebrospinal into greater prominence, the pineal gland gradually became dormant. The sympathetic system became increasingly subordinate to the rising powers of the cerebrospinal. And the skeleton form became further crystallized.

As the cerebrospinal continues to develop under the power of the will, the higher planes will once again be opened to the lifewave via the reactivated pineal gland and the balanced action of the pituitary body. However, this new development will be voluntary and controlled, because it will operate through the cerebrospinal system.

As the mind unfolds, the cerebrospinal will come into its adulthood, and vice versa. Although the cerebrospinal is the channel for the operations of the mental body, at our present state of evolution it is equally under the control of the astral body, the body of emotions. The mind, operating through the cerebrospinal, has not yet gained enough of its own dynamic power to withstand the influence of the carnal desires rising through the automatic functions of the sympathetic system.

These desires react through impulses upon the cerebrospinal, which means that it is frequently victimized by the uncontrolled desires and emotions of the astral nature. As the mental nature becomes increasingly stable under the impact of our developing will, the mind will begin to dominate the emotions and, in the slow process of time, will eventually bring the inner powerhouse of the sympathetic under its control.

You will then be able to govern the functions of your physical body by your mind. You will not then be subject to the illnesses which plague you now. Through the sympathetic operating as it does under the automatic control of the subconscious, you are at present subject to the diseases and torments of the physical form. You have not yet gained enough mental control to command the subconscious to perfect its workings through the sympathetic system.

The sympathetic, as you already know, works automatically under the influence of the subconscious as it in turn carries out the commands placed there by the waking conscious mind. Unwittingly so, it is true, for you never intentionally bring illness upon yourself. You do so by the negativity of your own conscious thinking. When the unruly giant, the subconscious, is brought under your mental control — when the two nervous systems begin to merge in their mystic marriage — then you are beginning not only to reach for but to attain some measure of godhood.

THE TWO HEAD GLANDS

With the further development of the cerebrospinal will also come the awakening of the dormant organs in the brain, and many of the brain cells which now are inactive. The pituitary body will become far more active than is obvious at present. (In our Lesson concerning the glands, we shall have much more to say about the functions of this powerful gland.) It will have combined with the pineal to open the inimitable third eye — the "eye of wisdom" in the you of tomorrow. You will gradually become as you were in the past.

The sympathetic system will harmonize with the cerebrospinal; the pineal gland will be no longer dormant, and the skeleton form will again become etherealized. But with your developed powers you will no longer be as a puppet, buffeted by the elements as we were in our early days. You will have become a reborn, regenerated, all-seeing, all-knowing god, commanding the elements through the power of your will.

The pituitary will become the physical organ for astral clairvoyance. It is this gland, working through the sympathetic system, which will act as a point of contact between the waking conscious mind and that of the astral form as we begin to remember our journeys into that Other Land. The pineal — the instrument of the mental body — will be the organ of thought transmission as we acquire the ability to transmit thoughts from one mind to another. Telepathy will come to the fore and its unfoldment will be through the pineal.

We possess an etheric brain, an astral brain and a mental brain. These are nonphysical counterparts of the physical brain corresponding to the higher vehicles. Memory of journeys taken in the astral cannot become a part of the waking conscious mind until connecting links and bridges have been forged between all these brains or forcefields.

Building these bridges must be through the nervous systems of the higher bodies, and will be accomplished by means of an active pituitary which will focus the vibrational waves of the higher planes upon and into the physical brain, much as a magnifying glass concentrates the heat from the sun upon any point of contact. We shall enlarge upon this idea when we begin our researches into the brain itself.

Until these developments unfold, the waking consciousness cannot become the instrument of the superconscious, for the superconscious cannot operate with full intensity until the two physical nervous systems — the sympathetic and the cerebrospinal — merge in their mystic marriage.

THE MYSTIC MARRIAGE OF THE TWO SYSTEMS

Ida, pingala and sushumna in the cerebrospinal system are involved in the entire mechanism of the spinal column. However, even though the spinal chakras are connected with the sympathetic system, such is not the case with one of the two centers in the head. The pituitary belongs to the sympathetic system, but the pineal belongs to the cerebrospinal. The brow chakra, involved with the pituitary, is a part of the sympathetic ... while the crown chakra, involved with the pineal, is a part of the cerebrospinal system.

Here we witness a harmonizing of the two nervous systems, and a hint of the coming marriage between them. Also the throat chakra is both positive and negative in polarity for it reflects the power generated in the medulla oblongata. It is in the medulla that pingala and ida — the positive and negative lines of force — cross with the fires and fluids of sushumna, creating the "cross of Golgotha" upon which the lower being is

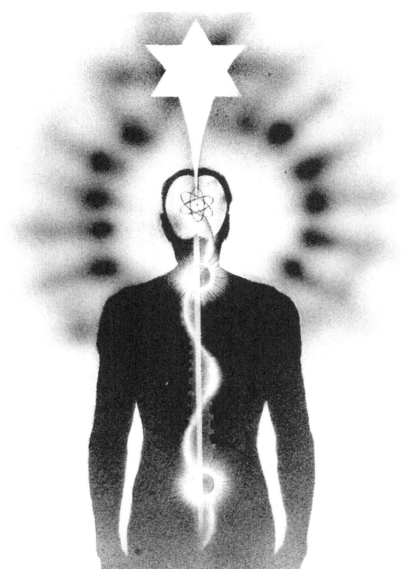

THE METAPHYSICAL CEREBROSPINAL NERVOUS SYSTEM
(back view)

The metaphysical cerebrospinal system consists of the brain, the spinal cord, the positive pingala, and the pineal gland. In our illustration we also depict the throat and navel chakras, which are both positive and negative, and belong both to the positive cerebrospinal and the negative sympathetic system. Therefore, we have drawn them in both light and dark. The navel, for instance, belongs to the negative sympathetic system, but indraws positive solar prana, making it both positive and negative. Thus the " marriage" of the two systems is already culminated in this particular chakra.

crucified to attain its ascension. The navel chakra also belongs to both nervous systems for, although it operates automatically under the functions of the sympathetic, it indraws positive solar prana from the sun, thereby becoming positive-negative in polarity.

Try to visualize the sympathetic system, consisting of the two cords of nerve plexuses running down the right and left sides of the body. Visualize them connected by the negative chakras along the spine and the brow or pituitary chakra in the head. Next visualize the cerebrospinal involving the ida, pingala and sushumna intertwining the length of the spinal column and including the crown or pineal chakra in the head.

Ida, the Black Serpent entwining the spine, is negative and the pituitary body is negative. It follows then that this negative channel must be prominently connected with the negative sympathetic system. The pituitary gland, which has registered a negative polarity for eons of time, is now beginning to register a slight positive polarity in its posterior section. One remote day in the lifewave's evolution this important gland will become a balanced seat of negative-positive power.

Suppose we take the sympathetic system and overlay it with the cerebrospinal. Now, indeed, we begin to see the picture. Now we see that some of the negative spinal chakras are registering positive polarity, and ida, a branch of the positive cerebrospinal system, is registering a negative polarity. Our illustration clearly discloses what we are attempting to teach: *the cerebrospinal system and the sympathetic system are indeed merging.*

The two systems will some day truly blend because ida, pingala and sushumna of the cerebrospinal system will have become completely enmeshed with the negative chakras, and vice versa. The positive of the cerebrospinal will have united with the negative of the sympathetic.

Intricate "bridges," such as the autonomic system, will have been created and gradually the two nervous systems will completely merge. Mind will have mastered matter. No longer will we be at the mercy of the innate workings of the subconscious operating through the sympathetic   system. Through your own unfolded powers you will manipulate your physical functions and control your emotional life.

Combining these two systems is the entire point of our present discussion. As the two nervous systems become more involved, the positive and negative forces operating in the two separate systems will become increasingly harmonized. When perfect equilibrium is achieved, kundalini will rise easily and naturally through sushumna, and humans will become Master souls.

The practice of Lama Yoga is a certain method of uniting the two systems. Thus Astarians should be among the vanguard of the human race to attain superior psychic and spiritual powers.

The mystic marriage of the nervous systems will culminate in the birth of the Christ-in-man, for as kundalini rises she will carry with her much of the generative

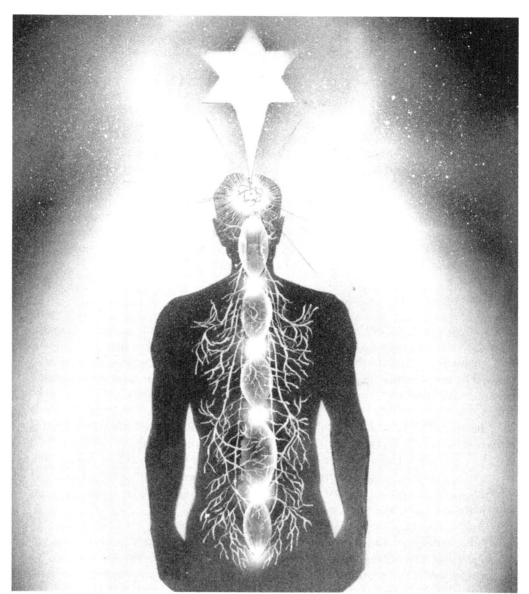

THE MYSTIC MARRIAGE OF THE TWO SYSTEMS

In future humanity the cerebrospinal and the sympathetic will have consummated their mystic marriage. We will mentally control the functions of the sympathetic, thereby bringing under our own conscious dominion the state of our physical being. We will control our health, eliminate and block the sensation of pain, and become master of our destiny. The negative forces of ida and the positive forces of pingala will have attained equilibrium to rise up the channel of sushumna, bringing cosmic consciousness to the lifewave.

powers of the lower force centers. As those powers are lifted to the brain and away from the reproductive organs, our mental potentialities will be realized and the carnal minded person of today will become the regenerated Master of tomorrow.

MYSTERY OF THE MAGIC WAND: THE CADUCEUS

In the days of the Mystery Schools, one of the dramas of the Greater Mysteries concerned the god Hermes, or Mercury, and his mysterious magic wand, the caduceus. As his famous rod of office, the caduceus was the source of Mercury's power to fly.

The super-eminent symbol did not belong exclusively to Mercury, however. It was often held in the hand of statues of the Assyrian goddess Cybele. It was used by the Egyptian god Anubis in initiation ceremonies. It was wielded by the Grecian goddess Aphrodite and the god Dionysus. So the symbol was universal.

What mystery did it symbolize?

In the Mystery Schools of Mu, Atlantis, Egypt and Greece the caduceus was often used to symbolize the whole person — physically, mentally, emotionally, psychically and spiritually. To clarify the mystery of the soul, the caduceus was overlaid by a cross. The cross represented the realm of matter and the physical form upon which the soul was "nailed" during its sojourn in the physical body.

The staff of the caduceus symbolized the spinal column. The entwining serpents represented the etheric channels ida and pingala. The human head was symbolized by the globe and the wings defined the various levels of the mind operating through the brain. In many of the ancient symbols the staff was depicted without the widespread wings but never without the entwining serpents. The wingless globe symbolized the soul without its unfolded superconscious mind.

In the writings of Madame Blavatsky she quotes a commentary from the esoteric doctrine: "*The trunk of the Asvattha (The Tree of Life and Being, the Rod of Caduceus) grows from and descends at every Beginning (every new Manvantara) from the two dark wings of the Swan (Hansa) of Life. The two Serpents, the ever-living and its illusion (spirit and matter) whose two heads grow from the one head between the wings, descend along the trunk, interlaced in close embrace. The two tails join on earth (the manifested universe) into one, and this is the great illusion, O Lanoo.*"

The serpents representing ida and pingala, the negative and the positive polarities, join together at the base of the caduceus just as they do in the spinal column, signifying that spirit and matter are united as one in the body, and from this union springs the Tree of Life and the Tree of the Knowledge of Good and Evil. The serpents also represent the cosmic forces of the sun and the moon, and are channels for their mystic influence.

The caduceus was often used during initiations to induce trance in the initiate and to symbolize the state of regeneration or purity. The staff, symbolizing the spinal column, simultaneously symbolized the upraised serpent of kundalini — the globe symbolizing the head and the outspread wings the attainment of the superconscious through regeneration. When we speak of regeneration we refer to raising or resurrecting the reproductive energies from the generative organs up the spinal cord into the brain. It is this upraised kundalini which transforms the human soul into a Master soul.

In the Mysteries the caduceus also symbolized the personified constellation Virgo. In the Mysteries which depicted the solar drama, the caduceus and cross symbolized the equator and equinoctial Colure, the great circle of the celestial sphere through the celestial poles and equinoxes, and the four elements — earth, air, fire and water — proceeding from a common center. The globe — a serpent with its tail in its mouth — became the emblem of the Supreme Deity. The cross, lacking the wings, became the Egyptian Tau cross, symbol of the upraised generative power in the initiate of the Mysteries.

Especially in the Egyptian Mysteries the serpent and cross were associated. In the temple of Isis at Philae a cross bearing a serpent is found on the Grand Staircase. On many Egyptian ruined temples are found two figures holding up a cross on top of which is an erect serpent. The Egyptian Crux Ansata is a cross with a coiled serpent above it.

THE COSMIC CADUCEUS

In some Mystery dramas the caduceus symbolized the lifewaves of humanity traversing the "Round of Tartarus" — the seven Rounds of involution and evolution the lifewave experiences after its departure from its etheric Garden of Eden until the time it reenters paradise.

The evolving lifewaves make seven revolutions around the seven globes of the seven world periods. We call the seven periods "Rounds." The cosmic caduceus symbolized this pilgrimage. Three Rounds are spent with the lifewaves descending steadily downward in involution. The first half of the Fourth Round is the lowest when humanity has reached the nadir of its Round in Tartarus. The last half of the Fourth Round sees the lifewave beginning its slow ascent in evolution: the journey back upward to the Godhead.

Humankind has now attained the last half of the Fourth Round. Humanity, leaving the darkness, is treading the upward pathway toward the light. But whereas the vast masses of humanity will travel slowly and painfully through the Rounds of evolution, the initiate will travel "the straight and narrow way" of initiation and liberation, symbolized by the staff of the caduceus. In a few lives the initiate will accomplish that which the millions of the masses require millenniums — even perhaps in this one incarnation the goal may be realized.

In our illustration, the Black Serpent represents the descending path of involution while the White represents the ascending path of evolution. The Fourth Round, the lowest, encompasses the tails of both serpents. This indicates some portion of humanity may still be descending in involution while some are already ascending the upward way of evolution. Therefore the conflicts.

When the Cosmic Door of this Fourth Round closes, *involution* will cease and *evolution* will accelerate. The lifewave of "saved" souls will turn its full force toward a return to the light.

THE "FALL" OF HUMANKIND

Astarians realize there are various interpretations of the Bible:

1. literal;

2. esoteric or hidden;

3. physiological as applied to our physical regeneration;

4. metaphysical;

5. historical. Let us analyze a certain Scripture in the esoteric sense.

In the days of humanity's youth upon this planet, when the gods walked among humankind, an admonition was issued accordingly:

Of every tree of the garden thou mayest freely eat. But of the Tree of the Knowledge of Good and Evil thou shalt not eat of it, for in the day that thou eatest thereof, thou shalt surely die. (Genesis 2:17)

Let us rewrite the Scripture in the light of our new understanding:

Of every tree of the garden (which is your body) *you may freely eat* (or, you may enjoy all the pleasures of the body). *But of the Tree of the Knowledge of Good and Evil* (the cerebrospinal system in the brain and the spinal column, extending to the base of the spine) *you shall not eat this fruit* (you must not use the fluids and substances of this Tree for generative purposes) *for in the day that you do* (when you rob the brain of its creative power by consuming the fruits of the Tree) *the higher powers shall surely die within you!*

In this interpretation the body becomes the Garden of Eden with the Tree of the Knowledge of Good and Evil — the cerebrospinal nervous system, including the etheric sushumna — growing "in the midst of it." To eat of the fruit of this sacred Tree meant to send down to the generative organs a portion of the creative force which, in those early days, still was held resident in the brain.

Man and woman were becoming aware of themselves in a sexual sense and were beginning to unite to reproduce their kind, the practice of which meant that

The Human Caduceus

the creative force in the head must fall to the generative organs. But although its fall divided the divine substance, still it enabled the soul to become a creator in and of itself, and to begin building its own important nervous system through which it was to travel out of nothingness into godhood.

To eat of the Tree of Knowledge, then, meant that the lifewave divided the creative power in the brain and sent part of it spiraling downward to the "land of darkness," the root of the spine. This was, in part, *the fall of man*, since from that time on we began to weave about our etheric forms a "coat of skin" and to become involved in dense matter, leaving behind the etheric realms — our Garden of Eden — in which we had heretofore resided.

Had humankind not eaten of the fruit, and had not the creative force fallen to the generative organs, the soul could not have become the evolving individual it is today — a spirit enmeshed in a material world of turmoil and pain in order to progress through conscious experience to our own individual perfection. It was, indeed, necessary that the higher powers then unfolded "surely die," so that we might focus our attention upon the "world of sweat" into which we were entering.

Thus came about the "fall" of man — the creative force fell within us and the etheric realms were closed to us as the body of dense matter began to crystallize around our etheric forms. Our higher spiritual powers did "die" and we must now, by unfolding them, lift the fruit of the Tree back to the brain and out of the generative organs, becoming the androgynous beings we were in the days of old — except we shall not reenter paradise as the innocent puppet-beings we were then, but as resurrected gods-in-glory.

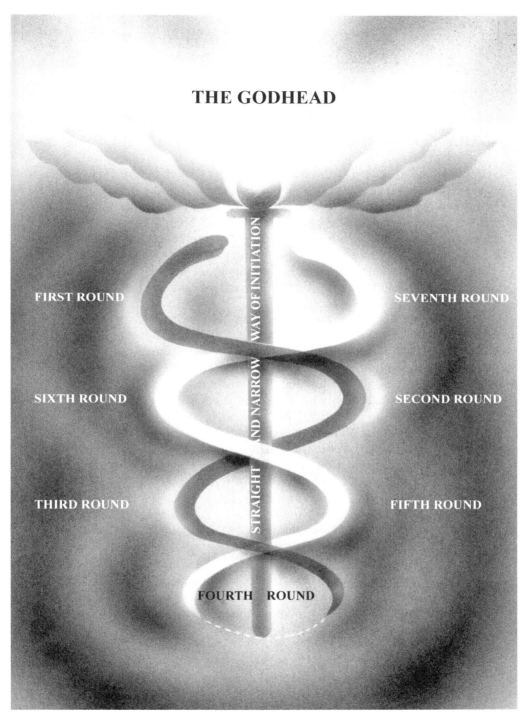

The Cosmic Caduceus

Supplementary Monograph

THE TRANSCENDENTAL POWER OF LOVE

For centuries, we people of this little Earth planet have made our God so little that we have expected very little. Usually we call upon God only in times of greatest adversities. It remains now for us to expand our vision and our expectations and allow that factor in our lives — the larger dream, the larger vision — to come into being, when we begin to envision a larger God and to expect mightier things from the Great Father-Mother. In this new age we are beginning to dream dreams with God on a godlike scale, rather than the meager little prison of self which scarcely dares to take a glimpse outside its windows to see wider horizons.

God has given us the key to our little prisons. He expects us to turn the key and to open the door which will lead us out into the vast freedom of the universe, out into the broad horizons of living — not thinking in our narrow, constricted way of life with its innumerable limitations, but a life with infinite expansions and possibilities, a life expressing infinite love, a life of infinite commitment to a principle of love-in-God which will inevitably meet all human needs, not only in this life but throughout eternity.

The key is turned through the drama of prayer-in-action, which is transcendental love. The only thing worth having in life is love, in that it transcends everything else. If you are interested in prayer power, then it follows that you will have to be interested in love power, because love is the key to it all. You will remember that Jesus once taught of this, the greatest of all laws, when he said, *Thou shalt love the Lord thy God with all thy heart, and with all thy soul, and with all thy mind, and with all thy strength ... and thou shalt love thy neighbour as thyself.* (Mark 12:30)

We speak not now of that mundane love so blithely offered by the shallow mind of humans, but of the love which produces miracles. These words of the Christ offer the freedom of the universe, the key to the kingdom of God, and give you the abundant life which everyone ought to receive. God-love is the kind which makes the power of God possible in its release.

All of Christ's ministry, with all its miracles, with all the light that has shined down the centuries, has come from that love released, and nothing else. It never was an intellectual process, although one may seek intellectually to understand. But if you are interested in prayer, if you are interested in healing, if you are interested in communion with God, if you are interested in the release of infinite power in your life, then you will have to break away from the intellect of the mind and come to the intuitional love factor in the heart, and be as a little child in the doing of it.

You are not here to manipulate God, but rather to allow God to manipulate you; to be so serene that the love of God shines out and brings into your life exactly what you would have in your life ... and, through you, blesses everyone else.

Each of us must walk the Eternal Highway, whether we like it or not. Since we must walk it, wouldn't it be a good idea to walk in the light of the power that made the journey possible? — in the spirit of God which is the "life" in every one of us? — to prepare ourselves for a future journey of increased awakening? — and to lift our vision away from this dreadful blindness that afflicts the entire race, in a society which we have helped to build?

We need to rearrange our values, and the greatest opportunity before us today is the exploration of the kingdom of love. Humankind is beginning to realize that love is the Great Law of the universe. Love is beyond and behind intellect. When you see a world manifesting, what you really see is the love of God manifesting form. The very life within you is love. And certainly, when you bring love to bear in a healing ministry of prayer, that is when miracles happen. They seldom occur when only intellect is involved, because love is that Something that is beyond words.

But *something* happens when we begin loving the Father-Mother and literally offering our lives to Them, and loving each other with that dynamic divine manifestation that shines out in us when we get very close to God. When we healers see a human disease melt away because we are able to generate and "stir up" the love of God, then we begin to understand that there is an awesome *something* in operation which is worthy of our devout attention. And when the world really sees love as the dynamic secret weapon, then will we begin to uncover this tremendous kingdom of love in the hearts and minds of all people and find that paradise on Earth which all the world is seeking.

The tragedy is that we are seeking paradise in the wrong way. We are not seeking it the "love" way. It is indeed true that few people calling themselves Christians ever really put true Christianity into action. Somehow we must bring this greater vision above the miracle of being. We must get away from simply drifting in our own little groove of life, and see ourselves as spiritual beings, living in a spiritual universe of infinite dimensions with infinite powers and resources at our disposal, and with the vision of God ahead to show us *who we are*, *what we are*, and *where we should be going*.

The real tragedy is that we become accustomed to ourselves as commonplace. Look at yourself. A miracle! Has it ever occurred to you that there isn't another *you* anywhere in the whole universe? Not in this world nor in any of the countless billions of other worlds out there in deepest space. Not another *you* anywhere in existence at any time, and there never will be. There is only *one you!* And that makes *you* unique.

Since there is only one you, then there is only one you to do whatever *you* have to do to bring into manifestation whatever the Father-Mother would have you do. This places you in an unbelievably wonderful position, and upon you incredible responsibility. It makes you responsible for the state of the world insofar as you are or are not fulfilling your destiny at this particular moment.

That is why we have to begin to dream our dreams with God, because it is the Father-Mother who has the perfect pattern for the perfect unfolding of everything that we are ready to do. The Divine Parents have called us into being, They know exactly what our true potentials are, know exactly where to lead us, and know how quickly They can take us to that fulfillment when we are awakened in that higher consciousness of love.

God never makes a mistake. The Father-Mother will carry you along toward paradise as rapidly as you will go. You will never receive a healing, never receive the spiritual impulses of a better life, unless you begin to be fruitful in the law of love. Apathy and compromise can have no place in your consciousness. When you make this love a reality in your life and put this dynamic power into action, you will see changes.

We are on the threshold of a great new age. Mighty forces are working all over the world to bring coalition, knowledge, guidance and wisdom to Earth, consummating the reality of heavenly powers and forces. The world is on the verge of the greatest spiritual revival in history.

Think! We have the knowledge — we know that dynamic prayer is a living force, and we know that never in all history has the world been in such a dangerous dilemma as it is today. We need some dramatic and some drastic intervention to put things right. In the midst of this terrible potential of disaster, there never was a moment in history so potent in its possibilities of supreme spiritual upliftment and revival. It can begin with *you* — if you will let the Holy Spirit set you on fire and allow the fire to spread.

When you release the true love of God in you and harness it with faith, then you have the power to heal, you have the power to save, you have the power to make the whole world new — because you have, in love and faith, the power to release the infinite perfection of God. You have the power to open wide the channels through which multitudes of angels can bring utopia into the lives of all humankind.

In these dangerous days you haven't time to be sick, you haven't time to be self-centered, to wallow in any kind of self-aggrandizement. You haven't time for self-seeking — for the world is hungry and yearning for those who will rise with a spiritual vision and be about the Father-Mother's business, sending out love right, left and center. When you begin to experience this kind of vision, you'll find yourself being healed of everything — illness, selfishness, hatred — because you'll forget about yourself and turn your whole being into the kingdom of love and loving people and in helping to heal and help others. In helping others — therein truly lies your own healing salvation. You will find that the energies you release are returned to you a thousandfold and healing comes mightily in the midst of it.

Many of us are ill because we are centering our thoughts completely around ourselves, our problems, our difficulties, our pains, our aggravations, our conflicts, our petty little affairs that happen in our everyday lives. And in the midst of them we lose sight of the vision, the incredible miracle of being, the majesty of being alive.

God has given you a gift — a sack of seeds, the seeds of love. The wise recipient accepts his or her gift and says, *"I will keep some for myself but the majority I will spread out into the heart of mother earth, for in so doing I will multiply my treasure."* *And you spread your seeds afar, and gather in your harvest, sufficient for your own needs and enough to share with many others.*

The selfish ones receive their gifts and store their precious seeds in their warehouses against the time of shortage — where the seeds mold and rot. They have not then any for themselves and none to share. The seeds of love always multiply when spread afar. They cannot be hoarded. They are the substance of the universe. The law of abundant return is the principle of God in action — sending forth, returning again, planting and harvesting, spreading and gathering, helping others and receiving your own healing and blessings.

You cannot claim the kingdom of God for yourself alone. Claim it you must! — but it must be done with your arms wide open, breathing it into your own being and sending it out again with all the dedication and faith you can command. As the God-force pours into you, through you and out into the lives of others — then does the power heal and bless you. If you try to hold it all to yourself, it becomes as a stagnant pool. The healing waters of love must be flowing waters. They must move ever outward again from you as you turn your thoughts and actions toward the betterment of your fellowbeing. You cannot help, then, but be healed yourself, or be lifted into a higher, better way of life, whether it be materially or spiritually. It need not manifest necessarily as physical healing — it may be healing of the heart or of the soul.

In so doing, you begin to know what divine energy really is, what vitality and strength truly are, for you are harnessed to the infinite powers of the universe which have only one purpose — to lift your life to an ever-ascending manifestation of fulfillment, and to fill your consciousness with the invincible powers of the spirit to bless everyone else.

YOUR MEDITATION

Go now and sit in a comfortable chair. Read these next words in a spirit of tense expectancy, for we are going to help you to commune with God.

Breathe one slow deep breath.

You are going to lift yourself in consciousness into the very Presence of God and see yourself at one with the Divine Being. You are not going to ask God to come and do something for you. You are going to lift yourself right out of this world with all its problems.

Come up into the adoration and worship and love of God and know that in this glory all things are indeed glorious. See yourself so filled with the power of spirit that its potency is released in the midst of you. Accept the wholeness of God without any qualifications, with no reservations. In the Presence of God, you should expect godlike manifestations, and nothing less.

You should expect the healing of *all* the causes of your past and present distress. The forgiveness of all your sins, if you like; the complete cleansing of your soul and your mind. The past is as dead as yesterday. In the consciousness of the love of God — which transcends all — you transcend *cause*. It is the highest state of consciousness you can ever attain.

GOD'S LOVE TRANSCENDS CAUSE!

If you can find the healing of cause, you will experience your healing now and immediately! You are in the Christ Consciousness at this moment, so you are entitled to express it. To express it you must know the truth that sets you free. You have to know your problems are solved, and that God is in the midst of the situation; that everything is in a state of divine order and perfect adjustment, spiritually, physically, mentally and materially; and that, right now, you are so full of God that any physical illness is healed! It cannot live where God is! Unless, as has been already mentioned, illness is a manifestation of past karma or a spiritual lesson which you have chosen to take upon yourself in this incarnation.

In your mind's eye, see yourself in a state of godlike perfection. See yourself as the most wonderful being on Earth, because it is God who is making you wonderful and whole. See yourself full of vitality and strength and health and joy and power, full of abundant life, eager to accomplish all your highest dreams. See yourself in a Christ-like expression — the real and wonderful *you*, the Christ in you, that wonderful *you* who is eager to expand and expend yourself so that somebody else might be advanced through your help.

That wonderful *you* who would never worry about the sacrifice of time in going clear across town to visit a sick friend in need; that wonderful *you* who doesn't mind going into your personal funds to see that some friend has a helping hand in a time of financial distress; that wonderful *you* who is ready to spend time in prayer for others; that wonderful *you* who doesn't count the cost, but knows the only thing that matters is that you are expending yourself in divine service.

In this meditation, see yourself as you would be with all the powers and resources of God at your disposal ... and make it so. If you are sick, then see the vision of *absolute perfection*. See the disease falling away from you — dissolving from within you, as you hold the pure White Light of the Christ all around yourself and permeate your entire being with it. All power is All Power, and it cannot be less than that!

All the quietness, all the love of God, all the power of God, lives within you. Establish the divine rhythm within yourself by taking another slow deep breath and become serene. Feel yourself going into a state of wholeness. Feel God's power acting upon you and through you. Feel God releasing divine healing throughout your being. Problems are dissolved in your mind, pains are dissolved in your body. These things are inevitable. You are filled with the radiance of Divine Perfection.

Feel near you now the presence of a Wondrous Being who has come to help you. Or a loved one drawing near from his or her estate on the other side of life.

Everything adjusts now to a state of divine order. Your problems, your aggravations, your troubles, your sicknesses — they are committed to the Father-Mother! And if you will hold to this consciousness, in the hours and days that follow this meditation, you will see them melt away and out of your life as the Hand of the Father-Mother works them away into nothingness.

If you know you are released from these things; if you are finished with them and with the responsibility of handling them — if you believe that all the infinite love and intelligence of the universe has now moved into your life, producing divine adjustments, sorting out your problems and solving them — if you believe that, then you can truly breathe a sigh of relief and say, "*Thank you, Father-Mother, it is done!*" For *it will be done!*

If you have an illness, I charge you in the names of all holy Master teachers to rise in wholeness and be done with it! Rise in the power of the spirit right now, this moment, and feel it surging through you. You are healed, you are whole! Your problems are lifted away and into the keeping of a Bigger Hand. Your pains have disappeared as you have been sitting there.

They must be gone because you cannot be in Divine Presence without something happening!

It has happened to you, as you have been indrawing the light.

Take another deep slow breath. Say aloud, "Thank You, Father-Mother."

Try this attunement again and again. It can happen! It will happen! It *must* happen!

God bless and keep you, beloved Astarian. *And may the Holy One Walk Ever With You*, is our prayer.

THE MYSTERY OF LIFE ...

... has puzzled scientist, theologian and philosopher throughout time. Lifelong studies of the objective and superficial are fruitless. But the mystical provides rays of understanding that lead from the maze of confusion to the way of realization.

It's an inner way ... a "know thyself" way...a leap in consciousness from the Self to the Cosmos.

In all of time there has never been an organized assemblage of mystical teachings to equal *Astara's Book of Life*. Your next two Lessons of the Second Degree carry you further along the path of Realization.

Lesson 4 — The Holy Breath, teaches of the inner "river of light," the Nadis, the science of the magnetic fluid, the secret of Tummo, and the purifying breath.

Lesson 5 — The Sphinx Within, describes the inner record of what you are and will become, "the mystic death" of initiation, traveling in the astral, reading the akashic records, entering the stream of divine Sound.

These Lessons provide the solutions to many mysteries. They offer a specialized knowledge that gives deep satisfaction in personal understanding. They gather the tangled webs of confusion and reweave them into the enduring fabric of wisdom.

ACHIEVEMENT IS THE CONSTANT COMPANION OF KNOWLEDGE.

God Whither?

Space!
I cannot tell where you are greatest;
Whether out there,
Or in here where my soul
Lies sleeping.
It stirs and wants to wake,
But I am afraid.
I cannot know
Which way to go;
Whether within or without
To find God.
But if He be everywhere
Then what matter!
Perhaps if I stand
Very still
He will find me.

— Earlyne

Do all you can and then some.

— Selected

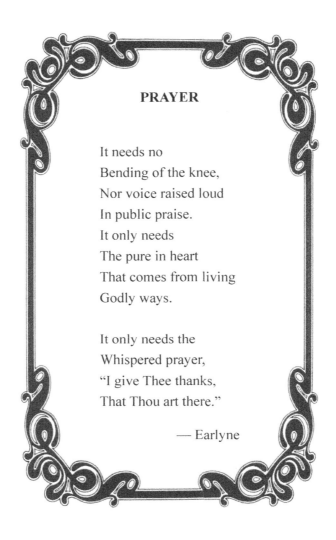

PRAYER

It needs no
Bending of the knee,
Nor voice raised loud
In public praise.
It only needs
The pure in heart
That comes from living
Godly ways.

It only needs the
Whispered prayer,
"I give Thee thanks,
That Thou art there."

— Earlyne

The Holy Breath

Second Degree — Lesson Four

THE VAGUS NERVE — RIVER OF LIGHT

If breath is the most important element of life to you, what is most important to breath?

Lungs? No — the *vagus nerve*. It is one of the little known heroes of your body mechanism.

There is no life without breath. And there is no breath without the vagus nerve. Like the director of a play who is not seen by the audience, the vagus nevertheless dominates the respiratory system. It is probably the paramount single nerve of your body. To both medical and esoteric scientists it is one of the supreme channels of life in the physical being.

To the esoteric scientist it is much more: it also is the channel for the holy breath, that mysterious inner breath known only to the yogis and those who have attained a high degree of inner spiritual enlightenment.

The vagus is called the *pneumogastric nerve* — *pneumo* being translated as "life-breath" by the initiates. *Gastro,* of course, refers to the stomach or the abdomen. This nerve is the channel for the breath already spoken about in connection with the yogic inner breath sometimes experienced by those engaged in the practice of Lama Yoga.

Following the breathing exercise, or during the ensuing meditation, the Astarian may find that the usual breathing process has become temporarily suspended, and a mysterious inner breathing mechanism has assumed control. It becomes unnecessary to breathe as we usually do. There is no indication of a breathing process whatever, yet one is aware that there is temporarily a motionless mechanism operating within. The passage of this internal holy breath — this "soul-breath" — by means of the vagus nerve.

It is obvious that all yogis use and understand this science of the inner breath in connection with their phenomenal activities, and in their spiritual attainments. For instance, the yogic practice of *pranayama* (the control of the breath) is intimately associated with regulating the functions of the vagus nerve; consciously suspending its automatic functions and power over the respiratory system and bringing them under the domination of the mind.

In other words, removing the vagus functions from the dominion of the sympathetic nervous system, and temporarily bringing them under the operation of the cerebrospinal system, or under the control of the waking conscious mind. This is no casual accomplishment when one considers that *all* the vital automatic functions of the human form operate under the command of the vagus nerve, since it regulates not only the breathing apparatus but also the heartbeat.

Temporarily removing the sympathetic system's control of the vagus enables the yogi to bring the heartbeat under conscious control, slowing it to a minimum. The functions of the radial nerves which lead directly to the pulse points in the wrists can be stopped. Also, by arresting the action of the vagus nerve which controls the respiratory system through nerve impulses, the yogi can be buried alive for a period of a few hours to several days.

By means of the vagus passing temporarily under the control of the cerebrospinal system, the yogi is able to inflict seemingly serious injury upon the physical form without the slightest evidence of pain and, in turn, instantaneously heal the self-inflicted wounds. We have seen this performed many times. We have watched as cheeks were penetrated by long pins. We have watched tongues being pierced. We have seen nails driven through the palms of hands as the yogi stood unflinching, obviously experiencing no pain.

Though certainly too sensational, this type of demonstration exhibits a remarkable mental control over both the cerebrospinal and the sympathetic systems and displays an astonishing mastery of the control of sensation impulses reaching the brain which normally would also register the sensation of pain through the vagus nerve. It demonstrates humankind's future ability to control the involuntary nervous system — the sympathetic — through the power of the will.

It must be remembered, of course, that the performance of these seeming "miracles" is not the ultimate purpose of mentally controlling the involuntary sympathetic system. The yogis call these phenomenal performances *siddhis*, and the energy of control should not be constantly exhausted in performing such demonstrations. The ultimate purpose of such a mental attainment is to direct these released energies toward a higher spiritual attainment, such as gaining Nirvana, or spiritual illumination.

Such demonstrations fulfill a purpose only when they are done to show others what a person *can* attain, and to teach "the way" to earnest seekers. The ultimate purpose

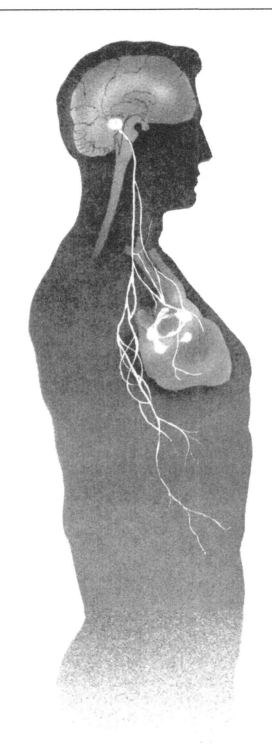

THE VAGUS PATHWAY CONNECTING THE HEAD AND HEART

of the yogi is not to promiscuously display supernatural powers, but to attain at-one-ment with the Infinite. The acquired supernatural powers are a natural by-product of this supreme effort.

The vagus is the tower of strength in the automatic sympathetic system, but will be the principal channel through which the human being will unite the sympathetic with the cerebrospinal system and become a spiritual master.

The vagus rises out of the medulla oblongata at the base of the brain, and courses downward through the neck to pierce the heart and abdomen. The nerve consists of two main cords, or fibers, in one trunk. Really it should be referred to as the *vagi* nerve, because of this double cord, but we usually refer to the entire trunk including both cords as the vagus nerve.

One branch anchors in the heart and is called the "pulse-point," or "pace-maker." Of the two cords, the one on the right is by far the more powerful, and although its most prominent terminal point is in the heart, there are branches of it which connect with other nerves leading not only into the solar plexus center but even into the pelvis.

We should correctly refer to the vagus nerve as the "inhibitory nerve." Because of its inhibiting action upon the heart it is often called the "braking" nerve, as opposed to another nerve called the "accelerating" nerve which is rooted also in the medulla, and extends to the heart. The accelerating nerve does all that its name implies, while the vagus acts as a brake on the nerve impulses reaching the heart.

Scientists are now quite familiar with the exoteric functions of the vagus nerve. But they are not cognizant of its power as it operates under the mental control of a master yogi. Nor are they familiar with the abdominal or holy breath which manifests through it.

We shall have more to say regarding this vagus nerve when we begin our teachings concerning the *aka cord*, or the *antahkarana* — the bridge connecting the human being to the High Self. It would be out of place to comment here. Suffice to say this eminent vagus nerve channel is one of the most prominent channels over which we must build the link between our waking conscious and superconscious minds, the cord or stream of life existing between each of us and our Oversoul.

The vagus is the bridge connecting mental impressions which rise from the heart to the brain. Usually inspiration and first impressions are dispatched from the Oversoul which is connected so dramatically through the sutratma, or life cord, to the heart center. These messages are received through the heart center and flashed from there to the head center via the vagus. It is only after these intuitional thought impulses reach the brain that human reason and logic take over, and many times will overshadow the first impressions received from the Oversoul, and one is turned away from spiritual guidance.

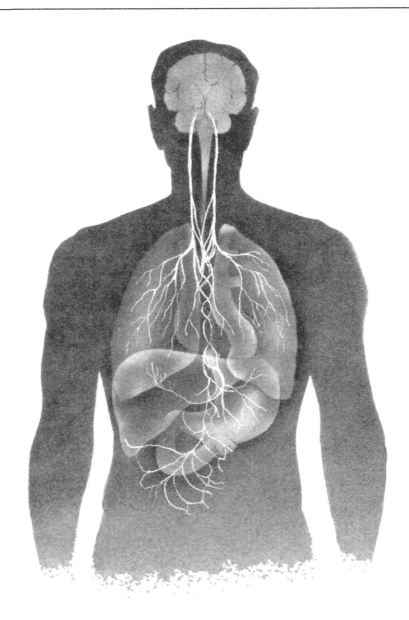

THE VAGUS BRANCHES — RIVERS OF LIFE

The vagus nerve rises out of the medulla oblongata and brain stem and courses downward through the neck to pierce the heart and abdomen. One branch of it terminates at the "pulse-point" in the heart. Another extends on down to the abdomen. This nerve completely controls the respiratory system, creating of it the most important one nerve in the body, for without precise eso-teric knowledge and training, we cannot physically exist without breathing.

The physical permanent seed atom lies directly over the pulse-point of the heart which clearly indicates that this atom, so efficacious in the physical life of the human being, lies just at the terminal point of the vagus nerve. This makes the vagus, in part, the channel of the life cord which extends from the Monad to the heart pulse-point. The vagus courses upward from the heart to join the sushumna near the throat, and from thence proceeds upward into the medulla oblongata. Thus it is a direct connection between the heart and the head, and plays a supreme role not only in our physical life but also in death.

At the time of death the heart seed atom is loosed from its anchorage at the pulse-point in the heart, and begins its journey up the vagus on its way to departure from the physical form. It may depart simultaneously with the mental and astral seed atoms if death is sudden. But it is more usual for the mental and astral atoms to have departed prior to the time the heart seed atom begins its journey.

The heart ceases to beat when the heart seed atom departs its home in the pulse-point, but life does not entirely cease until it has traveled up the vagus, entered the sushumna in the throat, ascended through the medulla oblongata and outward through the top of the head. With the departure of this atom, the sutratma or "silver cord" is loosed, and the life principle is completely withdrawn from the physical form. It is indeed "dead."

Thus the vagus is a most important part of the silver cord. It is the royal highway for the entrance and exit of the physical permanent seed atom in the heart, as well as the channel for the holy breath.

It is a supreme branch of the Tree of Life in the human body.

THE NERVOUS SYSTEMS AND THE NERVE FLUID

Just as there is constant circulation of the blood through the arteries and veins of the body, so there is constantly circulating through the nervous systems a substance called *nerve fluid*. This fluid is generated mostly within the body itself and is composed of various chemicals manufactured in the bone marrow, the glands, and the nerves. The power or impotence of this fluid helps determine whether an individual is either dynamic, forceful and magnetic, or is lackluster and languid. This nerve fluid, flowing through the nervous systems, carries with it the constant circulation of the physical ethers.

It must always be remembered that there is an etheric counterpart to the physical nervous system called the *nadis*. Throughout the nadis flow the four physical ethers — the electric, pranic, light and mental reflecting ethers. (See *Lesson 13, First Degree*.) This outer nervous system is, in fact, an externalization of the inner nerve network. This network of threads of energy is designed according to a pattern

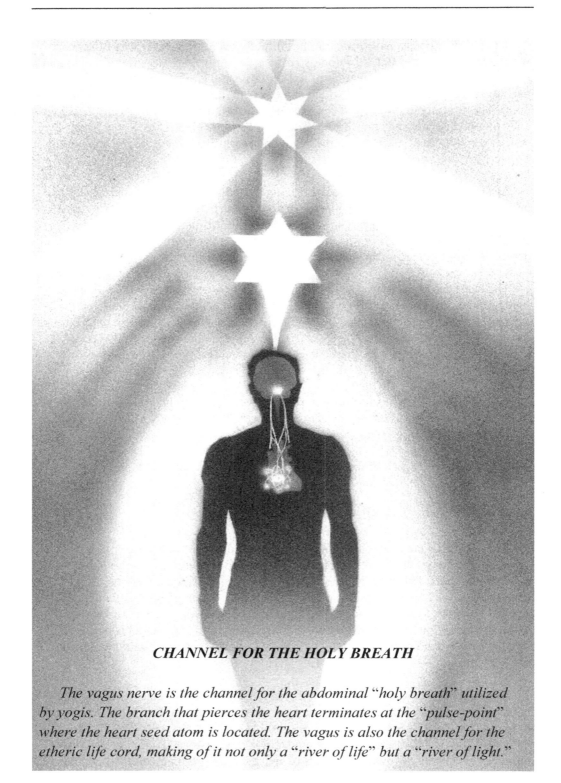

CHANNEL FOR THE HOLY BREATH

The vagus nerve is the channel for the abdominal "holy breath" utilized by yogis. The branch that pierces the heart terminates at the "pulse-point" where the heart seed atom is located. The vagus is also the channel for the etheric life cord, making of it not only a "river of life" but a "river of light."

which reflects the personality ray of every individual. According to this pattern, the physical nervous system will be built during the embryonic life, and according to its development, sensitivity and structure, the soul is able to function either as a genius or an ordinary mortal. The nadis determines the entire quality of the nervous system.

The nadis counterpart of the nervous system is composed of the four ethers just named. A healer must never forget the relationship between the nadis and the physical nervous system composed of the solids, liquids and gases of the dense physical plane.

Much disease is created because the connecting bridges between the physical and the etheric nervous systems have become obstructed, and a charge of nerve fluid from a healer is the surest method of restoring harmony and circulation between them. In the First Degree, you will recall, we mentioned that the bridges between these two bodies were the chakras, and that healing was accomplished when the chakras were "plugged in" properly. It is also necessary that the chakras of the astral and mental bodies be properly attuned.

An important association of the etheric nadis is the endocrine glandular system because the chakras are the glands of the etheric body. The glands of the physical form are the internal force centers of the chakras. In other words, the glands are the physical counterparts of the etheric chakras.

Medical science is now on the threshold of recognizing the existence of the etheric body with its nervous system (the nadis) and force centers (the chakras). When this happens it will completely revolutionize modern healing methods.

There are three systems which are principal aspects of humankind's divinity, and through their operation we have become what we are today. By means of their expression we in turn express either genius, mediocrity, or far less than we might. In some faraway, glorious future when these systems have become balanced and coordinated, the pattern of the inner being will reflect perfection in the outer being.

Disease will be outgrown, outlived, and we will manifest the god-Selves we are to become. The electromagnetic lifeforce will pour through the entire body by means of a *balanced, coordinated endocrine system* which reflects the powerful inflow of nerve force, and the perfect release of the proper elements into the *bloodstream*. When the bloodstream, working both through the glands and the permanent seed atoms, expresses without carrying germs of past karma, the bloodstream and the nervous system will reflect radiant perfection throughout the physical form.

THE ETHERIC NERVOUS SYSTEM — THE NADIS

At the present time, imbalance between the nadis and the physical nervous system seems to be causing a serious amount of disharmony. In some disciples the nadis is in a complete state of chaos. Some of the etheric nerve channels are operating at full force, unhindered and even overstimulated, but this current of electric fluid is hampered in other parts of the body by blocked nerve channels which arrest the flow of energy. Many obstructions develop in the chakras themselves, which in turn cause the glands to react unfavorably.

There is a never-ending battle in the present human form as the over-stimulated nadis discharges powerful currents of nerve fluid which meets with dammed up channels. Forcing the etheric fluid through the nadis causes a reflex action in the physical systems and they become inflamed and congested. When this happens, the nerve fluid cannot flow freely and we become the victim of disharmony between the two nervous systems.

The practice of Lama Yoga plays a vital role in attaining coordination and equilibrium between the nadis, the endocrine system, the blood stream, and the physical nervous systems.

This is why Astarian teachings have never encouraged stimulating the negative spinal chakras, but instead have concentrated upon vivifying the head centers. To awaken the spinal chakras usually overstimulates the etheric nadis, and creates an imbalance in the physical nervous and glandular systems, thereby releasing impurities in the bloodstream which the slower sympathetic system is not able to cast out.

The wise disciple of yoga concentrates upon Lama Yoga or other balanced forms of yoga, keeping the attention centered upon awakening the positive head centers. This proper brain stimulation brings a complete balance of all the forces in the physical form.

It is advisable for a healer to recognize the importance of the nerve fluid. It can be vitalized by the cosmic rays of the sun. All four physical ethers also may be utilized to enhance its power.

The ethers enter by various chakras. Prana, for instance, or the pranic ether, pervades our atmosphere and, as energy from the sun, is constantly streaming into the navel chakra. From the navel chakra the pranic emanations are sent into the solar plexus, there to be converted into nerve fluid which surges through the nervous systems much as electric currents flow through a wiring system.

This prana is the vital fluid which feeds life to the muscles and organs. Prana is the carrier of life to the entire body. Without it we die. It is the vitality in the blood. It is the "oil" without which the mechanism of the body breaks down. It is the electric current without which the brain cannot operate. It is the prana in the oxygen of the air we breathe which enables the lungs to contract and expand. It is, in short, our lifestream.

Prana inbreathed is not the same substance we call magnetism, or nerve fluid, which is generated in the body and which flows along the nerve channels. The nerve fluid is the conveyor of prana, by means of which prana circulates along the nerves much as the blood circulates through the veins.

THE SCIENCE OF THE MAGNETIC FLUID

It is through nerve fluid and prana, streaming from the palms of the hands, that a healer directs healing force toward the patient. It is the flow of this magnetism into the patient's body which will restore it to wholeness and bring the healing so desired.

Highly developed clairvoyants are able to see powerful currents of nerve ether emanating from the hands of a healer. These singular individuals have an abundance of this important personal magnetism. The magnetic person is one who can charge an entire room just through his or her presence, due to the dynamic flow of the nerve fluid. It is sometimes so highly charged that it is as if an electric current flows from the healer to permeate the auras of others.

The reality and secret of the magnetic fluid of the nervous system was known long before that marvelous mystic-physician, Anton Mesmer, ever discovered the essence he termed "animal" magnetism. All the ancient Masters were aware of it and were skilled in its use in their rites of initiation in the Mystery Schools of Mu, Atlantis, ancient Egypt and Greece.

The science of magnetic fluid was known to Hermes, Pythagoras, Plato, and all the thaumaturgists of ancient times. The alchemists knew well its power. The hierophants in the Mystery Schools used their knowledge of the fluid to induce hypnotic states in their candidates. Remember, this is the occult hypnotism related to the cerebrospinal system and the higher superconscious mind and not the type so often practiced today in connection with the sympathetic system and the subconscious mind.

The mystic Druids of ancient Europe understood the science of this mysterious magnetism, and how to use it in connection with their healing ceremonies. They were highly skilled in charging amulets with fluidic magnetism. They frequently used branches of mistletoe in their healing, as well as the magnetic lodestone. All esoteric physicians of old exercised the power of the lodestone in restoring balance to the electrical emanations in the human body.

Paracelsus and Descartes also were adept in the use of fluidic magnetism. They used both the lodestone and man-made magnets in accomplishing their healing miracles. Kercher and Fludd were familiar with the magnetic fluid. These great mystics realized that all living things possessed magnetic poles. They discovered what they called the magnetic field surrounding the human body, and they also found that magnetic streams flow in powerful radiations from all its extremities, particularly the hands.

In his investigation of what he called animal magnetism, Mesmer discovered that his hands emitted a magnetic quality, as did the natural magnets or lodestones with which he began his experiments. He discovered that he could accomplish astonishing healings by manipulations with his hands. He realized full well the source of human magnetism and its relation to the nervous system. The scientific world of today continues to ignore the healing magnetism of the lodestone as well as the natural magnetism of the human body. To ignore in no way dispels the fact of its existence.

The lodestone can either withdraw disease from the body through magnetism, or can attract into the body important elements from the ethers. Nerve fluid can also be stimulated by the aura of pine or eucalyptus trees. It could be helpful for a patient suffering from nervous disorders to retire for a while to a retreat surrounded by pine or eucalyptus trees. The nerves readily absorb the auric emanations of these particular trees, and depleted or inflamed nerves may again become harmonized and healed as the auric emanations enter into and regenerate the nerve fluid. Fresh fallen dew also contains much of this mystic power, and it would be wise for anyone suffering from a disturbed or depleted nervous system to place a cloth in the open so that dew can permeate it and then, after drying it, use the cloth as a healing magnet.

THE HEALING FLUID IN THE FORM OF WHITE LIGHT

It is the magnetic force in the nerve fluid that enables the healer to accomplish the cure. The magnetic currents flowing out through the radial nerves in the hands can be manipulated by the mind, which is the method we use. The magnetic force, by mental effort, is projected through the ethers to reach any Astarian, near or far. Distance is no obstacle.

The magnetic healing force is sent in the form of the White Light which can penetrate the ailing body of a faraway Astarian and help restore health. It will permeate the body as surely as if it were medicine injected by hypodermic needle. It will immediately enter the nerve fluid of the nervous system, and will be infused throughout the nervous systems and the blood, helping restore the body to wholeness. If a complete healing cannot occur because of some blockage in the subconscious mind, or because of karmic debt, or because of a chosen spiritual pathway, still some betterment is gained if the Astarian can mentally open to this White Light.

The White Light, then, is the etheric electromagnetic current flowing out of the nerve fluid of the healer. That is why we most earnestly urge you to keep healing petitions coming to headquarters where they are used as a vital contact. Without a healing petition, we must project the healing current through the ethers by our own mental efforts, creating the line of contact between ourselves and you. This effort requires intense mental energy whereas if we have your petition, there is already established a thread of contact, and along this etheric thread the electromagnetism more easily flows to reach and revitalize your physical form. Any healer must be constantly charging the nervous system with nerve force to keep the supply perpetually flowing outward.

This is the method employed by Zoser. He uses our physical forms (Robert, Earlyne, Sita and other Astarian healers), as transmitters and focal points of force through which to convey the White Light via the ethers to reach you.

This mysterious essence we call nerve fluid is of tremendous importance to the entire body for without it the nervous systems are not operative. It is the absence of nerve fluid which is observable in the case of paralysis, or a "stroke." Somewhere, somehow, the electricity and magnetism of the nerve fluid is blocked from entering certain parts of the nervous system. Thus this part of the physical form becomes inert and without sensation of any kind.

It is emanations of this nerve fluid radiating from the body which create an aura of vitality in a healthy body. We call this the "health aura." Lines of the vital force radiate straight outward in every direction so long as the body manifests good health. During illness the lines bend perceptibly downward, devoid of both prana and ether. They remain so until health is restored by means of renewed sources of vital force, or nerve fluid. The powerful streams of a healthy aura will vibrate outward from the body for a matter of several inches in some instances, especially from a highly magnetic personality.

It is this vital force which is utilized by fire walkers of the South Pacific Islands. They are adept at releasing the nerve fluid and surrounding their bodies, including the soles of their feet, to insulate against the heat of the flames. Many are equally adept at transferring this same vital protective force to others in the fire processional, who may not be capable of performing the feat themselves.

NERVE FLUID AND HYPNOTISM

It is through the operation of vital nerve force that hypnotism often occurs. The operator, through mind power alone, injects currents of etheric magnetism into the sympathetic nerve stream of the subject, permeating the subject's nerve fluid with the hypnotist's etheric substance. Since the sympathetic system is the agent of the subconscious mind, the hypnotist is then in control of the subject's subconscious. *However, the hypnotist is not in control of the higher mind which operates through the cerebrospinal system* — and this is important to remember. This represents the difference between *ordinary* hypnotism and *esoteric* hypnotism.

The hierophants in the temples of the Mysteries *were* capable of influencing the nerve force, not only of the sympathetic system but the cerebrospinal as well, allowing them to assume control of the superconscious minds of their candidates. This made it possible for their initiates-to-be to establish contact with their own Oversouls; to experience the most glorious personal events; to travel through the higher planes and remember the teachings received; and finally, to attain initiations in the astral and mental worlds.

As you know, the cerebrospinal system reaches into the brain and extends down the spinal cord. Therefore the hierophants worked directly through the brain and mental body, whereas the ordinary hypnotist never reaches this important center at all, but is concerned solely with the sympathetic system by means of the negative spinal chakras.

Of course the hypnotists themselves, in the majority, are usually ignorant of the law operating in their own science, but they should be aware that they are controlling the subconscious only. It should be noted, too, that by means of hypnotism and trance, by skillfully manipulating the flow of nerve force, the most marvelous healings could occur since the operator has the subconscious mind of the subject receptive to suggestion. There is no better method by which the healer could command the subconscious to bring about a healing of the patient.

Two things are necessary in effecting a healing:

1. Overcoming the previous negative command received by the subconscious mind of the patient.

2. Stirring up a vital flow of the White Light or pranic energy throughout the sympathetic nervous system, and removing existing obstructions.

As we have already indicated, many diseases are created because the conscious mind has given a negative command to the subconscious which begins carrying it out. We have explained, too, that for healings to manifest, obstructions in the etheric nervous system, the nadis, must be removed.

We employ both methods, not by hypnotism, but by speaking to the subconscious mind of a sleeping Astarian who needs healing, and infusing the nervous system with a vital charge of prana.

If the subconscious can be encouraged to accept the positive command of healing, and if we can remove the obstructions in the nervous system with a powerful charge of White Light, instantaneous healing may result. In the majority of cases it requires many such commands to overpower the negative thoughtform so firmly implanted in the subconscious.

When the two steps can be accomplished, a healing *usually* results. It does not always last, of course, if the petitioner continues to live in the manner which brought about the disease. If the old fears return, the same anxieties, the eternal irritations, the wrong foods — if the patient does not "go and sin no more" — then the healing may be in vain. Nevertheless, a healing *usually* results when the subconscious can be persuaded to accept a powerful healing command, and when the nerve fluid can be properly magnetized and distributed throughout the physical and etheric forms.

NERVE FLUID FOLLOWS THOUGHT

In previous Lessons we have said that energy follows thought. *Nerve fluid also follows thought. Fluidic magnetism is subject to human will power and mental direction.*

We have also said that the cerebrospinal is under the direct control of the mental body and the sympathetic is the channel for the astral body. Desires welling up from the sympathetic find their way to the mental body by means of impulses within the cerebrospinal, whose paramount seat of activity is the brain. The energy of the nerve fluid flows into the brain as a thought is placed there through mental impulse.

The blood carries a perpetual stream of mental images, placed there by impulses and impressions from contacts with the outside world which reverberate upon the senses, as well as the picture images flowing out of the heart seed atom. These minute images are carried along the bloodstream much as a leaf would float on the surface of a river. They also enter the nerve fluid and, by means of it and the blood, are carried into the brain.

If the mental image is vivid enough, and the mental activities surrounding the picture image are vigorous enough, the nerve fluid quickly increases its flow into the brain. During periods of deep study or intense meditation, the blood, as well as the nerve fluid, are driven to the seat of greatest activity which, at this time, would be the brain. Partaking of a heavy meal will send both the blood and the nerve fluid to the stomach. Often the need for sleep is felt following a heavy meal, because the nerve fluid has withdrawn from the brain almost completely to concentrate its activities in the digestive tract.

During sleep, both the blood and the nerve fluid flow languidly into the brain because thought is absent. The greatest intensity of their activity is centered in other areas of the body during sleep.

ETHERIC BODY VS. ASTRAL-MENTAL BODIES

Throughout the entire busyness of your day, the activities of your astral and mental bodies are constantly bombarding the cells of your dense body with impulses. Every thought and every desire strains against tissues and cells, often devitalizing them. While this is going on, the etheric body, the body of vital prana and energy, endeavors unceasingly to pour into the physical form the vitality needed to restore harmony and prevent any destructive processes.

In a sense it might be said that there is a constant tension between the etheric body and the astral-mental bodies. The function of the etheric body is to build, build, build the dense physical form through the channel of the sympathetic nervous system. The tendency of the astral-mental bodies is to project perpetual currents of emotional-mental impulses into the bloodstream, some of which are unintentionally destructive to the physical form.

Thus the etheric vital body and the astral-mental bodies seem ever at odds, one to build, the other to destroy. Although destruction is not the purpose, the cells and tissues of the physical form will respond according to the quality of the desire-thought impulses entering the bloodstream through the astral-mental bodies. If the qualities of the etheric vital body and the astral-mental are too differenet, there may ensue a battle between the two, always a losing one on the side of the etheric vital body.

Were it possible for the etheric body to perpetually pour a sufficient amount of energy into the nerve fluid, there would be no need for us ever to sleep. Its power is not sufficient, however, so the time arrives when the physical body must collapse into sleep, during which time the astral-mental bodies are withdrawn.

It is at this time that the etheric body expresses its unrestricted capacity to restore the physical form to its former vitality. Thus sleep is an interval of highest and most intense inner activity, for the nerve fluids are infiltrating the destroyed or depleted tissues, cells and muscles, rebuilding and revitalizing them. The more active the etheric body in its restorative process, the greater the benefit to the slumbering physical form.

Sleep, then, is the greatest of all restoratives. It is far more potent than any medicine. Nerve fluid, containing vital prana, can bring about a complete healing and it works most efficiently when the physical form is asleep.

We would not have you think that it is desirable, however, to withdraw the desire and thought impulses indefinitely, for to do so would give the etheric-vital body full sway. It not only would preserve the physical form for longevity but *could* bring about continued growth through the glandular system, which would result in a race of giants. Such was the state of humankind before the astral-mental bodies became developed through evolution. In the early days, when the etheric body reigned supreme, we possessed a giant-sized physical form.

Were the etheric body to operate with full intensity, all the nervous energy and nerve fluid would be applied toward the continuous building of the physical form, and no vital energy whatever would be given toward the development of the mind through the astral body. Growth and body preservation would be the instinctive and principal activities, with no thought processes involved. Even though at the present time desires are often of a lower nature, the impingements of the desire-mental bodies are necessary to check the intensive building of the etheric-vital body.

A balanced activity of the three bodies — the etheric, astral and mental — is to be greatly desired. Today the astral-mental bodies are considerably more powerful in their operations and in their destructive activities, but when the desires and emotions become stabilized and the mind expresses quiet serenity rather than worry, hate, anxiety and fear, people will discover that we constantly remain in a state of energetic wakefulness, needing little sleep to recuperate. Our forms may again exhibit both mental and physical perfection.

We will have overcome death ... for that is all death is: an ultimate winning of the eternal battle between the bodies, the ultimate destruction of the physical form by the tumultuous emotional and mental conflicts of the astral-mental bodies.

Supplementary Monograph

NERVE FLUID AND TUMMO

Some master yogis are able to accomplish the art of transmuting the generative energies into mind power. By the power of will they lift the creative reproductive energies through the spinal cord into the head. This requires intense concentration and mind power, and only a master yogi is able to accomplish it.

Using the creative essence of the generative glands in order to create by the power of the mind is called *Kriya Sakti* in Sanskrit. The Tibetans call it *Tummo*.

Tummo awakens the etheric nerve fluid within the nadis, Tummo refers to the method the yogi uses in extracting prana from the oxygen breathed into the body, and storing it in the nervous system to be utilized in transmuting the generative energies into the cosmic, fiery energy which is sent spiraling up the spinal column to the head. Prana is also sent into numerous subsidiary psychic-etheric nerves which act as channels to transmit the nerve fluid into the etheric nervous system as well as the physical. The nerves carry the prana throughout the body and distribute it to every organ.

The art of Tummo can be practiced only by a very advanced disciple or an adept. It involves a detailed ritual of yoga including postures, breathing, mental control, visualization, mastery over the elements such as fire, cold, etc., the forming of particular types of thought-forms, deep meditation, one-pointed concentration, a knowledge of the etheric nervous system, control of the nerve fluid in both the etheric and the physical nervous systems and the transmutation of the nerve fluids. One must also be celibate, for the art of Tummo depends completely on the yogi's ability to transmute ALL the sexual energies into the fiery ethers of the spine. It can be seen readily that the practice of Tummo is not for the neophyte.

Tibetan yogis learning the art of Tummo must temporarily dwell far removed from cities and sites of noise and confusion. They must seek complete solitude, preferably amid the wilds of nature, such as on a remote mountain top or in the midst of a forest, near a stream of water. This withdrawal is not necessarily of long duration, but only until the yogi masters the science of the art. Once mastered, he or she can return to daily work, and Tummo can be practiced anywhere.

It is by perfecting Tummo that the yogi begins, little by little, to develop control over the etheric and psychic nerve fluid which flows like a river of life throughout the nadis. It very subtly pervades every atom of the body, until the yogic power of endurance is gradually acquired so far as the elements are concerned.

Once mastering the art, this Tummo yogi is able to live in extreme cold, clad in very little. It is not that the yogi trains the mind constantly to endure suffering, but rather that the body is so completely warmed by the pervading fiery psychic energy in the nadis that it has no need for outer garments but rather generates an abundance of bodily heat from within.

Writings about the Master Kuthumi describe the period in his life when he mastered the art of Tummo. He was trained under the direct guidance of his own great guru, along with several other initiates. When one of them felt himself ready to be tested, his name was entered in what we would call a contest or a competition. He and other fellow initiates who were entering the contest were then escorted by their guru to the side of a body of water. A lake was selected which was frozen over, and they were seated on the shore.

A hole was cut in the ice and the guru dipped the robe of the initiate in the icy water. The initiate then wrapped it around his body and sat, cross-legged, mentally directing the heat of the cosmic fire of the nervous system toward drying the robe. As soon as his robe became dried, it was dipped again, and the same procedure followed. The contest lasted through the night until daybreak, and at a certain given time — perhaps sunrise — the contest was brought to a close. The contestant who had dried his robe the most times was acclaimed the winner.

An initiate undergoing such training had one goal: to be recognized as a *Repa*. To be worthy of belonging to the Order of the Repas, a contestant had to dry his robe at least three times during the contest. He was then entitled to wear the White Cotton Robe. Only a Repa could belong to the Order of the Cotton Clad Ones, and only the Cotton Clad Ones were those who had mastered Tummo.

Another test required of the Repa during the training was to be seated cross-legged in the snow and attempt to melt a large circle of surrounding snow. The Repa melting the greatest amount of snow was proclaimed winner. The Repa must also eventually be able to control and become immune to fire.

The fire contest was always performed in the midst of summer heat, and each contestant sat directly under the noonday sun, surrounded by four fires, each being placed at one of the four cardinal points of the compass. The fires were built up gradually by the guru until they reached intensity to burn the initiate badly who had not become, through the process of Tummo, immune to heat. Of course the initiate could withdraw at anytime, it was not a matter of compulsion, nor were they ever allowed to bring harm to themselves. It was definitely not a contest of enduring pain or suffering. It was a matter of mental training over the physical ethers of the body.

No initiate was ever obligated to submit to such a test, but entered through choice and could withdraw at any moment. The proper training would see the initiate through the trial with no pain whatever and no harm to the physical form. Having once mastered the fire contest, the initiate was then trained to walk on or through fire itself without physical injury.

Master Kuthumi attained such mastery over his body as to be able to transmute the solids, liquids and gases into a substance which withstands the elements of the physical plane of life.

The secret of Tummo is not only to raise kundalini from the base of the spine, but to raise the Chrism of regeneration up through sushumna as a fiery gas. This channel is quite impassable until it is completely cleansed of all barriers and impurities.

In the ordinary person this etheric cord is so obstructed as to bar even the passage of prana. Impurities and obstructions are so numerous in the entire nervous system that prana is prevented from moving freely through the nadis, particularly through sushumna.

Once the nervous systems, both physical and etheric, are cleared of the impure blockages, then and only then can prana pervade the entire system. Once the powerful forces of prana can pour down sushumna the Chrism Oil can easily be drawn upward in the form of cosmic fire.

Lama Yoga is an excellent method of charging the entire body with vital fluid. It aids in equalizing the vital fluids of both nervous systems. The straight spinal column and expanded diaphragm during the breathing portion of Lama Yoga help carry the electric and magnetic charges throughout the body.

Directing prana down sushumna is a positive attempt to reach the generative powers at the base of the spine. The entire practice of Lama Yoga, including breathing and meditation, vitalizes both nervous systems with vigorous charges of vital nerve fluid, and begins its flow through sushumna.

Thus the daily practice of Lama Yoga is a definite method of eventually attaining Tummo, and in the meantime the disciple completely changes the vibrations of the physical form from corruption to perfection.

PURIFYING BREATH

In the initiate the positive and negative etheric nerve currents have achieved a rhythmic flow. The positive force flows through the positive nerve channel (pingala) for approximately one hour, after which the pineal gland in the Third Eye in the brain automatically closes a valve at the root of the right nostril. This causes the negative force to flow through the negative spinal channel (ida) for one hour, after which it reverses again. This is the desired balance for both physical and spiritual well-being.

There are few today who possess this desired balance, due both to polluted air and erroneous habits in everyday life and thinking. The valves at the root of the nostrils are either damaged or do not respond as they should because of the impotency of the pineal gland and the resulting deterioration of the Third Eye in modern human beings. It has never been trained by the subconscious to respond automatically, and that is the purpose of the *Purifying Breath*.

Because the valves do not respond, some people are too negative, exhibiting undue fear, guilt, docility, weakness, lack of vitality. Some are too positive, exhibiting aggressiveness, boldness, greed for power, domination over others. Between the two, the balanced superbeing — the ultimate Astarian or seeker — exhibits courage, spiritual strength, love, serenity, humility, kindness, and an inner sustaining power. The Purifying Breath helps perfect this desired balance. The following constitutes *one* Breath:

1. Sit or stand with the spine held erect. Completely exhale to empty lungs of impure air.

2. Close the right nostril with the thumb of your right hand.

3. Inhale through your left nostril to the count of 4.

4. Close left nostril with right forefinger, hold breath to count of 16.

5. Raise thumb from right nostril, exhale to count of 8.

6. Repeat by leaving forefinger on left nostril and inhaling through the right nostril to the count of 4, etc.

Try not to force this exercise in any way, but keep the breathing as normal as possible. Should the counts listed seem to strain your breaths, lower the count to that which is comfortable for you — for instance, 2-8-4, if you wish.

The exercise is so apparently simple that one is apt to be deceived as to its effective power, which is so DEFINITE it must NOT be performed too long. Repeat the exercise during the day, if you desire, but do not perform over four Breaths at any one time. To do so occasionally would not be dangerous but it must not *habitually* be carried beyond this count. The disciple who will not heed warnings concerning these "simple" yogic exercises is only an extremely foolish aspirant who is likely to lose their way.

In practicing this Purifying Breath, do not make the common error of attempting to discover just how much air you can inhale, or how long you can "hold" the breath. This is no endurance contest. It is meant to build, not to destroy.

The value of this simple breathing exercise cannot be measured. By equalizing the nerve fluid it:

1. tranquilizes the nerves;

2. eases tension;

3. induces sleep;

4. helps to balance the flow of hormones.

It can be of incomparable benefit for your physical well-being and your spiritual unfoldment.

The Sphinx Within

Second Degree — Lesson Five

THE INDIVIDUAL BOOK OF JUDGMENT

The history of human beings is the history of the glands. The story of evolution, the story of personal and spiritual progress, is written unmistakably and indelibly in the glandular system. It tells a tale concerning the personality, as undeniable and as definite as each unique thumbprint.

One who can read the glandular activities of an individual can read that person physically, mentally, emotionally, psychically and spiritually — inside and out. The endocrine system is each person's individual, personal akashic record, and Book of Judgment, for as a person thinks and feels, so does the glandular system react — and as the glandular system reacts, so does that person think and feel. The two processes are so intimately intertwined as to be indistinguishable.

The endocrine system, so far as esoteric scientists are concerned, consists of:

1. glands possessing ducts;

2. glands possessing no ducts, called ductless glands.

The glands possessing ducts release their substances into the ducts which carry the secretions either to the surface of the body or the alimentary canal. The ductless glands, on the other hand, release their secretions directly into the bloodstream or the lymph, whence they are carried all over the physical body.

The principal endocrine glands are:

The *pineal* and *pituitary* in the head.

The *parathyroid*, the *thyroid* and the *thymus* in the throat and thoracic region.

The *spleen*, the *adrenals* and the *liver* in the solar plexus and abdominal area.

The *testes* in the male and the *ovaries* in the female in the sacral area.

The liver, spleen and reproductive organs are not considered endocrine glands by some glandular specialists. We include them however, even though they *do* have a function outside the usual ductless activities. With or without ducts, all these important glands emit secretions which affect the entire physiological structure of the human body. Thus they must be included in our research.

All glands are organized groups of cells. They possess the uncanny ability to extract certain substances from the blood and the lymph, to change them through some mysterious alchemical activity of their own — either by adding new chemical substances or using the materials from the blood to manufacture an entirely new type of substance — and then release it back into the bloodstream.

Since these secretions are distributed throughout the body, they exert their influence upon glands, cells, organs and tissues far removed from the gland expelling them. The influence of the pituitary, for instance, may be intense in the reproductive organs at the base of the spine as the bloodstream carries certain substances to that point.

Glandular activities are conducted with such incredible wisdom that the individual glands know which secretions are meant for them and which are to be passed along to some other gland. Thus the secretions meant for the reproductive organs will be received and utilized only by those and not by other glands. Some secretions, of course, are meant to influence *all* the glands.

The physical form is a most intricate, excellent alchemical laboratory and the endocrine glands are the points of highest chemical activities. Since humankind's earliest beginnings, our fundamental needs always have been met by a wise Creator. As the human form, through interminable lengths of space and time, attained higher stages of physical perfection and the evolutionary cycles brought perpetual mental development, so did the Creator begin to construct another spiritual center, manifesting as another gland.

Through the new gland the evolving form received the forces, substances, essences and hormones necessary to supply it with its changing needs. Thus the glands have developed, and as we attain ever higher degrees of evolution, the glands will manifest increasing perfection, and more may slowly evolve to serve us in our greater expression.

The glandular system can be compared to the nervous system in that both release "messages" which influence all bodily activities. Both are systems of intercommunication similar to powerful telephonic networks, and both release their chemical messages into their particular channels. That which is emitted by the nervous

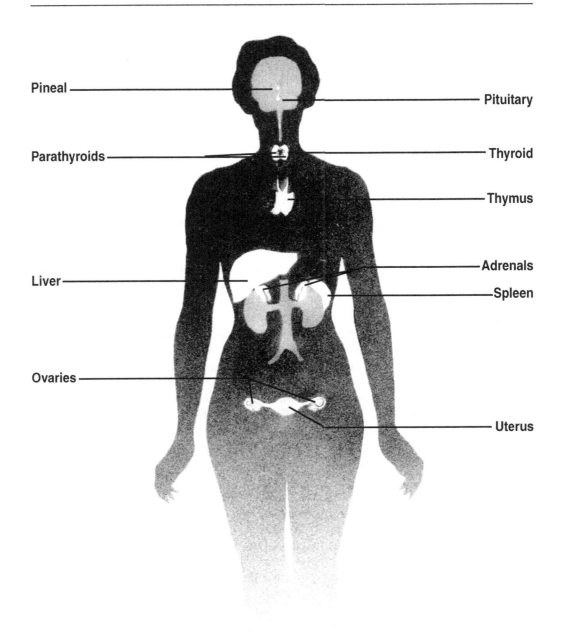

Pineal

Parathyroids

Liver

Ovaries

Pituitary

Thyroid

Thymus

Adrenals

Spleen

Uterus

THE SPHINX WITHIN

The endocrine system is the "sphinx" within ... the unfathomable enigma confronting and confounding medical science. The human being becomes the "creature having dominion over all the Earth," as we were ordained to do, in the exact proportion as we dominate our physiological endocrine functions.

system is called *nerve fluid*. The substances emitted by the endocrines are called *hormones*.

The word "endocrine" is a combination of two Greek words: *endon*, meaning "within" and *krinein*, meaning "to separate," which implies at once that endocrine refers to that which operates simultaneously with-in one unit, but also acts separately. This is a perfect description of the endocrine system. Each gland has its separate function and is capable of performing its own operation and producing its own mysterious hormonal fluid. Yet at the same time they all combine to function as one unit, consolidating intricate alchemical operations.

The word hormone is derived from the Greek word meaning "to arouse" or to "set in action" or "to stimulate." This adequately describes the glandular secretions since hormones released from one gland produce a stimulating effect upon other glands. Thus, again, the entire glandular system operates as one compact unit.

THE MYSTICAL ASPECT OF THE ENDOCRINES

We have said that the history of the glands is the history of humankind. That history is still in the process of being written. It is not completed by any means, nor will it be until our evolution is complete. As humankind evolves, so will the glands, and as the glands evolve, so will humankind.

At present we are the slaves of our endocrines in that the brain cells not only receive nourishment from the glandular secretions, but their functional processes are ordained by these secretions as well. The inner struggle of the lower human being with the Oversoul is the result of the influence of the endocrine secretions in the brain. As the Oversoul or superconscious mind gradually dominates the mental functions of the lower human being, the brain cells are increasingly activated, challenging the endocrines toward perpetual evolution.

We ourselves must overcome the yoke of slavery imposed upon us by the endocrines as they, through personality heredity, hold us to our karmic past. We *can* control the activities of the glandular system — but only with powerful personal effort, both mentally and emotionally, and few are endowed with such powers.

The birth of all NEW ideas comes from a source outside the endocrines — the radiant Oversoul. The influence of the Oversoul upon the manifesting personality is indicated by the degree that the individual utilizes the inflow of new mental concepts and gives credence to new ideas. To that degree is one freed from habitual enslavement to the endocrines.

The person who is afraid to express new thoughts and ideas in his or her life and who follows in the dogmatic footsteps of habit-bound leaders is one we call an "endocrine slave." Any personality who surges ahead of the masses with new age ideas, either in business, personal affairs or in spiritual undertakings, can be recognized as one who is overcoming the domination of the glandular system.

This is especially true of the religion a person follows. So long as one willingly subjects oneself to the domination of a "religious" leader who propounds psychological fears, just so long will this person remain a slave of the endocrines. The free soul, on the other hand, is the one who finds spiritual comfort and progression in the religion which gives free will, freedom from fear and a choice of one's creeds.

Animals are always slaves of the physiological functions of their endocrine secretions. And they cannot in any sense liberate themselves from these hormonal influences, because the endocrines themselves are the channels for the animalistic instincts which pour out from the group soul dominating the particular species to which each belongs. These instincts are the true guardians of the animal kingdom.

But, as a human possessing its *own* soul, the one who refuses to think independantly, who turns away from expanded mental horizons, whose eyes seek not the effulgent glory of spiritual self-unfoldment, is limiting his or her own potential.

We become the "creature having dominion over all the Earth," in the exact proportion that we dominate our physiological endocrine functions. Each person does this through development of personal will power as we give birth to new thought patterns, as we strive to erase past karmic records and open ourselves to receive wisdom from spiritual leaders who urge us toward the freedom of our own soul.

The endocrine system is indeed the *SPHINX* within — the unfathomable enigma confronting and confounding medical science.

Only as the medical practitioner of tomorrow discovers the presence, the esoteric aspect and the integration of the seven most powerful systems within this creature called the human being, can we completely understand ourselves.These seven systems are:

1. the nervous system;

2. the nadis, the etheric nervous system;

3. the etheric body;

4. the chakras, the glands of the etheric body;

5. the endocrine system;

6. the three permanent seed atoms;

7. the bloodstream (about which we shall write later).

THE PHYSICAL SEED ATOM IN THE HEART

We have explained in Lesson Fourteen, First Degree, about the three permanent atoms:

1. *the physical seed atom* in the heart, composed of physical plane energies;

2. *the astral-emotional seed atom* in the solar plexus, composed of astral substance;

3. *the mental seed atom* in the pineal gland, composed of substance from the mental plane.

We become co-creators with God only as we gradually liberate ourselves from the influence of our glandular secretions. We are held to this chain of slavery by our inherited karma, registering first through the heart seed atom and then through the glands. But our future freedom will well depend upon three things:

1. The use we make of our own individual will power as we, through spiritual means, strive to overcome the influence of past karma in our lives.

2. Our attempts to balance the chaotic flow of undesirable picture images released by the heart seed atom, with the powerful constructive picture images of the present as they are released by the mental and the astral seed atoms.

3. The constructive way we utilize the hormonal secretions of our glands.

Our inner urges — which drive us either upward or downward, forward or backward, to love, to hate, to feel everything that we experience within — rise up from the endocrine glandular system as it receives the picture images distributed by the heart seed atom into the bloodstream.

THE SEED ATOMS ARE DISPENSERS OF KARMA

To clarify the picture more completely, let's consider again the biblical scripture: *The sins of the fathers are visited upon the children even unto the fourth generation.* As we previously explained, this does not refer to our earthly "fathers" and their earthly "sins." This would imply that *we* must personally bear the karmic burden and responsibility of our parents, grandparents and indeed our forefathers. This would be a flagrant miscarriage of divine justice.

It means that we ourselves are the "parents" of our own future, whether it be good or bad, according to our actions in this present life, and that we today are the "child" of what

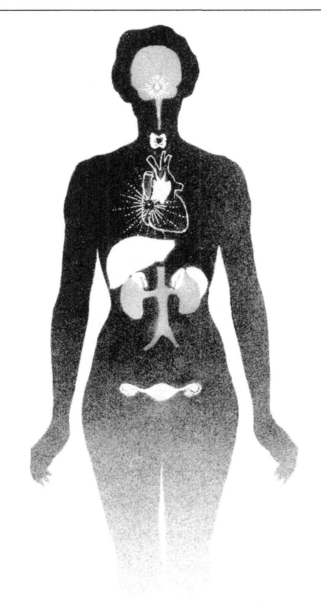

THE HEART SEED ATOM AND THE ENDOCRINE SYSTEM

The heart seed atom is the true controller of the endocrine functions, as it sends its karmic picture images via the bloodstream to the queen pituitary. She emits, then, her commands to the glandular system, bringing radiant health or disharmony to the physical form according to the karmic directive received. Thus you indeed "reap what YOU sow" through this incomparable system of divine justice.

we fathered, the actions we created, in past incarnations, even unto four incarnations ago. It means that we might now be reaping our karmic rewards or punishments earned by *ourselves* as far back as four "generations," as it is symbolized in the *Bible*.

To exemplify further, let us say that four incarnations ago you *deliberately* committed some deed which cost some fellow being his eyesight. It inevitably follows that in *some* lifetime you must pay your debt. You must balance your cosmic books — you must reap what you have sown. Since cosmic law demands that karmic records be made even within four "generations" this lifetime closes the cycle during which you must "clear" your record, balance your cosmic books and erase all karmic traces of deeds committed four incarnations ago.

So at some time during this incarnation the heart seed atom will begin releasing to the glands its atomic picture images bearing the message of eye weakness. As the glands receive this message it does not necessarily follow that you must completely lose your eyesight. But the glands will automatically begin to withhold from the bloodstream some needed hormone which will register as a general weakening throughout the body.

If your eyes have been particularly abused during this incarnation, then they most surely would be affected, possibly seriously. But if you have taken care to preserve their power and strength, the hormone deficiency would affect some other weaker organ. In other words, the deficiency would revert to and attack the organ in your physical form which exhibited the greatest weakness. It might be the heart or the kidneys or the liver or gall bladder — and not the eyes at all. Wherever your weakness lies, there will develop your ailment.

One very important point must be made particularly clear and that is: *When an illness befalls you, look first for an immediate physical cause and not for a long-ago karmic cause!* Never, never accept any condition, weakness or illness as being karma against which you can neither cope nor hope.

Karma extending back four incarnations is rare. This teaching is presented only because it does occasionally happen. BUT in the vast majority of cases the cause of any illness can be traced to some very present karmic action in this incarnation such as bad diet, undesirable liquids, stress, worry or confusion, even faulty elimination, or some equally common current cause.

There are also the equally devastating seeds born of hate, prejudice, anger, jealousy and avarice.

PERSONAL CHOICE OF KARMA

It is seldom that a karmic condition will extend over a period of the "permitted" four incarnations. It usually will be erased in the same lifetime the deeds are committed. Much depends upon the quality of the deeds. If one is a hardened criminal, it may well require four incarnations to blot this record — for the heart seed atom to release the atomic picture images at a rate bearable to this soul who has perpetrated such heinous deeds against other human beings.

Let us use the eyes as our example again. Let us assume that in a certain lifetime you blinded someone, not accidentally but with evil intent and purpose. Then before you incarnate again, you may make your own decision concerning your next incarnations in discharging your karmic debt.

When the time approaches for your incarnation following the one in which your crime was committed, your Celestial Guardian may remind you that you carry a karmic debt of blindness. You may have a choice of whether or not you wish to endure one life of complete blindness, or four lives of partial blindness. Many of us are given choices in these matters so that it can truly be said that God places no more upon us than we can endure. The things which sometime seem "unbearable" are conditions which we ourselves may have chosen.

The seed atom in the heart is the true controller of the entire body — the king of destiny in every sense of the word. The atom with its "file" of karmic atomic particles holds us completely in its power, yet at the same time it is only a record of what we have done to ourselves, The endocrines can manifest only that which the seed atom will allow, and the seed atom is, in turn, only a "storage file" of what we have made of ourselves in the past.

As the seed atom slowly becomes cleared of its dismal record of the past, we gradually will become liberated from our slavery to the endocrines, and the endocrines will grant us ever-increasing freedom. It is as if the endocrines were a council of sages in the human form which says to the personality inhabiting the body: "*Prove to us that you have the will power to overcome the world, and we will then give you our full support in carrying out every new plan, all your new ideals, helping you in every way to rejoice in your hard-won freedom from our rhythms and cycles of destiny.*"

The endocrine system is the person's inheritance of the past. The results manifesting in the individual through the glandular system have their cause in the roots of previous lives and foreshadow the person that is to be. It must be understood, of course, when we make this statement, that the glandular system is only *the Book* of the Record, and not the "writer" of the Record. It can manifest only that which is released to it by the seed atom, and the seed atom is only the instrument of the incarnating personality who is the true creator of the Record.

The network of intercommunication between the glands, seed atoms, and bloodstream, as they combine to help us in our evolution, is witness to incredible wisdom. Certain glandular conditions are an invitation to a life of crime — and other glandular conditions open the gates to godhood. Certain glandular conditions help create a genius — others develop a less-than-average intellect.

Each person can rise only as high as his or her individual glandular system, operating under higher influences, will allow. The glandular system is the "outer" voice of our past karma; the seed atom is the "inner."

The glandular system is also *our BOOK OF JUDGMENT so far as our future is concerned.* What we think and do in this present life will determine the glandular system we will manifest in our next incarnation.

The glandular secretions, operating through the nervous systems, mirror the degree of our personal magnetism. Depending upon the nerve fluid as it impinges on the endocrines, we become a dynamic personality or a nondescript individual. As the glands go, so we go. We are victims of our endocrine systems and the rulers, simultaneously.

THE ENDOCRINES AND THE MIND

The endocrine system is the agent of the subconscious mind, operating under orders from the pituitary who receives her commands from the heart seed atom. With future evolvement of the cerebrospinal, the agent of the superconscious, we will direct with our waking conscious mind the flow of the endocrine secretions into our systems, increasing and decreasing them as needed for our true and perfect life expression.

As you develop your two highest senses — clairvoyance and intuition — through the pineal and the pituitary glands, just so will you bring your cerebrospinal nervous system into increasing power as your superconscious mind begins to make its presence felt in your outer life.

The pituitary and pineal glands are the physical focal points for the activity of the spirit within. The glands located in the trunk of the body are the vehicles through which the lower aspect — the personality — manifests under orders from the pituitary.

The progress of the glands in the trunk will be the story of the regenerative process as we leave the limited material scope of our five senses and reach toward the development of our sixth and seventh senses, controlled by the pineal and the pituitary in the head.

The three glandular centers most prominently active in the personality of today are:

1. the brow chakra, with the anterior pituitary activated;

2. the solar plexus with the liver, the seat of baser emotions, activated;

3. the root chakra, at the base of the spine, with the reproductive organs activated.

As the glandular system, operating in conjunction with the evolving nervous system, becomes more balanced and integrated, the prominent centers will be:

1. the Third Eye, including the pituitary and the pineal combined in their more spiritual functions;

2. the heart center, activating the thymus gland, and transmuting the solar plexus emotions into divine love;

3. the sacral and coccygeal centers, with the adrenals and spleen balanced and equalized in their positive-negative hormone flow and activities.

With the dissipation of undesirable karmic picture images in the heart seed atom, and with the unfolding powers of the superconscious mind, we will cease to be dominated by our endocrines, victims of our own recorded past mistakes, and will become the guides of our future destinies. It will be a happy day when humankind has finally erased the greatest portion of our unpleasant karma. The tremendous evolutionary strides will become evident in our ever-accelerating pace toward immortality and perfection.

THE SEED ATOM, THE GLANDS AND DEATH

Even though we have covered the death process in the First Degree, a brief repetition might be in order so far as the glandular action is concerned since this Lesson relates to the glands.

When the physical seed atom in the heart, which carries in itself the pattern of death as well as life, releases the elements which notify the endocrine system that death of the physical form is imminent, the glands respond and inject into the blood stream a mysterious substance which gathers in ever-increasing power around the heart center.

This mysterious "death hormone," in the final analysis, is the basic cause of death. Flowing throughout the glandular system by means of the blood, it labors to loosen the etheric nervous system — the nadis — so that the etheric form may depart gently. This detachment of the etheric form starts in the minor nerve centers behind the eyes. As it is gradually freed, the entire spiritual body gravitates toward the head centers through the process of magnetic attraction, and begins its action of complete withdrawal.

There is a simultaneous activity in progress as the mental seed atom withdraws from the physical form. Usually the consciousness cord breaks with the departure of the mental atom, followed by the departure of the emotional seed atom.

The final effort of the death hormone is to free the heart seed atom from the surrounding cells and atoms of the physical form. It eventually carries the atom upward through the vagus nerve to the head center, then upward through the silver cord, as the spiritual form slowly withdraws. With the passing of the heart seed atom, the silver cord breaks and the physical form is indeed dead.

Supplementary Monograph

THE MYSTIC DEATH

In the Holy Bible and other scriptures there are several references to "the sound of many waters" heard while being "in the Spirit," and listening to the "sound of the trumpet." Very near the beginning of his *Book of The Revelation*, John of Patmos writes: *I was in the Spirit on the Lord's day, and heard behind me a great voice, as of a trumpet.* (Revelation 1:10)

With the development of the higher bodies — the astral, mental, and causal — these spiritual Sounds become clearer and transmit a deeper sense of ecstasy. This is possible because the higher vehicles serve as finer instruments of attunement to the keynotes of the universe.

In the Mysteries, during a candidate's first initiations, the Hierophant would place him or her in a deep hypnotic trance and, using mystical powers, would unite the candidate with the divine Sound. In this hypnotic state the Hierophant would help the candidate escape temporarily from the physical body to gain knowledge on the upper planes. Returning to the body, the candidate thus completely understood death and the afterlife. This experience, in the Mysteries, was called the "mystic death." In later initiations the initiate, through contact with the divine Sound, attained the transforming "second birth."

During the mystic death, the candidate actually passed through an experience closely resembling what we term "death." The conscious awareness in the inner worlds, however, removed all fear of actual death from the mind ... in fact, made the candidate eager to experience the mystic death again and again, and look forward to real death with anticipation rather than dread. The Astarian who practices Lama Yoga attempts to bring about the same mystic death experience by the development of your own mental and spiritual powers and your attunement to the divine Sound — the Holy Nahd.

When the initiate Paul said: *I die daily,* (I Corinthians 15:31), he referred to this mystic death which he experienced frequently ... meaning he could leave his body at will for journeys into the higher planes. In his second letter to the Corinthians he refers to his experiences in a guarded manner by saying:

I knew a man in Christ above fourteen years ago, (whether in the body, I cannot tell; or whether out of the body, I cannot tell: God knoweth;) such an one caught up to the third heaven. And I knew such a man, (whether in the body, or out of the body, I cannot tell: God knoweth;) how that he was caught up into paradise, and heard unspeakable words, which it is not lawful for a man to utter. (II Corinthians 12:2-4)

The practice of Lama Yoga and the Holy Nahd could well unfold this inner power. However, persistent attunement to mystical and esoteric studies can also confer the same inner power upon the Astarian who does *not* practice Lama Yoga. Developing the ability to merge with the Sound, you too, may indeed find that you are able to expand your consciousness to encompass the astral, the mental, the causal — and even, under certain circumstances, the Buddhic plane.

This Supplement is meant to give the Astarian candidate for initiation some pointers which might help you better to attain these goals; to offer a better understanding of the "inner journey," what to expect and what the inner journey really means.

THE UNLIMITED POTENTIAL

You may not wish to carry Lama Yoga to the point of a conscious "out-of-body" experience for fear you may be unable to re-enter your physical body. This should NEVER be a matter of grave concern, for as long as the silver cord connected to the physical remains intact, *nothing* can prevent your re-entry.

The silver cord breaks only at the moment of physical death and *only* the process of death can sever it. Therefore, set your fears at rest. Your main consideration is to bring a sharper remembrance of the inner mystical experience to the conscious mind.

However, should you experience fright or discomfort in any of your journeys, you have only to turn your attention earthward again and you will be automatically pulled back toward your body immediately, no matter how far away you may find yourself.

You must always — and this is important — you must always *immediately write down all that you remember*. If you do not, no matter how vivid it may seem at the time, it will slip rapidly away, and later you will be unable to recall much that might prove to be extremely important.

OVERCOMING THE "OBSTRUCTION CONSCIOUSNESS"

Let us consider *first* the prospect of *astral* consciousness and establish guideposts for the Astarian who already may be consciously crossing the threshold into the astral world.

Try not to hold steadfastly to any preconceived idea about what you are going to discover there. Release from your mind any notions about hell-fire and brimstone, the devil, golden streets and harps. Try to approach your wider visions "as a child" — open minded, eager to learn.

One of the first things you discover about the astral is that there are no obstacles. It is part of your normal consciousness to fear fire, falls from heights, impacts with any object, drowning ... but in spiritual journeys these concerns may be completely dismissed.

It requires considerable mental training to learn this elementary astral lesson. Until you experience it you will not know, for instance, that your astral body can pass directly through a mountain, if you so desire. You may even penetrate the Earth, investigating the inner workings of the planet.

However, you CANNOT do these things so long as your consciousness considers them obstructions, for you will place your own limitations upon yourself and your experiences.

For instance, you will be unable to pass through a wall in your home while "in your spiritual body" unless you first learn that it *can* be done by actually doing it. Once accomplished, it becomes part of your consciousness. Never accomplished, you will be convinced that it cannot be done. It requires considerable courage to overcome subconscious fears. So an early lesson to learn concerning the astral is that it is an "unobstructed universe."

It is important to remember that your astral vision may be out of focus until you have enjoyed considerable experience there. Thus if someone requests a description of your journey, instead of adopting a definite attitude about what life is like in the astral, be flexible in your opinions, ready to admit that you are a neophyte ... if you are ... and that further experience may prove your first impressions entirely wrong.

READING THE AKASHIC RECORDS

Let us say that you have an intense desire to read the akashic records. All the seven planes of life interpenetrate each other, and therefore someone on the physical plane *could* come in rapport with the substance from the higher planes since it lies all about you, awaiting your sensitivity to it. (See Lesson Ten, First Degree.)

Every thought, word and deed of yours is recorded in the ethers of the Buddhic plane, the record of which is sometimes called the *Book of Judgment.*

A sage once wrote:

> *I hear a voice that cries, "Alas, alas!*
> *Whatever hath been written shall remain,*

Nor be erased nor written o'er again;
The unwritten only still belongs to thee,
Take heed, and ponder well
What that shall be!"

We have said that a complete record is found on the Buddhic plane. A *reflection* of these true akashic records may be found on the astral. A lesser reflection is also found on the physical, ensouled in the mental reflecting ether.

It should be remembered always that a *reflection* of anything is not always a perfect image. This is also true of these mystic records, and the disciple who attempts to "read" them must remember that you are viewing only the etheric or astral reflection of the actual records. You are "reading" from an inaccurate reproduction which cannot present a perfect picture of the real words, thoughts and deeds originally expressed.

Only a Master who has fully developed the causal body would be able to view the true records of the Buddhic plane.

Now, how do we go about reading these records?

READING THE BOOK OF LIFE

Infinite Intelligence, it appears, constructed a human television set inside the head millenniums before we learned to build a mechanical replica. The Third Eye — including the pineal, the pituitary, the third ventricle, and the optic thalamus — truly compares with an incredible television set. The Eye, when properly attuned, captures the sights and sounds of the higher planes.

The yogi practices concentration upon an object in order to procure knowledge of that object. This yogic practice is to be applied regarding the study of the akashic records. While sitting in meditation, project a powerful concentration of mental energy toward the object of your investigation, holding to the intense desire that the records reveal some knowledge about that object or situation.

This is not to say that you will send your mind-power in any given direction, to any given locale. You will simply hold fast to your desire. Let no outer disturbance sway your mind. Faithful concentration WILL bring revelations to you. You may view the records either subjectively or objectively.

One of two things may occur:

1. you may step out of your body and view the inner world objectively;

2. you may remain conscious in your physical form and view the scenes subjectively.

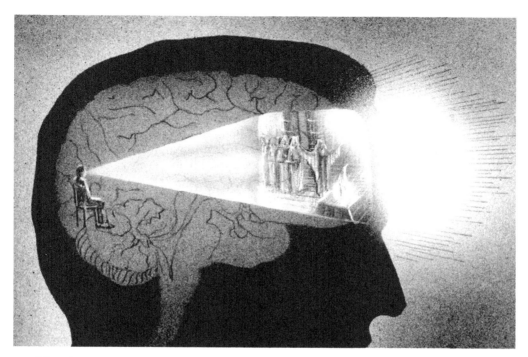

The objective view will most probably be seen while you are on a spiritual journey. It will seem as if you suddenly find yourself living in other surroundings with activities going on about you, with people strangely familiar enacting vaguely familiar scenes, with yourself as a part of the scenes. It will seem as real to you as your earth life. An entire lifetime with all its struggles, loves, sorrows and joys might be enacted, or the scenes might shift from one life to another, with you always participating.

When you regain your normal consciousness you will recall all that you witnessed but it will seem as though you had a vivid dream. You will know, of course, that it was no dream but an experience in projected consciousness. "Dream," however, is the only word which can describe the sensation you are apt to experience. This will be viewing the scenes *objectively*.

The subjective view is witnessed while remaining consciously in the physical body. It will appear to you as if there is a movie screen just inside your forehead, and you are witnessing the passing review from the back of your head. Indeed, it may seem as if you yourself are standing inside your own head, near the back, watching scenes unroll on a tiny screen on the inner side of your forehead.

You will have the sensation of sitting in a movie, or before a television set or computer screen, watching yourself portray a role in a motion picture. You will recognize yourself but will feel separate and apart from the "self" you are viewing. Just as before, you may follow one complete lifetime, or the scenes may change, skipping from one lifetime to another.

In these experiences you may find a study of historic records to be of vast interest. You may desire revelations concerning lost civilizations or some particular personality in history. These and other objectives CAN be achieved with power and patience.

However, whether you wish this type of revelation or whether you wish to gain information about your own past lives, a warning MUST be voiced. Be *extremely* cautious about discussing your findings. Particularly about your own past lives, *KEEP SILENT.* The mark of the neophyte or of one who is "off on a wrong track" is one who too eagerly proclaims who he was in some past life. It is extremely unlikely that you can "tune in" with your own past, in your early experiments, even though you may see many scenes moving before your vision.

It is most important, especially in this particular investigation, to abolish from your mind any preconceived notions as to who you may have been. Try to become indifferent about it, for truly it matters very little. Who you are and what you are *today* is the important thing to remember. A strong idea or hope on your part as to who you might have been can throw your whole vision of the records out of focus, for you will be forced to view them through the shadow of thoughtforms created by your own desires.

Always view with distrust any would-be spiritual teacher who claims to have access to the akashic records and who is eager to enlighten you about your former incarnations. Only the wise can gain access to the *true* records, and the wise would avoid disclosing such information about yourself. When you are ready to bear such knowledge — when you have gained a proper measure of spiritual unfoldment — your own Oversoul will reveal it to you.

MELTING INTO THE SOUND

Let us say that you wish to soar up and up, far beyond the confines of the astral, beyond the mental, the causal, and into the radiant celestial realms. The surest means of attaining such heights is to merge with the current of the divine Sound. And the best way to merge with the Sound — the Holy Nahd — is to float inward on the mental energy currents of AUM.

To better open the inner faculties to hear the divine Sound, one must close off the outer faculties. It is better to close your eyes, put stoppers in your ears and lock the tongue in order for the inner channels to open. If the eyes remain open much of the needed mental energy is dissipated outward in the use of the sense faculty of seeing. The same is true of *hearing and tasting.*

Locking the tongue means to turn it upward and touch the palate, then forcing the tip backward as far as possible. This will close the throat, forcing the upflowing spinal creative energies into the brain centers, and the brain dews downward into the sushumna. More will be given concerning this when we teach of Pad Nirvana, the next Step of Lama Yoga.

MELTING INTO THE SOUND

Eventually, as the power builds and builds, there cannot help but be pressure against the doorway in the top of the skull, the doorway of the Brahmarandra — the crown chakra — which, opening, carries the disciple into the divine Current of the Holy Nahd.

If you find it difficult to lock the physical tongue, then lock the tongue of your thoughts, speaking mentally over and over the chant of AUM, which is in effect calling the Lord's name over and over.

It is better to close your eyes and concentrate on the point midway inside your head than it is to find an outer object to gaze upon, for in the latter the energy is pouring outward to center upon the object instead of inward to center upon the divine Sound.

Energy follows thought, and we want the energy currents flowing inward. If you require an object upon which to concentrate, imagine an inner light shining inside your head. Keep your gaze centered upon the light. Or imagine that the Master's eyes are just inside your head and you are gazing into them.

Hold to these three steps:

1.　With the eyes closed, keep trying to see the eyes of the Master in the center of the head.

2.　With the tongue locked, keep mentally repeating the word AUM.

3.　With the ears closed, keep struggling to hear the inner Sound of the divine Current.

Thus the mental energy cannot ebb away through the nine openings in the physical form, but will be captured and held in the center of the head, becoming increasingly powerful as the mind focuses mental power there.

Eventually, as the power builds and builds, there cannot help but be pressure against the doorway in the top of the skull, the doorway of the Brahmarandra — the crown chakra — which, opening, carries the disciple into the divine Current of the Holy Nahd.

When the narrow gate of the crown chakra is opened, when the veil of the inner temple is rent, the soul vision passes upward into the different planes even though the physical body and even the consciousness remain in the physical, aware of all its physical surroundings.

The Current carries the inner vision upward through the astral plane, through the mental plane, and even through the higher causal plane. There it stands on the brink of the Buddhic or intuitional plane. This is the plane of the Pure Light.

The inner vision can proceed no higher into this Buddhic plane without a downpouring grace from the Formless One who presides over that plane. Receiving that grace, the inner vision proceeds on upward into the Light of the celestial spheres. Its destination is the plane called the *Sach Khand*.

Be it understood that this passage into the higher planes may require countless attempts, and no disciple can cross the vast inner spaces alone. You must have contacted the Master within yourself and have gained access to the higher realms by a downpouring of grace from those spheres of Light.

The disciple cannot enter the radiant Light alone. You must be accompanied by a Master who has preceded you and who knows the way; who knows how to pierce the barriers which block the entrance to these planes — an entrance not of matter but of Light so effulgent the disciple could not bear its glory unless accompanied and shielded by a Master guide.

REWARDS OF ATTAINMENT

Once one has merged with the Holy Sound by diving deeply into the brain through Lama Yoga, continual *practice* brings many benefits. A supreme peace falls upon that disciple as the sweetest dew from heaven, being absorbed into the mind and consciousness and nerves. All feelings of nervousness, hurry, tension, stress and strain gradually disappear and a strange serenity pervades.

Developing the power of the mind through intense concentration upon the Holy Sound brings healing of the body and the ability to overcome and transcend physical pain.

One realizes the littleness of *I* and the greatness of *the One*. Thus the ego merges with the One. The ego is thus eliminated and the soul is liberated from attachments.

Merging the little I with the One is totally different from the many practices offered by many so-called psychics and religious leaders today. Their goal is a greater development of the ego, a practice of gainful purposes, a "get this and get that" development, which fails utterly to liberate the soul but rather creates deeper bondage. "Holding the thought" to attain earthly things is one of the very worst practices for the disciple who would attain union with God through the Holy Word, the divine Sound.

Going within and concentrating, seeking inner union with God, is a far different cry than "holding the thought" for a new Cadillac. Once the disciple has attained the divine Sound and merged into the current of the divine Stream, the things of Earth that you *need* come easily to you, for you will never walk alone again.

We have only touched upon merging with the Holy Nahd. When we enter later Degree Lessons, and our teachings concerning salvation, we shall have much more to say about this. We shall teach of salvation through vicarious atonement, salvation through initiation, and salvation through liberation: the path through the Sound Current of the Holy Nahd.

YOUR NEXT LESSONS

LESSON 6, HUMAN BEING — MASTER OF DESTINY OR VICTIM OF FATE: Explains the relation between the glands, the emotions, the chakras, the seed atoms and everyday behavior. Tells how to overcome karmic influences and physiological cycles on your journey toward Mastership; how to control the physical, emotional and mental seed atoms and become the Living Philosopher's Stone.

LESSON 7, QUEEN PITUITARY AND HER FALLEN LORD, PINEAL: The queen of your inner world is the pituitary gland. Learn how the mystic "dew" of pituitary can transform person into Master; how the spiritual antenna of pineal can be stimulated so that higher plane contacts are possible. Learn how pineal, which with pituitary forms the center of the Third Eye, comes to spiritual birth through mystic union with pituitary.

LESSON 8, THE BIRTH OF THE THIRD EYE: Learn of the cosmic television station in the brain, or "the thousand petaled lotus"; how the mystic marriage of pituitary and pineal brings the opening of the Third Eye. Tells what experiences you will encounter when the Third Eye is properly and truly opened. Gives methods for unfolding this All Seeing Eye.

LESSON 9, TREASURES ON THE TREE OF LIFE: How to stimulate the spirillae in the pineal and temporarily dissolve the etheric web in the Crown Chakra. The four powers we acquired with our "fall" into matter. The true "immaculate conception" in the Third Eye. The glands and our coming longevity.

LESSON 10, THE BODY OF KARMA AND ITS LIFE FORCE: Transmuting the forces of the three lower centers. The health aura and the seven force streams. The body, the human atom, and our relationship to the elemental atoms and the celestial atoms.

QUOTATIONS...

Some men grow old striving to be great, too busy to plant seeds of small moments.

• • • • • • • • • • • •

After a lifetime of striving, when we arrive at old age there is only one thing we can truly say that we possess, and that is that which we had from the beginning: Time. We always have eternity.

• • • • • • • • • • • •

After I am gone, perhaps it cannot be said that I attained. Only let it be said that I believed what I taught.

• • • • • • • • • • • •

Truth is that which lights a stone but is not the stone.

— Earlyne

I Am ...

I am yesterday.

I am gone from you forever.

I am the last of a long procession of days,
    streaming behind you, away from you,
    pouring into mist and obscurity,
    and at last into the ocean of oblivion.

I depart from you, yet I am ever with you.

Once I was called tomorrow, and was virgin pure ...
    Then I became your bride and was named today ...
    Now I am yesterday, and carry upon me the
    eternal record of our togetherness ...

I am one of the leaves of a growing book.
    There are many pages before me.

Someday you will turn us all over, and read us,
    and know what you are.

I am rich, for I have wisdom.

I bore you a child, and left him with you.
    His name is experience.

I am yesterday ... yet I am the same as today
    and forever ...

For I am you ... and you cannot escape from yourself.

— Selected

Human Being --
Master of Destiny or Victim of Fate

Second Degree — Lesson Six

MEDICAL SCIENCE AND THE ENDOCRINES

We must remember that the scientific study of the endocrines — endocrinology — is still relatively young. Research was begun in the early part of the 20th century. Medical minds that have devotedly explored the mysteries of the glands have concluded that the glandular system is at once the dictator, the controller and the guardian of our physical destinies.

Esoteric scientists agree with them on this point, except that whereas medical minds limit their understanding to the physical form, the mystic carries research far beyond the cells, atoms, framework and operations of the physical and into the domain of higher bodies, and the soul inhabiting them.

Endocrinologists (gland specialists) should be assiduously attempting to discover the underlying cause of the difference between the endocrine system of the animal and that of the human. Such probings would carry them over the threshold of esoteric science and reveal the presence of the etheric body, the chakras and the nadis.

Although human beings will die with the removal of any one of several of the glands, it has been discovered that animals may be robbed of a great share of their glands without any obvious resulting tragedy. Even though only a small portion of each endocrine may be left, it apparently continues to function as before, and empties a sufficient amount of secretions into the bloodstream to enable the animal to continue normal life.

Why this difference?

Because, as we have already said, the animal operates under the influence of a group soul and is not spiritually individualized. Therefore, *the chakras are absent in the animal.*

Group souls utilize the endocrines as channels to direct life energies into the form of the animal. However, under this automatic direction, the forces flow with or without the glandular operations. Animals need no spiritual centers, such as chakras, for they are "fed" with life energies through the etheric life cord connecting them to their parental group soul.

The human being, on the other hand, is a completely individualized unit. By our own efforts we must "build" bridges and channels which link us to our own life cord, to our own Oversoul, the source of our very life.

Chakras are etheric focal points of life energy in the etheric form. They evolve and are stimulated through efforts of the individual. The endocrines are the physical counterparts. They are the centers through which the energies and life properties flow from the vital etheric body into the physical form. To destroy one of the endocrines means that an important bridge between the physical and its source of vital life has been destroyed. The result is death unless a synthetic hormone substance, similar to that produced by the missing gland, is injected into the bloodstream.

The fact that we die when our glands are removed, and animals do not, should proclaim the presence of some mysterious inner SOMETHING connected most prominently to our lifeforces and the endocrine system. Mystics declare this presence to be the etheric body with all its properties ... particularly, in this case, the spiritual chakras.

When the existence of the etheric form is once established, medical minds will be able more clearly to understand the mysterious sphinx within and its secretions into the bloodstream. For upon those functions will depend the progress of the future human being as he or she evolves out of the human kingdom into the kingdom of the superhuman and realizes the glorious heritage of regeneration and immortality.

Some small portion of humanity paid dearly in order for medical science to learn the value of the endocrine system. There was complete ignorance concerning these glands until the present century, and many unfortunate people became victims of that ignorance when medical doctors, not knowing the importance of the glands, either destroyed or removed them. Through the tragic process of trial and error they discovered that removal brought almost immediate death or, if not death, an extremely undesirable reaction.

They learned that, when it became necessary to remove a vital gland, a substitute synthetic chemical hormone must be injected into the bloodstream at regular intervals, else the physical body dies. This procedure is practiced today and has saved countless lives.

In their years of trial and error it was learned that removal of the pancreas caused death. Removal of the adrenals caused death. The removal of the thyroid caused either death or cretinism, deforming the body and severely limiting the mind. Removal of the pituitary resulted in infantilism in children, and impotency in adults. Removal of the thymus resulted in premature sexual development. Removal of the gonads resulted in sex infantilism in children, and atrophy of the secondary sexual characteristics in adults.

They learned that the parathyroids are directly connected with the functions of the nervous system, and that their removal caused death. The result of the removal of the pineal gland is not even today obvious to the limited vision of the physician. But a mystic well knows that a physical terminal for the transmission of higher intelligence has been removed and, though it causes no outer physical reaction such as death, it most surely limits the intuitional potentials of the individual. A vital terminal of the Third Eye will have been eliminated.

Medical science shares with mystics the knowledge that children's entire physical growth, as well as their emotional qualities, depend upon the nature of the endocrine activity. It is also known that as individuals grow from childhood to adulthood, some glandular secretions diminish while others increase. This accounts for remarkable personality changes as the individual leaves childhood for puberty and puberty for adulthood. Whatever gland is most active at any given time will dominate the personality characteristics. If a gland, during the process of growing up, becomes overstimulated, the personality can become completely changed from that previously exhibited.

Medical scientists know that the endocrines control facial characteristics, hair, stature, and all things pertaining to general make-up of the physical body. They understand how the glands cause abnormal conditions. They know that glandular disorders produce obesity, deformities of the body and mind, giantism, malfunctions of the reproductive organs and many mental disorders. They know that severe mental limitation is traced directly to malfunctioning of the glands. They are beginning to perceive that personal magnetism, intellectual strength and moral character are also intricately involved in the operations of the endocrines. They are only beginning to suspect that genius, too, is related to glandular operations.

They understand almost everything about the endocrines except HOW. The question is *how* does the endocrine system govern and control our destinies? And why? Even the most learned of our medical minds possess only meager knowledge of this most marvelous mechanism called the human being, insofar as our glandular systems are concerned. The esotericist understands that the answers lie in the heart seed atom, the chakras, the nadis, and all the higher principles we possess.

HEALING AND THE ENDOCRINES

Until medical minds recognize the existence of the etheric body and all its functions — until they gain some knowledge of the seed atoms, which are the "bosses" of the endocrines — they will only blindly grope for the cause of our diseases and physical disorders.

At the present stage of people's spiritual understanding, we dare not teach of healing exclusively through chakras. To create an increased flow of spiritual force into glands not yet properly evolved to harmonize with those powerful forces, is to cause congestion of the nerves and glands.

The intensity of this type of healing force must depend upon the evolutionary status of the individual glandular system through which it must be absorbed, and the glandular system cannot properly operate beyond the spiritual status of the etheric and the astral-emotional chakras. To drive beyond its present capabilities is to result in congestion of the ethers, rather than a healing.

In our healing work, we stimulate the flow of the *nerve fluids* — *not* that of the glandular substance. To stimulate the nerve fluids, as we do with our prayers, causes a natural reaction in the glands themselves and they equalize their operations, distributing the necessary glandular substance into the bloodstream according to their own incomparable wisdom.

The endocrines are like God — they will not be fooled and they are not respecters of persons. They simply mirror your activities and desires and emotions. Many spiritual scientists and practitioners attempt to heal by suggesting away or denying the existence of a disease. And they often successfully convince the subconscious minds of their patients that there is no disease. If conviction be strong enough, the deep inhibitions within will be dissolved and healing will result. But if the inhibitions remain buried regardless of the removal of pain, the disease is still there and will manifest again in some other manner.

We also use this same "affirmation method" in our healing and recommend that you use the Astarian affirmation especially when you desire healing. But understanding the power of the seed atoms upon the sympathetic nervous system and the subconscious mind, we also encourage some method of erasing the seed inhibitions. (See *Lesson Six, First Degree.*) The point is to clear the subconscious of complexes and erase any remaining feelings of guilt, fear or anxiety.

On the other hand, a physician may choose the administration of a drug or the removal of an offending organ by surgery. This approach is often valid, but occasionally it is misguided for it may leave seed inhibitions still buried deeply in the subconscious to manifest again in some other illness.

There are times, of course, when removal of an organ is correct, but at the same time, a wise medical scientist will recognize that there are inner complexes, conflicts and inhibitions to be dealt with, else illness may manifest again.

One of the most common causes of illness is the inadequacy of the glands under the impact of human being's baser emotions. Why do we continually urge you to strive for mental tranquility ... to serve others ... to continually build your mental and soul powers through study or meditation? Because these methods, too, dissolve the seed inhibitions in the subconscious.

If one continually expresses greed, exhibits aggressiveness in the struggle to gain more prestige, manifests *only* materiality by perpetually thinking of wealth and all that it entails, constantly expresses envy of those who possess more, eternally engages in enterprises which cause harm to others in order to promote self gain, constantly fears that which one does not understand, and in general lives under too high a mental tension, then the glandular system, a complete victim of the "germs" of the picture images of the seed atoms, begins to manifest illness.

It usually will register first in the digestive tract. Anger, fear, envy, jealousy, nervous tension, violent emotions, and strain of any kind cause an immediate slowing down of the glandular functions and the digestive tract ceases its peristaltic activity. Such cessation causes food fermentation which eventually spreads toxins throughout the entire body. The result is illness. Perhaps the illness is not obvious enough to be called such, and becomes a definite cause for alarm only if the negative causes persist.

Teachers, ministers, and physicians should be somewhat familiar with the esoteric functionings of the glands and the results involved. A teacher who is equipped with this important knowledge can understand better the infantile impulses exhibited in the schoolroom, can understand also the absence of desirable motivations. A knowledge of child psychology alone will not answer the need. Until and unless the teacher understands the operation of the glandular system and its effect upon the outer life, he or she cannot be completely equipped as a guide and counselor.

A minister without the qualities of a teacher will be completely anachronous in the evolving new age which has already dawned. It is not enough that one decry the sins of his flock from a strictly moral standpoint. A minister must also be able to understand the practical reasons behind these "sins," other than that a person is either good or evil, depending upon one's inclinations.

The Christian minister of the future who urges followers to come forward and be "saved by the blood" would do well to understand the mystical significance of the phrase, and all that the "saving blood" implies. It may be important indeed to be "saved" by the blood — but it is also important to understand the elements which flow in the blood which occasion that "saving."

Medical people, of course, do their utmost to understand the functions of the glands, but they would do well, too, to look beyond the physical manifestations of these mysterious little giants in the body. Until they understand the presence of the etheric form and its all-important chakras, they cannot pierce the veil of darkness in this new age of medicine. Physicians MUST cease being content in doctoring "effects." They must search beyond the dense physical form and learn to deal with CAUSES.

A Second Degree Astarian cannot help radiating from the entire being some evidence of the study of these Lessons. Your mind automatically reacts in response to the knowledge gained. You continue to benefit as your superconscious mind gradually assumes automatic control over all the inner activities of your mysterious dense physical form.

THE ENDOCRINES AND THE EMOTIONS

The emotions are related perceptibly to the functionings of the glands; and the changes that occur in the individual are all part of endocrine system processes.

The glandular system reacts immediately when one exhibits emotions such as envy, worry, jealousy in unhealthy ways rather than learning healthy ways to allow these emotions to flow through and away from you. It becomes inoperative and inefficient when one is inappropriately angry or hates someone. It is indeed more blessed to let revenge go by, forgetting that which has caused distress, for to seek to balance the scales by personal retribution destroys the seeker.

When a spiritual teacher cautions the disciple to cease worrying, it is not a trivial platitude, but very sage advice. The teacher well knows the effect of worry upon the glandular system and that it can lead only to disturbance within.

Fear is the greatest of all destroyers. We deplore its use in some orthodox religions. It is abhorrent to teach that a person is born a lost sinner and a wicked wretch, that unless one conforms to some particular preacher's creeds he or she will burn eternally in hell-fire after departing this earthly plane. To plant such iniquitous fears in the mind is to inhibit spiritual expressions that are the potentials of every seeker.

Such fears and the guilt implanted in the mind of the masses by the teachings of many orthodox religions have resulted in an endocrine imbalance in a large portion of humanity and have delayed our spiritual evolution for many hundreds of years. Such fears and guilts *must* be removed. *Love of God* must replace *fear of God*, and we must come to know ourselves, thereby understanding better both the god-Self within and the universal God.

It is only when fear and the resulting phobias are gradually erased from the subconscious mind that the endocrines will be able to bring the full power of the brain into activity. All the presently inactive brain cells will be brought into operation. A person employing complete brain capacity is indeed a true leader.

One of our principal purposes is to erase the seeds of fear and inappropriate guilt from the minds of Astarians everywhere ... fear of God, fear of hell-fire, fear of death, fear of life ... and to plant instead the seeds of divine love.

WOMAN, GLANDULAR CHEMISTRY AND EMOTIONAL CYCLES

Glandular secretions determine a great deal more than the physiological functions of the body. They also have a distinct bearing upon the personality and characteristics exhibited.

Consider the emotional cycles endured under the direct impact and influence of the glands and the changing chemistry of the physical form. One of the most evident of these cycles and its obvious reaction is the cycle of reproduction in the female. Understanding this important cycle may help you better to relate the activity of the glands to your everyday life, whether male or female; and it is for this reason that we have included this discussion here.

Around the age of puberty, around fourteen years, the pituitary gland receives a mysterious "message" from some *source*. We recognize it to be the heart seed atom. Upon receipt of this message, the pituitary begins to secrete minute particles of a hormone substance into the bloodstream. The bloodstream carries this hormone into the reproductive organs where it begins to stimulate the female ovaries, the growth of female breasts, the maturing of the sex organs, changes in the bone structure and fatty tissues which transform and mold the female figure. A shapeless, long-legged, boyish creature is almost overnight transformed into a radiant young woman.

The ovaries, under further stimulation from the pituitary, begin their long program of menstruation. With this development of the menstrual cycle, which continues until the woman is middle-aged, comes the ability of the ovaries to produce the female hormone called *estrogen*. This important hormone flows forcefully through the bloodstream for approximately fifteen days following her menstruation, and during those days she will experience well-being, mental alertness and a drive toward some beneficent goal. About thirteen to fifteen days following her menstruation period the ovum or female reproductive egg leaves the ovary to journey to the uterus for possible impregnation.

It leaves behind a protective follicle which, once it releases the ovum, becomes a temporary gland called the *corpus luteum*. This temporary gland, following the departure of the ovum, begins to release into the bloodstream a second very important female hormone called *progesterone*.

Woman is, in a certain sense, the slave of these two female hormones, estrogen and progesterone. The two secretions in their dual flow can cause some women, during the period of approximately five days, to display a tendency toward negativity, passiveness, inertia and receptivity. It is during these five days — from thirteen to fifteen days following menstruation — that she usually conceives because of the presence of the ripened ovum or egg in the uterus. Medical science now declares that it is not possible for woman to conceive except during these five "ripe" days, and it is upon this premise that the modern "rhythm" cycle of birth control is based.

Following these five ripe days which bring the woman near to her menstrual period again, the flow of the estrogen and the progesterone will decrease sharply, automatically preparing the uterus for its process of casting out of the body the "lining" which would have been utilized in the event of impregnation. The elimination of this lining is what we call menstruation, occurring monthly when the female egg fails its goal of impregnation.

The important point here is that during those few days prior to her menstruation, when the female hormones are at an extremely low ebb and the glands have dropped sharply in their output, a woman can enter a difficult time. Her nerves, denied their needed hormonal secretions, may become taut and tense.

As soon as the menstrual flow begins, the estrogen hormone flows abundantly again, releasing the tension. It is important for a woman to understand these cycles — usually a period of from two to four days prior to her menstrual period.

The female reproductive cycle is only one example of the power and influence of the glandular system in our lives.

THE ENDOCRINES AND THE CHAKRAS

A human being is a duality, possessing both a "body celestial and a body terrestrial." Reason must present the fact that there are points of contact or intercommunication between these two. Since the physical form is quite dead without the functions of the soul within, it is obvious that the soul must have some means of transmitting its power over and into the dense physical form.

Mystics have long recognized the glands to be these points of contact in the physical form, and the chakras in the etheric form. They know that underlying the endocrine system are the chakric spiritual centers, without which the endocrine system is inoperative. The chakras are the channels through which the glands express.

Medical minds are but dimly aware of this as yet. Given time, they cannot help arriving at a better understanding of the glandular system, and the fact that glands are obtaining their power and authority from some indiscernible source. This they will ultimately come to know as the heart seed atom.

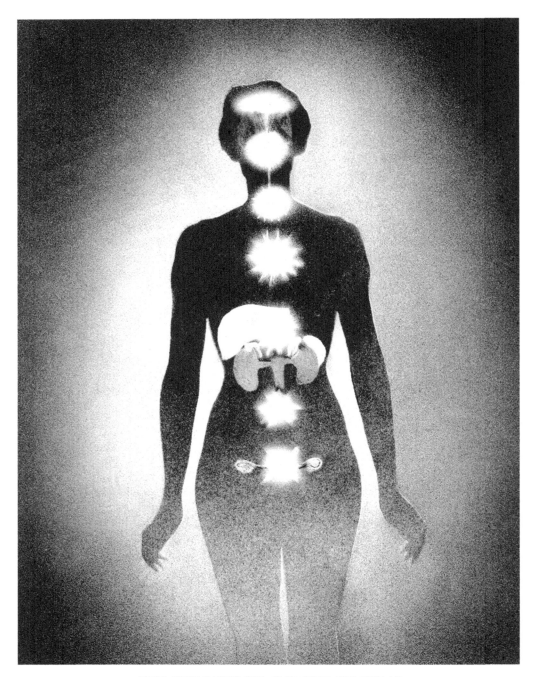

THE ENDOCRINES AND THE CHAKRAS

The etheric chakras are the glands of the etheric body. The glands of the physical form are the crystallized counterparts and instruments for the chakras.

The heart seed atom is the powerhouse, but the chakras are the centers through which the power MUST flow. Although the seed atom governs the glands completely, still there MUST be established channels or centers of force through which the hormones and chemical secretions and ethers flow to bring the "waters of life" to the physical form. These are the chakras which act as "dams," holding tremendous power within themselves and releasing it into the physical body through the endocrines.

Having one of the chakras out of harmony with its representative gland is like trying to heat an electric iron without having it attached to the source of power. The chakra is the source of power into which the gland must be "plugged," else there can be no lifeforce flowing through into the physical form. If all the chakras and endocrines are out of harmony it is like having a fuse blown in your house. You simply cannot get any light and your house is in darkness.

The lifeforce cannot flow through the etheric nadis and into the physical nerves and glands if the valves or connecting bridges between the glands and chakras are inoperative. The body then becomes diseased. There is no light there. We are disconnected from our source of vitality, energy and lifeforce and our bodies cannot be "filled with light" until we harmonize the etheric body and the physical form through the glands and chakras. Otherwise the life current is impeded. The channels are not open to allow the lifeforce to carry the ethers into the physical form. Without them the body dies.

> *When we evolve to the time when the glands harmonize perfectly with the spiritual chakras, we will exhibit physical perfection. This means the heart seed atom will be purified of accumulated bad karma.*

If a medical scientist could study a Master through the revealing exposures of x-ray, s/he would be startled to discover a perfectly coordinated and balanced endocrine system which s/he has seldom witnessed. S/He might even be able to discern faint evidence of the etheric chakras operating through the glands, and distributing perfectly and faultlessly the energies and hormones of the glandular and nervous systems.

Science would discover a balanced flow of the nerve fluid throughout the entire body, and perceive no trace of disease in the Master's form, for the evenly distributed energies, nerve fluids and glandular hormones would evidence perfection.

In this sense the glands are not causes, but effects. They represent the effects of inner spiritual and physical causes. When the chakras, or any of the higher spiritual centers operating through the glandular system, exhibit a balanced state of energy receptivity and distribution, then the physical form manifests perfect health and perfect evolutionary progress.

Until the spiritual centers become properly developed and the endocrines, in turn, are balanced and can direct a continual flow of life energy throughout the physical form, the glands cannot supply the proper hormones for physical perfection. They cannot guard the body against disease. They cannot fight against the ravages of perpetual decay. They are completely inadequate in their present state.

> *However, the endocrines are only the physical reflections of the spiritual chakras, and the chakras, in turn, only mirror the spiritual progress of the individual soul. So until most people decide to look to their spiritual development, which will automatically develop the chakras, they will be the victim of their own spiritual inertia.*

It must constantly be remembered that the development of the chakras parallels the development of the endocrine glands. Both reflect the evolutionary progression attained by the individual. The Astarian should always keep in mind that the physical in all things is a reflection of the spiritual.

To attempt to gain perfection in the physical form, of itself, is a misguided approach. One must seek first spiritual progression through all phases. One should spend time tranquilizing the mind through spiritual meditations, erasing traits of weakness in one's character, and building strength from within; thinking of service to humanity and trying, without giving undivided attention to it, to purify the physical form through pure food, drink and air, and exercise. To concentrate the entire attention upon restoring the physical through physical means alone is like trying to mend a broken egg.

THE ENDOCRINES AND ADDICTIONS

In past Lessons we have urged Astarians to break the tobacco habit. Since our subject is the glands and since there is a glandular reaction from the use of tobacco, we should refer to smoking again so that you will understand that we are not speaking from a moral viewpoint but a spiritual one.

The bloodstream carries the lifeforce throughout the physical form, but it is not the blood itself which creates the lifeforce. It is the mysterious essences of the breath within the blood, indrawn from the atmosphere about us. One of the important properties of the breath is oxygen. Iron in the blood must be supplied with oxygen continuously, or else we die.

Any school child knows that slow-burning fires produce deadly carbon monoxide gas. All fires release this poisonous gas, but in a rapidly burning fire it is consumed. It is only when the fire is one of slow combustion that the carbon monoxide is not consumed and escapes into surrounding atmosphere. If enclosed, it fills the air rapidly and anyone inhaling it will die.

Smokers are coming to realize that a cigar, cigarette or pipe is in reality a slow-burning fire producing an amazing amount of carbon monoxide. As the smoke and all the ingredients of tobacco are inhaled by the smoker, one also inhales minute particles of lethal gas.

We have just spoken about the iron in the blood and its need for oxygen. Between these two there is a magnetic attraction, and the iron in the blood attracts oxygen to itself with the potency of a powerful magnet. However, carbon monoxide is more attractive to iron than is oxygen, and as the carbon monoxide from a cigarette, cigar or pipe is inhaled into the lungs, the iron in the blood draws the monoxide gases into the bloodstream.

This strange affinity of iron for carbon monoxide, rather than the oxygen so needed, results in these poisons being carried throughout the entire body. The decrease in the supply of needed oxygen results in destructive effects, the most devastating of which are upon the glands.

Carbon monoxide inhalation causes all glands to slow down, and they simply cannot release their important secretions and hormones. The principal gland affected is the pituitary which in turn affects the reproductive organs.

The excessive smoking indulged in by present humanity will surely bring destructive effects upon future generations. Many men and women will become sterile in this and future incarnations. The effect upon the glands is a gradual process, but the glands will be damaged and, though the damage will not be eternally irreparable, it may require future incarnations to restore them to balance.

To say that smoking affects the pituitary and reproductive organs is only half the story. People simply cannot reach spiritual heights as long as they are the victims of tobacco, for the impure bloodstream will be a stagnant, impeded channel of disease rather than a river of life. The glandular secretions, marvelous as they are, fight a losing battle against the powerful carbon monoxide gases. The smoker can never hope to attain the superconscious state because the bloodstream, glandular system and nervous system are helpless to evolve.

And what of alcohol and drugs? First, considering alcohol, let us say that a person has consumed a drink. It affects principally the pituitary gland. This amazing controller of the subconscious, ever alert to damage in her domain, sends out an emergency alarm to all the other glands which begin working with increased activity to evict the invading poison.

Research tests have shown that the senses and reactions to them are decelerated. But this sudden charge of energy gives a false sensation of upliftment and well-being, and makes the other drinks seem most attractive. Attempting to overcome the disastrous effect of alcohol, all the glands continue to pour their increased portions of hormones and secretions into the system. They seldom win in the battle and finally collapse in their efforts. The poison pervading every atom of the physical form eventually overwhelms the complete system, and the person becomes intoxicated.

The result experienced the following day is an actual illness, not only from poisons having gained entrance into every cell, but from the over-stimulation of all the glands until they have exhausted their supply of secretions. They cannot cope with the challenge required of them at this low ebb, and the person must recover normalcy painfully and slowly as the glands readjust to their normal function. If this happens continually, the effect of alcohol upon the glandular system leads eventually to complete destruction of physical and mental faculties. This same scenario occurs with the use of drugs as well.

And what of the prescription drugs we depend on so much for our modern healing? An oral dose or hypodermic of most of these drugs causes increased stimulation of one or all the glands, or nerve fluid, and it is this which encourages healing. It is not the drug itself, but only its action upon the important glandular and nervous systems in the physical form — even the etheric body itself — which paves the way for the healing to manifest.

RECONCILING THE PHYSIOLOGICAL WITH THE MYSTICAL

When humanity, beginning with the adolescent mind, is taught to transmute creative energy into a dynamic force operative in the life of every human, its constructive expression can bring about a complete re-magnetization of the endocrine system, and the individual begins to express love, tolerance and kindness in daily life.

We have previously indicated that it is possible to master the glandular influence in your life, but we have also made a seemingly contradictory statement. We have said:

1. we are the slave of our past karmic picture images as they are injected into the bloodstream and work their influence first upon the chakras and then, through them, the endocrines;

and

2. we are potential Masters and captains of our fate.

How can we equate these two diverse statements? Are we masters of our fate, or are we slaves to physiological cycles? Is it possible for us to overcome and eliminate the influence of karmic picture images in our lives and avoid karmic debt, or must we be submissive to our fate and cease any struggle toward victory?

There are steps that you *can* take to overcome karmic influences and chemical physiological cycles in your life, and progress toward Mastership.

Step One: Removal of "seed inhibitions," resulting from the effect of picture images of the past flowing out of the heart seed atom.

Step Two: Scientific prayer.

Step Three: Conservation of the propagative energies.

Step Four: Seeking every possible aid on the physical level.

Step Five: Practicing daily meditation, to tranquilize the mental body, gain mastery over thoughts, allow only the pure to find permanent lodging in your mind.

Step Six: Learning to express emotions in a healthy balanced way.

Let us consider each step.

Step One: Removal of the "Seed Inhibitions"

We have explained that the heart seed atom releases picture images created in the *past,* while the astral seed atom and the mental seed atom release picture images created by your present actions.

Inhibitions are planted in the subconscious by the release of picture images of the past. They arouse those indwelling and enigmatical fears, complexes and phobias that find their way into the waking conscious and mingle in the bloodstream with the picture images of the present. Which of these control your outer life will depend upon which of the picture images contain the greater power — those of the past or those of the present.

You can destroy the power in those of the past by persistent affirmations of perfection, persistent visualization of perfection, persistent expressions of love.

The power of inhibitions and complexes can also be destroyed by raising them out of the realm of the subconscious and bringing them to the surface of the waking conscious mind, there to be talked through. This procedure may be accomplished by counseling with either a trusted minister, a priest in a confessional, or a rabbi; through dealing with difficult issues with a reliable therapist or psychologist; or by writing your "confession" to us with a request that it be burned after we have prayed over it.

Also to be considered is nocturnal persuasion: playing products that convince the subconscious of your desire for perfection, that help you let go of fears, doubts and guilt.

Step Two: The Use of Scientific Prayer

For the ordinary person who is not familiar with the teachings revealed through Astara or other similar schools, prayer is often completely empty of purpose. This person usually does not even believe in divine healing. If this person does pray the prayers may be devoid of power, are negative and are empty of direction. In the case of karmic debts of long standing, such as we have described previously, this type of prayer will avail little. As an Astarian, you will begin to put cosmic law into operation for yourself.

1. You will begin immediately to use the Astarian method of surrounding yourself with the pure White Light.

2. You will direct powerful streams of the White Light to the afflicted area of your body with your own mind power, and you will ask the assistance of higher beings, including the spiritual leader of any religion to which you may belong, in attaining your goal.

3. You will write to Astara to ask for healing prayers. You understand that this action of asking is a very necessary part of a mystical magic which has brought help and healing to countless thousands. The cosmic law seldom inaugurates any action to help anyone who will not take the first step forward to obtain help. That step is *to ask, to knock, to seek,* acknowledging the presence of a greater power.

4. You will try to develop more powerful faith, more willingness to co-create your future with the Divine Source.

5. Recognizing that love can overcome all things, you will attempt as mystic Buddhism and all great religions teach, to express right action, right thinking, right emotions, to overbalance the influence of the atomic picture images within.

Step Three: Regeneration

The self-preservation impulse is the greatest force in the human being. The creative urge is second, and is expressed in many ways other than through a sexual relationship. We have said that the creative force released by the reproductive organs when not dissipated through sexual intercourse can be directed upward to express in increased mental powers. Dissipation of these creative forces through excessive sex siphons much needed power from one of the brain's most potent sources.

To attempt celibacy, however, is equally destructive unless one is intelligently guided in the proper method of conserving these creative forces. They *can* be lifted to the brain if one possesses a complete understanding of the science of regeneration. Further along in our studies such teachings will be given for those who desire to master this most ancient art of physical and spiritual regeneration.

Until it can be mastered, one is wise to discover some constructive release for the creative force through mental and physical activities. Painting, teaching, singing, study, riding, playing, dancing, tennis, swimming, writing — any sort of strenuous activity which consumes either physical or mental energy will simultaneously consume the creative force and dissipate the discharges of creative energy resulting in the propagative urge. Given enough of these activities, the body will fall into its own conservative rhythm in connection with sexual activities.

To avoid confusion it would be important to explain that to suppress the creative urge by denying sexual activity does not necessarily imply that it automatically is lifted to the brain centers. Unless deliberately channeled into some constructive activity it can become only inhibited in its expression, causing a restlessness and gnawing discontent toward everything and everybody.

Creative forces *will* be expressed, whether through sex, through creative physical or mental activities or, if continually denied these two channels, through negative destructivity such as crime, excessive drinking, or some other equally undesirable trait. The suppressed creative force will go "underground" and manifest in some negative manner — even mental imbalance.

Thus, unless one is trained for celibacy, a wise procedure is simply to abstain from excessive sexual activities, and to turn a share of the creative force toward physical and mental creative activities.

Step Four: The Physical Level

First of all, when illness threatens, you may wish to consult a physician for this particular method of healing. At least you may wish to have a doctor diagnose your case to discover the medical opinion regarding the *cause* of your difficulties. It may lie purely in the physical realm and not be a karmic problem at all.

Second, you may wish to turn to the natural method of healing such as the use of herbs, adjustments by chiropractors, treatment by a naturopath, use of natural vitamins, health juices, fasting, heat therapy, ultrasonic therapy, mineral baths, acupuncture or any of the countless methods along metaphysical lines. Many people today are combining these two sources of healing with very beneficial results.

Steps Five And Six:
Expressing Right Action, Right Emotions, Right Thoughts

First, let us consider the case of the common cold which has perplexed the physician for untold decades. In attempting to combat and conquer this most baffling of all human diseases, medical scientists have arrived at two conclusions regarding its cause:

1. exposure to the elements such as drafts, cold, rains, winds;

2. exposure to contagious germs and viruses.

Now which of these two is correct? The answer eludes the physician who has discovered that many exposed to the elements do *not* catch a cold, but will become the victim of a germ. And many, on the other hand, exposed to the germs will overcome their influence but will fall victim to the draft. While yet others, exposed to both, will escape the disease entirely. What, then, is the answer?

The physician has found it in immunization. The person who has built up the proper immunity against both these causes will throw off the disease. The person who has not, will fall victim to it. The idea of immunization exemplifies what we are attempting to teach.

How does this discussion of the common cold help us to understand the functioning of karmic picture images in our lives, and how to eliminate or balance their effect? The flow of picture images represents the germs in our bodies ... while the effort on our part to overcome them represents our immunization program. Right thinking, right feeling, and right action are the antibodies which can build up an immunity in us which *can* offset the influence of the karmic germs.

The Biblical admonition to "overcome evil with good" describes it exactly. And viewed from this standpoint it becomes not a dull platitude at all, but a power-packed *rule for victory.* As the good which you do begins to outweigh the effect of the picture images, you begin to master all aspects of your life, whether they be physical, mental, or spiritual. You are like a tree "planted by the water" — you shall not be moved by the fluctuating currents of your everyday life.

Your goal is, indeed, to overcome evil with good. Remember, the picture images are of vibratory substance, and an *overwhelming portion of powerful, good vibrations* streaming out of the

a. astral seed atom in the solar plexus and the

b. mental seed atom in the brain,

can completely dissipate the charges of vibratory substance in the karmic picture images pouring from the

c. physical seed atom in the heart.

It requires the will power of near mastership to accomplish this goal. It requires concentrated effort, unswerving faith, and an understanding of what is actually occurring physiologically in your body. It requires supreme mental training to attain the desired result, for the impulses rising from the subconscious as the voice of your past are extremely potent, and there are few who will even attempt to overcome them through their own will. But it *can* be done.

In some far-distant, wonderful day you will bring all your intricate inner systems into harmonious coordination, will become the perfected fivefold person — perfect physically, emotionally, spiritually, psychically and mentally. As this perfection begins to register, so shall the life within become the light without. You shall become "one that dwelleth in the secret place of the Most High" and you shall go no more out of the Divine Parent's House.

SUMMATION

The nadis, operative in the etheric body, is a complete counterpart of the nervous system of the physical form. Both the etheric nervous system and the physical operate through the endocrine system. The nerve fluids help produce the power in the glands which enables them, with incredible wisdom, to emit their mysterious hormones into the bloodstream, which then conveys to all parts of the body the secretions of all three systems — the etheric nadis, the physical endocrines, and the physical nervous system. All three use the bloodstream as a means of intercommunication between the centers of activity in the physical form.

The heart seed atom also conveys its atomic picture images of karma, both past and present, into the bloodstream which carries them first to the spiritual chakras, through which they are registered upon the physical endocrine system. The chakras, then, are the direct instruments of karma operating hand-in-hand under the influence of the seed atom in the heart.

Any individual's progress depends on the spiritual and physical experiences gained in past lives. The endocrine gland of the physical form can reflect only the degree of perfection manifested by its etheric counterpart, the chakra of the etheric body, and also the similar force center or chakra in the higher astral and mental bodies. The higher spiritual centers in turn reflect only that degree of evolutionary progress attained by the individual incarnating soul.

The glands are an outward expression of the spiritual chakras. The spiritual chakras are centers of force through which cosmic energies flow. Since the glands are only an outer manifestation of spiritual centers, they are a physical LIVING RECORD of the degree of evolution attained by the individual.

They can express only the strength, power and spiritual potency with which the individual has endowed them in previous incarnations. The character of one's conduct and behavior in past lives is recorded in the endocrine system and can manifest only such perfection as the soul has attained in past efforts.

The chakras are focal points of both soul and physical energy, and depending upon how high an estate the soul has attained in evolutionary spiritual progress, just so will the chakras be able to manifest perfected streams of energy. And just so, in turn, will

THE "LIVING PHILOSOPHER'S STONE"

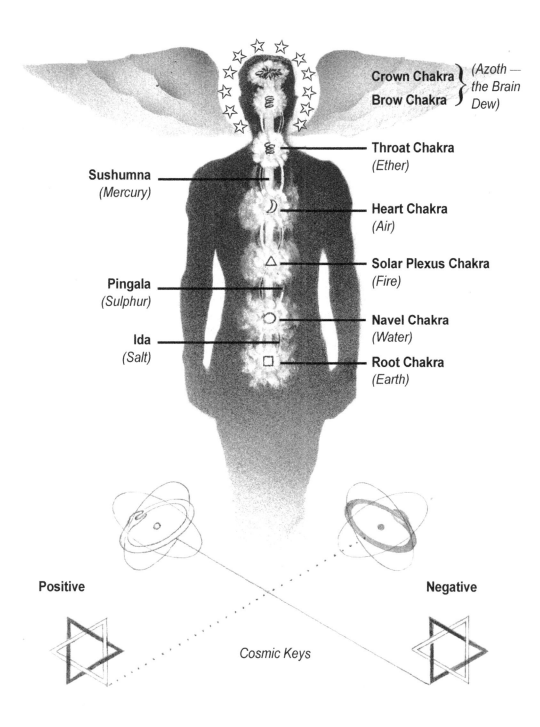

Crown Chakra ⎫ (Azoth —
Brow Chakra ⎭ the Brain Dew)

Throat Chakra
(Ether)

Sushumna
(Mercury)

Heart Chakra
(Air)

Solar Plexus Chakra
(Fire)

Pingala
(Sulphur)

Navel Chakra
(Water)

Ida
(Salt)

Root Chakra
(Earth)

Positive

Negative

Cosmic Keys

the endocrines express the perfect flow of the life principle throughout the physical form. The goal of the future is to bring the chakras toward a state of perfection, which will automatically bring reflected improvement in the glandular system.

If the chakras are increasingly stimulated through spiritual activities and thinking, such as meditation, studies, proper living and altruistic services, so will they begin to manifest the same condition of stimulation in their counterparts, the physical glands. The endocrine system will begin to express perfect harmony as it releases more spiritualized essences, chemicals and hormones into the bloodstream and nervous system.

Thus it can truly be said that as we awaken spiritually, so does the glandular system express perfection and power, and as this power is released, so do we begin to express more and more our great connection with the Divine Source.

Queen Pituitary and Her Fallen Lord, Pineal

Second Degree — Lesson Seven

PITUITARY — QUEEN OF YOUR INNER WORLD

In this Lesson, we present teachings about the physical functions of the glands that will lay the groundwork for the esoteric teachings which follow. You will better understand the esoteric teachings if you understand basic physical functions.

At our present evolutionary status, both medical and esoteric science recognize the pituitary as the master gland of the physical body. She holds the entire kingdom of your inner world in her domain. Her commands are obeyed promptly and without question by all the other glands.

The pituitary is sometimes called the *hypophysis* gland. It is approximately the size of a pea, and is located behind the root of the nose, suspended from the base of the brain like a fruit attached to a tiny stalk. It is divided into two prominent lobes: the anterior or frontal lobe, and the posterior or rear lobe.

The pituitary body has a double origin. The anterior lobe is an upgrowth of the pharynx. In the course of evolution it became attached to the under surface of the brain. Fusion with the posterior lobe caused the gland itself to lose its connection with the alimentary canal, so far as medical science is concerned. Esoteric science, however, still recognizes this important connection between the mouth and the anterior lobe of the pituitary, and we shall enlarge upon this idea later.

The posterior lobe is a downgrowth of the brain itself and has a direct connection, through the third ventricle, to the spinal cord and the fires of the spinal sushumna.

The importance of this master gland to all the physiological processes of the body is witnessed by the fact that the Creator has seen fit to surround and protect it with a solid, bony cup into which it fits, called the *sella turcica* or Turkish Saddle.

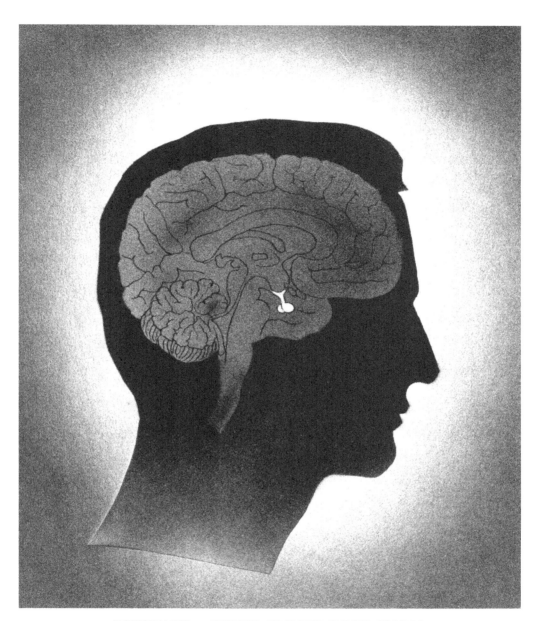

PITUITARY — QUEEN OF YOUR INNER WORLD

Pituitary is the master gland of the body. It is divided into two important lobes: the anterior or frontal lobe, and the posterior or rear lobe. The anterior lobe controls the automatic physiological functions of the physical body. The post-lobe is connected with the functions of the Oversoul, and the superconscious mind.

Removal of the gland itself does not directly cause death, but a very rapid weakening of the physical body. Other glands begin a slow deterioration, possibly resulting in death.

Malfunctioning of the gland produces tragic phenomena. If over-stimulation or enlargement of the gland occurs in a child, the result is growth to giant size. If the overstimulation occurs after the physical form has already assumed adult stature, then the form will not grow taller, but various parts of the skeleton will be affected such as the bony ridges over the eyes, the jawbones and cheekbones. The hands and feet will also assume enlarged proportions.

Understimulation, on the other hand, will produce a dwarfed child. In some cases pituitary insufficiency produces obesity. Many excessively obese children who lead unhappy, tragic young lives could be spared much of their misery if taken to an endocrinologist and given pituitary glandular feedings. These will usually restore the child to average size.

Pituitary insufficiency in the adult also produces obesity. Many adults who, around middle age, become the victims of excessive fat, unevenly distributed over the body, would do well to consult an endocrinologist for advice concerning the possibility of glandular treatments. During menopause in the female, all the ductless glands diminish their activity, under the command of pituitary. The thyroid may become completely atrophied, causing a serious condition called *myxedema*.

THE ANTERIOR LOBE OF THE PITUITARY

An adequate description of the activities of the anterior lobe would be to say that it controls the physiological functions of the physical form. This lobe emits many important hormones, without which the body could not properly function:

1. *The Growth Hormone* — which controls balanced development of the physical form; the structure of the skeleton — height, weight and breadth in particular.

2. *The Sex Hormone* — which, entering the bloodstream, is carried directly to the ovaries and testes, stimulating the gonadotrophic hormone in the male, and the ovarian hormones in the female. Under the stimulation created by hormones from the anterior lobe, the sex glands begin to grow, to function, and finally to mature.

3. *The Lactogenic Hormone* — whose function is to cause the secretion of milk in the female mammary glands during and directly following the period of gestation.

Other glands affected very directly by the hormones of the anterior lobe are the thyroid, the adrenals and the parathyroid glands. When the pituitary is damaged or diseased, the thyroid, the adrenals and the parathyroids become degenerated. The stimulation of the thyroid depends completely upon the pituitary secretions and, if these cease, the thyroid becomes practically atrophied.

Removal of the pituitary before puberty causes the reproductive organs to remain completely infantile, and further development of the sexual characteristics ceases. In the male, the voice fails to develop, hair will not grow on the face, the testes atrophy and genesis of the sperm ceases as well as further hormone production.

In the female, the ovic egg fails to mature and no follicles form. There is no further hormone production and the menstrual cycle fails to begin. If the gland is removed during early pregnancy, the result is miscarriage or natural abortion.

Glandular secretions and extracts can, of course, be injected into the bloodstream, counteracting all these effects. With these injections, the male characteristics develop, the menstrual cycles continue in the female, pregnancies proceed normally, as well as all other bodily functions usually under the control of the pituitary.

One realizes immediately, then, that the anterior lobe is in complete control of the reproductive organs, which is to say that all sexual development and functions are influenced by the hormones reaching these reproductive glands from the pituitary. This explains why, from a mystical standpoint, it is not wise to excessively dissipate the reproductive energies, since to do so causes a direct influence upon the powers of the pituitary, resulting in mental fatigue, loss of mind power, and noted inefficiency in all mental functions.

THE POSTERIOR LOBE

The posterior lobe, which we shall call the post-lobe for brevity, is composed of gland tissue and nerve cells and is a downgrowth of the brain itself, developing from the lining cells of the third ventricle. Medical science defines the post-lobe as:

1. the regulator of the oxidative processes in the muscles;

2. the controller of water metabolism;

3. the controller of heat production;

4. the controller of blood pressure;

5. the stimulator of intestinal movements;

6. the stimulator of the kidneys;

7. the instigator of muscular contractions of the uterus at time of childbirth through the flow of the magical hormone called *pituitrin*.

Mysticism has nothing to do with the first six items, but about the seventh — the flow of pituitrin — we have much to say.

Post-lobe and Pituitrin

Medical scientists stand in awe before the evidence of the influence of this divine essence. They are familiar with its physiological functions, its effect upon the uterus during and after childbirth, how it causes the muscles to contract and eventually expel the child from the mother's womb, then immediately to contract the muscles back to normal size.

With these functions they are more than familiar. But they remain amazed at the power of the mother's love aroused by the flow of this oily substance into her bloodstream — a love so intense as to cause her to sacrifice her very life to save that of her young; tender enough to keep her consecrated to a perpetual vigil over her own, or fierce enough to turn her into a fighting tigress if protection is necessary.

Increased portions of this pituitrin can change a ruthless, war-minded, brute into a calm, reasoning, peace-loving individual. It can transform a vicious, mercenary, heartless female into a warmhearted, tender woman, strongly devoted to motherhood and world-lovingness. Behavior, in general, in any individual can be radically changed by the increase or decrease of this most excellent "elixir of love."

Pituitrin influences the entire nervous system, creating its unfailing reaction either of greater kindness, soul love and compassion when increased; or hatred, greed, jealousy, violence when it is decreased.

Medical scientists have witnessed its incredible transforming influence upon human behavior but they cannot explain the why and the how of it. Mystics know the secret of the flow of the holy oil, and its marriage with the cosmic fires of sushumna.

Pituitrin and the Moon Cycle

Since we acknowledge the human being to be a miniature universe, we then recognize each gland to represent an interior star or planet. The priest-physician Paracelsus understood this mystery well for he taught: *Heaven operates within us. Each star in our solar system has a special influence over an interior star.* He declared that the sun ruled the pineal gland; the moon the pituitary; and Mercury, messenger between gods and humans, the thyroid which is the bridge connecting the personality with the soul and spirit.

Medical science scoffs at these "superstitions" — yet it cannot ignore the fact that the glands operate somewhat in cycles and these cycles, controlled by the pituitary, harmonize with certain cycles of the moon. During certain of these mysterious moon cycles the pituitary injects increased portions of pituitrin into the bloodstream and nervous system, which is intended to arouse spiritual powers — just as there are physical cycles relating to sleep, sex, thought power, energies, etc.

Our spiritual evolution depends largely upon our response to this spiritual impulse. The majority misinterprets the impulse and directs the flow of increased power into completely physical channels — misinterpreting it for the sexual urge. In others it arouses a drive toward personal ambition. In yet others it stirs a deep, lonely longing in the soul to such a degree as to result in melancholy.

In some it may externalize as exaltation and elation, such as the sudden urge to have a social fling or to entertain lavishly. Individuals react in varied ways to this cyclic flow of the oily essence.

The mystic recognizes it at once as the spiritual impulse and turns thoughts and activities immediately into a spiritual channel, the better to benefit by the precious "waters of eternal life." You may enter more intense meditation, or you may express it through painting, writing, or some other creative, artistic, constructive channel. According to the manner in which the individual responds, so will the oil increase in potency, remain the same, or decrease in power.

If you react spiritually and attempt to maintain the flow in the bloodstream, you will in time be able to hold the power of one cycle until a new cycle begins, thus ensuring a constant stream of both spiritual and psychic forces. This, of course, may require many years of training. But when one attains this cyclic rhythm there will come a spiritual quickening within, just as there is a quickening in the physical embryo at a certain time of its development in the mother's womb. The spiritual quickening results in increased levels of consciousness, of psychic potentials and increased magnetic power of the personality.

Post-lobe Influence in Our Future

The post-lobe, connected with the third ventricle, is in turn, indirectly connected with the spinal column. The post-lobe, then, is the terminal point in the head for the upward flow of the spinal fluids and fires once they pass the "guard" at the gateway, the medulla oblongata. It follows, too, that the spinal essences are influenced by the downflow of pituitary substances. Thus, through sushumna, the royal road to godhood, flow the true fires and waters of eternal life, all of which influence or are influenced by the secretions of the post-lobe of queen pituitary.

Pituitrin, our most important feminine-negative brain dew, cannot gain its ultimate power until it unites with the fires which burn at the base of the spine in kundalini, and in the reproductive centers. Only when the pituitary can mix her pituitrin with the creative forces rising through sushumna from the root chakra, will she be able to transmit her auric emanations in sufficient quantity to arouse and permanently resurrect her crucified god, the pineal.

It seems expedient that we mention the means by which the post-lobe of pituitary may best be stimulated:

1. through zealous study in a continuous and burning search for truth;

2. through the practice of Lama Yoga, or other spiritually oriented yoga practice;

3. through meditation, beseeching the assistance of your Oversoul, opening the way for a downpouring of cosmic power from on High through the sutratmic silver cord which joins you with your Oversoul;

4. the practice of universal love for ALL of God's creatures.

Arousing the post-lobe results in myriad reactions. First, an increased flow of pituitrin in the bloodstream causes the personality to exhibit more divine qualities. Second, the stimulation arouses the spirillae in the heart of the crown chakra and intensifies their activities.

The spirillae (about which we shall teach later) act as a magnet, drawing the fires of kundalini upward through sushumna. As these fires ascend and strike the post-lobe, they unite with pituitrin and from this union flows the radiations of cosmic power from pituitary toward her mate, pineal.

Pituitrin is also urged into greater activity through the spiritual experiences of the personality and the direct downpouring of power from the Oversoul via the sutratmic silver cord.

At our present level of spiritual evolution, it is important to concentrate our entire attention upon arousing the pituitary to her fullest intensity, for *IT IS THROUGH HER INFLUENCE, AND HERS ALONE, THAT THE PINEAL AND CROWN CHAKRA GAIN THEIR MATURITY, RESULTING IN MASTERSHIP FOR THE STRIVING DISCIPLE.* It is also through her influence alone that the cosmic fires of kundalini rise through sushumna.

Just as we all must come into physical manifestation through the labors of woman, so must we be brought into spiritual birth through the spiritual labors of the feminine pituitary. Pineal represents divine wisdom. Pituitary represents divine love. Divine wisdom can *NEVER* manifest without first being baptized and brought to birth through divine love. Pineal can *NEVER* be aroused to spiritual perfection, except it be through the stimulation and labors of pituitary.

In the Mysteries of old, the female hierophant often represented pituitary, for the ancients understood well that only through the efforts of pituitary would the fallen god, pineal, be resurrected.

In the majority of individuals kundalini has been raised out of the root chakra to dominate the solar plexus, the center of carnal emotions, where humankind is polarized at present. The next stage of development will be raising the fires from the solar plexus to the heart center. We will then begin to express increasing degrees of spiritual love for our fellow beings.

In some souls, where the intellect has become overemphasized, kundalini will bypass the heart center and begin to stimulate the throat center. In these instances we have one who is too busy expressing intellectualism and self-aggrandizement to bother with compassion, mercy, humility, kindness, or sympathy in any way.

This indicates a small degree of wisdom without love. It is intellect operating alone. It is knowledge without understanding; pride without humility. It is ruthless cunning. It is selfishness without the qualities of mercy. The spiritual malfunction must be corrected before the individual can evolve further along the spiritual path.

This malfunction cannot occur in the head centers, for the brow and crown chakras are lifted beyond the reach of the personality and into that of the spirit. True wisdom cannot be wisdom without love. Love is the mother of wisdom, and without it, true wisdom does not exist.

PITUITARY AND THE INFUNDIBULUM

It is important to note that the post-lobe is attached to the third ventricle by the stalk which medical science calls the *infundibulum*. You will see in our illustration that we depict a small passageway or channel running through the infundibulum stalk, connecting the post-lobe with the third ventricle.

Medical science believes there to be a connecting link between the post-lobe and the third brain ventricle during infancy, but closed in the adult. We cannot agree, for mystics know of the presence of the brain ethers and dews and their influence upon the spiritual life of the disciple.

Observe the illustration and note the presence of this tiny channel. We call it the *zu-tube* or river of light — the pathway of azoth.

The spiritual ethers from the Oversoul descend into the brain cells and seep, like ink in a blotter, into many brain cavities, one of which is the third ventricle. There they are held captive and evaporate unless the disciple begins to evolve spiritually. Where the lower-minded individual is concerned, medical science is correct — the infundibulum IS closed. But not in the unfolding disciple.

Under spiritual influence the ethers begin to flow in minute portions from the third ventricle, via the zu-tube, into the post-lobe where they cause a stimulation of pituitrin.

THE POST-LOBE, THE THIRD VENTRICLE AND THE CONNECTING "ZU-TUBE"

The infundibulum is the channel extending between the post-lobe of pituitary and the third ventricle of the brain. We call it the "zu-tube" of consciousness. As the brain dews seep into the third ventricle from the Oversoul, they pass via the infundibulum "zu-tube" into the post-lobe of pituitary, there to stimulate the hormonal flow of pituitrin, the essence of divine love.

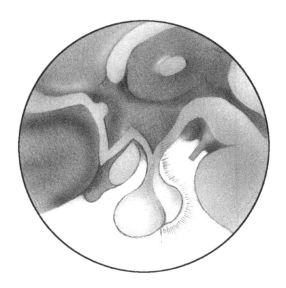

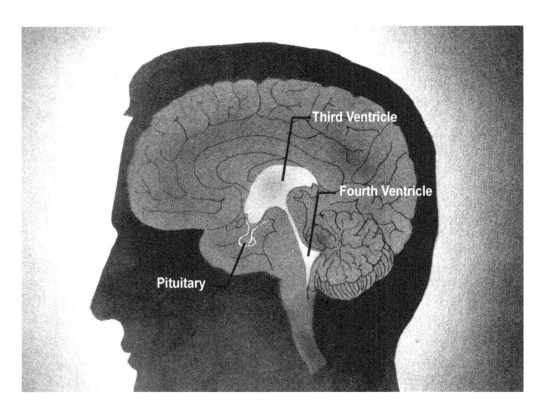

Knowing this, mystics acknowledge a definite connection between the third ventricle and the post-lobe which, under certain conditions, becomes increasingly opened according to the spiritual progression of the individual.

THE PINEAL GLAND

Medical science stands even more in wonder concerning the pineal gland. Most scientists declare that it has no practical physical function whatever. Mystics see a mysterious connection between this "atrophied" gland and the sex glands. They recognize a threefold interplay between the pineal, the thymus (the gland between the shoulder blades) and the sex glands, in that during the early years of life, before puberty, the pineal-thymus glands seem to inhibit the development of the sex glands until the proper time for their normal development.

Around puberty, (about fourteen years of age) these two glands — the pineal and the thymus — seem to atrophy altogether and, with the ceasing of their mysterious functions, the generative organs begin to develop and mature.

Medical scientists admit their complete ignorance of the exact nature and functions of both these glands, except for this fragmentary knowledge. They confess their genuine perplexity as to *how* these two glands control sexual development, but they do recognize the connection between them and the sex glands. There *is* a connection, but the pineal and the thymus do not inhibit the development of the sex glands directly.

They both, however, use the same creative forces in building their powers as do sex glands. That is, all three — the pineal, the thymus and the sex glands — utilize the same creative forces to gain their maturity: the sex glands to develop power to reproduce, and the pineal-thymus to develop the power to create with the mind.

As the child reaches puberty, the developing sex glands begin to attract *all* the creative pranic energies downward to themselves, preventing further development of the pineal and the thymus. Thus, in order for the sex glands to mature, these two higher centers are robbed of their "inheritance" and they apparently atrophy and cease to function.

In the regenerated person, or the advanced soul, the thymus and pineal glands will become reactivated to develop the two higher chakras by inhibiting the flow of creative forces to the root chakra. When one begins to transfer the reproductive energies to the head, the generative glands will begin to atrophy and the thymus and pineal will begin to manifest their divine powers.

Until we decide, however, to "tithe" one-tenth of our "treasures" — the creative energies — to God, or to the higher chakras, we will be a wanderer in life's

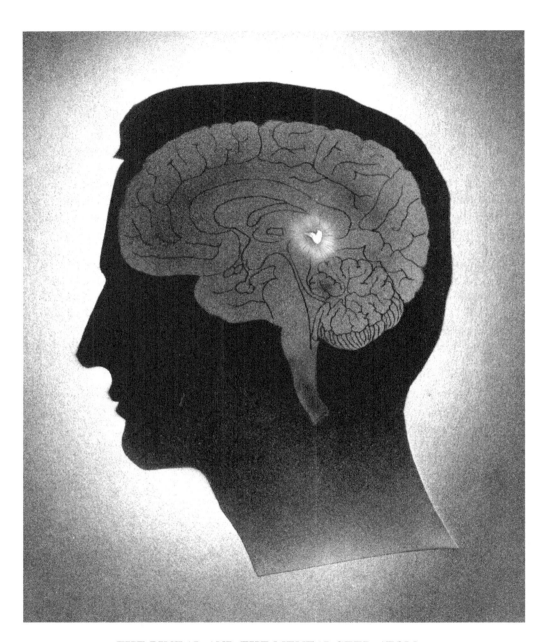

THE PINEAL AND THE MENTAL SEED ATOM

The pineal gland lies on the opposite side of the third ventricle from pituitary. It is the seat of the intellect, the "home" of the mental seed atom and contact point of the mental body in human beings.

wilderness and a prodigal child, not yet turned homeward to the Father-Mother's house. It is not required that seekers become celibate ... only that we give our "tithe" toward the development of the higher centers.

THE ACTIVE HEAD CHAKRAS IN CHILDHOOD

Since the Third Eye — containing both the pineal and the pituitary — is active during the early years of life, usually the first seven, it is through this center that the child many times beholds inhabitants of another world. They even play with unseen playmates, describe the colors around them and the objects of the invisible realms.

An unwise parent often punishes a child for his or her innocent declaration of the presence of unseen things, causing fear, confusion and insecurity in the young mind, since the child HAS seen and felt something from other planes of life. A withdrawal into oneself is the usual reaction of this unfortunate, sensitive child — unfortunate because of well-meaning, but unwise parents who fail to understand the presence of the opened Third Eye which, by the time puberty is gained, will have retreated into the skull. The sutures of the head will have closed over it much as a door closes on the Higher Worlds.

MEDICAL SCIENCE AND THE PINEAL

Medical science declares that the pineal is a remnant of a parietal eye in the primordial amphibian. Cells are discovered in the pineal which are like the cells in the retina of the human eye, thus suggesting even to these scientists that the pineal once was an organ of sight.

The pineal developed as an outgrowth of the third ventricle and is located near the junction of the third ventricle and the midbrain. It is shaped like a pine cone and is reddish-gray in color. In size the pineal compares to a large grain of wheat, being smaller than the pituitary.

Medical science is handicapped in its research concerning this diminutive gland, for it is difficult to reach without causing injury to the brain. But the fact that science finds no positive function of the gland should not imply that its importance is lessened. Under no circumstances can the pineal be considered permanently atrophied, deteriorated or degenerated, for its principle functions lie outside the realm of the physical. What medical minds fail to discern, even with mounting evidence before them, is that the pineal is the seat of the mind and the intellect, the home of the mental seed atom.

One case in particular is that of a five-year-old boy who very suddenly began to mature both physically and mentally. He was brought to a clinic in Germany to be examined and studied. He exhibited the physical form and mind of an adult and had ceased to perform as a child in any way. He died a few weeks after admission into the clinic, and an autopsy revealed the presence of a tumor on the pineal gland. The *malfunction of the gland* had transformed the child suddenly into an adult, yet the field of medicine failed to heed the lesson taught by this tragic occurrence. But we wonder if it truly was a tragedy.

Perhaps the soul which inhabited the body of the child came to Earth for the sole purpose of demonstrating to the world of science that a connection does exist between the pineal and the mind. If so, the real tragedy lies not in his death, but in the failure of science to recognize the phenomenon and in the soul-sacrifice of the being who gave his life in vain, seeking to teach the lesson that *the pineal is a focal point of the mind.*

Careful observation should have revealed that normal stimulation of the pineal cannot alone produce growth of either the physical form or development of sex characteristics. As medical science already knows, it accomplishes the exact opposite, in that sexual development does not begin until *after* the pineal apparently ceases some mysterious function which inhibits that sexual development until the time of puberty.

Therefore, the only connection between the pineal and the development of sexual attributes can be said to be that of a mysterious control over the reproductive glands to prevent premature development. After puberty the sex glands require the major portion of the creative force to further their normal growth, leaving the pineal center without the needed source of its further development.

There are child geniuses whom we witness every day demonstrating the new age trend toward pineal development — young wizards in the fields of mathematics, electronics, biochemistry, nuclear physics. It is obvious, in observing these remarkable children, that it is possible for the pineal to develop mental powers without any undesirable traits being discernible in the functioning of the physical form. These children are normal in every way; only their minds are in advance of their earthly years, demonstrating the stimulated pineal in magnificent operation.

But we must point out that when we say the pineal is denied its "nourishment" as the sexual characteristics develop, we do not mean to imply that IF A PERSON UNFOLDS UNUSUAL INTELLECTUAL POWERS, HE OR SHE MUST OF NECESSITY DISPLAY A WEAKENED PHYSICAL FORM OR IMPOTENCY, BECAUSE THIS IS NOT TRUE.

If we direct even a small portion of the creative energies upward through sushumna to the brain cells and the pineal chakra, then we receive downpouring mental stimulus from the higher mental body, the causal, residing in the overshadowing Oversoul. This results in increased powers, not only in the seat of the mind in the pineal but also in the creative centers in the root chakra and in the thymus, the youth-retaining gland.

It is important to note that even with the stimulation of the pineal it does not necessarily follow that the individual is advanced spiritually. She or he simply displays above average mental powers. *It requires a simultaneous development of the entire Third Eye* to produce advanced degrees of spirituality as well as mentality, and not the action of the stimulated pineal alone. Spirituality implies love as well as wisdom, which must embrace the feminine pituitary and the entire surrounding forcefield of the mental and causal human being, as well as the masculine pineal.

Many esoteric teachers proclaim the pineal to be the most important gland, in a spiritual sense. We at Astara do not agree with this opinion, particularly at this stage of our evolution. In the person of the future, the pineal will rise to its majestic heights, but never will it predominate over the pituitary for *both will rank of equal importance* in bringing humankind to our ultimate perfection and in constituting the Third Eye.

And only as they *both* evolve will the Third Eye realize its ultimate potential. Thus we do not designate the pineal gland alone to constitute the Third Eye. It is, rather, the "eye of the soul," for the pineal is, indeed, the seat of the soul in the physical body. But the entire Third Eye area, including the pituitary, is the "eye of the Oversoul."

> *Without pituitary, pineal cannot attain spiritual birth. It cannot gain spiritual heights until its harmonious marriage with queen pituitary. It is from the mystic union of these two that the Divine is born within, and it is the birth of this inner divine spark of light which will bring humankind into the ultimate kingdom of God.*

THE MENTAL SEED ATOM AND THE SPIRILLAE

The only thing that makes the pineal, of itself, a most important center is the presence of the seven spirillae and the mental seed atom in its heart. Let us first discuss the mental seed atom which holds the record of your complete mental development through the past ages of your existence as an individualized soul.

It is not the victim of your mental karma. Whatever mental "sins" you have committed have been transferred, as a record, to the heart seed atom to act upon your future as karmic retribution. The mental atom simply exists as a record of your mental development so far, just as you exist in an overall form as an adult, signifying that you have passed out of childhood and become an adult.

Whatever you have gained of mental powers is also registered in the pineal atom. Since your mental "sins" are not recorded there — but register simply as a mental deficiency — this seed atom can be said to be similar to the causal forcefield in that only the mental good you have developed is recorded. Thus, if your pineal gland is retarded, it simply signifies that you have not used your mind to its full capacity in past incarnations; that you neglected opportunities to develop mental potentials, for only mental development will register in this seed atom. The record of *how* or *why* you failed to accomplish more mental development is not recorded, but simply the record of what you *did* develop mentally.

Also buried in the heart of the pineal lie seven radiant crystal atoms, each of which contains a central energy-mass called a *spirilla*. These seven spirillae surround the mental seed atom. Our long journey from night to light carries us through seven Rounds of evolution, and one spirilla evolves with each succeeding Round.

At the present time humankind is involved in the fourth Round of our evolutionary arc, and is in the process of gradually activating the fourth spirilla in the pineal. This spirilla is the link between waking consciousness on the physical plane and consciousness on the *astral plane*. When the fourth spirilla becomes fully active, you will "see" with your astral vision, and "hear" with you astral hearing. You will be well on your way to accomplishing perceptive attunement to the higher worlds which lie about you.

You will retain a memory of your journeys into the astral during your hours of sleep, some vague and some vivid. Quickened fourth spirilla activation will be accomplished by many Astarian disciples in the coming new age, through their steadfast practice of Lama Yoga or other yogic disciplines or through devoted study of mind-stimulating spiritual teachings. Through this pineal stimulation, some are already able to catch occasional glimpses of Spiritual Teachers who usually appear in their etheric forms; are able to dream dreams of their past incarnations and see visions of future events to their profit and progression.

* * * * * * * * * * * * * * * * *

THE SEVEN SPIRILLAE

Buried deep in the heart of the pineal lie seven crystal atoms which contain a central energy-mass we call a spirilla. One spirilla becomes active as humankind passes through each of the required seven Rounds of evolution. Since we are now in our fourth evolutionary Round, we show only four spirillae active with the remaining three in a state of dormancy.

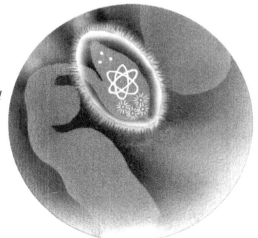

Since the mental seed atom must be more developed for the disciple to bring back memories of experiences on the *mental plane*, this accomplishment can occur only with the awakening of the fifth of the seven spirillae.

The development of this fifth spirilla, along with the pineal gland, belongs actually to the next Round of evolution and it is not expected that the mass of humanity attain this evolvement in the foreseeable future. It is a rare individual who can now bring the fifth spirilla into activation; who can retain memories of mental plane encounters; who can experience the spiritual ecstasies related to the future development of the pineal gland. At our present evolutionary status we can catch only momentary glimpses of that ultimate glory, can enjoy only fleeting instances on the crest of time in that state of expanded consciousness which lifts us into paradise.

When the lifewave has completed all seven of the Rounds through which we must travel, the seven crystal spirillae will, through natural evolvement, attain a high estate of perfection and we will be able to function on the physical, astral and mental planes, with no break in consciousness.

If medical scientists could successfully open a living person's head without injury and carefully examine the pineal, they would observe a glow of light radiating from it. This light is that of the mental seed atom surrounded by the seven crystal spirillae. An autopsy, on the other hand, reveals no light issuing from the gland because these spirillae crystallize after the soul departs the physical. Medical scientists know them as the mysterious "calcium salts" and "brain sands" found in the gland after death.

The light of the pineal is the contact point of the Oversoul, the kingdom of the mind in human beings. We shall speak further concerning the spirillae in another Lesson when we probe the mysteries of the heart. Suffice to say that the gradual development of the spirillae in the pineal causes an increased flow of pituitrin, which helps transform a person into a saint.

THE WIRELESS RADAR ANTENNA OF THE PINEAL

Through the infundibulum, or zu-tube, pass the essences, brain dews and waters of eternal life from the third ventricle into the pituitary, and vice versa.

The pineal also possesses such a "tube." The stalk which attaches the pineal to the third ventricle is called the *habenular commissure*. This "sound-tube" projects outward from the opposite side of the pineal — that is, it is found on the opposite side of the connecting stalk.

Do you remember the tiny wire protuberances on the crystal radio receiving sets of many years ago which vibrated under stimulation of radio waves? This pineal "wireless" antenna can be compared to that wire protuberance for it, too, registers the vibrations of sounds — but not of the physical vibratory range.

The sounds registered upon this infinitesimal pineal antenna are those of the cosmic ethers about us, sounds which, for the most part, are "tuned out" of our consciousness and can be heard only through the vibrations of the Third Eye.

This pineal receiving set also responds to the influence of the etheric "waters" sent toward it from the post-lobe of the pituitary, and from the cosmic fires which travel upward through sushumna from the root chakra. It also registers the influence of the Oversoul, the seat of which is found in the heart of the thousand-petaled lotus, the crown chakra. We shall have more to teach about this pineal antenna as we progress deeper into our esoteric teachings concerning the Third Eye and our evolving cosmic consciousness.

* * * * * * * * * * * * * * * * *

THE PINEAL ANTENNA

The pineal radio antenna extends into the fourth ventricle. This "sending-receiving" transmitter of cosmic fire registers any spiritual contact or influence from the Oversoul and superconscious mind or kundalini fire. It also responds to the flow of pituitrin from pituitary. Under stimulation the pineal rises to an erect position and the pineal antenna, lifted to an upright position, vibrates with immeasurable speed. It is this pineal "resurrection" which helps to bring cosmic consciousness to the disciple.

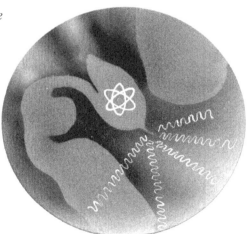

Supplementary Monograph

SOUND AND VIBRATION

There are many teachings concerning the *Voice of the Silence* — and the term seems a contradiction. *Voice* indicates the presence of sound and *silence* the absence of it. But this apparent contradiction reveals a treasure-laden teaching.

First we must understand that vibration itself, any oscillating or back and forth movement, creates sound. Even light waves create sound though they seem silent to the physical ear.

Silence, then, is not the absence of *all* sound but only the absence of the kind which the physical ear is able to perceive. The ear registers only that sound which lies in the vibratory range between approximately 30 to 30,000 vibrations per second. Frequencies below and above that vibratory rate constitute silence to the physical sense of hearing. So the Voice of the Silence is sound which the physical ear does not hear but which, according to the mystic, may be heard by the inner ear. We might call it cosmic sound, or the Voice of God, or the symphony of the spheres, or other names depending upon which aspect of it we are considering.

It is fascinating to note that a complete absence of physical sound frequently results in emotional disturbance on the normal personality level. Were you to enter a darkened anechoic (echoless) chamber at an outer space research center where, inside thick concrete, soundproofed walls there was a complete absence of physical sound and light, you would suffer an emotional and mental breakdown in less than an hour. The personality level cannot remain stable in the absence of sound and light.

But if in this same chamber you found it possible to shift the center of your consciousness to a higher level, where you would be attuned to the presence of sound and light of a higher vibration, which no amount of sound and light proofing could nullify, you would maintain your equilibrium. You would be sustained, as it were, by the Voice of the Silence.

Now let us apply this same idea to your everyday world. We have adapted ourselves to the sound level of the physical domain, though many scientists are concerned that this level is increasing so rapidly that we cannot keep pace with its destructive impact upon our emotions. We are suffering from too much vibration in the 30 to 30,000 per second range. We suggest that we each need the counterbalancing benefit of the Voice of the Silence which you obtain through the various meditative practices offered by Astara, and other centers of light. This is one aspect, one of gaining stability in your physical environment.

A second aspect, probably more important to you, is the opportunity for spiritual, mental and emotional growth which the Voice of the Silence offers you. The Voice of the Silence is the repository of eternal and spiritual essence. When you convert some portion of this higher essence to the level of your everyday self you improve as a personality and you increase your spiritual growth.

A school girl at a science fair demonstrated the effect of sound on plants. Those grown to the accompaniment of discordant music were not nearly as large nor luxuriant as plants grown to the accompaniment of melodious music. This, of course, was upon the purely physical level. Apply the same concept to your mental, emotional and spiritual reactions. Does it not indicate that your growth on these higher levels will be benefited when you frequently attune yourself to the music of the spheres?

In music when two notes are in tune with each other they vibrate as one. If they are played slightly out of tune an annoying throbbing sound results — the two notes are "in phase" and together in vibration for a split second, then "out of phase" or slightly distinct from each other, wavering back and forth between these two states. If placed still further out of tune, the wavering back and forth between being in phase and out ceases, and the two become completely separate from each other — two separate vibrational notes, or sound entities, without any relationship or common vibration.

Is there not a similar phenomenon in the relation between God and human beings? If we never lift our minds to the level of God vibration, then we and God are almost completely separate entities. If one is occasionally in tune with God, then one wavers back and forth between being in phase and out of phase with the Infinite. But if you are in tune with God, then the two vibrate as one. You are the same note, on different octaves to be sure, but the same note nevertheless.

For two sounds of nearly the same pitch to be heard together, the number of beats per second must be equal to the difference of frequencies of the two sources. When there is a great difference in the frequencies there is no distinguishable clear note to be heard. This is why we can get no clear message from the Oversoul when the entire consciousness is centered on the low self, the personality. Wherever the consciousness is centered, there the lifeforce and the mind force are active. Consciousness is a state of vibration.

The pineal antenna is the physical plane listening post for the Voice of the Silence. It is the terminal point at which the silent sound of the upper dimensions becomes audible, not to the physical ear but to your consciousness. It registers vibratory waves of higher than 30,000 vibrations per second and, through the mysterious alchemy of the inner self, makes another world, indeed another universe, available to you.

YOUR SPIRITUAL TELESCOPE

It is difficult for science to admit the presence of unseen worlds surrounding us because we cannot witness them with our physical senses. But science readily admits that the telescope, microscope and various ultrasonic instruments have revealed whole universes of new life previously imperceptible to our unaided senses. Science should be able to concede that we might also possess little known powers of mind which become to us what the microscope is to the biologist, and what the telescope is to the astronomer.

These human mental powers have not as yet become reliably developed to the degree that science can forge a workable law upon them. It remains, then, for Astarians simply to proceed with the development of this mental power and gain as much knowledge of the unseen worlds as is possible through the inner instrument which hears the Voice of the Silence.

It cannot be too strongly emphasized that along with this unfolding power must be built nobility of character and balance of mind.

It is far better to possess only your five objective physical senses — seeing, hearing, smelling, tasting, feeling — and good common sense and sanity, than it is to unfold the higher senses which reveal glimpses of the unseen worlds and at the same time develop psychic problems. Seership should be the integration of the personality, not the destruction of it.

And so the path of Astarianry leads not only toward Self-realization — the union of the low self with the High Self, or Oversoul — but at the same time it firmly integrates the whole being.

One does not blend one's consciousness with the vibratory frequencies of the Oversoul overnight. It is a slow growth. One who walks from a darkened room into the full brilliance of the sun is temporarily blinded. The consciousness must adjust to the full impact of the light. So must the spiritual light be entered gradually so that its power may be absorbed. This slow-growing disciple bathes daily in the higher frequencies until able to withstand the heat of the Divine Fire. Your soul note slowly attunes to the Infinite and you and God are one.

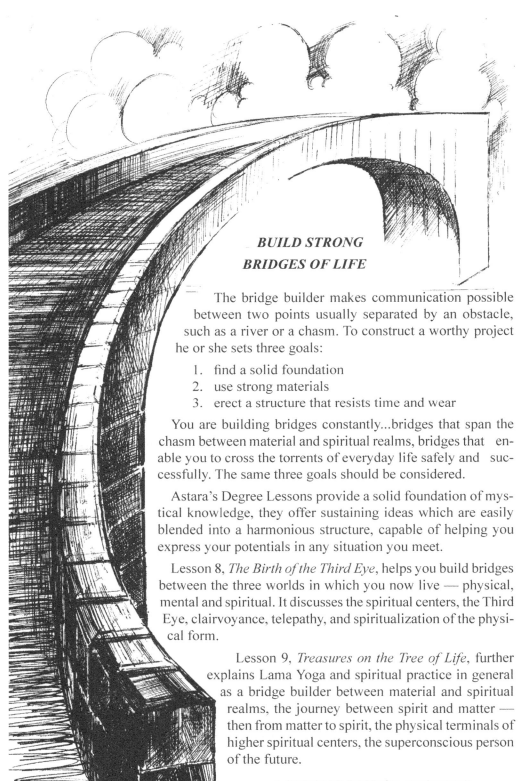

BUILD STRONG
BRIDGES OF LIFE

The bridge builder makes communication possible between two points usually separated by an obstacle, such as a river or a chasm. To construct a worthy project he or she sets three goals:

1. find a solid foundation
2. use strong materials
3. erect a structure that resists time and wear

You are building bridges constantly...bridges that span the chasm between material and spiritual realms, bridges that enable you to cross the torrents of everyday life safely and successfully. The same three goals should be considered.

Astara's Degree Lessons provide a solid foundation of mystical knowledge, they offer sustaining ideas which are easily blended into a harmonious structure, capable of helping you express your potentials in any situation you meet.

Lesson 8, *The Birth of the Third Eye*, helps you build bridges between the three worlds in which you now live — physical, mental and spiritual. It discusses the spiritual centers, the Third Eye, clairvoyance, telepathy, and spiritualization of the physical form.

Lesson 9, *Treasures on the Tree of Life*, further explains Lama Yoga and spiritual practice in general as a bridge builder between material and spiritual realms, the journey between spirit and matter — then from matter to spirit, the physical terminals of higher spiritual centers, the superconscious person of the future.

A STRONG BRIDGE ENSURES
A SAFE PASSAGE

THE FENCE AND THE AMBULANCE

'Twas a dangerous cliff, as they freely confessed,
　　Though to walk near its crest was most pleasant;
For over its terrible edge had slipped
　　A duke and many a peasant.
So the people said something would have to be done,
　　Though their projects did not at all tally;
Said some, "Put a fence around the edge of the cliff";
　　Some, "An ambulance down in the valley."

And the cry of the ambulance carried the day,
　　For it spread thru the neighboring city;
The cliff is all right if you're careful, they said;
　　But each heart was brimful of pity
For those who had slipped o'er the terrible cliff;
　　And the peasants in highway and alley,
Gave pound and gave pence, not to put up the fence,
　　But the ambulance down in the valley.

"For the cliff is all right if you're careful," they said,
　　"And if folks ever slip, or are dropping,
It isn't the slipping that hurts them so much
　　As the shock down below when they're stopping."
Then an old sage remarked: "It's a marvel to me,
　　That folks give far more attention
To repairing results, than to stopping the cause;
　　They'd far, far better aim at prevention."

"Oh, he's a fanatic!" the others rejoined,
　　"Dispense with the ambulance, never!
He'd dispense with all charities, too, if he could;
　　But, no, we'll protect forever.
Aren't we picking folks up, just as fast as they fall;
　　And shall this man dictate to us; shall he?
Why should people of sense stop to put up a fence,
　　When their ambulance works in the valley."

— Anon.

Quotations ...

Let your soul be rooted in things
beyond time and sight.
~ Earlyne

* * * * * * *

We cannot do a good deed, or give to others, without
receiving a blessing. Even then we do not do it for the reward
of the blessing, but for the quiet peace that steals into the heart
with the simple doing of a little good.
~ Earlyne

* * * * * * *

Give to the world a masterpiece.
At least let all souls say ~
"She gave her best."
~ Earlyne

The Birth of the Third Eye

Second Degree — Lesson Eight

THE BROW CHAKRA AND THE PITUITARY

Always remember that when we speak of the spiritual evolvement and functions of the pituitary we do not refer to the physical gland alone but also to its etheric counterpart and the entire forcefield surrounding it which we call, in its entirety, the brow chakra. This is sometimes referred to as the *ajna* center.

The two lobes of the pituitary gland, the anterior and postlobe, are represented in the brow chakra as two petals of a flower. However, they do not resemble a flower as much as the other chakras. The two petals are opened in the forcefield of the chakra much like the outspread wings of a bird. In the Egyptian Mysteries the brow chakra was depicted as the "wings of the hawk."

In the Mysteries of Solomon in Egypt the radiant Queen of Sheba, so dearly beloved by him, represented the feminine pituitary body. She was the queen of her entire domain and all bowed to her command. Even as her gifts to Solomon were "priceless pearls," just so are the gifts she bestows now upon any seeker who will receive them. As queen pituitary she is considered the incomparable treasure in the physical temple and the emanations from her storehouse represent priceless pearls to the human form she inhabits.

Through her workings, she brings the Tree of Life to its ultimate fruition. The "mystic marriage" in the head cannot be consummated until this feminine principle, the Queen of Sheba, glorious upon her veiled throne in the pituitary, gains enough of her innate power to produce the awakening of Solomon, the pineal. From their union is born the rare gift of spiritual wisdom.

The brow chakra covers not only the location of the pituitary gland but extends forward to a point between the eyebrows, slightly above the eyes. Another point of the forcefield extends backward to connect with the spinal cord directly, making

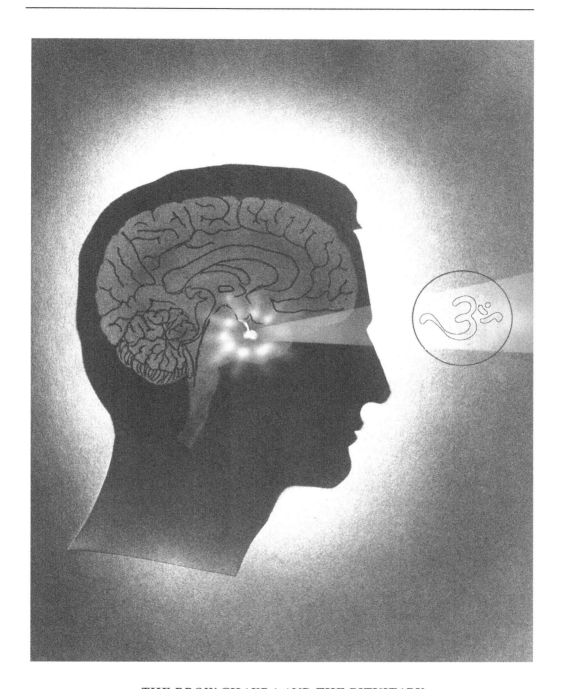

THE BROW CHAKRA AND THE PITUITARY

The brow chakra covers not only the location of the pituitary gland, but extends forward to a point directly between the eyebrows. Another extends backward to connect with the spinal cord directly, making the postlobe of pituitary one of the terminal points for the cosmic fires which travel up and down sushumna.

the postlobe of the pituitary one of the terminal points for the cosmic fires which travel up and down sushumna. It is the spiritualized ethers and dews of the brow chakra which must blend with these cosmic fires before you can attain your ultimate perfection.

We have already said that the anterior lobe of pituitary developed as an elongation of a primeval mouth and is a direct continuance of the alimentary canal. We have said that the posterior lobe is directly connected with an outlet to the etheric sushumna. Picturing this, the Astarian can be aware that the pituitary and the brow chakra lie as a bridge between the negative creative forces rising from the root chakra and the creative forces pouring from the mouth through the power of the spoken word.

It is through this avenue that much of the creative energy burning in the root chakra and now dissipated through excessive sexual activity will, in the fullness of time, be transferred to the throat chakra. This important chakra is destined to become the principal creative center as the human race learns how to create through visualization and the power of the spoken word. These "risen" creative powers will be dominated by the awakened Third Eye and the combined fires of the spiritual bodies.

THE CROWN CHAKRA AND THE PINEAL GLAND

The pineal gland occupies a place in the head which causes it to be aligned to the crown chakra, the highest spiritual center. This chakra is called the thousand-petaled lotus, the *Brahmarandra,* the gateway of the gods and goddesses.

The crown chakra extends far beyond the area of the pineal gland. This pineal region is but the point of contact in the brain. The crown chakra actually occupies not only the top part of the head, but extends upward to cover the surrounding area when the soul has unfolded spiritually. It also encompasses the fourth ventricle and the brain stem, two highly spiritual nerve centers.

THE TRUE HEART CENTER

In the bosom of the thousand-petaled lotus of the crown chakra lies what we call the true heart center. We call this head-heart center the seven-pointed star in the heart of the lotus, because its upturned petals closely resemble the points of a star. It is the brilliant jewel of the Brahmarandra, the crown chakra. It is connected very intimately with the heart and the heart chakra.

It is well to remember that there is the twelve-petaled lotus in the causal forcefield above the head. But the seven-pointed star in the thousand-petaled lotus refers solely to the heart of the crown chakra, the contact point of the Oversoul.

THE CROWN CHAKRA AND THE PINEAL

The pineal gland lies at a point directly in the center of the head and is aligned to the highest spiritual center, the crown chakra. The crown chakra occupies not only the area of the pineal but extends to cover the lobes of the brain, the brain stem, and the third and fourth ventricles. Its upward extension reaches beyond the head to encompass the surrounding area, when the soul has unfolded spiritually. In this thousand-petaled lotus lies the true heart center.

The bridge which links the heart center and the head-heart center is the vagus nerve, that mystical nerve utilized by the Oversoul as the channel for the flow of spiritualized nerve force.

As pineal is aroused by the subtle urgings of pituitary, the Oversoul sends an outpouring of divine essence into the heart center, via the vagus nerve. And as the initiate transfers the emotional desires from the solar plexus into the heart chakra, the heart center will, in turn, begin to project, via the vagus, its own divine essences to reach the pineal chakra. The flow of these spiritualized forces will constitute the building of the "antahkarana thread" between the two heart centers — the physical heart center and the head-heart center in the star in the thousand-petaled lotus.

We have said that the Monad finds its contact point in the physical seed atom in the heart. As you advance in your efforts toward Mastership, the Monadic spiritual powers will shift upward through the vagus, and will have their focal point of expression in the throat chakra. In the completely regenerated initiate of the future, however, the Monadic spiritual powers will eventually abandon the throat center for the crown chakra, until ultimately the divine spirit will find its contact in the heart of the thousand-petaled lotus.

Only in a highly advanced soul is the thousand-petaled chakra functioning in a balanced manner. Only when the pineal and pituitary bodies are harmoniously joined in their mystic marriage and the soul has "become that which it is," will the center petals of the thousand-petaled lotus be lifted upward to receive the downpouring of spiritual light from higher planes through the Third Eye center.

The upturned petals will project rays of light from the top of the head, causing it to be surrounded by a glowing halo such as was depicted around the heads of spiritual leaders in paintings by illumined artists of old.

THE ALL-SEEING EYE

The wondrous All-Seeing Eye ... the Third Eye ... is not simply one gland, or even two, but a combination of various centers which include:

1. the pineal gland;

2. the postlobe of pituitary;

3. the third ventricle;

4. the optic thalamus.

We have said that the postlobe of pituitary is one of our most important spiritual centers, for it is the seat of *divine love*, releasing in minute quantities the substance called pituitrin, esoterically the holy oil of initiation.

We have said that the pineal is the home of the mental seed atom, the seat of the mind, and the ultimate seat of *divine wisdom*. Observation of our illustration will reveal that the third ventricle lies like an open "lake" between the two glands, where the Mother pituitary and the Father pineal unite to give birth to their child, the Divine Spirit within. This birth brings the radiance of divine light to the nerve center of the Third Eye — the optic thalamus. It is this tremendous network of optic nerves and channels which constitutes the "body" of the All-Seeing Eye.

The Cosmic Television Station Within Us

If the layperson finds it difficult to understand the intricate electronic operations of earth plane television or computers, then the modus operandi of a cosmic telecasting station becomes almost incomprehensible. We find it difficult to understand that the ethers are constantly pulsating with sounds, pictures and activities, making no apparent impression on the senses until one seats oneself before a mechanical box, pushes several buttons and tunes in the desired wavelength or channel. How is it that this device we call television can accomplish what the marvelous brain centers cannot?

Can humans outdo the Divine?

It becomes obvious that, in constructing television, we are simply duplicating in a crude, mechanical manner the "blueprint" of what we subconsciously understand to be a part of ourselves — our incomparable Third Eye.

For that is what the Third Eye really is, a built-in cosmic television or computer, designed to tune in certain "channels" of the cosmos, as the soul aligns itself with the proper micro-wavelengths.

Since the operations of the Eye are not unlike those of the   audio-video camera, let us make crude comparisons. Considering the entire Third Eye, we understand the postlobe of pituitary to be the lens of the cosmic camera through which must pass the "divine light rays" — traveling across the third ventricle to reach the film, the pineal gland. The "picture" is then developed in the developing fluid of the optic thalamus, and lo! the soul has tuned in to the telecasting channels of the higher worlds.

The "sounds" of this most incredible camera-device are registered by the pineal antenna — that minute protuberance which resembles the wire receiver on antiquated crystal radio receiving sets. Under stimulation from the cosmic fires of the fourth ventricle and the postlobe of pituitary, it begins to vibrate, spinning round and round like the revolving arc of a radar set, slowly at first, with its revolutions registering space sounds just as television sets register our earth sounds.

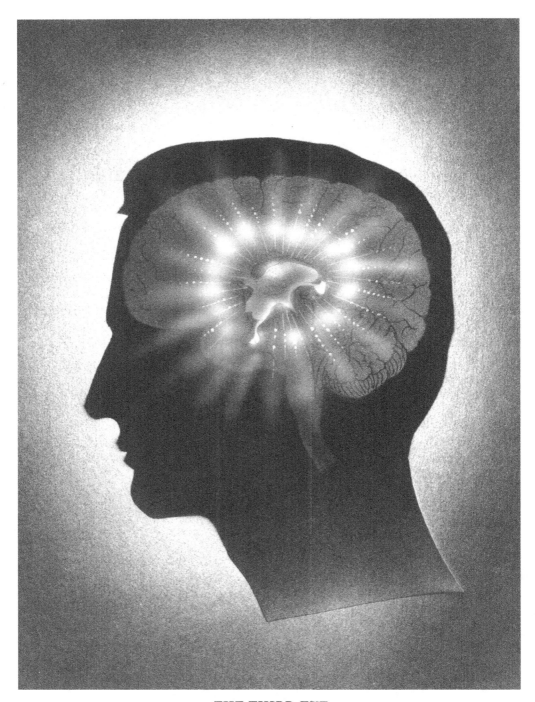

THE THIRD EYE

The Third Eye consists of the optic thalamus, the third ventricle, the pineal gland and the postlobe of pituitary.

When the ethers of the brain unite with the fires of sushumna, the sounds received by the pineal antenna differ in quality as you, the seeker, advance in your spiritual attunements. Especially during the meditations of Lama Yoga, you are apt to tune in to this mystic ladder of sounds.

When the fires of sushumna have aroused the root chakra, one of the first sounds to register is a mysterious humming sound similar to the hum of busy bees. Some of the higher chakras will register other sounds, one of which is like that of a sweet-sounding harp, echoing over deep chasms. Or the chiming of a deep-toned gong. Or a church bell.

When the pineal antenna begins to register the sound of roaring waters, it most surely indicates that the head centers are reaching some degree of alignment and attunement to the cosmic forces swirling about us.

When the component parts of the *cosmic camera* eventually come into focus, the disciple will be able to open the Third Eye at will to receive the blessings of the higher worlds. The love of the divine mother, pituitary, will have coaxed the wisdom of the divine father, pineal, into action. As divine love and wisdom unite in the head centers, the majestic All-Seeing Eye opens and the Candle of the Divine, the optic thalamus, is flooded with light. The disciple experiences illumination. The universe opens before you and you momentarily *know* God.

The camera of the Third Eye will have photographed and recorded its contact with divinity, and your entire being will be flooded with light. *If thine eye be single, thy whole body will be filled with light.*

Understanding that the Third Eye consists of considerably more than the pineal gland, the mystics of old referred to the entire Third Eye as the All-Seeing Eye, the Eye Single, the Eye of Odin, the Eye of Horus, the Eye of the Lord, the Eye of Shiva, the Eye of Dangma.

The mystic "mark upon the forehead" of disciples of the hierarchy and the Order of Melchizedek refers to no physical marking but to the radiations shining from the Third Eye as it attains a high state of spiritual unfoldment. This progression is signified by the "mark" peculiar only to initiates who have attained some degree of enlightenment.

The mark, taking the form of a luminous light, can be discerned only by seers, prophets and other initiates, and distinguishes the possessor as a "light bearer." Many Astarian disciples wear the mark without being in the slightest aware of it, though in the majority the light is burning only dimly.

When you who have "eyes with which to see" witness the presence of the light, it signifies to you that the soul force has begun to dominate the personality. In the majority, the personality by far dictates the daily life of the individual. The normal person usually lives according to the petty whims and desires of the limited selfish personality. In those who wear the mark is found the submission of the personality to the soul as the characteristics of the soul force ... humility, kindness, tolerance, unselfishness ... begin to dominate the life of the initiate.

The initiate, seeing the sign of the unfolding light, recognizes that the Oversoul, taking advantage of the stimulated pineal, is sending charges of divine essence to the postlobe of pituitary, which register in the brain as the mystic brain dews.

These exude into the optic thalamus through the crown chakra which contains, among other things, the head centers of the claustrum, the *external capsule*, the *lenticular nucleus* and the *internal capsule*. The latter is a funnel-like group of nerve fibers which enter the cerebrum of the brain itself, and are reinforced by fibers from the optic thalamus which, in the spiritual seeker, converge upward.

Through these important head centers the dews finally coagulate to form the mystic chemical water which enters the optic thalamus itself. From there it seeps into the third ventricle and, in the evolving disciple who has opened some of the doors of the inner temple, finds its way into the postlobe of pituitary through the *zu-tube*.

Once this mystic dew enters the postlobe it causes stimulation of the mystic hormone pituitrin. Every stimulation of this love-force results in increasing domination of the personality by the Oversoul. This dominance is signified by the glow of the mystic mark upon the forehead. The disciple is "anointed with oil" — which is to say, the pituitrin, the oil of the lamp of God, is flowing through to the Eye which, when touched by the fires of sushumna, blazes forth in illumined glory.

THE HISTORIC THIRD EYE

It was in the Lemurian epoch that the Third Eye, of which the pineal is the actual remnant, was functioning at its highest perfection. In the lifewave's early days the entire Third Eye was opened, but only to the astral and etheric realms, and not to the glories of the upper worlds, since humanity had not developed the mental qualities necessary for contact with higher planes.

Since the two physical eyes had not yet developed a proper focus to the material world, the Third Eye found its principal interests in the etheric and astral realms. As the lifewave evolved physically and advanced into the Atlantean Age, the developing brain cells caused a gradual closing of the Third Eye. The two physical eyes, gaining in development and focusing powers, were bringing the physical realm into greater prominence, as the etheric and astral planes became increasingly blurred in our dimming spiritual vision.

Eventually the sutures of the bony structure closed over the brain centers of the Great Eye, and the nerves of the optic thalamus extended forward to the frontal portion of the head to stimulate development of the physical eyes. With the enclosure of the pineal gland, the visions of the other worlds were lost, and we must now "see through a glass darkly" until, through our own individually developed powers, we open once again the channels which lead to light, through the crown and brow chakras.

The "dark glass" through which we behold life now is the clouded "lens" of the cosmic camera, the postlobe of struggling pituitary, who carries on her vast duties under innumerable hazards and travails. She is indeed in cosmic labor as she attempts to fulfill her obligations to her lower kingdom, the physical form, over which she presides through the subconscious mind, and simultaneously struggles to awaken her dormant lord, the sleeping pineal, king of her upper kingdom.

THE SYMBOLIC THIRD EYE

In the ancient Mysteries of Greece, the initiates carried a staff known as the *Thyrsus*. The Thyrsus was symbolic of the spinal column, the etheric nervous system, and the opened Third Eye. It consisted of a staff entwined with vines of ivy and grape. The entwining vines symbolized the nadis, or etheric nervous system. Atop the staff was a golden object similar to a pine cone, shaped like an upturned triangle. From the heart of the triangle one vine extended downward, ending in the middle of the staff, signifying the vagus nerve which extends between the Third Eye and the heart center.

The triangular pine cone symbolized the pineal and Third Eye, and only those who were striving to open the Eye were privileged to carry the Thyrsus, although they were not necessarily initiates of the Greater Mysteries.

In the Greater Egyptian Mysteries, the initiates wore their identifying symbol upon the head. Their headdress contained the upraised head of a cobra, with a tiny extended tongue. This symbol was particularly apropos because, seen clairvoyantly, the opened Third Eye atop the upright spinal column closely resembles the raised cobra, with the extended tongue symbolizing the antenna of the pineal, vibrating vigorously when stimulated.

Only the initiate-priest or priestess who had opened the Third Eye was privileged to wear the serpent symbol, and indeed these sages of the Mysteries were called "the Serpents" — the Wise Ones. Jesus reveals his knowledge of these sages when he admonished his disciples: "Be ye wise as Serpents but gentle as the dove."

The Native American also possessed knowledge of the opened All-Seeing Eye, for the colorful eagle feather headdress of the chief symbolized the beauty and magnitude of the human aura when the Third Eye was activated. Clairvoyant vision had revealed to the Native American initiate the radiant colors rippling from above the head and down the spine when the Third Eye was opened, and he attempted to imitate this magnificent auric splendor in his headdress. Only chiefs and tribal healers were allowed to wear this feathered glory, which symbolized wisdom — and chiefs and tribal healers were chosen only after proving their psychic and spiritual prowess.

THE OPENING OF THE THIRD EYE

When the individual begins to activate the pituitary-brow chakra, either through the slow process of natural evolution or acceleration through disciplinary training such as the Astarian disciple follows, the oversoul responds by sending a direct flow of spiritual power downward to permeate the brain cells as brain dew.

Since the prime purpose of the pituitary is to arouse the dormant pineal and return it to full power, she takes every opportunity to exert influence upon her sleeping mate. Thus when you use any of the methods given in these Lessons to stimulate pituitary she, in turn, reacting to this stimulation, attracts to herself a downpouring from the Oversoul as the spiritualized force sweeps into the brain cells.

Taking advantage of her increased powers, she directs toward the pineal gland little charges of magnetism which radiate in tiny circles or riplets of light. These riplets, a silvery-rose in color, pulsate outward in an ever-widening radius, traversing the "lake" of the third ventricle to reach her fallen partner.

As the light impulses pulsate outward wave upon wave, the pineal begins to rouse out of its dormant state. Its flabby, paste-like substance becomes firm. Its pale coloring absorbs the rosy hues from pituitary and, enhancing them, begins to exude flame-like rays of its own. The pineal antenna begins to whir and hum and vibrate at an immeasurable speed which increases the light of the fires until the gland radiates with such brilliance as to be dazzling to those who have "eyes to see."

The drama now continues to unfold.

This radiating force begins to attract the cosmic fires of kundalini from the root chakra. They are drawn upward to first be purified in the medulla oblongata, and from there to swirl into the fourth ventricle of the brain. Ordinarily they are stopped here, for the pineal in its flabby, sleeping state acts as a closed gateway between the fourth and third ventricles.

The chemical fires of the spine, entering the fourth ventricle, usually cannot mix with the etheric waters of the third ventricle. Only in pineal's "raised state" is the gateway lifted, allowing the chemical forces of the two brain ventricles to rush together.

Only when the pineal "valve" is erected, allowing the essences of both the fourth and third ventricles to combine, is there free circulation of the powerful brain ethers and dews with the cosmic fires of the spine. Under such stimulus the Third Eye becomes a living chemical laboratory within.

Through the stimulation of pituitary pouring out her divine love essence, and the pineal projecting and receiving waves of spiritual power from the Oversoul, plus the "explosion" of the brain ethers, oils and dews mixing with the cosmic fires of kundalini rushing up sushumna — under such tremendous vibratory frequency, the Third Eye momentarily opens, lifting the disciple into the very heights of ecstasy.

There may be a slight dizzy sensation just prior to the opening, as the fires of kundalini rise. Then, as the tremendous Eye "slides" open, it is like having the top of the head removed. The entire universe is exposed to one's own being. The wisdom of the divine pours down into the brain, and the disciple becomes one-with-God, illumined with light.

The light of the "burning" crown chakra streams up and out of the head not unlike the electrical arc lights used at some gala movie premiere ... the arc light of the chakra turning unceasingly, sending its beams far beyond the auric forcefield. You, the disciple, sense an indescribable sensation of light force beaming from the top of your head, as well as powerful charges of light streaming down into your brain.

The top of your head is "dissolved" and your mind expands to encompass the entire universe. Such a state of mental and spiritual awareness cannot be endured for long, for the vibrations are so powerful as to destroy the brain cells at our present evolutionary level. The sensation gradually ebbs. The pituitary relaxes her stimulation, the tension of the erected pineal subsides as it assumes once more its flabby condition, kundalini returns to her own chakra ...

... And the great Third Eye closes.

Although the outer appearance of the disciple may appear unchanged, you will never be the same after such an incomparable spiritual experience. You will well understand why you could not live continuously in such a state of consciousness, for should you be given these expanded mental powers before you have brought your emotional-desire nature under control, a fit of anger could completely shatter your mind. Much as you may long for perpetual union with the divine, even so, you can realize the wisdom of slow growth toward such a state.

In the vast majority, an occasional gentle stimulant from pituitary is all that ever reaches the region of the pineal. But as Astarians begin to utilize their mystic knowledge they will increasingly put to use some of the Astarian practices which serve to bring the gland to her full status.

Continued development of pituitary by any of these sure, safe methods will result eventually in the power to resurrect *at will* the sleeping pineal, to open the Third Eye, to enter cosmic consciousness voluntarily and reach upward into divine-regions. You cannot attain this, however, until you can unite the spiritual forces in yourself and until you use a portion of the sexual propagative energies toward spiritual regeneration.

In an evolutionary sense, the crown chakra represents spirit and the root chakra represents matter in the physical form. Between these two forces there rages an eternal war, fought on the battleground of the solar plexus. At the present, matter is the victor and will be so as long as you dissipate the lifeforce in the generative organs. Ultimately, however, as you begin to attain increasing mental development, the stimulated pituitary will magnetically attract upward some of these generative forces.

Each time she succeeds in arousing pineal even minutely, some portion of generative power has been lifted up the spinal column to activate more brain cells. The obvious result is an increased lighting of the crown chakra as the fires of kundalini are gradually transferred from the root chakra to the head. Ultimately spirit must win in this interminable battle of Armageddon, and matter will surrender its hold upon the creative forces. You will have "overcome the world" and can enter again your lost paradise — your Garden of Eden — as will the entire lifewave.

THE THIRD EYE AND HEALING

As you know, we work with what we call the White Light in sending healing to Astarians all over the world. What is this White Light and how do we utilize it in performing apparent healing miracles?

It is the power, created by the will of the healer, in the Third Eye. It is composed of spinal fluids and fires drawn upward from the root chakra, spiritualized in the mystic center of the medulla oblongata, then combined with the pranic and mental reflecting ethers and the brain dews. The combination of these magnetic and electric energies creates a white cloud of powerful cosmic energy that glows like a radiant, swirling vortex of light in the Third Eye.

These energies are subject to the direction of the creator — the healer. The purpose of creating the White Light is to direct it to another who is in need of healing or, of course, toward healing oneself.

This force that pours from the Third Eye through the brow- pituitary chakra like a sparkling, transparent beam of light, may be directed into the upraised hands of the concentrating healer and out into the ethers surrounding the hands. (See Lesson One, First Degree.)

If you wish to be a dedicated healer, you will need to be a "mental chemist" of the first magnitude. Using the powers of your own mind you will create the mystic formula of the White Light, consisting of:

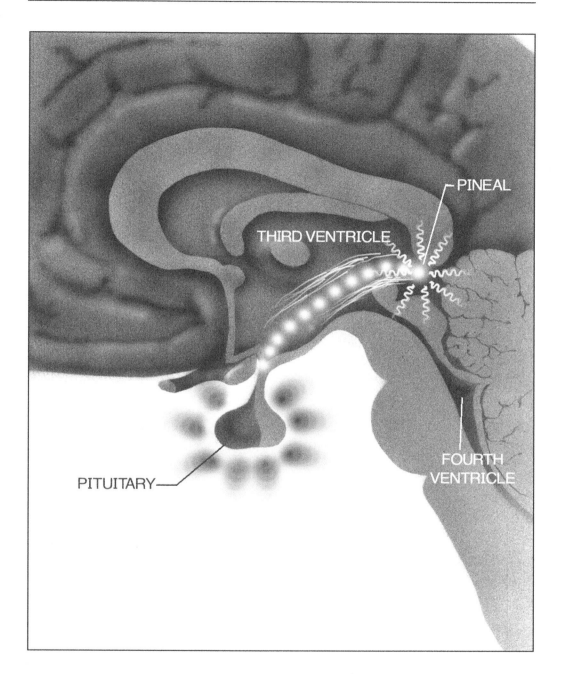

QUEEN PITUITARY AND HER SLEEPING MATE, PINEAL

The sleeping king of the inner world, pineal, cannot be resurrected except through the efforts of queen pituitary. She sends her rays to arouse him whenever you, the incarnate personality, allow her to release a flow of pituitrin, the hormonal elixir of love, toward him. She receives this opportunity only through your spiritual efforts.

1. the creative forces flowing upward from the root chakra which contain the lifeforce of the physical body;

2. the pranic forces drawn into the body by slow, concentrated breathing, which contain the lifeforce of the etheric body;

3. the mental reflecting ether also drawn in from the surrounding ethers, which enables you to visualize perfection in the body of your patient.

How can you discern whether or not you are using these particular forces and are successful? We can only say that every one of these forces is subject to mental direction and if you, as a healer, concentrate intensely enough you cannot help but create some kind of healing thoughtform of White Light.

It is of immeasurable help if, when sending healing, you can work with some object which has been connected to the petitioner, such as healing petitions which Astara issues to Astarians everywhere.

Possessing no petition or other object, it is then necessary for you to project the White Light through the ethers to your petitioner with no directing or connecting "wire" between you unless you yourself create one through tremendous mental effort.

If you possess some object the petitioner has touched the connecting thread is already established and you can direct your full attention to building a more powerful cloud of White Light.

During the process of building and directing the White Light you should avoid speaking, even to affirm perfection or to count, for to do so is to use mental energy which cannot help but detract from the concentration necessary to hold the White Light steady and powerful.

When you feel you have created an outflow of the White Light to your patient to the best of your ability, then you may proceed with your visualization process. You may engage in spiritual chants and affirmations, decreeing and visualizing the perfection of your patient. You will no longer be creating the White Light in the Third Eye but will be giving your undivided attention to your visualization activities, sending the healing forces pouring outward from the upraised palms of both hands.

If you anticipate becoming a healer you would do well to recognize the importance of activating the Third Eye, and one sure way of doing so is through the practice of Lama Yoga, which acts directly upon the postlobe of the pituitary.

As every Degree Astarian knows, Lama Yoga is divided in three parts, the latter of which is a meditation exercise involving focusing mental attention upon the Third

Eye. (Other steps will come later.) Since the pineal can be stimulated only through the efforts of the pituitary, you would do well to direct your attention upon the point directly behind the center of the eyebrows, toward the center of the head, for this will approximate the location of the pituitary-pineal Third Eye area.

Once you stimulate the Third Eye, you automatically become a healer. Your very presence will result in a healing effect upon any depleted person in your midst even without your awareness. If you, however, are conscious of your healing powers and at the same time concentrate on intensifying the activities of the Third Eye, you can create a tremendous power which, flowing from your brow into your hands and on outward along the etheric cord to reach the patient, has the potential to effect a miraculous and instantaneous healing.

THE POWERS OF THE UNFOLDED THIRD EYE

It requires the stimulation of the spirillae in the pineal gland through the activation of pineal by pituitary to bring *mental plane* experiences into the waking consciousness. Therefore it requires development of both these glands, plus all the other factors involved to bring about the opening of the entire Third Eye, resulting in true spiritual powers in the unfolding Astarian.

As the Third Eye begins to become operative, the etheric, astral and mental webs woven so intricately about the brow and crown chakras begin to loose their hold on the brain cells, subjecting them to the downflow of spiritual energies and mystic dews streaming from the divine Monad and Oversoul through the sutratmic silver cord. As you become increasingly receptive to these energies, along with your perpetually increasing brain cell power, you will:

1. begin to live in three worlds at once, to remember your experiences upon the astral and mental planes;

2. begin to "see" with clairvoyant vision and to "hear" with clairaudient hearing;

3. begin to utilize thought transference in your daily life;

4. begin gradually to etherealize the dense physical form.

Each of these future acquirements deserves our consideration.

The Initiate's Life in Three Worlds

With the gradual opening of the Third Eye, you become dimly aware that during your seeming visions or vivid dreams you are or have been traveling in higher worlds. You may vaguely remember people whom you have met during the journey, places visited, classes attended, lessons learned. You may bring back at first only fragmentary remembrances of these astral-mental plane experiences, but you eventually come to a realization that something unusual is happening within yourself and that your dreams are not truly dreams at all, but flashes of your experiences in the higher planes.

Gradually you will become more mentally alert on the physical plane during your daytime hours, and joyously awake upon the inner planes during the hours when your physical body sleeps. You will be able to recall your journeys and to live consciously in three worlds simultaneously, to be an inhabitant of the higher planes while yet abiding on earth.

This double life causes no fatigue, for the etheric body restores the physical to renewed strength just as it does now through sleep. The activity of the higher bodies in no way affects the restoration of the physical, or uses the energies needed for physical plane activities. Actually, as these two bodies become increasingly perfected and attuned, they in turn reflect the increasing perfection of the Oversoul.

At the present stage of evolutionary development, you are like television sets tuned in to static. The ethers about us are filled with other worlds, other beings, other sounds, but we cannot perceive them. At present we are victims of the beating wavelength of time and space, unable to "tune in" to those we would desire, or to "tune out" those we would avoid.

It is only through development of the Third Eye that you will be able, of yourself, to control your destiny, to occupy that place in time and space desirable to you. As the Third Eye gains further maturity, so will your dreams, your visions, your intuitions — until some day — or in some life — you will be capable of reading the Akashic Records of the future as well as the past; of becoming your own priest or priestess, your own prophet and guide.

You will be able to interpret your perceptions as either foreshadowings of future disasters or "fore-glowings" of future happiness, and will guide your individual life accordingly. For one is not a victim of destiny or fate except if one so wills it, or submits, without the effort of personal will power, to the ebb and flow of the unpredictable tides of time and life.

Your Future Powers of Clairvoyance

When we speak of clairvoyance, we include the faculty of clairaudience, for the true clairvoyant will hear as well as see visions of other worlds and far-distant earth scenes, just as movie film records the sounds of a motion picture as well as the scenes.

Perfected clairvoyance signifies that the All-Seeing Eye is opened and operating. As the fortunate and illumined initiate possessing this faculty you are or will be able to discern without actually seeing, for you see with your inner sight. Your perceptions seem to come into your brain by means of an opened doorway in the top of your head, for the visions of the Third Eye have nothing to do with the vision of the two physical eyes. One may be nearsighted, farsighted, even altogether blind and still possess the ability to "see" through a wall, a mountain, or even to the other side of the universe. For the vision of the Third Eye is that of a cosmic x-ray machine, tuning one in to divinity.

Utilizing the clairvoyant faculties of the Third Eye, a Master Teacher may direct vision, like a focused beam of brilliant light, to any desired point on Earth or in space at any given moment. Such a statement is apt to make any disciple apprehensive for fear that many undisciplined daily actions may be observed critically by this "Seeing Eye tyrant." Such is *not* the case. One who has developed such extended vision has not the slightest desire to be curious or to pry concerning personal events in your daily life, nor the time to occupy a highly developed mind with such activities.

The Master's beneficent duties are complex in many far-reaching areas, not only of this world but of the worlds surrounding ours. Thus such a Teacher has neither the time nor inclination to observe your conduct under the stress of your daily problems. S/he is concerned only with very major events in your life, and then only when invited to participate by a call from you.

Your Teacher is well able to discern from your image in the Hall of Images the degree of your spiritual progression, your general health condition, and whether or not you are in need. This is all that needs to be known. Your Teacher will focus attention upon you during the hours of your meditations or when you study or pray. But, unless you have sent a call through the ethers for help, never will your Teacher invade your private life. Even the beam of a Master's clairvoyant vision cannot pierce the surroundings of a locale unless there is receptivity there, created by your call. Not expecting perfection, your daily conduct will never be viewed critically. Tolerance and patience are virtues of such Teachers. They realize you have eternity in which to grow and overcome, just as they have had to do themselves.

We mention the clairvoyant powers of Teachers only to clarify the abilities *you* will one day possess. It is called *extended clairvoyance* and it enables the possessor to project one's vision to any point on Earth or in space whenever one desires to do so, and to will the powers of the ethers about one to serve one's needs.

Is clairvoyance the only gauge by which you can know whether or not your Third Eye is active? How are you to measure its evolution? Must you be clairvoyant? And if you are not ... if you have never seen a vision ... must you concede that the Third Eye is not in any sense activated?

It certainly should be understood that the powers of clairvoyance are not the only gauge of the status of the Third Eye, though often with its opening the disciple *will* become clairvoyant. The Third Eye is also an organ for *clairsentience*, or supreme intuition — that uncanny ability of *all-knowing* without knowing how you know; of knowing innately without studying to know; of knowing intuitively without reasoning and logic. Thus you need not despair if you have never seen a clairvoyant vision, for you may already have brought the Third Eye to a high degree of unfoldment.

With advanced clairsentient powers, you not only will be able to discern intuitively, perhaps even clairvoyantly, but you will be able to *know* all things, so far as *causes* are concerned, rather than experiencing simply the *effects*. For you will be able to "read" the true akashic records of the higher causal planes, not simply the reflected recordings of the astral.

When time evolves you to your full potential of clairsentience, which includes clairvoyance and clairaudience — when the brow and crown chakras, and the flow of cosmic energies have all blended in harmonious chemical balance in the laboratory of your brain — you will actually "see" with your entire body. For the one whose Eye is "single," the glories of heaven are revealed through the light which "fills one's entire body." The etheric, astral and mental force centers begin to harmonize and you begin to become a light unto yourself.

Thought Transference or Telepathy

In the fullness of time, as the Third Eye begins to become more operative in our daily lives, thought transference between minds will become fairly ordinary. This unfolded power will become possible through the development of the pineal antenna. This mystic mechanism will perform many feats:

a. It will receive messages *from* the minds of others here on Earth.

b. It will send messages *to* the minds of others here on Earth.

c. It will send to and receive messages from the minds of those dwelling in the unseen worlds about us.

d. It will receive messages from the Oversoul.

The science of thought transference and telepathy will come into its own in this new age, and the next hundred years will witness its usage and acceptance among us to a remarkable degree.

The Etherealization of the Dense Physical Form

As the Third Eye gradually evolves, you not only will begin the transference of the generative powers upward into the thymus and the pineal glands, but you will also begin to transfer the digestive operations of the body to the respiratory system.

The time will arrive, in some distant future, when we shall not require food for the nourishment of our physical bodies, as we do today. The needed chemical ethers in our food will be inhaled from the surrounding ethers and assimilated into our bloodstream and cells by the operations of the respiratory system. As our little earth globe moves into the ethers of the Aquarian magnetic field, the prana will become increasingly rarefied and filled with a substance containing more spiritual qualities. As the centuries pass, our ethers will contain an essence qualified to sustain our more purified physical forms.

This "manna from heaven" will be indrawn via the nostrils and the pores of the skin, from whence it will impinge upon the Third Eye. From this chemical laboratory it will be distributed throughout the entire body via the blood, just as the pituitary today distributes her all-important hormones.

Through this process of "respiratory" nourishment the dense physical form will become increasingly etherealized. The bony structure will gradually become refined to a more resilient construction. We will not regress to walking on all fours without a firmly crystallized upright spinal column, but rather we will use our more etherealized form to glide through the ethers instead of moving with the slow steps of our two physical feet.

Under the impact of our developing mental powers, we will learn how to propel our forms through space just as we now learn how to drive our cars or pilot our airplanes. Eventually we shall travel on the beam of thought. Mind, Mind, Mind! — operating through the powers of the opened Third Eye!

In those far-off days of glory we shall inhale life out of pranic and cosmic ethers about us; we shall direct the functionings of the physical form so that we shall never know sickness again; our bodies shall cease to be the cesspools of waste matter and taverns of disease we inhabit today and shall become temples of the living God.

These visions of the future may seem inconceivable now and will be better understood several lifetimes hence. All we can do at this particular time is to give you a fore-glowing of the glory of things to come, when the Third Eye shall be "single" and the soul will have become "that which it is."

Treasures on the Tree of Life

Second Degree — Lesson Nine

LAMA YOGA AND THE THIRD EYE

Gleaming upon the Tree of Life are the radiant treasures — the chakras — which, as you already know, are the etheric, astral and mental counterparts of the physical glands. The pineal is the most radiant jewel on the Tree of Knowledge. On the Tree of Life it is the pituitary. The two of them combine with the optic thalamus and the third ventricle of the brain to constitute the incomparable Third Eye. Let us first complete our teachings concerning the Third Eye before we embark upon our searchings into the spinal chakras — the jewels on the trunk of the Tree of Life.

The practice of Lama Yoga accomplishes many benefits, not only in the physical form but all the other bodies.

Among other things, it is a means of stimulating the fourth spirilla in the pineal. To bring this fourth spirilla to its perfection is the purpose of this particular Round of progression, as we have said. Since we have at present attained only a little beyond the halfway point, it requires some type of yogic training to stimulate this fourth spirilla prior to the time of its full maturity. It will mature in its slow evolutionary process unless some special effort is made toward an early development. Lama Yoga is, in our opinion, one excellent means of achieving this goal.

The practice of Lama Yoga also attracts a downflow of spiritual energy from the overshadowing Oversoul. Infusing the sutratma, it impinges not only upon the brow-pituitary chakra, but the pineal itself, causing an increase in the flow of its hormonal secretions and the vibratory waves about it. The pineal may be further stimulated by certain chants and mantras, particularly the AUM chant in the practice of Lama Yoga.

The pineal may also be stimulated through devotion to study. Any brain currents, produced by intense thoughts, affect the pineal gland and the crown chakra due to the presence of the mental seed atom in the pineal. Development through Lama Yoga or study of the Degree Lessons actually is a protection to the disciple against undesirable development. To explain, we must teach again of the webs that are woven so intricately around the brow and crown chakras.

As you know, there is an etheric web interpenetrating each of the chakras, composed of the four physical ethers. However, concentrated around the pineal and pituitary there is added protection in the form of an additional web composed of atoms from the higher astral planes. To disturb these two webs prematurely, before you, the disciple, have attained some degree of Mastership, is to rend the veil of the Holy of Holies, leaving you exposed to most undesirable influences of the lower astral planes. Too often you become the victim of these influences, mistakenly believing that you are in touch with divinity.

It is not possible that danger can assail the sincere Astarian disciple if you seek to fulfill the steps of the Formula given in the First Degree. In your meditations and contemplations, only the astral web is affected. The web composed of etheric atoms remains intact, protecting you from undesirable influences of the lower astral planes. The momentary dissolution of the astral web brings you in contact with the higher astral, the mental, sometimes causal, and even the celestial realms. It is accomplished with the utmost protection to you because it is a voluntary accomplishment, and such contacts with higher planes are subject to your own will and direction.

The more closely you become attuned to the higher planes, the less are you exposed to lower plane influences. The light that rays out around you, resulting from the perpetual stimulation of the brow and crown chakras, is a repellent force to inhabitants of the lower planes. They avoid you, for contact with you is vibrationally painful to them. With the increase of light about you, the disciple gains increasing protection from the influences of the lower astral planes.

We have spoken of the "dissolution" of the protective astral web in such a manner as to lead to possible confusion. We have seemed to indicate that, with the practice of Lama Yoga, it completely dissolves. Such is not the case.

The astral web itself does not permanently disappear, leaving the disciple constantly exposed to the higher plane vibrations. Such an exposure, even to the higher planes, could be most undesirable. A bombardment of thoughts, even from such a high source, could prevent one from carrying out one's earth mission, and such a contact, without the power to voluntarily control it, would be shattering to one's nervous system.

What actually happens is that the disciple, through the practice of Lama Yoga and the stimulation of the pituitary, *temporarily* dissolves the atoms of the astral web, in that they are raised in their vibratory essence out of the astral plane and transmuted into mental plane substance, or even into causal substance.

The astral web acts as a whirling vortex under pituitary stimulation, but as the stimulation subsides, the atoms of the web return to their normal vibration, closing the "door" to the higher planes.

Permanent dissolution of the protective webs occurs only when the disciple becomes the Master. The etheric atoms are transmuted and are absorbed into the atoms of the higher astral web. The Master radiates such a light as to become invulnerable to the lower planes. There may be occasions when a deliberate contact with others less fortunate who are dwelling in the lower depths of astral life is desired. But again, a Master would be invulnerable to harm during those contacts.

If an aspirant engages in a negative low form of psychic development such as automatic writing over an extended period of time, instead of pursuing spiritual unfoldment through a positive method such as Lama Yoga, one is inviting psychic disaster. Such negative unfoldment may open the lower spinal chakras through destruction of the protective etheric webs, and the unfortunate victim may be unable to "close the door" on the undesirable influences, the voices, which may plague him or her. It is possible to restore the webs in the majority of cases, but it requires perpetual striving. The Astarian is urged to concentrate upon the practice of Lama Yoga and/or spiritual study and meditation in your efforts toward spiritual and psychic unfoldment, for therein such dangers are avoided. Once one attains a measure of spiritual attainment, automatic writing becomes a fairly safe channel of communication.

THE TRUE "FALL" OF THE HUMAN BEING

We mentioned the "fall of the human being" previously. We shall enlarge now upon those earlier ideas and discuss one symbolic meaning of the story of Adam and Eve.

The drama of Adam and Eve and their ejection from paradise as it was portrayed in the Mystery Schools of ancient Mu and Atlantis, sometimes symbolized the drama of pineal and pituitary, the eternal male-female within the individual.

In this drama, Adam and Eve reside in the Garden of Eden, the brain. The Tree of the Knowledge of Good and Evil which stood in the midst of the Garden is represented by the cerebrospinal nervous system containing the spinal column with its etheric sushumna. Adam and Eve — the pineal and pituitary — were warned not to "eat of the fruit of this Tree" or, in other words, not to use the sexual forces flowing in the generative organs, for if they did so, "in that day they would surely die."

It was through the influence of the feminine pituitary that the soul fell from its estate in its Garden of paradise. Disregarding the command and opening the valve of her posterior lobe which links to the spinal cord, pituitary drew unto herself a portion of the generative powers. Thus she partook of the fruit of the Tree of the Knowledge of Good and Evil. This was the "apple" which Eve persuaded Adam, the pineal, to eat with her. This was her first creative activity, and her stimulations of pineal caused the mental seed atom to "fall" from its residing place in the heart of the lotus of the Oversoul above the head, and find its abode in the pineal gland of the head, bringing with it the seed of mind which the soul was to develop in itself.

After partaking of the fruit, Adam and Eve were then driven from their Garden and did surely "die." That is, although the pituitary and pineal glands themselves remained in the brain, their spiritual powers were cut off. Eve, or kundalini, the world Mother, fled to the lower regions and assumed her place in kanda at the base of the spine. Adam took his place in the prostatic-root chakra.

A "cherubim with a flaming sword" was placed at the gateway to the Garden to prevent their reentry. This flaming sword, "which turns ever to the right and left," is represented by the fires of the eternal altar in the medulla oblongata which block the reentrance of the generative creative powers into the brain *until each soul has so developed its brain power to be able to utilize them properly.*

Thus in the early days of human development, the innate powers of pineal and pituitary "fell" to the reproductive centers, and the mental seed atom "fell" into the pineal from the heart of the Oversoul. But the portion of the "apple" which pituitary consumed remained an everlasting part of the head region and became the brain of developing humankind, the home of the mental seed atom, the seat of the mind.

The spiritual powers of both the pituitary and pineal atrophied as these two forces assumed their places in the reproductive centers, but the mental development of the lifewave was begun, for the Divine Being not only said: *"... in that day you shall surely die,"* but also said: *"... Behold! the man has become like one of Us, to know good and evil!"*

Humankind gained four things with its fall into matter:

1. the presence of the permanent mental seed atom in the pineal which would enable the soul to evolve its own individual mind;

2. the presence of generative power in the head which was to enable the soul to develop brain cells;

3. the potential to evolve a cerebrospinal nervous system through which the senses were to come into birth;

4. the power to create one's own "likeness" — to reproduce children through physical channels as they are reproduced today.

The mystery in the drama of the Fall of the Human Being must be realized in the knowledge that without the Fall — the division of the generative powers between the head centers and the root centers — individuals of this lifewave could never have developed their own minds, their own brain power; would never have been able to reproduce their kind. The lifewave of souls would have remained ever under the tutelage and guardianship of the Higher Beings who had watched over it until it was able to become its own guardian.

With the Fall, although the soul's spiritual powers became dormant and it was cut off from visions and contacts with the higher worlds about it, the soul was able to begin construction of its own brain cells and the development of its individual mental body. Gradually it began to assume its own place in the cosmic plan of the divine Maker, and assume its own personal responsibilities through its developing knowledge of *good and evil* as each soul, through the "sweat of its brow," fought its way toward its divine inheritance and individuality.

With the Fall, the lifewave emerged from a state of spiritual puppetism, held in necessary bondage by the Great Beings who watched over it, into its own individual estate, to progress through its long journey out of darkness into light. The lifewave "fell" from the etheric planes as our physical forms gradually began to take on their "coats of skin." Our spiritual powers closed off as our physical senses — our physical seeing, hearing, tasting, feeling and smelling — began to develop through our evolving cerebrospinal nervous system.

The lifewave is only now beginning to gain some partial reentry to its lost paradise as we learn how to lift the generative fires out of the reproductive centers and into the brain via sushumna. The fires of the flaming sword of the cherubim in the medulla oblongata, placed there for our own protection, must give way before the greater fires of sushumna, as each soul develops its own powers and gains its own right to reenter its lost Eden.

But each soul will return as a god or goddess in its own right, developed and made possible only through its own endeavors and through its own experiences in the valley of its seeking. We will have gained our godhood through the "sweat of our brows," or the dews of the brow chakra, the pituitrin hormone of the pituitary chakra, the oil of divine love within which flows only under the impact of our tears, our joys, our heartbreaks, our spiritual triumphs, as individual souls plod their weary way upward from the shadowland of earth to the shining heights of heaven and our lost paradise.

TREASURES ON THE TREE OF LIFE

We have fully discussed two of the most important treasures — the pineal and pituitary. It is now advisable that we study the remaining glands from both a physical and an esoteric standpoint so that you may better understand the importance of them, their corresponding chakras, and the part they play not only in your present physical incarnation, but in your own personal eternity ahead. These remaining glands are:

the thyroid (the throat chakra);

the thymus (the heart chakra);

the adrenals (connected with the root chakra);

the liver (the solar plexus chakra);

the spleen (the splenic-navel chakra);

the reproductive organs (the root chakra).

THE THYROID GLAND

This organ, as do most of the endocrine glands, consists of two lobes. One lies along the right side of the trachea, or windpipe, and one on the left. They are connected across the front of the windpipe. The entire gland weighs about two ounces and its color is dark red. The length varies between two and three inches. It is larger in the female than in the male, and tends to shrink as one reaches middle age.

The thyroid is one of the most important chemical laboratories in the entire body. Unfortunate disabilities occur when this important glandular center is unbalanced or diseased. In one condition, called myxedema, the entire muscular and nervous systems are impaired. Convulsions usually occur, and ultimately the mind is affected. The symptoms of this dread disease do not occur if, in the removal of this important gland, only a small portion is left behind or, failing that, thyroid glandular feedings be given to substitute for removal of the gland itself.

Disease of the thyroid sometimes results in retardation of mental, physical and sexual development. If untreated, sufferers seldom exceed the intelligence of a child of five and never attain sexual maturity. Thyroid disease affects also the rate of cellular oxidation and bodily heat production.

A profuse network of blood vessels surrounding and penetrating the follicles of the gland are the receivers of its hormone secretions. These hormones contain a relatively large quantity of iodine, an important factor in controlling physical well-being. Thyroid iodine is also the builder of brain cells. It supplies electric conductivity to the brain. The secretions of the thyroid, an energy producing gland, influence the action of the adrenal glands, causing them to pour out needed body energies. It produces iron for the blood and phosphorus for the nerves and brain centers. Phosphorus in the brain cells attracts from the surrounding ethers many etheric qualities needed to develop spirituality. The thyroid gland is most intimately connected with the temperament of the individual. Depending on the normalcy of the thyroid, one will be either a pleasing personality who is cheerful, happy, pleasant to be with — or moody, cross, irritable.

The thyroid is also connected with the aging process. If and when you learn to regulate and stimulate certain thyroid and parathyroid secretions, you will have learned how to extend your youth.

The thyroid hormone capable of producing longevity is still strange to medical science, for it has not yet come to maturity in the physical functions of the body. The pituitary releases a particular type of hormone stimulating to the thyroid, thereby creating an intimacy between these two glands. There is also a powerful connection between the thyroid and the reproductive organs. When x-ray is applied to the thyroid, it may impair its function and make the individual sterile.

THE THROAT CHAKRA

The throat chakra superimposes the thyroid gland, which is a connecting link between the pituitary and the reproductive organs in the root chakra. Located toward the back of the neck and head, and extending into the medulla oblongata, the throat chakra is an important center in the distribution of creative energy. It is highly stimulated in artistic persons. The term "artist" includes all persons in whom creativity combines the emotions and the mind — the actor, dancer, singer, writer, sculptor, speaker, painter, psychic, designer, and many others. At times, every one of us falls in this "artist" category, at least temporarily.

Whereas the act of physical creativity combines many physical and emotional energies, other types of creativity combine emotional and mental energies predominantly. As an example, renowned artists frequently become temporarily celibate, renouncing sexual activity during the weeks required to produce an important painting or other work of art. They may not do this consciously. However, they do discover (as do artists in other fields) that the sexual urge is dissolved into, or negated by, a different kind of creative expression.

In most supersensitive, artistic beings there is a superabundance of creative force flowing through their systems, for their creative expressions cause an upward "pull" on the normal function of the reproductive organs. When this occurs, there are two possible results.

In one instance the individual may completely deny the higher form of creativity, with its tendency toward spiritual expression, and channel the entire force toward sex,

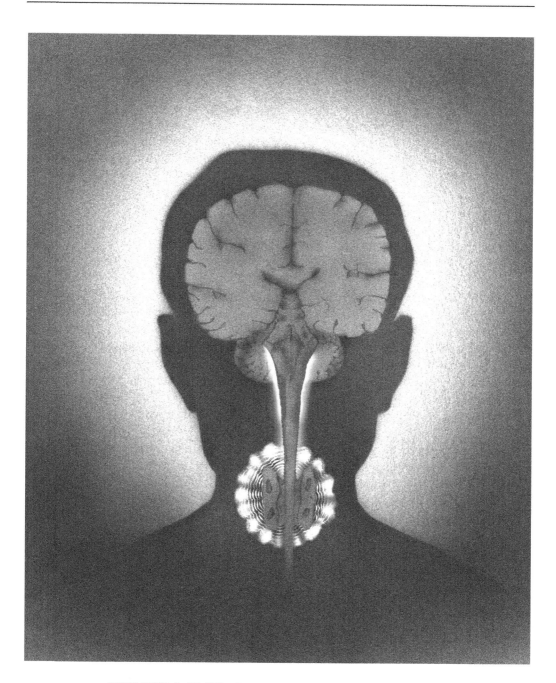

THE THROAT CHAKRA AND THE THYROID GLAND

The throat chakra includes the thyroid gland, the parathyroid glands, and extends upward to encompass the medulla oblongata. The chakra covers both the throat and the neck and connects directly with the important brain stem and fourth ventricle of the brain just above the medulla.

a diversion of the natural flow of this particular energy. The results are unfortunate, in that a permanent or at least a long term spiritual creation is never realized — and a very temporary short term pleasure is substituted.

In the other instance, the individual expresses the creative flow to the best of one's ability. This utilizes the uprising energies in the manner in which they were intended, not limited to procreation of the human form or a physical and emotional expression of love. When the energy takes its natural course, beauty in one form or another is the result. In addition, higher vibratory essences are incorporated into the material world around us.

This is not to say that the average person, or even the great creative artist, should deny sex in his or her life. It is only to point out that higher purposes are never served when the energy from the root chakra is denied higher expression completely.

The throat chakra might well be considered a point of decision. You decide what or what not to say in certain social situations. You also decide whether or not the flow of creative energy from the root chakra will be allowed outer expression through and above the throat chakra or will be directed downward again toward the lower centers in purely physical expression. One future goal of humanity is to transfer the creative powers upward from the sacral centers through the throat chakra. The creative force is meant to be raised to the brain centers — not ingathered in the throat center or directed downward again toward the lower centers in purely physical expression.

Since the throat center is a direct link between the brain and the generative region, it follows that it becomes superactive in the distribution of creative energies. But just as these energies should be raised out of the root chakra, they should also be raised out of the throat chakra. Its journey upward should culminate in the Third Eye in the brain, opening it in illumination.

The creative energies of the perfected soul of the future will be raised through the throat chakra, it is true. But they will be transmuted energies, employed in creative and not sexual activities.

REPRODUCTIVE POWERS OF FUTURE HUMANITY

The perfected person of the future will be able to reproduce offspring through the power of the spoken word through the throat chakra, and the power of mental visualization through the developed Third Eye, even as reproduction today is manifested through the lower organs and lower centers.

This, at the present stage of your evolution, may sound fantastic and unbelievable. However, we plant it only as a seed thought. You may accept or reject it as you see fit.

This activity will not transpire for many ages to come when the creative Word will again manifest on the physical plane through the powers of a more evolved humanity.

When you thus attain you will no longer be victim of the lower worlds, bound and chained to lower carnal desires. You will be regent of the skies, of the higher planes, through the power of the creative WORD, as the throat chakra becomes the outward expression of the inner powers unfolded by the Third Eye.

If you are incredulous at our teaching then ponder birth as we understand it today. A seed is planted in the female womb. On the "scaffolding" of the etheric body inside the womb the cells and atoms of the dense infant physical form are infused and built as the period of gestation proceeds under the auspices of the subconscious mind of the mother — building, building, building, without any conscious effort or knowledge on the part of her waking conscious mind.

At the supreme moment of birth the personality image, involving the higher bodies and faculties of the incoming entity, enters through the crown chakra of the tiny new form in one tremendous, overwhelming Breath of Life. Through the bloodstream, the nervous systems, the chakras and the endocrine system, these higher bodies are "nailed to the cross of matter" of the physical form for another incarnation upon Earth.

In the future the creative powers in the root chakra and generative centers will be gradually transferred to and transmuted in the throat chakra. As these energies are raised through the etheric spinal cord, the throat chakra will become increasingly active. Is it so strange, then, to realize that humans will create with their own mental powers, and their own spoken word, the etheric body of a new incoming entity and, by these same mental powers, build upon it the cells and atoms of the new physical form?

If you can bring the thoughtform you have created into objective manifestation, you will have created a form worthy of being inhabited by the higher bodies, just as the subconscious mind of woman now supplies all the life-giving properties to the form building in her womb. The difference is that it will be supplied with life energies by the *conscious* and *superconscious minds*, rather than the subconscious mind as happens today. It is as simple as that.

The thoughtform of the new body will be created outside the sphere of the female form, however, and the physical cells and atoms of a new physical form will be mentally infused upon the etheric matrix, to be inhabited at the proper time by the higher bodies and the soul of some incoming ego. Meditation upon this mental reproduction process will make it seem logical and simple, as indeed it will be when our mental powers unfold, and we are truly able to bring into objective manifestation our own created thoughtforms.

Pursuing these studies arouses many questions. They will require thoughtful answers. First, will the creator of the thoughtform of the new body mold it according to *his or her* desires, or will the karma of the incoming entity affect and influence the new body?

The answer is that the creator of the thoughtform will only supply the *energies* necessary to create the cells and atoms of the new form. Its shape and degree of perfection will always lie in the realm of karma. It must assume either beauty or defect according to the laws of cause and effect established by the incoming ego regardless of the mental powers of the one creating the thoughtform. Only the *energies* necessary to build the body can be created, not the pattern of the body itself. The creator can, of course, cause features which resemble itself, just as the subconscious minds of both parents of the present day often cause the child of their physical creation to resemble themselves.

But in many cases at present, the physical resemblance vanishes after the age of twenty-one when the mental body of the child takes more complete command of its physical form. It should also be remembered that by the time the soul has evolved the mental powers which make it capable of creating by the mental processes, its physical vehicle will have become so perfected, such a thing of beauty, that there need be no fear of a less than healthy physical form coming into birth. All past unpleasant karma will have been dissolved from the heart seed atom, and all physical forms will be creations of wonder and delight. Thus the creator of the thoughtform will not be as bound by the laws of karma as now.

The second question of supreme importance is: How will the "seed" be planted? Today the seed is planted by the entrance of the male sperm into the female ovum. How shall this be accomplished in regenerated humans?

A full and comprehensive explanation must wait until we arrive at the time in our studies when it seems more fitting for us to discuss the solar seed and the lunar seed which come into being in the regenerated soul. You will also possess a double spinal cord and both male and female reproductive organs within yourself. You will have become the TRUE divine hermaphrodite, possessing a positive seed and a negative egg, which will unite under the power of the mind, the Word, and the visualization of the combined Third Eye and the throat chakra.

At our present level, the heart and throat chakras are the two most affected by this process. This, in part, explains the increased visibility and human rights movement with regard to homosexuals. As they take their places on the world scene, we see an increased sensibility and advanced level of evolution among many. Just like heterosexuals, there are those who are less evolved than others, but many exhibit notable talents, compassion and creativity. Science has begun to help us understand the physical basis for this, from distinct differences in regions of the brain to biochemical differences caused by differing hormone levels. Yet regardless of causation, this presents the first faint evidence of how a new paradigm can evolve in the human race; one indication we are headed toward becoming once again unisexual — the body reflecting its Creator, in Whom ultimate Oneness is fully expressed.

Through the ages, many spiritual traditions have recognized and honored the unique characteristics of homosexuals. Likewise, renowned homosexuals have contributed greatly to various aspects of society, including philosophy and spirituality. Consider Michelangelo, Leonardo de Vinci, Socrates, Tchaikovsky, Oscar Wilde, Frank Capra, Walt Whitman, Dag Hammerskjald, T. E. Lawrence, Sappho, Emily Dickinson, Gertrude Stein, Willa Cather, Richard the Lion Hearted, James I of Britain, and Hans Christian Anderson.

It is now clear that homosexuals come into this life with a specific distinction in their genes, chromosomes, brain and biochemistry, which offers them the opportunity to help create inner balance of the male and female energies present within every human being - perhaps a planned pattern of evolutionary development for the entire human race. If this is true, isn't it time we stopped discriminating against a group of people who may well be representing the creative and spiritual potential within us all?

A hermaphrodite is one having both male and female qualities in one form, but whose reproductive powers lie in the Third Eye and not the root chakra, as in humans today. The male and female properties will be represented by the pineal and pituitary glands, and their union will not only bring illumination but will enable the soul to reproduce through the powers of the throat chakra, combining the glandular hormones — a male seed and a female egg — with the power of the creative Word as it proceeds out of the throat chakra.

This transaction will represent the true *immaculate conception* in humans. We shall teach further about this in later Lessons. To do so now would carry us far afield from our present subject, which concerns the throat chakra.

In the School at Crotona, the Teacher Pythagoras presented a profound teaching concerning the chakras. This Master was particularly aware of the future importance and powers of the throat chakra, and toward the development of these powers he gave his supreme attention. He recognized the destructive processes of the generative energies in the lives of so many, even among his own disciples, and he set about transmuting these destructive energies into constructive creations by stimulating the throat chakra.

This was the true purpose of the two year period of silence imposed upon his disciples — to concentrate the creative powers and energies toward a rapid development of the throat chakra. This increased development caused an upflow of the generative energies from the root chakra, so that it was easy for his disciples to become celibates, to conserve their generative powers and to direct them toward creative endeavors. By so doing, they simultaneously increased the development of their brain cells and called into higher vibrations all the mental powers they were capable of attaining.

Apollonius of Tyana was another Master who imposed upon himself a vow of silence. Perhaps practiced without a mystical understanding, nonetheless, this same vow of silence is practiced by some orders of monks and nuns in both the Christian and Buddhist traditions and can be beneficial in the same way. Nonuse of the throat chakra through perpetual silence, combined with the practice of celibacy, preserved its power and caused a tremendous stimulation of this creative center.

THE THYMUS GLAND

We have already referred to one important aspect of the thymus gland: its triune connection with both the pineal gland and the reproductive organs. We taught that each child is born with an extremely active thymus gland. It remains so until around the age of seven, at which time it begins its regressive period. By the time the child reaches the age of puberty, the thymus has apparently ceased to function and, so far as medical science can ascertain, is of no further service to the physical form. Future research will find this idea untrue as science begins its probings into the mysteries of the thymus and discovers many of its potentials.

The thymus is an indispensable factor in the life of a newborn baby. It produces defensive cells that enable the body to develop immunity to infection. Without this immunity normal life would be impossible except in a completely sterile environment. For the first three months the thymus labors to manufacture immunizing cells which it dispatches through the bloodstream to the spleen, bone marrow and lymph glands. There these cells begin either to reproduce themselves or convert other cells into immunizers. Within three months, the thymus has established antibody-producing plants throughout the body.

The discovery that the thymus initiates the body's complex immunity reactions began a vast field of research into the operations of a gland which, for centuries, scientists dismissed as an insignificant, purposeless mass of tissue behind the breastbone.

More important to us are the metaphysical functions of this important gland which we covered only to a limited extent. We shall now approach the subject more thoroughly for it is imperative that you understand more about this mysterious center.

At birth the gland is located deep in the neck. It is significant to note that as the infant reaches childhood and puberty the gland slips further down in the body until it ultimately resides in the chest cavity just above the heart. We call this to your attention

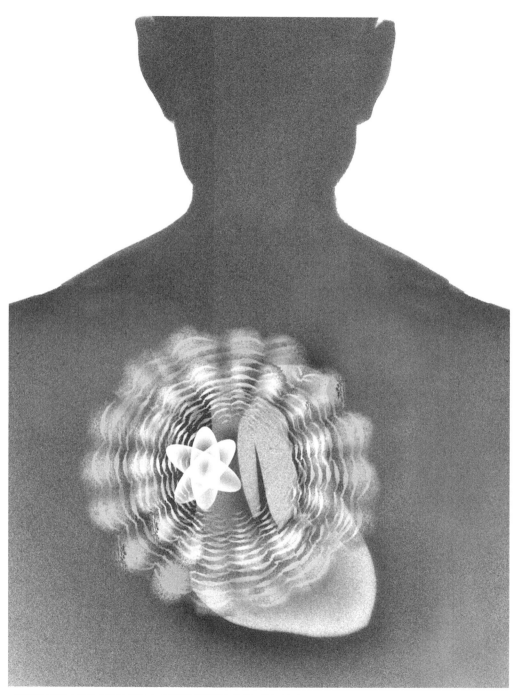

THE HEART CHAKRA, THE THYMUS GLAND, AND THE HEART SEED ATOM

The heart chakra includes the thymus gland, a portion of the heart itself, and the physical heart seed atom located in the upper right venticle of the heart.

to point out that what remains of the thymus in the adult lies almost directly between the shoulder blades in the back — the exact location of what we call the heart chakra.

It is true that in the heart chakra is the physical heart seed atom, located in the upper right lobe of the heart itself, but the chakra extends to encompass the area between the shoulder blades which is where the "atrophied" thymus lies. Thus the actual heart chakra is the area of the heart seed atom *and* the thymus gland.

To what mystery in humans does this information relate? It brings the thymus into ever-increasing prominence to the mystic. Although the thymus itself does somewhat atrophy at time of puberty, the heart chakra it helps to represent most certainly remains active.

The Thymus and the Mental Body

From an esoteric standpoint the thymus is directly connected with the mental body and mental development during the early years of childhood. Its removal during childhood affects development of the brain cells and the pituitary itself, directly influencing not only intellectual growth but physical as well.

The thymus is the instrument of the mental body until the brain cells develop around the fourteenth year (the time of puberty) and are able to bear the strain of mental development, after which time the atrophying processes of the gland begin.

As the mental body gains an ever-increasing hold upon the physical form, the forces active in the thymus are raised to and embedded in the gray matter of the brain. Thus the seat of the mental body is transferred to the brain and out of the thymus. When the transference is complete, the etheric umbilical cord joining the child to both mother and father is finally broken and the child becomes an individualized "I."

This applies equally to adopted children and those who, for various reasons may never have met one or more of their biological parents. The connection to the biological parents remains, even though they may be deceased. Only after the personality begins to detach itself from the parents does the mental body become infused enough in the physical form to be capable of performing mental powers producing what we call "memory."

The "birth" of the mental body actually transpires around the age of seven, but does not assume enough of its powers to become capable of "individualization" until around fourteen. At that time, when the etheric umbilical cord connecting the child to its parents is broken, the mental body enters a more active period and at twenty-one the soul assumes its full mental responsibilities. One's mind continues its development, and attains its full maturity around the age of forty-nine.

Thus much of the mental powers of the child flow to it through the thymus umbilical cord, attached to both parents, until the age of fourteen. With the breaking of this thymus cord at puberty, the remaining mental forces are raised to the brain and receive any further development through the individualized Trees of Life and Knowledge rooted in the individual's sutratmic silver cord. Henceforth the soul is connected only to its own Oversoul and Monad, and has become an individualized "I," an independent being. The thymus gland, the entrance point of the mental energies until that time, begins to atrophy, and the sex glands begin their development and functioning.

At the age of forty-nine, the soul can either begin an increased mental development through its superconscious mind, or it can begin to experience a decrease in mental efficiency as the brain cells begin to atrophy as did the thymus gland — not completely but extensively. If one does not transmute some of the generative, creative forces of one's life upward to the brain, then the mental force — the creative powers once found in the thymus gland which were transferred to the brain at puberty — will begin to withdraw into the reservoir of the supercon-scious forcefield above the head, causing a partial atrophy of the brain cells in old age. One will become senile, displaying the same mental capabilities one exhibited as a child.

We have previously pointed out that there is a definite triune connection between the pineal, the thymus and the reproductive organs. Medical science has discovered several things concerning the thymus:

1.   It is active in the infant and child and atrophies apparently when the child attains the age of puberty (around fourteen).

2.   After puberty, when the thymus becomes atrophied, the reproductive organs in both the male and the female begin to develop to bring the child into physical and sexual maturity. Therefore science concludes that the thymus activities must act as a "brake" upon the sexual glands, until the proper age. At puberty the reproductive organs begin to consume *all* the creative forces to further their own development, leaving the pineal and thymus to atrophy for lack of lifeforces.

3.   Medical science states, too, that *when the thymus fails to atrophy* at puberty, extremely undesirable effects are registered upon the individual:

a.   Immaturity of body, mind and sexual characteristics.

b.   If the thymus continues to remain operative the reproductive organs do not attain their maturity nor does the generative force become operative in the individual. The postpuberty active thymus causes the throat chakra to become prematurely stimulated.

c. Repeated chest x-ray treatments administered to children could cause problems. The thymus may shrink, causing the reproductive organs to develop prematurely and abnormally.

d. Immaturity of mind frequently occurs. Medical science recognizes a significant connection between the pineal, the thymus and the mind. They state that the thymus is responsible for mental weaknesses if it fails to atrophy.

But thymo-centrics are victims of an unfortunate glandular development. Some wish to correct its influence in their lives. Frequently an operation upon the generative organs and the intake of glandular substance are necessary.

We have said that the regenerated person of the future will be the one in whom the thymus remains active. Yet medical science suggests that an active thymus in an adult can cause difficulties. How can we reconcile this?

Medical scientists are quick to admit their confusion concerning the mysterious functions of the thymus gland. They have failed to recognize the spiritual significance of this important center. It represents to the mystic, however, the heart chakra in the etheric body, and even though the physical gland atrophies at the time of puberty, such is not true of the etheric counterpart, the heart chakra, which continues its full activity.

Reconciling "Fantasy" with Fact

First of all, let us speak of the normal spiritual evolutionary processes, so that we may better understand the abnormal. As we have taught previously, almost the entirety of humanity's mental attention is at present polarized in the solar plexus seat of emotion-desires. The lifewave is completely ruled by desires, not by reasoning, logic, or will power. The next evolutionary action in our spiritual progression is a gradual transference of the kundalini force out of the solar plexus chakra into the heart-thymus chakra. There in the laboratory of the heart, the desire force will be transmuted into the essence of divine love. Purified in the heart, kundalini will then rise into the throat chakra, a powerful vortex of creative energy.

This is the normal procedure and what should occur in each individual. However, there are those who struggle on the spiritual pathway. As is many times the case, as the new age ethers pour their influence upon individuals of today, the force which would normally find residence in the awakening heart chakra finds no harmony there because the individual continues to remain victim of undesirable karmic picture images pouring out of its seed atom.

The majority have not begun to equalize the flow of these "bad" picture images of past karma with a flow of beneficent picture images created by the good karma of their present lives. In other words, they are not doing enough good in this present life and the "bad" karmic picture images flowing out of the heart seed atom into the bloodstream dominate their lives and *prevent the development of the heart chakra.*

If kundalini, rising into the undeveloped heart chakra, finds no harmonious residence there, it may rise prematurely into the throat chakra.

When the rampant kundalini force strikes the throat chakra it finds it equally unprepared for this flow of "unbalanced" creative force. It is "unbalanced" because it should have been transmuted in the chakra of the heart; it should have been cleansed and purified in the ethers of Nirvanic love force found only in an awakened heart chakra. Failing to find the heart laboratory awakened and prepared, it has rushed on upward to the throat chakra and there it becomes a raging torrent of undirected creative force.

In those whose karmic picture images have prevented a normal spiritual development of the heart chakra, the creative force in an unprepared throat chakra becomes uncontrollable.

What has happened in the heart chakra? The unchecked flow of undesirable karmic picture images prevents, as we have said, a normal development of the heart chakra. The thymus gland which usually atrophies at puberty, remains active under the impact of this karmic force. This soul, rather than directing its life pattern toward a good life, has set its mind toward negativity, and the mental creative force in the thymus fails to rise to the head.

The thymus, rather than the pineal and reproductive organs, uses the creative force in the body, and the pineal and reproductive organs fall short of their normal development. The individual fails to develop normal sexual growth. The throat chakra becomes prematurely stimulated instead. The soul has given way to the influence of the karma of its past rather than attempting to overcome it in this life by setting its face toward better things.

In the person of the future the heart seed atom will have discharged the majority of its undesirable karmic picture images. The heart-thymus chakra will develop normally. The creative kundalini force, rising out of the solar plexus, will find an awakened heart chakra awaiting it, and from there it will proceed upward into a prepared throat center. It will be highly desirable that the thymus remain active after puberty because there will remain no undesirable karmic force in the heart seed atom to deter its spiritual development. The active thymus in the person of the future will ensure a supremely developed heart chakra.

A complete comprehension of our explanation will depend upon an understanding of the workings of the heart seed atom and the karmic picture images.

The person whose thymus remains active after puberty CAN struggle through negativity, or become a creative genius of the highest magnitude. It depends entirely upon how each soul chooses to use the creative forces of its life, how it surrenders to the influence of the picture images in its heart seed atom, or how it uses its own mental and spiritual powers to overcome their influence in its life.

Fortunate is the child who is born to parents with an understanding of these laws; who can set the child's face toward spiritual activities; who can direct its feet away from negative attractions; who can teach the child constructively.

THE ADRENAL GLANDS

The adrenal glands are located on the right and left sides of the body and sit like a cap on the top of each kidney. In size they are about as big as the tip end of the forefinger, being about an inch and a half in length. Although the weight of the adrenals varies, they usually weigh about half an ounce each. The adrenals are composed of two parts, an outer portion and an inner portion. The outer is called the *adrenal cortex* and the inner is called the *adrenal medulla.*

It has been thought and taught by the medical profession that the adrenalin secretion of the adrenal medulla is responsible for the rush of vital energy necessary in times of stress. Because of this belief, the adrenals have been called the "fight or flight" glands — the "shock" glands of the body — releasing the adrenalin necessary to help one face emergency situations calling one to do battle or to flee from danger. It is erroneous to credit the adrenals completely with this energy supply, however.

The adrenals alone cannot supply this excessive output without a sudden outpouring of iodine from the thyroid which, in turn, cannot operate in crises without a command from the high and mighty pituitary. And so, although the needed adrenalin itself pours out of the adrenals, we must again bow to pituitary who commands a release of iodine from the thyroid, which indirectly causes a flow of this "emergency" hormone from the adrenals.

Removal of the adrenal medulla itself will not result in death, but removal of the complete gland will, unless the proper glandular substitute is available.

Attainment and the Adrenals

An excessive supply of adrenalin when the body is not under duress can result in sexual excesses, selfish aggressiveness, ruthlessness in attaining driving ambitions, high tension, and a beligerant attitude. Although the adrenals can be counted upon to supply a temporary excessive flow of energy in emergencies, still the supply can become depleted, and the individual who lives under continuous stress for any degree of time is storing for oneself a sure and certain karma of a physical nature.

You cannot be mentally or emotionally tense a high percentage of time without calling into action these adrenal "shock" glands which, under continuous stimulation, pour into the bloodstream an excessive supply of adrenalin. This keeps the body perpetually burning at an intense pace. Sooner or later, the glands collapse under such constant high pressure and you then become victim of your own temperament. You must pay your karmic debt of supreme fatigue, nervous breakdown, mental exhaustion, heart malfunction, and complete bodily susceptibility to all forms of karmic disease.

The same is true of the overaggressive and ambitious individual who lives under a perpetual drive to "live better than the Joneses." You, and you alone, must pay the price of your aggressive progression. If you are this type of individual, who treads your earthly pathway winning your own goals over the broken spirits and shattered dreams of your fellow travelers, who are so intent upon outdoing and making a competitive race of every physical goal and endeavor, are destined to be the victim of your own creation when the day of adrenalin exhaustion arrives and the pituitary withholds her command to release the needed excessive hormones. You are cut off from your source, and must pay your karmic price for your emotionalism, your temperamental aggressiveness, and your overambitious heart.

If, in past incarnations, you have earned the right to "obtain" in this particular lifetime, you will be granted enough excessive adrenalin by pituitary to enable the adrenals to release the necessary flow of hormones which contribute liberally to brain development and mental powers. You — fortunate individual — will steadily and constantly "obtain and attain" with little obvious effort on your own, and without displaying selfish aggression.

Here again, we see the heart seed atom at work. These karmic rewards will be of your own accomplishment. They will be due you for past good deeds, past kindnesses in already-lived incarnations. The beneficent picture images flowing out of the heart seed atom give the pituitary her cue to release sufficient adrenalin to enable you to attain your goals.

You find that you need not constantly exert yourself to keep the adrenalin flowing. The flow will be automatic. Once a goal is established in your mind the adrenals, under command of pituitary, release a sufficient supply of their precious hormone into the system to keep it well-tuned to the project at hand, and to keep the brain waves washed in ethers which stimulate brain power and mental endurance. Thus you will constantly succeed without an outward struggle or a constant battle or a competitive attitude toward your fellowbeings.

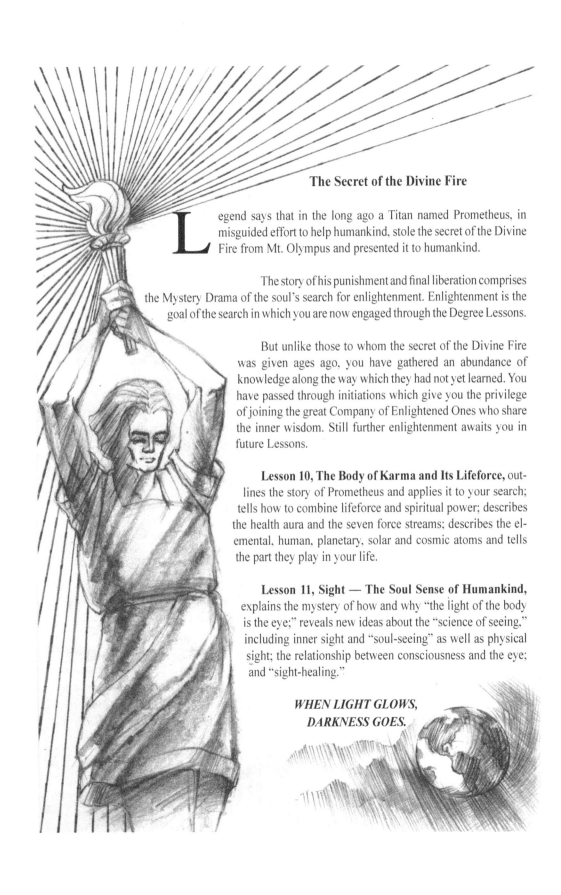

The Secret of the Divine Fire

Legend says that in the long ago a Titan named Prometheus, in misguided effort to help humankind, stole the secret of the Divine Fire from Mt. Olympus and presented it to humankind.

The story of his punishment and final liberation comprises the Mystery Drama of the soul's search for enlightenment. Enlightenment is the goal of the search in which you are now engaged through the Degree Lessons.

But unlike those to whom the secret of the Divine Fire was given ages ago, you have gathered an abundance of knowledge along the way which they had not yet learned. You have passed through initiations which give you the privilege of joining the great Company of Enlightened Ones who share the inner wisdom. Still further enlightenment awaits you in future Lessons.

Lesson 10, The Body of Karma and Its Lifeforce, outlines the story of Prometheus and applies it to your search; tells how to combine lifeforce and spiritual power; describes the health aura and the seven force streams; describes the elemental, human, planetary, solar and cosmic atoms and tells the part they play in your life.

Lesson 11, Sight — The Soul Sense of Humankind, explains the mystery of how and why "the light of the body is the eye;" reveals new ideas about the "science of seeing," including inner sight and "soul-seeing" as well as physical sight; the relationship between consciousness and the eye; and "sight-healing."

*WHEN LIGHT GLOWS,
DARKNESS GOES.*

He Who Knows Not

Life never led but to
Death.
But for the light-filled
Heart
There is peaceful anticipation.
For him who knows not
There is death-dread.
But he who knows
And he who knows not~
Both must go.
Since this is so
Wise is the one who,
Not knowing,
Admits not knowing
And seeks to know.

~Earlyne

THE OLD VIOLIN

'Twas battered and scarred, and the auctioneer
    Thought it scarcely worth his while
To waste much time on the old violin,
    But held it up with a smile.
"What am I bid, good folks," he cried,
    "Who'll start bidding for me?
A dollar, a dollar — now two, only two —
    Two dollars, and who'll make it three?

"Three dollars once, three dollars twice,
    Going for three —" but no!
From the room far back a gray-haired man
    Came forward and picked up the bow;
Then wiping the dust from the old violin
    And tightening up the strings,
He played a melody, pure and sweet,
    As sweet as an angel sings.

The music ceased, and the auctioneer
    With a voice that was quiet and low,
Said: "What am I bid for the old violin?"
    And he held it up with the bow.
"A thousand dollars — and who'll make it two?
    Two thousand — and who'll make it three?
Three thousand once and three thousand twice
    And going and gone," said he.

The people cheered, but some of them cried,
    "We do not quite understand —
What changed its worth?" The man replied,
    "The touch of the Master's hand."
And many a man with a life out of tune,
    And battered and torn with sin,
Is auctioned cheap to the thoughtless crowd,
    Much like the old violin.

A "mess of pottage," a glass of wine,
    A game and he travels on,
He's going once, and going twice,
    He's going — and almost gone!
But the Master comes, and the foolish crowd
    Never can quite understand
The worth of a soul, and the change that's wrought
    By the touch of the Master's Hand.

— Maurice Francis Egan

The Body of Karma and Its Lifeforce

Second Degree — Lesson Ten

THE SEAT OF HUMAN DESIRE — THE LIVER

When thinking in terms of occult anatomy, one might be inclined to overlook the importance of the liver. However, its functions are among the most important of the human form, both from a physiological and an esoteric viewpoint.

As esoteric scientists we must list the liver as a vital part of the endocrine glandular system, although it is not usually considered so. It is the largest gland in the body. The approximate weight is three and one-half pounds. It is about ten or twelve inches in length. It lies just below the diaphragm and is divided into two lobes — the right lobe being about six times larger than the left.

The liver evolved in the human form because a storage place and a distributing station for food were needed. As a distributing station and a purifying house, it breaks food into particles and types them for different functions throughout the body. That which the body needs, the liver differentiates and directs into circulation. That which is useless is committed to waste, and that which is needed for bile is extracted for that purpose.

The iodine secretions released by the thyroid are utilized to the ultimate by the processes of the liver, and without the iodine substance, the liver does not function properly. There is an incomparable wisdom to these operations, controlled by the subconscious mind, beyond our conscious understanding.

THE SOLAR PLEXUS CHAKRA

It is in the solar plexus area of the liver that we find the astral body exercising its principal seat of activity. It is in the apex of the great lobe of the liver where the astral-emotional seed atom is buried. This knowledge brings the liver into increased importance. Medical science recognizes it to be the seat of emotions, although it is unaware of the presence of the seed atom there.

Since the liver is the focal point of the astral body it must be apparent that it thus becomes the principal organ in the body subject to diseases through our emotions. Suppressed frustration, hatred, bitterness, revenge, produce diseases or malfunctions of the liver which also result in diseases in other organs or areas. These emotional impulses command the subconscious to react, and the reactions center in or through the liver.

The astral seed atom in the apex of the liver is the seat of lower desires. It is in this "abdominal brain" that we find the carnal mind attuned at our present level of spiritual progression. The disciple who seeks spiritual attainment must come to a full realization that the forces of transmutation must first calm, cleanse and purify the solar plexus chakra before the heart chakra can be fully activated.

Otherwise, regardless of how evolved the heart chakra may become, there will ensue a perpetual struggle as the desires of the lower nature well up from the seed atom in the liver to pull the desires of the heart down to this level. Only by constantly practicing will power can the disciple overcome the dynamic force of the carnal desires in the astral seed atom.

At our present level of evolution, humanity lives with its thoughts and emotions governed principally through the abdominal brain, all revolving around desire — all types of desire, spiritual as well as selfish. This makes the solar plexus the most active of all the chakras. Many of our present emotions relate to ourselves, and some are of a selfish nature.

It is true that the next highest chakra, the heart, is evolving increasing activity as we enter the Aquarian Age. As it gradually awakens, the emotions of the solar plexus will become somewhat conditioned by the essences emanating from the heart laboratory. Only as we begin to realize more fully that we help ourselves when we help others, will the energies of emotion become tinctured with the essences of the heart.

Even though we will continue for an interminable time to think first of ourselves, still we must eventually come to a balancing of the Buddhic love nature with our desire nature, as we slowly construct the etheric bridge between these two chakras.

Since energy follows thought it must be realized that great surges of mental power follow the emotional desires born in the solar plexus chakra. There must be, then, an expression of these energies, either upward into the heart chakra to be transmuted, or outward in physical expression.

Much to be desired, of course, is the art of mental transmutation if the disciple can so master it, but under no circumstances should you dam up the emotional energies in the liver and leave them to stagnate in this boiling caldron of carnal creation. To do this is to plant in the subconscious mind the beginnings of disease, for suppressed desires or emotions are like the seeds in a garden, and they must bear their harvest in some sort of outward expression.

There is a key word to utilize in this transmuting art and that word is *forgive*. Forgiving an offense releases all karmic influence from the emotions, and causes the power in the emotions to fade away into nothingness. A second word to remember is *forget*. To forgive and forget is the surest means of transmuting the lower nature to a higher vibration.

If the transmutation cannot be accomplished mentally, then find vigorous physical work temporarily until the body can absorb the turbulent outpouring of hormones. Dig in the garden, walk around the block, scrub the floor, iron clothes, wash the car. Engage in any purely physical activity that will exhaust the body — anything that will relax taut muscles and tense nerves, that will burn up swirling negative energies, that will restore the mind to calmness and some degree of tranquility.

THE LEGEND OF PROMETHEUS

There is a legend from antiquity which bears a relation to our studies concerning the astral seed atom and the liver.

During a conclave of the gods and goddesses on Mount Olympus, Prometheus the Titan requested that he be allowed to bring a portion of the divine Fire down and present it to humanity in order to help free it from its sins. The father of the gods, Zeus, refused his petition on the grounds that humanity was not yet ready to be given the secrets of the Fire. Feeling compassion for humanity, however, Prometheus stole the Fire and, placing it in the hollow stalk of a fennel plant, brought it down to Earth and revealed the secret to humankind. However, Zeus was correct. Mortals, learning of this Fire and being unprepared for its secret, misused it and lit not the divine creative force in the fennel stalk — the spinal cord — but lighted instead the fires of the astral body in the liver.

The gods, seeing so powerful a secret utilized destructively by an early lifewave of humans whose minds were not yet matured sufficiently to understand its true significance, took back the secret to hold until humankind was prepared to receive it. Zeus, in his wrath against Prometheus, ordered him to be chained to the rocky crags of Mount Kazbeck, the Caucasian Mount. He commanded that a vulture be sent to devour his liver daily, and each night that which had been devoured would be replaced, so that the punishment would be interminable. And the god Hermes spoke these words to Prometheus:

> *To such labors look thou for no*
> *termination until some god shall appear*
> *as a substitute in thy pangs, and shall*
> *be willing to go both to gloomy Hades*
> *and to the murky depths around Tartarus.*

The one who finally was to liberate Prometheus was Herakles, or Hercules, the Greek name for this god. His liberation came when Hercules descended to Hades and went the "Round of Tartarus." He killed the vulture and delivered Prometheus. The gods permitted Hercules to perform these acts of mercy, and Zeus grasped the opportunity of liberating Prometheus and allowing him to gain immortality among the gods.

What does this Mystery drama of Prometheus mean to students of the esoteric? Let us say that the conclave of the gods and goddesses, referred to in the myth, relates to a conclave of the Master Teachers who walked among early humankind. Let us say that Zeus represented the hierophant and that Prometheus, a neophyte among Teachers, asked permission to reveal to uninitiated humanity the secret of regeneration and illumination by the divine Fire in the spinal cord, or "hollow fennel stalk."

Zeus, the leader of the great beings who came to Earth from higher realms — discerning that humanity was not yet evolved enough to receive and constructively utilize the secret — forbade it. But Prometheus ignored his admonition and revealed this most marvelous,but dangerous, of the secrets of the Mysteries to uninitiated disciples of the early Mystery Temples.

Zeus was correct in his discernment that humanity was not yet prepared to receive such power. So the gods and goddesses, to prevent further sacrilege, took back into the archives of the Mysteries the secret documents Prometheus had stolen. However, much harm had been done. Many of the early disciples, receiving the secret, misused it, causing incalculable destruction not only on Earth itself but among many other unprepared disciples as well as the profane.

Prometheus was expelled from the Mystery Schools, and told that, following his death, he must suffer in the astral worlds until every one of the misguided ones whom he had injured by revealing the secret prematurely had righted all the wrongs committed through ignorant knowledge of the Fire. Since much of the destruction

of Atlantis was caused by ignorant and evil use of this Fire, the punishment of Prometheus extended almost interminably. It ended only when another of the Masters, Hercules, descended from the higher planes to help bring the light to those who had performed the destruction through its misusage.

Prometheus Symbolizes Humankind

There is much symbolism in this legend. Prometheus, in one sense, symbolizes one who chains him or herself to the material plane of life, enduring long ages of suffering through the astral seed atom in the liver which is the recording book of all lower desires. This person comes back into rebirth again and again to be tortured through the destruction of his or her own solar plexus chakra by the perpetual dissipation of the creative forces through lower desires, symbolized by the consuming "vulture." The liver, or solar plexus chakra, is restored again and again in the legend, only to be repeatedly eaten away by the vulture. This perpetual drama symbolizes our seeming determination to suffer perpetually through a satisfaction of our carnal desires. The suffering will continue just as long as humankind continues the creation of astral impulses in the seed atom of the liver.

As humankind evolves, each person must gradually come to know that he or she is the cause of his or her own suffering and, through the seed atom in the liver, ultimately will come regeneration. For the secret of the divine Fire, given so prematurely to early humanity, was the secret of regeneration through raising the kundalini fires to the head chakras and the preservation of the creative forces in the root chakra.

Humanity was in no way prepared for such knowledge. The secret is only now being revealed to select disciples among humanity by the "Serpents" of the Mysteries, for we are only now becoming fit instruments to receive the Fire and to cope with the power of the secret. We are only now becoming capable of attaining perfection. And even now the secret can be revealed only partially.

The astral body and its astral seed atom represent the body of karma. The coarser atoms of this body combine to make humankind's true lower body, called the *kama-rupa*. Kama-rupa, the lower aspect of the astral body, dominates completely at the present stage of evolution. It is vitalized through the solar plexus chakra.

This desire body is the very lowest manifestation, and is humankind's own creation. We have not only created this body of lower desires but in so doing we have become its slave. The creation has gained power over the creator. The higher body of aspirations is called the true astral body. This body, without the presence of kama-rupa, is radiant and beautiful.

In some distant future, the astral seed atom will have become cleansed of its impurities and become transmuted, as lower desires are tinctured by the developing love forces in the heart, and the astral atom will dissolve into nothingness. It will have become completely "lifted" into the laboratory of the heart and will be no more. It will manifest as a radiating center of light.

The atoms of the desire body, the kama-rupa, will be transmuted into the shining astral body, the body of aspirations. Ultimately, in turn, this astral body will be overshadowed and absorbed by the evolving causal as humankind attains perfection. As the causal form is evolved, so do the astral qualities become transfigured. Our desires will express as divine Love. Our passion will become compassion, and we will attain our Mastership. Our astral form will dissolve into the causal and will be no more. We will have "overcome the earth."

THE SPLEEN AND THE SPLENIC-NAVEL CHAKRA

The spleen is a ductless gland. Its shape is similar to a mushroom. It is located on the left side of the body near the liver. It weighs about seven ounces, is about five inches in length, and is three to four inches in width. Its size varies in individuals.

One of the principal physical functions of the spleen is to destroy the red blood cells after they have fulfilled their necessary activities in the bloodstream. The life of the average red cell is approximately three weeks, after which it eventually is destroyed. The spleen then sends the remaining pigments into the liver where the body transforms them into bile. They are then reabsorbed from the digestive tract, which sends them into the marrow of the bone to be used again for the formation of new blood cells. The function of the spleen, then, is very intimately associated with the blood.

Removal of the spleen will not result in death. There are subsidiary spleens in various locations in the body which, if the primary spleen is destroyed, will assume its functions. From a purely physical standpoint the spleen can be said to be a factory in which cellular elements of the blood are renewed and elements of the blood which have discharged their usefulness are destroyed or remade.

You already know that the physical form is penetrated by its etheric double and that the seat of principal activity of this etheric body is the splenic-navel chakra. Whereas the spleen, from a physical standpoint, is tremendously concerned with the production and distribution of the human blood, from an esoteric standpoint it is the distributing center of the vital solar forces of the etheric body.

It is a transforming station of the first magnitude. Attracting all the solar forces from surrounding cosmic ethers, it transforms them into the vibrational qualities and etheric properties necessary to the individual, stepping down the power of the infinite to harmonize with the needs of finite humankind.

The Seven Force Streams

Through this important chakra pass all the solar prana of the ethers, bringing lifeforce, vitality, nerve fluid and even blood. Solar prana enters the splenic-navel chakra first. From there it is transformed into seven streams of differentiated energy. Mystics recognize these seven streams as the seven rays of physical energy in the body: the violet ray, the blue ray, the yellow, the green, the red, the orange, and another we term the White Ray.

We shall not enter into a lengthy teaching concerning these rays at the present time. They will be dealt with more completely in later discussions. They must, however, be considered in this present Lesson, for they are distinctly connected with the operation of the spleen and the splenic-navel chakra.

The rays distribute vital lifeforce throughout the physical form by means of the nervous system. Without this activity, the physical form would be quite dead. Thus we feel safe in saying that, *from a purely physical standpoint*, the navel chakra is perhaps the most necessary of all the chakras for the duration of a person's life on the earth plane.

These rays of energy have nothing to do with spirituality, except as one of them, the White Ray, influences indirectly the flow of spiritual forces.

One of the rays issues from the navel chakra to reach the bone marrow and the liver in whose laboratories it is combined with oxygen, iron and other mysterious properties to be manufactured into blood. Another is directed downward to activate the reproductive centers. Without the flow of this ray, the gonads and prostate in the male cease to produce the fluids necessary to accomplish their reproductive purpose. It is also this ray which establishes the growth of the ovum in the female ovary.

If the flow of this ray is blocked in its passage to the reproductive glands, the person can be sterile. For even though the sperm or the ovum be perfect, if it is not permeated with the red pranic ray it contains no lifeforce.

The rays as they radiate through the spleen are in no way spiritual. They are concerned only with the biological and physiological aspects of the physical form — and the ethers which flow into and through the navel chakra are all of a material plane substance. They are vitally necessary to life, but are not necessarily important to spiritual progression and development. The spiritual rays emanate from the heart and head chakras and not the spleen — except, as we have said, the White Ray.

Sushumna, that etheric channel which rises through the center of the spinal cord, is penetrated by yet another channel called *Chitrini*, which is "as fine as a spider's thread." It is via this incomparably delicate thread that the White Ray flows to reach the pineal and pituitary chakras. It is this one ray, transmuted into nerve fluid, which indirectly influences spiritual development, for without the flow of nerve fluid, the mental body has no attaching link to the physical form.

THE LIFEFORCE OF THE BODY OF KARMA

The navel chakra is very closely aligned with the solar plexus chakra. The vital forces of the spleen give vitality and life to the desire-emotions in the solar plexus. To express it another way, let us say that the kama-rupa (desire body) is given life and vitality through the vital solar prana issuing from the navel chakra. This is no deprecation of the navel chakra. It simply implies that the splenic prana vitalizes that center upon which humankind focuses utmost attention.

Energy follows thought. Never forget this. At present our thoughts are centered in the solar plexus. Therefore the navel chakra supplies that center with its vital force, to give life and substance to lower desires.

The navel chakra is the seat of the etheric body and the solar plexus the seat of the astral. The spleen is the battleground where a constant war is waged between the astral forces of the desire body and the pranic ethers pouring into the navel chakra from the surrounding atmosphere.

How a person feels in his or her mind, whether happy, whether angry, whether s/he is the victim of fear, worry, jealousy, greed, all these reflect most definitely in the navel chakra and affect the radiating rays before they can be distributed to all parts of the body. Thus if a person, let us say, is the victim of worry, the spleen will be affected by negative charges which meet head-on the inrushing vital force from the surrounding atmosphere. Since the negative charges are given birth in the liver, where the "worry" is given life, the liver is also involved in these negative emotions.

The negative charges flow out of the liver and into the spleen, and the positive solar forces flow into the spleen from the ethers. There they meet. Because prana is always subject to our direction and influence, the positive solar prana flowing into the spleen always is nullified by the negative charges of worry.

Therefore, the vital pranic force is depleted and negatively charged before it even begins its radiations through the nervous systems, before it becomes differentiated into the streams of the seven rays. Instead of carrying vigorous vitality to replenish and restore the devitalized cells and atoms of the physical form, the rays and fluids which flow into the nervous systems will already be negatively polarized by worry.

This person then becomes far less able to solve the problem, become completely devitalized, robbed of positive mental energy, irritable and deficient. Hate or anger produces the same result.

It was once popular to refer to such a person as one who was exhibiting "a bad spleen," who was "venting his spleen." The point we are making, however, is that the emotions very definitely affect the vital pranic processes of the etheric body as it is recharged constantly by the inflow of solar prana through the navel chakra. It would be important to learn to identify your emotions and learn to express them in helpful, positive ways and let them go. Keep them flowing in order to exhibit the "splenic disposition" that is your heritage.

The Navel Chakra and The Health Aura

The spleen constantly attempts to eject and burn up the toxins of the body, laboring to keep it energized and vitalized. Whereas most medical scientists look upon the gland as a waste disposal unit, the esotericist regards it as a channel for purifying, energizing and vitalizing incoming prana and etheric fluids.

To medical scientists the function of the spleen remains somewhat of an enigma. They have not yet discovered its full function, nor will they until they realize the significance of the spiritual activities of its etheric counterpart, the navel chakra.

The health aura is nothing more than a forcefield surrounding the human body, composed of a continuation of radiating energy which flows from the spleen to reach every cell. The health aura extends beyond the periphery of the physical body in radiating lines of pranic force. They project from every pore. If the body expresses health, the pranic radiations will extend vibrantly erect, but if they droop they very clearly signal a lack of vitality, and that the navel chakra is not functioning at its highest capabilities.

To deny entry of the vital pranic ether would be like withholding oxygen from the lungs. The body would perish very shortly. The flow of solar prana through the nervous system is electric in nature. The nervous system is lifeless without it. The brain formation may be perfect, the nervous system may be formed perfectly, but if either is denied the flow of this electric nerve fluid, the inhabiting soul cannot express life in the physical form.

The pranic fluid represents to the nervous system what electricity represents to the telegraph system. The entire telegraph system may be in perfect working order, but messages cannot be transmitted unless electricity is available in the lines. This is exactly the case with the physical form. Without the flow of pranic electric ether through the nerves, the body dies.

When one is enjoying health, undesirable germs and toxins pass out along these radiating straight lines of the health aura and are ejected from the body into the surrounding ethers. When ill health strikes and the rays are too devitalized to project straight outward, germs and toxins cannot pass out and away from the body.

They remain in the circulatory system, making the struggle to regain health much more difficult, subjecting the individual to danger of infections and contagious viruses which may be in the atmosphere. They have no opportunity of entering the spleen of one whose health aura is such that the pranic streams of vital force flow vibrantly outward.

But our important point here is that the pranic rays are subject to mental direction. It is possible, even imperative, that mental effort be perpetually used in directing positive thought force throughout the physical form. This prevents any negative influence upon the navel chakra and the incoming solar prana in our surrounding ethers.

A mind pulsing with negative forces created by unexpressed fears, worries and anger will attract negative forces. When the mind does not express these emotions in a healthy way there is a definite reaction on the solar plexus and navel chakras. In an automatic endeavor to barricade the body against negative influences in the ethers, which would be attracted into the body through the open gateway of the spleen, the navel chakra automatically attempts a partial closure.

It is valiantly protecting the body against the onslaught of these negative etheric energies. This obstruction of the navel chakra causes a deficiency of vital fluid and the result is that the lines of energy, streaming out from the body in the health aura, decline downward, signifying that the body is depleted of vital lifeforce.

Until the mind identifies, accepts and expresses emotions again in a healthy way, the navel chakra remains protectively sealed against the inflow of negative atmospheric ethers. Not completely, of course, since complete closure would result in death. When the mind, through positive expression of all emotions becomes serene and peaceful, emanating positive energy, the navel chakra will open its barricade to attract harmonizing positive energies. The health aura will once again radiate the lines of living force which, in themselves, are one of our principal guardians against negativity, disease and undesirable thoughtforms pervading the ethers.

Medical science asserts that much of the bodily poisons and toxins are eliminated through the pores of the skin. The truth is, they are ejected from the body through the streams of force of the health aura, which project from every pore — and NOT from the actual pores themselves. The pores are only the physical outlets for the auric health emanations. The toxins cannot be eliminated if the radiations are limp and depleted, or if the body is devitalized as a result of blocking or denying one's emotions because the navel chakra is constricted and not functioning to its full capacity.

Again it is important to remember that the pranic forces are amenable to the mind and the will. Thus the Astarian, learning of the health aura and its radiating streams of vitality, would do well to direct mentally increased portions of prana through the navel chakra into every cell of the body, and send it outward in powerful rays, thus expelling any toxic wastes that might attract disease. Many of Astara's Supplementary Lessons are written with this idea in mind — that of creating powerful thoughtforms of positive energy through the physical body and its health aura.

Control can be accomplished through the power of mind. One can direct prana to accomplish one's own healing and increased vitality by concentrating on the health aura. Establishing a radiant health aura builds an impenetrable wall of protection and nothing but positive forces can enter such a splenic forcefield of light.

A person with dynamic willpower can also direct currents of this vital ether outward from him/herself to encompass someone else who is in need of healing. It requires considerable mental training, but it is extremely effective. This is one of the methods utilized by Astarian healers in accomplishing our healings.

THE REPRODUCTIVE ORGANS

The reproductive organs are the primary sex organs. They are the testes in the male and the ovaries in the female. These generative organs produce the spermatozoon from the male testes and the ovum from the female ovaries. They also secrete a number of important hormones without which the sperm and the ovum, regardless of how perfect they may be in themselves, cannot cause growth of the embryo in the womb.

The Male Testes

In the male, the sperm begins to develop at puberty and, from that time forward, producing the sperm is the primary activity of the testes. The prostate gland and the seminal vesicles supply a fluid which, when mixed with the sperm, constitutes the semen of the male. It is this semen which, entering the female reproductive passages, is the carrier or "container" of the sperm which causes conception to occur.

The functions of the testes are:

1. production of sperm;

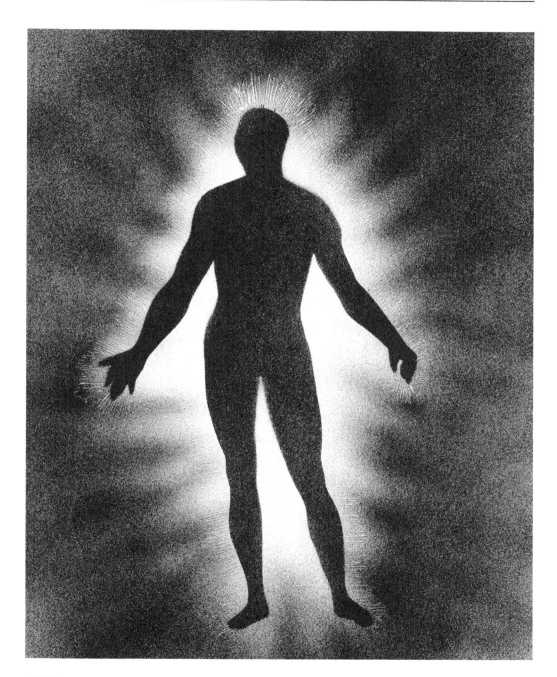

THE RADIANT HEALTH AURA
    The radiant health aura depicts the powerful streams of light energy pouring out of the physical form in lines of force extending outward and upward. These resplendent auric rays protect the disciple from negative forces in the surrounding ethers.

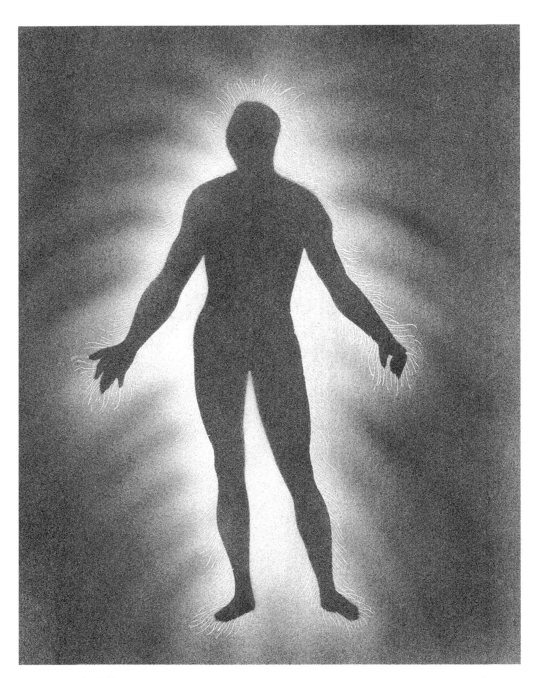

THE DEPLETED HEALTH AURA

The depleted health aura indicates the rays of the nerve force deprived of their life-source, the solar prana. The disciple is struggling with negative emotions, causing a partial closure of the navel chakra and a cessation of the flow of light energy.

2. production of the male sex hormone which, in turn, reacts upon the entire personality by influencing secondary male characteristics, such as hair on the body and changing of the voice. The hormone also brings about development of the sex organs themselves, stimulates the sex drive and determines the cycle of sexual desire.

The Female Ovaries

The ovum in the ovaries also starts developing at the time of puberty. The cycle of ovulation begins several days following the menstrual period, which signifies that a mature ovum or female egg has slipped out of the ovary and has traveled into the fallopian tube which leads to the uterus. The ovum remains in the fallopian tube for about five days and, unless fertilized by a male sperm, disintegrates and disappears.

During intercourse, the male sperm, having been introduced into the female vagina, finds its way upward through the uterus and into the fallopian tube, there to encounter the female ovum where fertilization occurs. After fertilization, the egg, having absorbed the sperm, migrates downward from the fallopian tube and imbeds itself in the wall of the uterus where embryonic development begins.

The ovaries fulfill these functions:

1. produce ovum;

2. produce hormones which cause glandular changes in the uterus during menstrual cycles;

3. influence feminine characteristics, the sex drive and sex cycle;

4. secrete a hormone which influences the mammary glands after childbirth, bringing about milk secretion for her child.

These are only a few of their activities, the rest being connected closely with gestation and the reproductive cycles and activities.

We have given only a fundamental glimpse of the real teachings concerning the reproductive organs. We shall teach further concerning them, the root chakra, the prostate, the seminal fluids and the mysterious Chrism Oil of initiates when we enter our study of the regeneration of future humanity.

Supplementary Monograph

THE ATOM — DIVINE AND HUMAN

The true mystic is bounded on every side by opposition:

1. *The materialistic scientists* who declare there is nothing real which cannot be measured, seen, touched, smelled or cognized by the five senses. All else simply cannot exist. These scientists measure life, the universe and God to the extent of which their laboratory instruments are capable. Beyond that there is nothing — no thing. These scientists are not much concerned with the questions why or how; they simply posit a world of matter beyond which they will not consider.

2. *The dogmatic religionists* who posit a solar system built by a God who sits beyond it, watching people scurry about in daily activities, visiting His wrath or His love upon His little created mite, depending on the whim of the moment.

The mystic, on the other hand, realizes full well the value of the unseen and declares that the material universe and all that exists therein floats upon the ethers of the cosmos. To the mystic the seen is but the outer manifestation of that inner cosmic process.

The mystic believes God to be not only the Creator of the solar system but involved in it so intimately as to be inseparable from it. S/he places the Divine Being, also, in the heart of every person and believes humankind to be evolving toward godhood.

Thus we have the three concepts: that of the materialist, the religionist and the mystic. And the eternal quarrel is the conflict which exists among these three, though the true mystic does not enter the fray upon the same level as the scientist and the religionist. The mystic's weapons are not the arms of antagonism, envy, crude power and dominion.

One purpose of Astara's teachings is to present a more profound con-ception of life and its processes as it applies to the evolving human soul. It is our hope that the teachings eventually will be acceptable to both scientist and religionist.

Science is making great strides toward mysticism. It is engrossed at present in unraveling the mystery of the atom. Only a few years ago the atom was regarded as an indivisible unit of homogenous matter. Science has gradually altered this concept, and now recognizes the atom to be a center of energy — a nucleus of positive protons around which rotate smaller units of negative electrons — a miniature solar system operating under the law of attraction and repulsion.

And science now is hard upon the process of creating life itself. In this process science can hardly escape realizing there is another side to matter. And when scientists once concede there is a hidden, innate aspect to matter, they will have simultaneously concluded there is a spiritual world lying all about us.

But equally important is recognition of an evolving consciousness, a form of intelligence, whose means of evolution is through the outer form — whether it be the form of a person, a planet or a solar system.

This, then, is the mystic's concept. The mystic recognizes the two worlds — matter and spirit — and the evolution of consciousness through both worlds.

Since all of Astara's teachings are based on the concept, *As above, so below,* we must continue our searchings with this as our foundation ... beginning with the infinitesimal atom.

The atom evidences a degree of intelligence. It operates under a system of divine order ... certainly directed either by an inner intelligence or amenable to an outer intelligence. Atoms congregate into numerous combinations to become various elements, substances and forms — forms of minerals, vegetables, animals and ultimately the *body* of a human being.

Since the purpose of the atom is to create elements and substances which become forms, we must conclude that we operate under the same pattern. The body can be described as a large atom, the brain being the positive nucleus, and the chakras the focal points of negative electrons. Or, dealing strictly with the brain, we can designate the Third Eye as the sun of our personal solar system, surrounded by the twelve brain centers or "planets."

If the atom is an infinitesimal replica of something greater, then we must concede our planet to be yet another gigantic atom ... a forcefield in the atomic structure of a Great Being ... an electron or negative forcefield moving around its positive nucleus of energy — the sun. We must even recognize this solar system as being an atom or atomic structure in the body of yet a Greater Being — our Creator, our Supreme Being, our Divine Source.

The atom possesses different attributes and qualities. In its process of congregating and disintegrating to create the forms of the material world, it possesses the ability to select or reject, to attract and repel.

The nature of the atom is to be attracted to others of its kind in order to create a form. Since the ultimate form upon Earth is the form of the human being, then the ultimate purpose of the atom must be to manifest within this form — just as our ultimate purpose is to unite with God, to become a part of our Divine Parent. We could well be recognized as an atom in the Body of a Greater Being, just as our physical atom is a part of the substance which makes up our own physical form. If we are a larger cosmic atom, the entire purpose of our being is to keep changing our own atomic structure to be worthy of attraction into a more celestial forcefield in the Heavenly Being.

Once we each individually accept the possibility that we are a cosmic atom in the form of God, it behooves us to realize that the best way we can become at one with the heart or mind of God is to reorganize our own atomic structure and our alliance with our brothers and sisters, other human atoms.

We must not live as a thing apart from our fellows, selfishly contemplating that all that matters is our own little life. We must realize we are part of the whole, and that what hurts another human atom must also hurt us.

Thus you can dedicate your life to service without the least feeling of piety. You will seek to find your proper place in the world — the place where you best can shine to suit the purpose of your own soul's evolution. You will try to find yourself where you can best express the purpose of the Divine, which is to draw all human atoms upward into the mind of God. The law of the universe which calls the atoms into the building of forms, and which causes them to break up these forms to build greater forms, is the same basic law which governs the evolution of the humankind and of a solar system.

God, the Macrocosm, reflects in human beings, the human atom, and in the elemental atom, the microcosm.

When we say the atom displays a rudimentary form of intelligence, we must qualify that statement. Intelligence is demonstrated by the ability to recognize that which attracts and that which repels and to discriminate between the two. Certainly some measure of this power lies in the atom.

Since the purpose of all atomic matter is to aggregate into forms and to build increasingly better forms, we must concede the presence of intelligence guiding the dance of the atoms — their constant movement of building and disintegrating — until the sum total of nature, of the planet and its lifewave of humanity is realized.

All atoms, then, can be said to be expressing some form of intelligence: the chemical atom only obscurely so ... the human being, the larger atom, definitely so ... and the Heavenly Being or Solar Atom, expressing the Infinite Mind.

These searchings will lead us one day to an investigation of what we call group souls — the beings who have under their dominion the involution and evolution of the world of matter. Briefly stated, it is a group soul which guides certain atomic particles into the

Cosmic Atom

Solar Atom

Planetary Atom

Human Atom

Elemental Atom

THAT WHICH IS ABOVE IS LIKE UNTO THAT WHICH IS BELOW AND THAT WHICH IS BELOW IS LIKE UNTO THAT WHICH IS ABOVE' FOR THE PERFORMANCE OF THE MIRACLE OF THE ONE SUBSTANCE. (Hermes)

Our physical form is governed by the same physical laws that govern the minutest atom and the mightiest galaxy. But our consciousness is not limited by these laws. It can, if liberated from the confines of the physical senses, be pinpointed to the size of an atom or expanded to the vastness of a galaxy — without the aid of microscope or telescope.

building of the mineral kingdom. Another manifestation directs certain atomic particles into the formation of the vegetable kingdom. It is their intelligence which guides the atoms to form themselves into various structures — ever disintegrating and rebuilding.

Again, various group souls direct the intelligence displayed in the animal kingdom; that is, the animal displaying a marked degree of intelligence is reflecting an ability to operate under the superior guidance of the group soul of which it is a part. The human being, departing from the animal group soul, expresses as an individualized soul, creating karma and assuming the responsibilities for that karma.

Continuing our discussion of the life processes: the world of matter operates under the law of attraction and repulsion ... the law which integrates matter and spirit. Under this law, the forms of the world of matter are built up. The atoms combine into certain forms, disintegrate and combine again into more forms — the forms becoming ever more evolved and perfected.

Thus the various atoms create different kingdoms in nature — the mineral kingdom, the plant kingdom, the animal kingdom and the human kingdom — through the process of involution and evolution. Involution is the process of the lifeforces becoming involved in the world of matter; evolution is the process by which lifeforces liberate themselves from the world of matter.

This perpetual process is *the process of becoming!* The process of involution occurs during a period of time in which atoms envelop themselves with increasing limitations, perpetually descending ever deeper into matter. Having once arrived at the ultimate depth, they then proceed to adapt themselves for a certain time to their imprisonment, after which begins the process of evolution.

This expanding process requires the atom to disintegrate some forms constantly to perfect other forms until, having arrived at its ultimate height, or perfection, it transcends the world of matter to create the higher spheres and the forms thereof.

This same process is carried out in the human kingdom. The soul takes on a physical form. In the early days it rebels against its limitations, then succumbs to a period of adaptation. You, reaching maturity, express personal talents to achieve your desires. You utilize to the utmost your threefold form: the physical, the emotional and the mental.

Finally you arrive at the later stages in life when the soul, outgrowing the limitations and crystallizations of the form, begins to seek release, causing the form to become increasingly inadequate.

Then comes the time of that enigmatical experience we call death. The soul, shaking off its bonds of earth, escapes the imprisonment of the physical form, leaving it to disintegrate into the world of matter. The soul is released to function in a more adequate form.

The purpose of the atom of chemistry is to produce the finest form possible in the world of matter. The purpose of the human — the larger atom — is to expand your consciousness to its ultimate potential. The purpose of the cosmic atom — the solar system — is to perfect its kingdoms throughout the spheres of life.

The atom, building forms in the mineral kingdom, displays a discriminative selectivity. In the plant kingdom, a second quality appears — that of rudimentary responsiveness to love and attention. Plants have demonstrated this response under experimental tests. The atoms of the animal kingdom display the selectivity, the responsiveness and a developing quality of love, through instinct, operating under the guidance of group souls.

You, displaying all these qualities in increased degrees, display also the qualities of the individualized human soul. You dominate the other kingdoms and possess the potential of immortality. Through the process of intelligent will, you are the deity of your own little individual kingdom — your own personal solar system. You guide and control your kingdom according to your own responses to the immutable law of attraction and repulsion.

You hold in your own personal domain the care of your physical form, the control over your emotional nature and the karmic responsibility of your actions. You fully realize that you are not your form but that you exercise considerable control over its well-being and that when you, as a spirit, withdraw from your form, it disintegrates back to the "dust" of the plane of matter.

The Supreme Solar Deity evolves also, expressing His/Her evolutionary processes through the totality of the kingdoms of nature. In the human kingdom, the Divine Parent causes the buildup of religion, science and philosophies.

The lifewaves of humanity rise to great heights, expressing as evolved civilizations. They sink to the lower levels of consciousness as the Great Being sweeps into manifestation the lesser aware entities of lifewaves. These entities, both elementary and evolved, express as but atoms in the divine form, the older evolved souls reflecting divine glory and the younger souls their more basic evolutionary beginnings.

Sight --
The Soul-Sense of Humankind

Second Degree — Lesson Eleven

THE LIGHT OF THE BODY

When the Nazarene walked the ways of the world he taught of many mysteries. He taught of the eye. He said: *"The light of the body is the eye."* The people pondered. The priests were confounded.

What did the Master mean?

His meaning remains a mystery — for of all the physical senses you possess, sight is the most enigmatic. It performs unique functions on behalf of your body, soul and spirit which are not even realized by most persons, certainly not understood.

This electronic age is revealing some of nature's most closely guarded secrets. We can now begin to understand, scientifically, what the ancients knew without benefit of science — but the world of both electronics and medicine still stands perplexed before the baffling phenomenon of sight in God's creature — the human being.

It sees us "see" — it traces the operation of sight into our brains, into the cells of the cerebral cortex, the optic nerves, the optic thalamus. But the world of science cannot find the force or faculty that gives us the power to see with these cells. Both layperson and scientist still ask: *"What lies in these cells that enables us to see God's world around us?"*

Seeking the answer to this question is like trying to find "life." Where is it? Life! What is it? From whence came the mysterious force called life into a form that it animates? Does the gift of sight lie in our brain cells, or is it in that intangible possession called "consciousness" — this gift that lets us "see" the world? Lo, could the ancients have been right when they taught that the soul is the seat of sight?

As usual, we shall begin our journey of exploration with a physical description of our subject — the eye.

The eye is spherical in shape. Technically it is composed of three parts — the outer coat called the *cornea;* the middle coat, the *iris,* which also contains the *pupil;* and the inner structure, the *retina,* in which the lens is located.

The outer layer which contains the cornea is composed of fibrous tissue. The middle layer contains a network of blood vessels which supply the eye with blood. The inner layer is a muscle-containing structure from which the crystalline lens is suspended. Called the retina, it contains what are called rods and cones. The rods and cones are connected with the fibers of the optic nerve, and are particularly sensitive to light.

From an anatomical standpoint it is important to remember that the eye is not a separate part of one's being, but is integral with the entire physical form, and is affected by whatever affects the body. It is particularly allied with the stomach. That which upsets the stomach will invariably affect the eyes and vice versa.

We can be compared to a camera stalking through the world on its tripod (or actually bipod), forever taking motion pictures. In the eye mechanism and the brain lies the camera apparatus necessary for the multifarious sights of the world to be properly focused and adjusted in order for the individual to perceive life and the outer world.

The lens of the camera is comparable to the pupil and iris of the eye. The retina corresponds to the photographic plate. Beyond these technical similarities the eye itself differs from the camera, but we find other equivalences if we move to the consideration of the sight-registering mechanism in the brain.

The retina, which we have compared to the camera's photographic film, is the receiver of direct light rays. It is interlaced with filaments of the optic nerve and, through these tributaries, is connected directly with the optic nerve itself.

THE SCIENCE OF SEEING

We do not actually "see" with our eyes. The nerves of the eyes join with the two optic nerve tracts of the brain which carry the impulses inward to the occipital lobe of the brain. To again compare the eye with the camera: the eye photographs the sights of the world but the resulting visual impulses are transferred to different sections of the brain where they are registered, developed and perceived. Our eyes are only the cameras which "take" the photographs of our world. The vision lies in the optic nerve tracts and the nerve fibers which end in the *cortical retina* at the back of the head in the occipital area.

This statement is important enough to repeat: *The eye is only a camera which visually perceives the scenes of the surrounding world.* This cognition, which takes the form of electrochemical impulses, is then transferred into the optic thalamus which acts as a developing tray where the film of the pictures is developed. The image is then projected to the back of the head in the occipital lobe where the developed film with its image is actually seen.

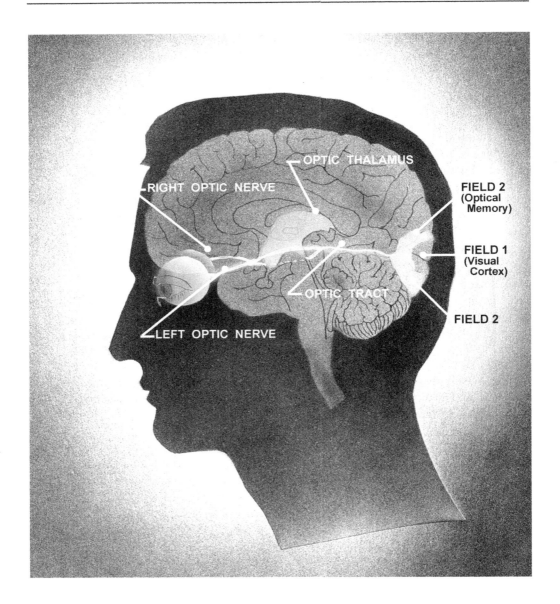

We do not see with our eyes. The eyes take pictures of the sights of our world, the images are developed in the optic thalamus, and then projected to the occipital lobe where the pictures are actually seen. FIELD 1 contains the cells of the lobe.

FIELD 2 contains the cells of optical memory. If FIELD 1 is destroyed, the individual is blind even though the eyes may be perfect. If FIELD 2 is destroyed, one can still see and observe an object but is unable to recognize it or attach any memory to it.

If the occipital area is injured, the individual becomes blind even though the eyes themselves remain organically and structurally perfect and intact, and even though the incoming film is developed perfectly in the optic thalamus. The individual cannot see simply because the cells of the cerebral cortex have lost their capacity to perceive and see.

The eyes — perhaps the most precious vehicles of all the senses — are God's special blessing, for particularly through the process of sight the soul is able to contact and gain experience from the physical world. Nature jealously guards these instruments of the soul by enclosing them completely in a bony structure.

We must remember that the soul is encased in a prisonhouse of material substance which we call the physical form. This human body can only become aware and conscious of the world about it through its senses — seeing, hearing, feeling, smelling, tasting — and the two higher senses which we classify as:

1. *clairvoyance,* sometimes called "inner seeing" or "soul-seeing," which encompasses *clairaudience* (inner hearing) and all the *sense* perceptions of the soul;

2. *clairsentience,* which is "inner knowing" or knowing without the usual process of sequential thinking, and encompasses all the *intuitive* qualities of the soul.

The actual physical seeing by the soul through the eyes is the soul's most important contact with the world, for our observance of the world about us creates an instinctive recognition of our limitations. The resulting discontent and frustration is interpreted as a desire for progression in every sense of the word — materially, physically and spiritually.

It is true that people seldom realize this struggle for freedom through their eyes. Nevertheless, everything we behold causes an instinctive yearning for something better, for freedom from frustrating bondage. That which one sees which belongs to oneself, seems more desirable if belonging to the other person. That which one sees which belongs to the other person, is not quite as perfect as one would have it if it belonged to oneself.

We admire and desire our neighbor's Cadillac, but if it were ours it would have a different color and better accessories. The architect regards his/her colleague's design and building as most wonderful ... but not quite as marvelous as s/he would have created it. The painter scrutinizes the canvas of a fellow artist, and sees many areas of improvement had it been his/her own handiwork.

We never find our complete satisfaction on the plane of Earth. The eyes contribute more than we realize to our eternal sense of dissatisfaction, for they continually rest upon something we desire ... only better. And this is the story of humankind's evolution and progression. Our drive for something better on the earth plane signifies the presence of *the soul within.* For we must attain, must struggle against our limitations, must eternally seek that which we see but do not possess. We call it divine discontent.

It is the interminable hunger of the soul yearning for fulfillment. It is good that human beings of Earth seek always to build a better earth plane, even though at present most reach only for improved material conditions. The soul, sensing a potentially better world about it, though unseen, attempts perpetually in its own way to re-create that better world out of the materials at its disposal. And this is good. Earth must be lifted up to heaven, and heaven must be duplicated among humans. Through the eyes of each person and the quest for desire-fulfillment this high goal attains some measure of realization.

THE ETHER AND THE EYE RAY

Although medical science is well equipped to handle the physical difficulties of the eyes, it is at a loss to truly understand and explain their complex mechanism. How is it that the eyes actually see the objective world? We know that the eyes themselves do not actually do the seeing. We know that perplexing mysteries are involved in the visual processes such as recognition, perception of the light, color, form, depth and distance. This aspect of human beings — sight — is still an unexplored and unexplained enigma.

Mysticism can explain more of the enigma, for it recognizes the presence of the four physical ethers about which we have taught: the electric, pranic, light and mental reflecting ethers. In the function of seeing, we automatically utilize the highest of these — the mental reflecting. This vaporous ocean of unseen substances is the actual carrier of the necessary emanations involved in the visual process.

Rays of electromagnetic energy, issuing from the eyes, meet etheric emanations issuing from the objects of the material plane. Through the flow of the mental reflecting ether, the eye rays register upon the lens and retina of the eye, calling into response the complete network of the optic nerve itself, from its laboratory near the posterior section of the brain. An actual ray of electromagnetic energy streams forth from the eyes where it contacts the mental reflecting ether of the atmosphere about us. This ether is, itself, charged with magnetism necessary to transmit the auric emanations of all objects into the ray from the eye.

The electromagnetic energies streaming from the eyes do not themselves meet actual objects of the objective physical world, but meet rather the emanations of the objects. The mental reflecting ether then acts as the vehicle for these emanations to the rays of the eyes, which "beam" the sights along the optic tracts back into the cells of the occipital lobe of the brain.

A crude comparison of this operation may be found in the way a pilot and the plane "ride the beam" to a landing at an airport. An electronic beam or ray is sent out from the airport. The plane's receptive mechanism receives and registers the emanations and the pilot follows it to a safe landing. Guided missiles sometimes operate on a similar principle.

The world of medical science is just beginning to become aware of the presence of the eye ray. In *Science Digest Magazine,* a number of years ago, a brief article

The electromagnetic energies streaming from the eyes do not themselves actually meet the material objects of the physical world, but meet rather the emanations thrown off by the objects into the ethers about us. The mental reflecting ether then acts as a carrier of these emanations to the rays of the eyes, which " beam " the sights along the optic tracts back into the cells of the occipital lobe of the brain, where the object — in this case a flower — is seen.

described the activities of Dr. Leo E. Lipetz, biophysicist at Ohio State University, who discovered the eyes emit energy in the form of "electrical charges." Dr. Lipetz, in his experiments, connected tiny wires to the nerve cells in eyes removed from dead animals. The eyes were then exposed to light and the electric current created by the eye cells was amplified about a million times. Electrical reactions were observed by watching a wavy line on an oscilloscope screen.

The experiments revealed that under normal room light, the eyes generate about one-hundred millionths of a volt of electricity. Exposure to sunlight tremendously increases the voltage. This increase affirms the presence of SOMETHING in the sunlit ethers about us which stimulates what we might call the electromagnetic potential of the eye ray and helps to make sight possible.

We mystics accept the presence of the mental reflecting ether as the causative agent of this increased power of the eye ray. We suggest that medical science consider recognizing three principles which might reinforce its comprehension of the science of sight:

1. The actuality of the mental reflecting ether;

2. The presence of the ray of electromagnetic light which flows outward from the eyes signifying the presence of *the soul within*. We submit that it is the soul, using the mental reflecting ether as it penetrates the brain cells and the atmosphere of our world, which "sees" through the eyes; which uses the power and force of this ether to register as "consciousness" upon the brain cells; which perceives and understands;

3. the fact that all physical objects emit emanations of force and are surrounded by invisible auric forcefields.

The presence of these three electronic energies, coalescing and interacting as a triadal unit, results in the phenomenon of vision.

"But," says the medical world, "animals also see! They share with human beings the faculty of sight. Does this, then, place them in a common kingdom?"

The differentiation is simple, when sought metaphysically. A shepherd and a sheep both stand viewing the same panorama. But they do not see the same picture. The sheep dimly realizes that before him stretches the fulfillment of his physical needs, his desire for pasture — and this is the extent of his vision. His complete constitution operates instinctively under the law of self-preservation, for he functions under the automatic control of the group soul of which he is a part. He possesses no individual soul-sense of his surroundings. He perceives no beauty before him. He "sees" not the "truth" about him. He senses only that his preservation instinct may here be satisfied.

The shepherd experiences innumerable reactions. S/He perceives the good of the pasture, the necessity of the water-stream, and the beauty of it all, the esthetic, indescribable wonder of the divine world. Wherein lies the difference? Not in the mechanism of the eyes but in the perceiving CONSCIOUSNESS. It has to be the level of consciousness present in the form.

The eyes are there in both the forms, and the eyes of both sheep and shepherd behold the same view. But what a difference in perception! One is instinctual animal perception. The other is the broad, far-reaching potential perception of the individual human soul, gazing out through the confines of the human form, with its comprehensive mechanism within. Consciousness, consciousness, consciousness! One is the limited

A shepherd and sheep both view the same panorama. But they see not the same picture. The sheep dimly senses a fulfillment of his physical need for pasture and water. The shepherd perceives much more. Wherein lies the difference? Not in the mechanism of the eyes but in the perceiving consciousness.

animal consciousness, operating under the group soul, expressing only the self-preservation instincts. The other is the consciousness of human beings, operating as an individualized spark of the divine Flame which is God, evolving through the individual god-powers as s/he see fit to express them.

SEEING WITHIN THE CONSCIOUSNESS

Again, the eyes themselves do not actually see. They are only the instruments of the brain which record the sightwaves through the eyes. An injury to a particular brain center will cause complete blindness even though the eyes are perfect and unimpaired.

Since we know the brain itself to be only an outer manifestation of an inner force, we then recognize that consciousness is behind both instruments — the brain *and* the eye. Since consciousness is an aspect of the soul, since the brain cannot function without the mind and since the eye cannot function without the brain, it behooves us to stand in awe before the force actually represented by this mystery which we call human sight.

The eye is vital to the soul as it operates through the brain. However, the mind, an aspect of that soul, must be attached to both the eyes and the brain if there is to be brainpower and seeing power, or mental and sight perception.

A blind genius may possess no faculty of sight, but may reveal depth of perception and wisdom far beyond the conscious awareness of the average sighted individual. Therefore, there is much more to our vision than our eyes. Again, *consciousness is the answer to it all.*

The eyes and the tissues of the brain are highly receptive to the spiritual energies pouring down through the sutratma and into the ventricles, creating what we call the brain dews. If a closed mind predominates and persists, it is very much as if the personality closed the door on the flow of spiritual energies into the head. In such cases, when the eyes and brain tissues cannot be stimulated by the inflow of spiritual energies, just so will their functions be restricted and even atrophied. If carried over a period of several incarnations, the result most surely will be physical blindness in some incarnation, either partially or completely.

Narrow-mindedness and closed-mindedness are words synonymous with the closing of the spiritual inflow through the sutratma into the crown chakra. Therefore, seeker, guard against these mental restrictions and never close your mind against the aspects of spiritual growth and truth. To do so means that you have partially closed off some ray of divine energy which might have been extremely beneficial to both your physical and spiritual well-being.

Blindness and eye difficulties are not always caused, of course, by the inability to "see" truth, so do not judge others accordingly. Some of the world's great mystics have suffered with eye and sight problems. In fact, few people escape them.

SIGHT HEALING AMONG THE ANCIENTS

In the days when Master-healers walked the Earth, their extensive knowledge of the eyes as the powerful instruments of the soul was utilized to its fullest. Patients in need of healing were not taken to a hospital, but rather to a temple of healing. Oh, for the return of the temple atmosphere for our sick! Our hospitals are scrupulously clean ... but in their sterility they are also devoid of many esthetic qualities which might help the individual attain healing.

In the days of old, the grand Master-physician sought to gain a knowledge of the patient's aura. He or she questioned the patient closely not only to obtain a better idea of what the patient was eating but also "what was eating the patient." S/he delved into the problems in the patient's mind; s/he sought to understand the patient's heart, not merely with a cardiograph, but rather with the skillful probing of a greater instrument, the human mind. For s/he was priest as well as physician, and s/he understood well the importance of a problem smoldering in the heart. The ancient Master-healer worked with the whole person, mind, body and spirit as some of today's physicians are beginning to do.

S/he determined the components of the patient's aura, for the highly developed priest-physician possessed both etheric and clairvoyant vision. S/he could usually discern the colors surrounding the patient and could read their unerring message or, understanding the inner conflict, could surmise the resulting colors of the aura. These auric colors revealed the cause of the illness. Thus he or she set to work not simply to heal the body, but to reach the whole person and restore perfect health.

In the healing temples, s/he resorted to metaphysical processes and surrounded the patient with soothing, healing colors. Beheld by the eyes of the patient, mental tranquility resulted. Healing through the eyes! ... an ancient custom, long fallen into disrepute to the indescribable loss of a suffering world.

THE SUN RAY AND THE EYE RAY

The Master-healer caused the patient to be placed daily under a canopy of therapeutic colored quartz, comparable to glass, exposed to the rays of the sun. The rays were filtered and diffused through certain colors which would supply the patient's needs, as indicated by the reading of the aura.

For instance, a patient, according to his or her auric colors, might be placed under the red ray. Thus s/he was not healed simply through color alone but through the flow of the solar ray tinctured by the color red, which is the ray of physical energy and strength. If a patient had lost the will to live, had given up the struggle, if s/he was faced with a problem so stirring as to result in hopelessness, then the flow of the solar red ray flooded the atoms of the physical form with renewed lifeforce, producing a powerful flow of adrenaline hormone throughout the system. It restored the instinctive will to live, of which the self-preservation instinct is a reflex.

Although the ray itself entered the physical form through the navel chakra, it was the conscious perception, through the sense of sight, which stirred the soul to the desire for continued physical life, love and the pursuit of happiness.

If a patient had suffered mental shock, despair, nervous tension, or any of the human ailments connected with emotional chaos, the blue ray was utilized to inspire and restore serenity and peace of mind.

Different color rays were used according to the auric diagnosis of the patient. If the clairvoyant healer-priest observed an overabundance of boiling muddy-red clouds in the aura, it was obvious that the unfortunate patient was seething inside with some long-standing hatred. Her heart was filled with bitterness, a longing for revenge, a deep and abiding resentment.

The White Ray was directed to this patient — a combination of the blue ray, the violet ray and a mysterious silver ray, produced by painting the quartz-glass with a certain silver chemical — until the auric emanations were stabilized. Then a subtle, diffused gold ray was gradually added to the White Ray, causing a surge of spiritual forces in the individual.

For those who doubt the potency of sun rays beamed on and through glass let them, if possible, visit the Museum of the Desert in Palm Springs, California. On display there is a collection of violet colored glass. This previously clear glass has actually turned purple by absorbing the ultraviolet ray of the sun!

If the atoms of inanimate glass can change colors under the impact of these solar rays, think what a metamorphosis can occur to and in the atoms of the living, responsive physical form. The chemistry of the cells can be transformed, the colors of the aura changed, and a complete healing effected.

In the healing temples the quartz canopy was designed to diffuse the direct rays of the sun to avoid burning the body and to bathe the patient in certain colors. The sun rays themselves were effective only to the degree they were able to influence the consciousness of the individual through the eyes, for the purpose was not only to equalize the body chemistry through the balanced flow of glandular hormones, but to restore peace to a troubled mind. Healing the body was of little value if the patient could not gain a causative healing of the mind and spirit as well.

THE SHRINE NICHE

Possessing this vital knowledge, the therapists created a shrine for each patient, situated so that it was constantly before the patient's eyes — a niche in the wall in which some object of worship or spiritual devotion could be placed. Carved images or paintings of a beautiful garden or a child's face, or a loved one, or a saint in prayer — anything that might appeal particularly to the individual, according to the diagnosis of the colors of the aura. In most cases statues of saints or Masters were placed in the niche-shrine, softly lighted to inspire devotion. Just as today a picture or statue of the Holy Virgin or the Master Jesus, the Buddha, an ancient goddess statue or an animal totem can lift some persons to spiritual heights, so were there placed before the view of the patient, likenesses of exalted ones who were revered by the patient.

The purpose was to fill the shrine with objects of beauty so that the eyes of the patient would behold only beauty. For the wise ones well understood the effective power of vision — healing through the eyes.

Sometimes a painting of the patient was placed in the niche, an image expressing radiant health, joy and happiness. For the healers were aware that the patient may have created a thought form of imperfection, and that this thought form had become a vital part of the aura. If the patient, for instance, had experienced a stroke and suffered partial paralysis, the power of his or her own fears and worries created a deformed thought form — ill, in pain, crippled, paralyzed, misshapen — negative in every manner.

Since energy follows thought, the undesirable thought form had been endowed with tremendous energy and, having become attached to the aura, was a continual source of negative force throughout the physical form. The healers well knew that they must destroy the misshapen thought form and replace it with one of beauty and perfection. Thus they often placed a picture of the patient depicting radiant happiness, abundant joy and unbounded energy directly before the eyes so that s/he could gaze upon it constantly. They knew that whatever the eyes beheld could influence his or her healing. The negative thought form gradually lost its lifeforce as the sufferer began to see him or herself healed and whole once more, and the powerful, beautiful thought form of the perfect self eventually replaced the previous creation of deformity.

Sometimes only a lighted candle was placed in the shrine. Sometimes a perfect flower, sometimes a glowing star, a reproduction of a loved one who had journeyed to the otherside. But usually it was a painting or statue of some revered saint, Master-king or queen or priest-physician.

In early Egypt, for instance, a likeness of Zoser was utilized for this beneficent purpose for many thousands of years, both during his life and after he had departed, for he was deified by his own people for at least three thousand years following his physical death. A picture or statue of this magnificent priest-healer-king, banked with flowers and softly lighted, could lift any suffering Egyptian to new spiritual heights, for Zoser was leader of both Upper and Lower Egypt. It was under his reign that Egypt was united as one kingdom, and wars between the two regions ceased. The Egyptians revered him as a god-king, and he was their principal object of worship.

In these healing temples, music was also utilized to its ultimate. Soft strains of muted music constantly pervaded the rooms of the patients. And during the hours of the night with the objects of beauty in the shrine glowing faintly with diffused light, the voice of some Master-healer always spoke gently and quietly to all the patients. The voice spoke words of encouragement, of the love of the Infinite Being, quoted verses of inspiration, prayers, affirmations, softly lifting the subconscious mind of the ailing one toward inner peace, physical wholeness, spiritual perfection.

HEALING THROUGH THOUGHTFORMS

In those days of the healing temples, no one was worthy to be called a therapeutic healer until, through personal inner development, she or he had fully stimulated, opened and brought under full control the Third Eye, for s/he had need of its powers in many of the spiritual functions, particularly in healing.

By and through evolved mental processes s/he was able to create a powerful thought form of beauty and color — a re-creation of him or herself. A thoughtform, of itself, is not difficult to produce — alas, we all are constantly creating and projecting some type of thoughtform into our existing auras, to either haunt or help us. But only through an opened and operating Third Eye is one able to pour streams of beneficent energy into a thoughtform with sufficient lifeforce to exert a benign influence upon a patient.

The Master-healer was able not only to create such a powerful thoughtform of him or herself, but to project it near a patient. The energized thoughtform was then employed as a transmitter of healing forces. This same practice is continued today. We healers of Astara frequently project thought forms of ourselves to the vicinity of some afflicted Astarian in order to direct more powerful charges of healing energies to him or her. We constantly attempt this projection to the best of our ability — which is by no means comparable to that of the Master-healers.

One may well ask why such a creation is necessary. Cannot the Master-healer just as well project the healing force itself to permeate the physical form of the patient? This, of course, is true. A Master-healer *can* project the healing force directly into the physical form of a patient, and it is very effective. But to transmit it thusly indicates that it must enter the patient's form by means of the navel chakra, carried by the solar pranic ethers. For the healer to create a powerful thoughtform of him or herself, on the other hand, and project it to the vicinity of a patient is to cause the healing force to flow directly into the light ray emitted by the patient's eyes and to enter the Third Eye area, thereby stimulating this more potent center in the physical form.

Again, healing through the eyes! For the entrance of the healing forces into the crown chakra of the patient through the mental reflecting ether rather than through the navel chakra and the pranic ether, causes a far more powerful stimulant of the nerve fluids because they react upon the mind and not simply upon the cells of the body.

If the healer is a powerful practitioner, he or she is able to construct a most marvelous and powerful thoughtform, to control it, to project and direct it wherever desired, and then through it to transmit dynamic charges of healing energies to reach the patient through the eye rays, and thus restore the patient to physical perfection.

This energized thoughtform of the Healer is, in some cases, as desirable as the appearance of the Healer, for it can be held steadfast and constant, emitting a perpetual stream of healing force. And this is the actual purpose of the thoughtform — to maintain a constant physical and mental rapport with the disciple, ill or well.

The point to be remembered is that such a thoughtform cannot be properly created and manipulated until the Third Eye of the healer is in active operation. Healing through the eye ray is far more effective than healing through the navel chakra. It can only be accomplished by the most adept of healers, working mentally and creatively with the powerful force of the mental reflecting ether, and with knowledge of all the cosmic laws involved.

THE EYE RAY OF THE MASTER

In previous Lessons when teaching of concentration and meditation, particularly in Lama Yoga, we stressed the importance of having a picture of some Master Teacher. During your meditations you should place the picture before you, just as if it were in a shrine, and concentrate upon the eyes of the Master. For even a picture of a Master can become so magnetized as to possess some of the radiance of the eye ray, and the great one can direct a current of healing force through the eyes of the picture, just as if it were him or herself. Your own eye ray, too, will penetrate the area of the eyes, blending its qualities with those streaming from the picture itself, and bringing you into definite and positive contact with the aura of the Master.

This eye contact is similar to dialing your chosen one by etheric telephone, for your call reaches him or her through the mental reflecting ether just as surely as if s/he heard

In the healing temples of old, the Master-healers built a niche-shrine in the wall, containing a statue of some belōved figure. Constant viewing of this vision of inspiration brought peace of mind and healing.

your voice call the Master's name. The very surest line of communication is through the concentrated study of the eyes as you consciously and willfully direct your own "eye beam" upon the picture. S/He can employ the created ray of light to transmit healing forces, to charge you with renewed magnetism, to energize your psychic centers, even to speak to you if you have silenced the disturbing sounds of the physical world about you and opened your inner ear to receive the sound of the Master's voice.

With the increased development of the Third Eye it is important to be acquainted with the power of the eye ray, for it surely will become a science to be dealt with and understood by scientific and esoteric researchers in the decades ahead. Just as the cosmic rays of the sun are now discernible, though unseen in a visual sense, so will eye rays become measurable and discernible. This will become an accomplished fact as the Third Eye gains unfoldment and significance among esoteric scientists.

EGYPTIANS AND THE EYE RAY

The ancient Egyptians believed emphatically in the eye ray. They taught that the eyes possess a special magical power; that they project a singular "fluid" by which they could repel harm or attract beneficent forces. The Egyptians placed such sacred interpretations upon the eye and its magic ray that they had amulets made of the Sacred Eye and called it the *Usa*. Wearing this magical eye around the necks of the living was purported to give health and soundness of sight and granted immunity from danger.

When mummifying their dead the Egyptians placed the Usa on the neck, a knuckle or the heart of the mummy. Or a small incision was made in the abdomen and the Usa inserted. Wearing the Usa purportedly protected the spirit of the dead. The symbolic Eye was usually made of gold, lapis lazuli or a popular green stone called feldspar. They also carved the Usa as the "Eye of Osiris" on coffins and sarcophagi. The large wooden sarcophagus resting in the middle of the Egyptian Room at the British Museum contains the Usa.

The Egyptians were so convinced of the power of the eye ray that their literature often depicts Ptah, the Father of the gods, bringing forth all the other gods from the ray of his eye, thus signifying that of all the emanations from the body, the eye ray was by far the most powerful and supreme.

In many ancient writings and monuments a nude Hercules is shown with a large eye on each breast and on each thigh, presumably to protect him from the malevolent glance of his enemy.

The "eye single" which Jesus mentioned in Matthew 6:22 is common to all races and religions. The Egyptians called it by many names — the *Eye of Horus*, the *Eye of Osiris,* and *Usa*. Sometimes the "inner seeing" faculty of the Masters is referred to as *the opened Eye of Dangma.* In Hindu philosophy it is called *the Eye of Siva.* In fact, this mystic symbol of the eye single can be found on so commonplace an object as an American one dollar bill, where it appears as the crown of the pyramid on the Great Seal of the United States.

The Lord Buddha developed the divine Eye at the twentieth hour of his vigil under the bo-tree; on the following morning he attained the supreme knowledge of Buddhahood.

THE VISION OF THE FUTURE

The visualizing processes of the person of the future are destined to undergo unbelievable changes. As the pituitary and pineal glands evolve in their spiritual operations, the optic nerves will acquire increased power, nerve force, and visualizing potential. Remember, too, the brain cells themselves involved in the mechanism of sight will be attaining intensified power as the mind expresses evolving and expanding soul power.

In the distant day when humankind has realized perfection, each person will "see" and perceive with and through the entire body, as we now *feel* with and through it. Sight will not be limited to the instrumentality of the eyes. They will simply be used as focal points in the phenomenon of sight. People will be aware of "seeing" and discerning through every cell in the body. This statement is difficult to accept and may be discarded by any who choose not to receive it. Only the evolutionary processes possess the answer.

In those distant dawning days of glory, our eyes will behold that which is already there but now unseen. The retina which now registers the lightwaves of our physical plane only, will then be equipped to register the lightwaves of yet a higher plane. The nerve forces and fluids of the optic nerve will conduct the lightwave impulses inward to impinge upon more evolved brain centers, which are involved in the process of sight, and we will perceive wondrous worlds about us. We do not now speak of clairvoyance, but of future *visual processes* through the sense instruments, the eyes.

Just as your ears can now receive only sounds in a certain vibratory octave, and are deaf to sounds registering above or below that vibratory range, just so are the eyes limited to certain vibratory octaves. In the future, as our new and evolving optical processes align with the mental reflecting ether surging now into the Aquarian field of expression, the vibratory scale will expand and the higher vibrations and waves of energy impinging upon our new vision capabilities will reveal new worlds to us.

The seat of spiritual vision in future human beings lies not in the physical eyes themselves, but with the gradual unfoldment and perfection of the supreme Third Eye in the crown chakra. Through this most excellent of organs we will glimpse heaven worlds. It is true that *eye hath not seen nor ear heard the things which God hath prepared for those that love Him.* The eye of the present surely has not, but the eyes of the future most definitely will discern these incomparable glories the Creator has prepared for those "who have eyes to see."

For us simply to "see" these higher worlds is not sufficient. We must of necessity evolve the other senses and emotions simultaneously. To see into other worlds is only to bring back to our normal consciousness fragmentary visions. To become completely *aware* of other worlds implies the simultaneous evolvement of all the other senses. Particularly essential is that of the heart chakra, as it radiates in the new human a love force unrealized by us today.

Polarized in the solar plexus chakra, carnal emotions hold us in an evolutionary status considerably "lower than the angels" — indeed often on a par with the animal kingdom. Only the transmutation of emotional force upward out of the solar plexus into the heart chakra can bring humankind to a rightful angelic heritage.

The spiritualized and rarefied ethers of the Aquarian Age are even now beginning to be perceived and sensed. As these tenuous ethers begin to intensify, our senses and emotions must become correspondingly spiritualized in order to harmonize and attune to the impacts of the new vibratory field beginning to eddy and swirl about us. Higher octaves of etheric force will bombard our atmosphere and our eyes, particularly, must become increasingly sensitized to these octaves for us to become receptive to the changing ethers around the planet Earth and ourselves.

Through our expanded vision we will experience not only increased physical vision but will discern the etheric wonders of our own
material world. We will be able to witness the etheric emanations of any object; will be able to visually penetrate the physical form of anyone and diagnose properly the cause of disease.

We will possess the ability to observe the health aura and colors emanating from the form of a patient, the inflow and outflow of pranic ether; x-ray vision, piercing the thickest wall of physical matter and substance; clairvoyant ability to extend our vision to objects and places halfway around the Earth.

All the other senses will be sharpened automatically. We will become telepathic, with the ability to project a thought along an etheric wave and maintain it under our direct control. We can thus transmit a thought to some other mind and brain and enhance it with charges of etheric energy.

Realizing full well that we reach Godward only through the development of our visionary potential and the unfolding Third Eye, the wise ones of the ancient temples of learning and initiation always symbolized wisdom by the glowing, radiant, opened All-Seeing Eye, indicative of the unfolded Third Eye. Ah truly, we have not seen and cannot yet know what God has in store for those who love the Divine Source!

AFTERTHOUGHT

I recall an incident occurring in our modern times which indicates we are becoming aware of healing methods employed in the healing temples of ancient times.

Dr. Karl Konig, superintendent of the Camphill Rudolf Steiner Schools in Scotland, conducted an amazing experiment with a tiny blind lad who was trained to "see" through his skin. The child was four years old when the experiment was begun. An extreme introvert, very thin, he spoke only a few words and phrases.

Dr. Konig placed him on a couch surrounded by a screen of white sheets. He caused colored lights to shine through on the boy. He thus lay in a flood of different colors which were changed at intervals.

The lad soon began to react to the treatment. He began to speak easily, he learned to use thought power by memorizing poetry, he learned to sing. The texture of his skin changed and he became healthy and energetic.

Another blind-deaf child was placed in a darkened room with beams of colored lights projected upon his eyes. He soon began to "see." A lighted candle was placed between him and his teacher. He "saw" his teacher's gestures and imitated them exactly. He could "see" objects at a distance of two or three yards.

These experiments indicate it is possible to "see" through the skin, particularly the forehead and cheeks. This conviction and these experiments prove much of what has been taught in this Lesson — that medical science of the present time will some day, little by little, revert to the wisdom of the ancients and discover how truly advanced and wise they were in restoring people to wholeness.

It also indicates the trueness of my statement that in the future human beings will "see" with the entire body as we now feel with it. We believe the nervous system will evolve sensitive centers of sight over the entire form and each person will, indeed, "see" through the skin — via the nerves.

SUGGESTIONS FOR SIGHT IMPROVEMENT

I submit suggestions to disciples for maintaining strong vision. They are by no means meant to replace the use of glasses. Others may wish to ignore the suggestions completely, finding the use of glasses adequate and satisfactory. The suggestions are given for those who may wish to make use of them.

SUGGESTION ONE: According to articles written by leading doctors and published in a prominent health magazine, *Prevention,* one should eat sunflower seeds daily and take natural organic Vitamin A. They both can be purchased at any health store, and both are excellent for the eyes.

SUGGESTION TWO: Take these simple exercises, (Dr. Bates) which can be done in five minutes — even before arising. Squeeze the eyes tightly three times. Pause between each squeeze to blink the eyes. After completing the three squeezes, blink the eyes for about fifty times, taking time to take deep breaths and releasing the breath through the mouth. Yawn deeply a few times. These exercises drive fresh blood into the cells and muscles of the eyes and release tensions.

Also, any time of the day or night, cover your closed eyes with your palms. Then *with your eyes closed,* imagine there is the face of a clock before you. Look first at its center. Then raise your eyes up to 12, then back to the center.

Next look far over at 3 o'clock, and back to the center.

Now look downward at 6 o'clock, and back to the center.

Then over at 9 o'clock, and back to the center.

Again at 12 o'clock and back at center.

These exercises are not meant to replace the advice of a medical doctor, but may do wonders for the eyes. This and other exercises are found in the book I have written, *The Eyes Have It.*

THE MYSTERY
OF THE PYRAMID

How many candidates in the Mysteries were raised to enlightenment in the chambers of the Great Pyramid? What eternal truths were brought to light in the seeming darkness of that man-made symbolic cavern?

We moderns will never know its full, fascinating history. But we do know that it was a symbol of and a place for initiation into the higher Mysteries.

There is a pyramid in each of us. It is the cave of the heart. In a unique way it is a symbol of and a place for our journey to a higher status of enlightenment ... our initiation.

Lesson 12, *The Cave of the Heart* tells us that there is an embryonic god or goddess in this inner recess, waiting to be brought to full consciousness. This esoteric study of the heart shows us how to become a "heart-thinker," and thereby rewrite the records in the inner   archives of the Self. It tells us how to clear the channel to the Oversoul.

Lesson 13, *Initiation and the Saving Blood* provides insight into the mysteries of the blood-stream. It explains the meaning of many mystical references in religious scriptures to the blood as a channel of life, energy, emotional expression, holy communion, and initiation. You will learn how the ancient dramas of the Greater Mysteries contain truths which are important to you today.

AS YOU CREATE YOUR DESTINY,
KNOWLEDGE IS A PRINCIPAL INGREDIENT.

LESSON 14, HEALING AND THE BLOOD: Contains arcane information concerning the invisible ethers and their place in healing, how they influence the bloodstream and the subconscious mind, how we react to influences from "outer" space, the cause of hereditary influences and the real meaning of blood kinship. Explains the new age, the new person and the new God. Learn of the two "great delights" toward which we are evolving.

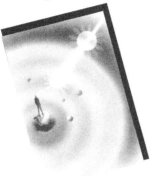

LESSON 15, THE SCIENCE OF SALVATION: *Beginning, God, Christ* — the words contain much that we cannot comprehend, yet there is much which could be understood if it were not for the sands which time, misunderstanding, error and deliberate falsehood have deposited upon them, dulling their glory and hiding their wisdom. The pages of this Lesson brush away the sand that you might see for yourself what lies beneath. For instance, learn of the five celestial rivers that flow from the plane of Divine Substance — spiritual energies which you can perceive or absorb.

LESSON 16, SALVATION AND MYSTIC CHRISTIANITY: To some the Christian-Judaic Bible is a mountain of confusion, to others an eternal monument of spirituality. It is indeed a book of Mysteries, and its dramas when rightly understood reveal life's significance. Learn what it really is to be the Lamb of God, to participate in the Passover, to partake of the Last Supper, to be crucified upon the heavenly cross, to experience the second birth and to find the inner New Testament.

THE SEED TIME

Lord, the shadow has passed by and
    Peace now fills my breast;
My days are warm with happiness,
    Thy love is manifest.

But I have been down in darkness
    Engulfed in my tear-walled gloom,
And I have drunk deep from the bitters
    Of the River Acheron.

Though the light on my path may diminish
    And the shadows once more fall,
I thank Thee for treasured moments
    And that light did come at all.

The strength and the wisdom garnered
    From these sweet days of calm
Will help me reach to others
    With strength and healing balm.

And when I enter my last sleep,
    And walk in higher Lands,
May others come and reap the seeds
    Planted by these weak hands.

— Earlyne

The Cave of the Heart

Second Degree — Lesson Twelve

OUR INNER PYRAMID

We pause in wonder and perplexity as we contemplate the Great Pyramid in the desert of Egypt.

But we stand even more in awe of the superb mechanism and construction of the human heart, after which the pyramid is patterned, for the human heart bears evidence of the supremacy of the Creator who constructed it.

It was a familiar fact to the ancient mystics that all the pyramid-temples were designed after the formation of the heart. Well did they know that only through initiatory rites, symbolizing the heart mystery, could the capstone of the pyramid in the human being find its place in the radiant Third Eye. It is a truth that we arrive at our godhood only through purification of the heart center. The divine fire in the "infernal world" at the base of the spine can rise only through the purified heart center to reach the "Holy Mount" in the head.

THE ANATOMY OF THE HEART

The heart is approximately five inches in length, three and one-half inches in breadth and two and one-half inches in thickness. It weighs from eight to twelve ounces. It is a muscle, divided into four cavities. The two lower cavities are called *ventricles* and the two upper cavities are called *auricles*. The pulse point, or that place in the heart where its beat originates, is found in the right auricle. The great vagus nerve leads from the pulse point upward to end in the medulla oblongata.

The first indication of life is the beating of the heart in the fetus forming in the mother's womb. It first becomes apparent around the third month of pregnancy. At this early stage the human embryonic heart resembles that which is found in the adult of the lowest vertebrates. As development continues, this single tube splits into two cavities, an auricle and a ventricle, at which stage it closely resembles the heart of the next higher vertebrates, the fish.

The next stage of development subdivides, bringing into existence three cavities which resemble the fully developed heart of the next higher vertebrate, the amphibian. In the final stages, subdivision occurs in the ventricle and the heart at birth contains four cavities.

This development only evidences again that the human embryo, during the months of formation, passes through all stages representative of various ascending vertebrates. This is the law of recapitulation in action, which teaches that in our embryonic development human beings repeat the process of the evolutionary history of humankind.

The heart does not lie upon the left side of the body as is so commonly supposed, but occupies a point very nearly in the middle　of the body in the thoracic cavity or chest, immediately above the diaphragm.

THE SEED ATOM IN THE HEART

We have said that the heart is a muscle, divided into four principal cavities — the upper auricles and the lower, larger, ventricles. In the upper right auricle lies the seat of one of the greatest mysteries — the mystery of life itself. For here is discovered the home of the physical permanent seed atom — the *Book of Life*, the record-bearer of each person's destiny.

Medical scientists, not yet recognizing the presence of the supreme seed atom, even so are amazed at the baffling mystery of life in the human heart. This tiny laboratory of life is known to them simply as the *pulse point*. Some call it the *sinus node*. Not understanding its mystery, they simply know that it "beats" life into the human being — that this pulse point is the "place" where life first originates in the fetus in the mother's womb and is the last to die when we depart the earthly realm. With cessation of the heart beat, life ceases to exist in the physical form.

Medical scientists could gain immeasurable understanding concerning this life center in the heart by perusal of ancient scriptures and writings, which reveal much of the heart's mystery and its significant occupant, the seed atom.

The mystery concerning the heart involves the sutratma or silver cord, and the physical seed atom buried at the pulse point. Concerning the silver cord, we have said that it extends from the divine Monad straight into the caverns of the heart. Though the sutratma itself continues down to the base of the spine, the life cord terminates in the pulse point. Thus the seat of life activity is located in the heart and focalizes in the area of the permanent heart seed atom.

THE HEART FLAME

The life cord within the sutratma extends from the divine Monad to the pulse-point in the heart. The heart seed atom is found in the pulse-point. It is surrounded by a miniature fire which is the perfect image of the Monad overshadowing you.

Surrounding the seed atom there blazes a miniature volcano of Divine Fire which reflects the perfect image of the divine Monad overshadowing you. This Fire actually radiates a "flame" about the size of a human thumb. The eminent physician and mystic, Paracelsus, left records of his scientific search for the "flame," and in his writings he tells in full of this evidence of divinity in the heart. He called the heart Fire *the Dweller in the heart equal in size to the last joint of a man's thumb.*

Paracelsus received his instructions concerning this heart flame from the Arabians who had written in their scientific records that: *If a certain point in the heart of a living animal be touched with the finger, the heat is so intense that a blister will result.* The Hindu mystic Sankaracharya describes the home of the Fire in the heart as *a light the size of the thumb in the cavity of the heart.*

The Upanishads say: *The soul dwells within us, a flame the size of a thumb. When it is known as the Lord of the past and the future, then ceases all fear.* And the Katha Upanishad: *Like a flame without smoke, the size of a thumb, is the soul; the Lord of the past and the future, the same both today and tomorrow.*

This image of the Divine Fire is simply a reflected replica of the divine being which you will one day become. It shines there in all its luminosity and glory as the deity manifesting in the activities of the human, yet sleeping in "sweet repose."

Most of the earlier mystics knew well the mystery of the heart, and the Dweller within. In the heart of its "flame" lies the imperceptible seed atom. The image of the Macrocosm is buried in this seed atom in your heart, just as the majestic oak is buried deep in the heart of the acorn. The electro-magnetic force operative in that single atom is the undifferentiated flame of divinity. This mysterious, electromagnetic force is the complete seed of life and without it the body would know no "life." All the other atoms of the body must harmonize with its cosmic vibratory "Sound."

It is in this secret cave of the heart that one of the most important initiations occurs. It cannot be realized until the embryonic spark of divinity in the cave awakens to full consciousness, and this cannot occur until the individual has purified the seed atom and the bloodstream of degenerate karmic picture images.

According to Paracelsus: *The human blood contains an airy, fiery spirit, and this spirit has its center in the heart, where it is most condensed and from which it radiates, and the radiating rays return to the heart.*

We have told you that this permanent physical seed atom carries a record of the karma of all your past lives so far as your physical forms are concerned. The astral seed atom in the solar plexus records the emotional record, and the mental seed atom in the pineal gland records the mental record.

Thus any errors and any perfections experienced in past lives are recorded in this physical heart seed atom just as surely as if they had been photographed by a camera and rolled into the atom like a miniature reel of a motion picture film. All things registered in this particular life as cause and effect or karma, will also record themselves in the corpuscles of the blood, which will carry them to the heart atom where they are indelibly recorded.

We have referred to the fire at the base of the spine as the divine fire, and we have said the flame in the heart is the seat of divine fire. The fire at the base of the spine is kundalini, and it does not become "divine" until it rises to be purified in the laboratory of the activated heart chakra. The fire in the heart, though it truly *is* the focal point of the divine fire in the human body, actually remains passive and fails to radiate divine qualities until *after* kundalini has been raised to, and purified in, the heart.

THE RECORD OF YOUR DESTINY

The heart seed atom bears the record of your destiny. Into it is ultimately poured all the attributes of the physical being, and it becomes your akashic record. The "germ pictures" of all past lives, which the ancients termed "spirits and demons," are released gradually throughout the bloodstream by the heart seed atom. Thus it is erroneous to say a child has inherited some weakness from a parent. It is more correct to say that the blood is carrying the weakness of the individual to the particular area which is responding.

For instance, should a mother have weak eyes and her child also evidences weak eyes, it may not be that the child has inherited the weak eyes of its mother. This would mark gross injustice on the part of our Creator. It would be more correct to assume that the child came into this present incarnation with the inherent weakness in its own physical form and, through the workings of the blood, fell under the influence of its "ancestors," which is to say, the influence of its own past bodies in past lives.

This is not to say that the same disease from which a person dies will again be part of the body in the next life, but it is to say that the blood will bear a record of the past, both good and bad. Thus each person will have an innate tendency toward any habitual problem or weakness. The blood, of course, picks it up from the seed atom which stores it in itself as a trait.

In the Scriptures, the Lord upbraided Samuel for his belief that God might be appeased in his judgment upon the wrongdoer who, in Samuel's eyes, committed outward signs of worship rather than living a true spiritual life. The Lord said: *"The Lord seeth not as man seeth, for man looketh on the outward appearance but the Lord looketh on the heart."* (1 Samuel 16:7) Samuel was aware that those possessing higher sight can discern the record of the physical life as it lies buried in the heart seed atom.

In Proverbs 4:23, we find this admonition: *Keep thy heart with all diligence; for out of it are the issues of life.* The writer of these momentous words must have been an initiate who was aware that out of the heart issued, in truth, the life record of our past, and in much wisdom admonished us to "keep our heart with all diligence," since by so doing the "stained" karmic record becomes gradually obliterated and replaced with a better record of spiritual life and attainment.

Once the seeker understands the import of the record of life held in the permanent atom, many things become revealed. You understand better the words of David when he said: *"Your heart shall live forever,"* meaning the perpetual record of your life is being forever written in the heart seed atom.

Thus do we also better understand the admonition, *As a man thinketh in heart, so is he.* For then we come to know that as you think in your heart so is registered therein your true nature, be it good or evil, for out of the seed atom will pour karmic pictures as constant reminders of your daily deeds and thoughts regardless of how you try to veil your true nature from the outer world.

The sage and the Master can read the record of the seed atom and know at a glance how a person "thinketh in the heart," whether that person be true or false. Could this, then, be what the Master Jesus referred to when he said: *"The kingdom of heaven is within you"?* No doubt he was also familiar with the teachings of the Upanishads which declare that *both heaven and Earth are found in the ethers of the heart.* The tiny reflection of your divine Self lies buried deep in the pulse point, surrounded by its own miniature forcefield, awaiting the "redemption" of the human body from mortal "sin" — recorded in the heart seed atom.

It has been asked that when medical science transplants hearts, will the new heart have a new seed atom? Would it affect one's karmic record? The answer is no, there will not be a new seed atom. The seed atom is not of dense physical substance. It only uses the heart as a home in the body because that organ is the pumping station for the blood which distributes the picture images of the seed atom throughout the body.

When a leg is lost, the etheric double of the leg remains. When a physical heart is removed and another transplanted in its place, the etheric chakra of the true heart remains, which is the real home of the atom. While one's karma is not transplanted along with the heart, certain qualities of the personality who donated the heart do sometimes seem to carry over into the organ recipient. These most often begin to diminish after the first few weeks of a successful transplant.

AN ESOTERIC STUDY OF THE HEART

The abdominal brain in the solar plexus chakra predominates humankind's decisions and thinking at the present stage of evolvement since we are the victims of our personality desires. The abdominal brain is the ruling center in the body *from an emotional and physical standpoint.* A person neither reasons completely with the head nor altruistically with the heart in the majority of cases, but is influenced by the domination of self-desires which lead always along the pathway of materiality, seldom upward toward spiritual attainment.

The heart chakra, between the shoulder blades, superimposes the heart. It is by far the most dominant center in the body today, *from a spiritual standpoint.*

Although the multitudes are ruled by the solar plexus brain, those who have become seekers are activating the heart chakra by raising and transmuting their desire energies into love energies by thinking with their hearts and not submitting to the persuasions of the solar plexus passions and emotions.

Through the end of the Piscean Age and as we move further into the Aquarian Age, the petals of the heart chakra have begun to unfold and turn upward toward the throat chakra. That is to say — the heart force center, composed of etheric and atomic particles, has been charged with positive activity, whereas previously only negative passivity existed. It has been a "stirring up of the gift of God" in singular individuals who faced the challenge of the search for God. All the chakric force centers when stirred into vibrational activity, actually resemble the upturned leaves of an unfolded lotus.

The flow of spiritual energies through these centers should rise freely through sushumna from kundalini to the head centers. When it is impeded the leaves of the lotus are denied their life source and, like the petals of an unopened bud, the chakra remains closed.

The root chakra, the splenic-navel chakra and the solar plexus chakra have pulsed with full and forceful activity as humankind has lived through evolutionary childhood. Lower passions have ruled most people and they have been more-than-willing victims of their desires.

Through countless incarnations in the flesh and through lessons learned in the bitter school of experience, the average person is being molded into the shape and glory of the god or goddess to be. We now begin to approach our decisions cautiously. We heed more readily the voice of conscience that speaks to us through the heart center.

We are beginning, through our own will and inclination, to raise the carnal-emotional energies from the solar plexus to the heart chakra where, under the power of the indwelling spiritual force, our passions are cooled and tempered. Our instincts are less impulsive and our   motives more altruistic.

We are beginning to weave the radiant bridge of light between the solar plexus chakra and the heart chakra, called the *antahkarana of the heart.* This stream of light energy, created solely by our own spiritual efforts, is the pathway over which kundalini will be raised. Along this electromagnetic bridge of energy kundalini can escape from its confines in the "infernal regions" of the root chakra and, through a process of transmutation, travel up sushumna to the upper region.

But it can progress no further upward than the antahkarana has been created, since kundalini must use the antahkarana as a bridge over which to travel.

In the course of evolution, humankind has constructed the antahkarana between the root and solar plexus chakras so that, in most individuals, kundalini no longer sleeps in passive repose in kanda at the base of the spine. It extends into the solar plexus chakra and smolders there like a partially active volcano.

Each person, through the power of his or her own will and spiritual efforts, must now construct a further span of the antahkarana between the solar plexus and the heart, providing a pathway over which kundalini may be raised into the heart center where the kundalini fires are transmuted first into altruistic ideas, then into selfless love, and finally into divine Love.

THE HEART THINKER

Since the heart chakra is the sun of the entire physical organism, just so will light begin to fill the aura of the heart-thinking disciple or seeker. It cannot escape being so, any more than the universe can escape the rays of the physical sun. The energy rays of the heart center will become increasingly dominant in the life of the heart thinker and, in just the degree that the light shines in the aura, will divine Love begin to be an obvious part of this seeker's world. As the heart lotus opens its petals to receive light from the head chakras, it signifies that the emotional nature and all the desires of the personality are blending harmoniously with the wisdom of the mind.

The heart-thinking disciple is usually one who is connected very closely to his or her unseen Teacher. You may not even be aware of the closeness with which your Master regards you, for the hierarchy still may be upon the inner plane activities of your life and not yet part of your outer waking consciousness. Nevertheless, you will be "a disciple in the Master's heart," which means the Master is using you to the fullest extent of your spiritual abilities in carrying on a great deal of inner plane activity.

The astral body of the heart-thinker no longer vibrates constantly with changing emotions, but becomes constant and steadfast in its purer and more radiant light. The bloodstream, which in earlier days picked up karmic picture images from the astral-emotional seed atom in the solar plexus, now finds fewer and fewer karmic patterns released through that atom, and an increasing number of higher types of karmic patterns emanating from the heart seed atom.

This is an automatic process, indicating there is increasing activity in the development of the cerebrospinal nervous system and that the subconscious mind is

THE THREE BRAINS

In addition to the cranial brain, we possess a solar plexus brain, and the root brain at the base of the spine. These last two are called "brains" in that they are powerful centers, influencing our minds and thoughts. At present, humankind is dominated by the solar plexus brain, which is shown fully unfolded. The heart center is shown inactive, as a closed lotus, but which will unfold to its full radiance. Note the cord extending between the solar brain and the heart. It is over this cord, created by our own efforts, that the energies must rise into the heart chakra and be transmuted. When this happens the heart chakra will radiate light and the solar brain will become inactive, just opposite to our present illustration.

being subjugated to the control of the waking conscious mind. The waking conscious is, to some extent, controlling the rampant sympathetic nervous system. The disciple begins to modify or regulate some of the functions of the body which have usually been more or less automatic.

When this is the focus of one's life, one becomes a yogi — which means he or she has united with god-powers to a degree and begins to master and control automatic functions of the subconscious mind. The nerve fluid becomes increasingly magnetic as the solar fire in the heart center radiates in ever-increasing activity. The magnetism of the aura cannot help continually attracting higher and better circumstances into his or her life.

As a Person Thinketh in His or Her Heart

First let us consider the process as it occurs in the solar plexus thinker. Let us say you are one who still thinks with the solar plexus brain and someone brings you a report concerning an unfortunate incident in the life of a friend. This friend has committed some misdeed, an error in judgment, for which the world sits in criticism and condemnation.

As you listen to the sorry tale by the one who feels it necessary to enlighten you, a thought of pleasure at someone else's mistake rises in your consciousness. The solar plexus thinker instinctively reacts this way. It seems a natural reaction, to sense pleasure in an error made by another. Perhaps you feel a surge of pity, but always there first is an inner sense of exultation that the mistake was made by someone else and not by you.

You immediately start sending your own added thought impetus of criticism, condemnation, pious judgment, intolerance — adding power to the dismal thoughtform already created in the aura of the unfortunate one. Perhaps you, in your own turn, pass along the story of the misdeed, adding to the troubles of your "sinning" brother or sister.

Let us now say that you are a *heart-thinking disciple* and you hear this same report. What, then, do you do? Immediately you send out an enveloping surge of soul love toward your struggling friend and attempt to absorb the complete aura of the undesirable thoughtform which surrounds this person.

You open your heart chakra as if it were a real door upon hinges, and you attempt to destroy the dark thoughtform completely by drawing it toward your own heart center. Once the thoughtform is anchored to you, you attempt to transmute its darkness into nothingness by the alchemy of heart love and surrounding your heart in White Light. You start immediately projecting a steady stream of love, kindness, forgiveness, upliftment and encouragement to your unhappy friend.

You speak words of kindness to the one who brought you the story, and tell this person you consider it possible this happening may well be within the karmic pattern of the unfortunate friend and that, since you are a disciple on the path, you are in no position to judge. Practicing heart-thinking, you will absorb all unpleasant things into the heart chakra and devitalize the negative thoughtform through the positive alchemy of your own heart love. This is a definite science which, *when practiced often and thoroughly, will become second nature with you.* You will never pass along gossip, you will never send back to anyone an unpleasant thoughtform. You will learn to fortify yourself strongly with love thoughts, harmony, peacefulness and beauty. In your everyday practical life you will be living the life of a heart-thinker. To feel a thought of criticism for another will be completely foreign to your nature. It is truly unbelievable what a transformation can come into your life as daily you practice this science of the heart — *the science of absorption and transformation.*

Your true status as a heart-thinker can be gauged by your actions in connection with your use of this science. You must not, under an emotional urge, go to your friend to deliver a lecture, to offer unsolicited advice, or to enlighten this friend concerning your own "noble" endeavors. This will be the surest indication that you are only a surface heart-thinker. You must think with and pray from your heart without objectively interfering in the affairs of others. If you are a spiritual leader in a ministerial or counseling capacity, then perhaps the struggling one will seek your advice, in which case you most surely can do this person service by offering whatever help you can.

Results of Heart-Thinking

When the heart center becomes completely awakened, it begins radiating spiritual energy toward the throat chakra and construction of the antahkarana is begun between these two centers. The antahkarana is the spiritual bridge we must build which will eventually extend from the heart to the Oversoul. It will travel via the vagus nerve first from the heart to the throat chakra, then upward through the crown chakra to fuse with the sutratma of the Oversoul.

As the bridge-building is carried out in practical everyday living, a transformation occurs in the life of the disciple which is obvious, usually, only to a watching and overshadowing Teacher. A golden mist appears around the head as the light of the crown chakra begins to radiate outward and upward. This will indicate to the Master that the disciple is prepared for intensified creative work, for the art of heart transmutation will already have been mastered.

Until a major degree of this science of heart alchemy has been mastered, no Teacher will trust a disciple with the usage of creative powers flowing from the throat chakra, for until the spiritual seeker becomes a heart-thinker and until the heart chakra is completely awakened, the seeker is involuntarily selfish, worldly, ambitious, vindictive and the victim of the solar plexus brain. Only when the heart center is completely opened will a Master trust a disciple with the creative powers of the throat chakra, for one can destroy as well as create through this all powerful center.

DEVELOPING EMPATHY

Becoming a heart-thinker is a personal matter with every seeker. Joining Astara, or any other esoteric school, cannot add one inch to the stature of your life. But practicing Astara's teachings can. Only you can accomplish this and it can be done only as you think in your heart. You will begin to recognize the awakening of the heart center as, within yourself, you develop what is known as *empathy*. Empathy can be compared somewhat with sympathy, except that it transcends it. To be empathetic with another is to be able to place yourself in their emotional and mental field of thought, and to feel in your own self their joy, their sorrow, their pain, their grief.

This is certainly far more than simply being sympathetic and understanding. It is actually to feel within yourself what the other is feeling. This is heart empathy and by this will the heart disciple be known. Only as you can keenly and actually *feel* what another fellow human is feeling can you demonstrate to what degree the heart center is actually opened.

As little by little the energy bridge between the solar plexus and heart chakra becomes strengthened, you will begin transmuting the energies of your personal desires into higher aspirations. Your passions become compassion, your carnal love, divine Love. Your longings embrace humanity and transcend thoughts of self. Even now the solar plexus center is shifting toward the heart center so that humankind, in developing divine Love nature, will concentrate the emotions principally around the heart. From there thought energies will be raised to the throat chakra and from there to the thousand-petaled lotus of the crown chakra.

COSMIC LONELINESS

Pouring through the sutratma is a constant downflow of spiritual energies. After the disciple has begun activating the heart chakra, these energies are concentrated in the vagus nerve. They constantly stimulate the chakric petals with spiritual force, coaxing them toward a gradual upward trend. We have already spoken of the effect of this spiritual energy in the life of the unfolding, upreaching disciple. It reacts as the "soul call from the boundless deep" which makes one feel utter aloneness on the godward pathway.

As the heart center begins to unfold there rises from it a feeling of unutterable loneliness and yearning. It causes the disciple to seek constantly for that which cannot be found here on the earth plane. S/he finds no satisfaction in the attainment of earthly gold. S/he finds no complete contentment in any earthly love. S/he forever yearns for that which is higher and that which alone can be grasped by the superconscious.

Only through the developing sense of intuition can the disciple understand that the loneliness experienced is the spark of divinity in the heart yearning to be once again united with the divine Monad which sent it forth. The spirit becomes homesick for its native land. The Prodigal Child longs to return to the Parent's home. Almost all Degree Astarians will have heard the Call and will have, to some extent, stirred the heart chakra into activity. Only as you couple your intellectual learning with your heart's yearning, will you be able ever to enter the Holy of Holies where you may find some answer to your cosmic loneliness.

THE HEART AND YOUR EMOTIONS

The transference of the solar plexus energies to the heart chakra is not without its tragedies and its difficulties. We speak of it reluctantly, but it must be obvious that one of the prominent diseases in the world today is known by such names as coronary thrombosis and angina pectoris, but which is popularly known simply as heart trouble.

Some of our greatest thinkers and leading disciples pass out of their physical bodies through heart failure. Also there is increasing difficulty with what we call mental ailments. To the discerning mystic the implication is that the heart and head centers have become unbalanced in raising solar plexus energies to the higher spiritual centers.

This is no criticism of the seekers who are victims of the so-called heart disease, for it is far better to overstimulate the heart energies than to refrain from stimulating them at all. The disciple who succumbs to heart trouble could indicate one who has overstimulated the heart chakra by sacrificing too much in service to humanity. This record of his/her discipleship will not mark this person as an unwise one but only as one who gave too freely.

Or it could indicate the opposite — one who refuses to manipulate the upflowing spiritual currents, and will not open the heart to or for others. The restricted and constricted etheric heart chakra finally manifests its obstruction in the physical heart, and it simply closes itself off from its source of life — the bloodstream — and the selfish individual dies of a heart attack.

Metaphysical reasons for heart failure usually fall into three categories:

1. The over-ambitious person who focuses all of life energies into gaining worldly desires. This person places too great a strain upon the heart center, caused by overstimulation of life energy flowing through one particular center, a force center not properly unfolded and prepared to receive such an impact.

2. The "cold" heart of one who closes off the heart center to the spiritual energies that seek to rise from the solar plexus, placing an unexpected strain upon a center too constricted to receive their inpourings.

3. The unfolded, but awakened heart center in one who gives too much in service
    to others. It not only seeks to house the upflow of spiritual energies from the
    solar plexus but to pour it out to a clamoring humanity who, without thinking,
    would drain both the spiritual and physical energies from this person.

The disciple-leader who understands that much of the work lies upon inner planes,
will guard against those who would place such a strain upon "giving" that life would be
cut short.

Since energy follows thought and since such a disciple will be thinking completely
with the heart, there could not help being an overstimulation of the all important heart
center which would carry this well-meaning one to an early demise.

OUR FUTURE POWERS OVER DESTINY

With humankind's ever-expanding consciousness we are acquiring more complete
control over the functions of our various organs. As a result of this conscious control
new development is occurring in the heart.

Again, the heart is a muscle. Our bodies possess both voluntary and involuntary
muscles. The voluntary muscles are controlled by the conscious mind and the will,
and operate as part of the cerebrospinal nervous system. They are the muscles in the
hands, arms, feet and all parts of the body that we mentally direct, at least to a partial
degree. These voluntary muscles contain fibers running both lengthwise and crosswise,
intersecting each other.

The involuntary muscles are those operating under the functions of the sympathetic
nervous system — such as excretion, digestion, respiration — muscles which operate
automatically without conscious effort, direction or thought. They are without the cross
fibers and are formed of lengthwise stripes. Usually the heart is listed as an involuntary
muscle, belonging to the sympathetic nervous system and under the control of the
subconscious mind.

But the heart is now developing muscular cross-stripes which indicates to both
medical and esoteric scientists that it is developing the capabilities of a voluntary muscle,
foreshadowing the day when we will consciously control the functions of our own hearts.
It will, at that far distant day, come partially under the dominion of the cerebrospinal
nervous system which means that, although it will still function automatically under the
direction of the subconscious, it will be subject to control by the conscious mind. We will
control the functions of our hearts by the power of our will when we desire to do so. The
heart will then be operating both objectively and subjectively.

The yogi — the holy one of the East — has proven time and again that one can
successfully live without the heart beating. He or she can start it or stop it at will — not
totally of course. By lifting the tongue so that it closes the air passages into the lungs

s/he can enter and remain in a state of suspended animation for long periods of time, even being buried in the ground. These souls have an extraordinary control over the functions of the body.

But what does all this mean to you and me — mystics in search of the soul? Of what possible significance is the knowledge that we will one day be able to consciously direct the beat of our hearts and the flow of the blood through this tremendous center of life? How will the conscious control of the flow of blood affect us as we approach our coming perfection? The possibilities are indeed startling.

In recent years medical physiologists have entered the realm of esoteric science in their amazing discovery that the cells of the brain seemingly record every occurrence in our daily lives as if they were filming some passing event. They have discovered, by the use of electric needles, that pressure on certain brain cells releases to the consciousness a complete re-run of past scenes and experiences. Of course they have not as yet entered so completely into the esoteric field that they recognize that it is not the brain cell at all which is the record-bearer. The memory patterns are produced by several means, namely:

1. the presence of the magnetic field of the superconscious above the head, composed of higher mental substance. This superconscious forcefield imposes itself upon the physical brain through the cerebral cortex, brain stem and the Third Eye;

2. the nerve fluid of the nervous system which forms, in part, that mystic substance known as the brain dew;

3. karmic pictures in the bloodstream transmitted to the brain area by impulses flowing out of the physical seed atom in the heart under the control of the subconscious mind, operating through the sympathetic nervous system.

Medical science has discovered that pressure of an electric needle upon certain brain cells can cause an epileptic seizure and/or can release to the memory consciousness, for instance, constant re-runs of a scene of tragedy upsetting enough to be considered as a cause behind insanity. They have also discovered that removal of these particular brain cells which seem to be the seat of this "remembrance" will apparently remove from the consciousness all traces of that unpleasant scene. This is a most marvelous discovery. Yet science is but bordering on the fringes of a higher truth.

We shall not proceed further with this discussion because we intend to consider it fully in future Lessons concerning the brain. However, it is important to mention these things here since there is a connection to the functions of the heart. They concern our future capabilities of conscious control over the flow of blood and the pulse beat.

It is not the brain cells alone which hold the scene of a past event, but rather the threads of mental reflecting ether connected to the cells which, stimulated by the flow of karmic pictures in the blood, release past scenes into activity, causing them to be brought to memory again and again. Esoteric scientists are aware of how the memory-recording ether in the brain cells is penetrated by karmic pictures in the blood, and sometimes produces epileptic seizures, schizophrenia and insanity.

Now let us say that a person has attained that stage of evolutionary development that enables him or her to control consciously the functions of the heart and the flow of blood into the brain area. The flow of blood will be controlled by the will, operating through the cerebrospinal nervous system, and since the heart will then have become a voluntary as well as involuntary muscle, s/he will possess the power to regulate the flow of blood to the brain. In time s/he will be able to withhold the flow of life-giving blood to certain cells which hold the thread of memory containing certain unpleasant episodes.

Sensing the approach of an epileptic seizure or upsetting memory, this person will be able to temporarily check the flow of blood from the heart to these particular brain cells until such time as the scenery of the unhappy episode can be erased so completely from the heart seed atom that it will not rise into prominence again in the consciousness. It will of course remain in the higher akashic records, but will be closed off from remembrance for this particular lifetime, at least.

Thus it will become possible to become free not only of these mental etheric reflections which rise up from within, but one will be able consciously to create and direct other karmic pictures of a more pleasant nature into the memory field of the brain, erasing unhappy records and changing your life entirely. One will not then be a puppet of one's subconscious memories as is true today, but will rather be the master over the waking conscious mind and the possessor of superconscious powers.

* * * * *

Supplementary Monograph

Step Four of Lama Yoga

OUR IMMEDIATE GOAL

Humanity of this planet is now in its fourth round of evolution: we have circled the cosmic scheme of the planets three times and are now halfway through the fourth round of the seven which we must travel in this present seven-round plan of evolution.

We have spoken to you of the seven bodies all human beings possess. The immediate purpose lying ahead in this particular round is the alignment of the bodies. We are concerned principally with: the physical body, which includes the etheric; the astral; the mental; and the causal, which includes the higher mental.

The first task of the mental body is to hold the astral and the physical in complete harmony. Once this alignment is accomplished, the next purpose is for the three lower bodies — the physical, astral, and mental — to become aligned with the Oversoul. Certain definite attainments are necessary to accomplish the latter:

    1. physical co-ordination;

    2. emotional stability;

    3. mental awareness, higher consciousness or self discipline.

With these accomplishments the result is an unobstructed channel directly from the Oversoul to the physical brain. And THAT is our present overall goal in the practice of Lama Yoga...an unimpeded channel from the soul to the Oversoul.

Three major centers in the brain are points of contact between the personality and the Oversoul. They are the pineal gland, the pituitary body, and the medulla oblongata. When the pineal and pituitary begin functioning in correlation, the medulla oblongata is stepped up in its own particular vibration to complete the process. Usually it is not until the fifth initiation that complete harmony exists between these three principal brain centers.

At that time the geometrical alignment of the bodies is completely realized, and Mastership has been attained. This supreme attainment is available to you *now*, if you will but grasp it. It actually expresses in your daily life at various intervals when you momentarily bring your complete being into perfect focus: when it happens spontaneously; in moments of deepest meditation; or in times of dire distress, when surges of supreme energy are necessary in a crisis.

The steps of Lama Yoga are selected with extreme care, and designed to produce a very definite result. They are meant to bring about the desired achievements of physical co-ordination, emotional stability, and mental awareness, higher consciousness and self discipline.

We suggest that the Step we now present not be shared with others. It should be incorporated into the practice of those who are thoroughly familiar with the previous steps of Lama Yoga and who have practiced them for some time. This is a very advanced yogic rite.

PAD NIRVANA

Between the pituitary body and the uvula at the back of your mouth is a little white hollow known in Sanskrit as the *Tircotee,* meaning the "inner tongue." The ancient initiates called it "Jacob's Ladder," the "10th door," the "sacred tongue," "ruska Jeebe" and "rechree mundra."

This inner tongue is the valve for irrigating the physical body with "holy waters" from the "spiritual lakes" or third and fourth ventricles. This inner tongue ends in the soft palate of the mouth. If you will look into a mirror and open your mouth wide you will discern the ending of the soft palate or the uvula. The uvula is the end of the inner tongue and is sometimes called the little snake.

The *corpus striatum* is the head of the little snake which is lying on the holy eggs or the optic thalamus. Advanced yogis perform an exercise known as *"Pad Nirvana"* in order to vibrate the little snake, the uvula, causing a tremendous increase of energy in all the brain cells and tissues, from whence it pours down throughout the entire physical body, bringing renewed physical, mental and spiritual powers.

While in front of the mirror, with mouth wide open, turn your tongue up and backward in an attempt to touch the little snake suspended there at the end of the soft palate. It will be difficult or perhaps impossible.

Now you are ready for the exercise: Sit quietly and close your eyes. Then close your ear "tabs" with your thumbs, as in the previous Step of Lama Yoga (see Lesson 17, First Degree). Rest your head in your hands, allowing the fingers to lie easily on each side of your head.

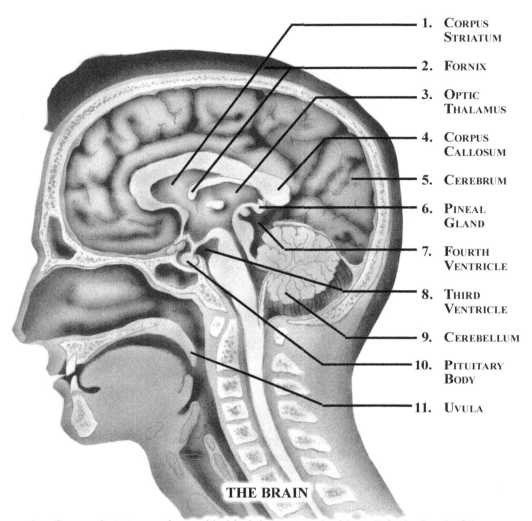

1. **CORPUS STRIATUM**
2. **FORNIX**
3. **OPTIC THALAMUS**
4. **CORPUS CALLOSUM**
5. **CEREBRUM**
6. **PINEAL GLAND**
7. **FOURTH VENTRICLE**
8. **THIRD VENTRICLE**
9. **CEREBELLUM**
10. **PITUITARY BODY**
11. **UVULA**

THE BRAIN

1. *Corpus Striatum* — located behind the septum lucidum. It is the head of the sleeping kundalini serpent (in the head region) which is lying on the holy eggs.
2. *Fornix* — Door of Brahm and the road to the cosmic.
3. *Optic Thalamus* — called the round eye, seat of the soul, the holy eggs, sacred seal, hidden door or holy temple.
4. *Corpus Callosum* — river of life.
5. *Cerebrum* — holy mountain or universal brain.
6. *Pineal Gland* — the male, positive pole.
7. *Fourth Ventricle* — spiritual lake of holy water, spiritual nourishment known in the Christian Bible as the cup of honey. Known to Greek philosophers as the nectar of life. Known to the Hindus as Amrat.
8. *Third Ventricle* — spiritual lake of holy water.
9. *Cerebellum* — seat of instinct.
10. *Pituitary Body* — the female, negative pole.
11. *Uvula* — the little snake

Now, still with eyes closed and ear tabs held shut, begin chanting *hoon, yang, yang, yang — hoon.* Keep the mouth almost closed during chanting, which causes it to be more of a hum than an actual chant, since it is the vibration we are after more than the words themselves. All the while you are humming, keep trying to reach the uvula with the tongue. The constant rubbing of the tongue against the palate will produce much saliva, which should simply be swallowed as the exercise proceeds.

Five minutes a day of this powerful chant can change the entire vibration of your physical body. But this is not all. The Third Eye, including the pineal and pituitary, will be stepped up in vibrational frequency. The valve locking the dam which holds the holy waters in the spiritual lakes in the third and fourth ventricles will be unlocked and the mysterious brain dews will pour down sushumna in the spinal column, carrying their healing potency all over the body, and charging the spinal chakras with cosmic power.

Therefore, this exercise is far more than a breathing exercise. It is an extremely powerful spiritual rite designed to help the Astarian light the cosmic fires in his or her own being.

* * *   * * *

You may find the first three Steps of Lama Yoga completely sufficient and may not wish to pursue any of these supplementary Steps. The first three Steps, which have previously been given, are the basics of Lama Yoga.

These further Steps are given for the Astarian who has the time and inclination for very serious yogic pursuits.

Initiation and the Saving Blood

Second Degree — Lesson Thirteen

ANATOMY OF THE BLOOD

The life is in the blood.

So says the Bible.

So said the ancient mystics.

So says medical science.

So says esoteric science.

And so say we.

A miraculous river of life surges through your veins. Perhaps you accept it with only casual interest, but it is a matter of life and death to every cell of your body — and therefore to you.

Each of your body's countless billions of cells depends upon this stream for:

1. the energy which enables it to function and reproduce itself;

2. the disposal of wastes and toxins which quickly and sometimes fatally poison if allowed to remain in the cell.

Thus it is in truth a river of life.

Bringing energy and disposing of waste materials constitutes the physiological commerce of the bloodstream. It means life to a population of cells which is many times the population of Earth. Thus it accomplishes more for you than all the Earth's waterways do for humankind.

Yet like all streams there are mysterious currents and constituents which are an ever-changing puzzle to those who study them. Some of these mysteries are known only to those who understand the esoteric.

Since the days when humankind first began to study itself, one of the most baffling enigmas has been the mysterious bloodstream and its contents. One of the reasons for this perplexity is that the blood is in a perpetual state of change and evolution — so much so that no sooner does science gain knowledge of one phase of this amazing river within than new mysteries become apparent. The riddle seems, therefore, never to be solved. New questions continually arise because the blood carries the eternal record of our evolutionary progress. As we constantly change and evolve, so does the bloodstream.

For this reason we must consider our study of the blood from the standpoint of the past, the present and the future. The past, when it was in a state of chaotic turbulence uncontrolled by the mind, influenced largely by tribal and animal instinct; the present, when it exists as a partially dammed up and partially free-flowing river, depending upon the state of one's emotional and mental life, yet containing some portion of its ultimate pure glory; and the future when it will eventually become a glorious stream of living light.

From the Christian religion we shall examine the mystical significance of the saving blood of the Christ, the redeeming blood of the Lamb, the significance of the blood of the Lord at the Last Supper, and the science of soul salvation as it relates to the blood. This mystical understanding is of significance to all seekers of any spiritual background or belief. There are many mysteries to be unveiled, but to understand better the esoteric properties and activities of the blood and how they relate to you and your spiritual progression, we must pause to consider briefly the exoteric anatomy of the blood.

The blood is composed of innumerable minute corpuscles and other enigmatic particles floating in a river of liquid composed of seven agents, three gross and four subtle.

The gross agents are:

1. carbonic acid;

2. oxygen;

3. nitrogen.

The subtle agents are the four physical ethers:

1. light ether;

2. pranic ether;

3. electric ether;

4. mental reflecting ether.

Medical science recognizes the presence of only the first three — carbonic acid, oxygen, and nitrogen. It realizes that in addition to these three agents other mysterious life-giving substances exist in the blood, but it has not yet recognized those substances to be the four physical ethers.

On the other hand, mysticism not only recognizes the existence of the four ethers, but finds it obvious that life could not exist without their presence in the blood.

Oxygen, for instance, a most important substance indrawn into the bloodstream from the atmosphere, is a derivative of the ethers themselves, without which the blood could not sustain the life of the body. The bloodstream contains plasma, two kinds of corpuscles — red and white — and the mysterious nuclei, the platelets.

The life is in the blood is an axiom proclaimed by all the mystics of old and is a truth so obvious that medical science must concur.

The principal function of the blood is as carrier of the breath, and the breath in turn acts as the carrier of the ethers of life throughout the system. Blood without breath is blood without life, and breath without the ethers is breath without life. Therefore, the sum of the idea is simply that:

1. The life-giving ethers in the atmosphere around us are taken into the body via the breath.

2. The ethers are carried throughout the body via the blood.

The blood is the agent of the life-giving ethers; therefore the life is indeed in the blood.

THE RED CELLS: BEARERS OF LIFE-GIVING OXYGEN

Your red blood cells outnumber white blood cells many hundreds of times. They are born in your bone marrow and the lymph nodes which lie in various places throughout the body.

The red blood cell lives for approximately three weeks and is eventually carried into the spleen where it is destroyed and decomposed. When red blood cells are first born in your bone marrow they are nucleated, which causes them to appear to be living structures. Just prior to the time they leave your bone marrow and enter the bloodstream to become a part of circulation, however, the nucleus is extruded and the cell becomes a mechanical object, a protoplasmatic filled with blood pigment. It is the blood pigment containing magnetic iron that attracts oxygen from the atmosphere around you. It is your red blood cells which carry oxygen from the lungs and throughout the body.

It is the lack of oxygen circulating throughout the body which causes inharmony among the cells and, under these conditions, dread diseases could begin. A bloodstream filled with life-giving oxygen will keep the cells of the body so charged with the proper magnetism that foreign growths stand little or no opportunity of originating or of sustaining life.

Normally red blood corpuscles are formed in the bone marrow in equal proportion to the destructive activity of the spleen. If the formation of the blood cells in the marrow overbalances the destruction in the spleen, or vice versa, then trouble results.

If the spleen destroys too few blood cells in proportion to their production, polycythemia follows. If too many white blood cells are released into the bloodstream, then we have a case of leukemia, or cancer of the blood. Anemia and leukemia are terms used by medical science to describe a condition which means that the red blood cells are either being destroyed too rapidly, or are not being produced in large enough quantities inside the bone marrow, and white cells are produced in excess.

Bone marrow actually can be injured or destroyed by bacterial poison. Foreign chemicals or serum containing potent toxins taken into the body (often in the form of drug injections) can injure the bone marrow, thus causing a decrease in the normal supply of red blood cells. Prolonged infections can also injure the bone marrow and curtail the production of red blood cells. The bone marrow also may be attacked by the growth of malignant tumors. Malignancy can cause the tissue of the bone marrow to be replaced by abnormal tissue which cannot properly build the red corpuscles necessary for sustaining life.

Under normal conditions anemia can be corrected through an increase of iron in the bloodstream. Iron may be obtained through fresh air, sunshine and proper nutrition, namely, those foods which contain iron.

A few foods rich in iron include apples, bananas, soybeans, spinach, dandelion greens, beet greens, mustard greens, blackstrap molasses. The iron stimulates production of red blood cells in the bone marrow.

The intake of any green foods containing chlorophyll is a most excellent means of increasing the iron content. Although chlorophyll itself does not contain iron, it does contain magnesium, which attracts great quantities of solar iron from the atmosphere.

Iron in the blood is an all-important substance, not only the presence of iron from the physical dimensions of life, but the solar iron of the pranic atmospheres about us.

The influence of the Oversoul upon your personality is considerably diminished or enhanced depending upon the amount of solar iron in your blood.

Solar iron is attracted to your bloodstream through the agency of the nerve fluids in your nervous system. This nerve fluid contains a magnetism which draws solar iron from the pranic atmosphere. If your nervous system is healthy, its magnetic force is capable of attracting increased portions of solar iron, assuring perpetual contact with your Oversoul.

The power of the nerve fluid depends in turn upon the degree of regeneration in the human being. When we say regeneration we refer to the conservation of the propagative fluids which operate throughout the nervous system as well as in the blood.

One secret of good, healthy blood is the inhalation of pure oxygen. As you inhale oxygen it passes from your lungs into the bloodstream and charges your body with constant new life and energy. With each exhalation, poisons and toxins pass out of your body. You lose some of these impurities through the cells or pores as well, but a major part of this body-building, body-cleansing job is performed by the heart and lungs — the heart purifying the blood which passes through it, and the lungs discharging toxins through the breath.

THE WHITE CORPUSCLES: DEFENDERS AND DESTROYERS

The majority of white corpuscles are manufactured in the spleen. The blood picks them up as it flows through the spleen, carrying them first to the solar plexus-liver area and from there into the bloodstream. A few white corpuscles are born in the bone marrow and the lymph glands.

Opinions differ as to the basic function of the white corpuscle. Some think these cells are the result of one's negative actions; that they only make their appearance as a person discharges poison into the system through wrong thinking, evil deeds, wrong foods and violent emotional experiences. Others declare the white corpuscle to be the spiritual police officer of the body, and we concur in this esoteric interpretation.

Perhaps it is true that the white corpuscles, or cells, are created *because* of one's negative thinking but not by one's negative thinking. Since people do think negatively, since they do commit unwise deeds, since they do eat wrong foods, since they do experience emotional upsets, it is good that the body can produce white corpuscles which rush to the scene of destruction created by these upheavals and help bring the physical system back to a state of harmony.

It is not true that the emotions cause or create white corpuscles.

People can contribute to their problems and
diseases through the mind and the emotions.

It is the job of these white cells to control and destroy such   poisons and diseases before they destroy the body. The white corpuscles well up from seeming nothingness and wander through the bloodstream until an invader attacks the body. Their function is to rush to the site of infection and fight valiantly to destroy and absorb undesirable bacteria into themselves.

The presence of fever in the body indicates an increase of white corpuscles. Esoteric scientists believe most firmly that fever aids in fighting infection. Medical science would do well to consider that it may be a mistake to reduce fever in the majority of cases.

Fever, plus the presence of white corpuscles, only indicates the body itself is attempting to destroy the infection. Fever — heat in the blood — is nature's way of burning out infection in cooperation with a marked increase of white corpuscles which rush to the scene of infection to combat it.

White corpuscles also have a disintegrating effect upon foreign matter or objects. Let us say that a splinter lodges beneath the flesh of the finger. White corpuscles rush immediately to the wound and attempt to dissolve it. If they are not successful, they begin to eat into the tissue around the splinter, causing it to liquify. Liquified tissue is called "pus." The splinter can then be removed later along with the pus. Pus is not an undesirable substance, but is nature's way of destroying foreign objects and healing wounds. Once this job is completed the body is restored to normalcy.

BLOOD AND ENERGY

It is the energy in the bloodstream which makes the blood susceptible to our thoughts and emotions. These energies are controlled by the vasomotor nerves located in the brain. These nerves regulate the distribution of blood throughout the body. If a person is engaged in concentrated mental activity, the blood will be drawn to the brain, the seat of that activity, through the vasomotor nerves which send the blood flowing rapidly through the cerebral vessels.

When a meal is consumed the vasomotor nerves, on the other hand, direct the blood to the center of activity which at that time is the digestive tract, the stomach, the liver, the salivary glands and the pancreas. They become dilated with an increased supply of blood in order to carry out their digestive function in the intestinal area.

During this period when the digestive tract is being supplied with the additional amount of blood to complete its operations, the supply to the brain is lessened. The blood vessels there are temporarily constricted and deprived of an adequate supply of blood. This causes a resistance to the thinking processes and the individual is apt to become sleepy. It is not wise to arrange a study period directly following a meal, for under concentrated thought processes the brain requires tremendous quantities of blood to function at full capacity.

After eating, the muscles also are deprived of their usual supply of blood. Thus, a sports program also should not closely follow a meal. In physical exercise the muscles and skin require a generous supply of blood. If one engages in vigorous swimming or games immediately after eating, the muscles can experience a severe cramp.

During sleep blood is partially withdrawn from the brain and its activity is decreased. The etheric double, the body of vitality, is engaged in other parts of the physical form restoring wholeness to the cells, charging them with new lifeforce and renewed energy.

In summer when the body is apt to become overheated or when a fever rages, the vasomotor nerves dilate the blood vessels of the skin through which perspiration flows to release the heat.

Energy follows thought, or the seat of the greatest activity at any given moment. Blood follows the energy, since energy penetrates and permeates the blood.

THE BLOOD AND YOUR EMOTIONS

The emotions operate in and through certain atoms in the physical form which are composed of substance from the astral plane — the astral atoms. As you know, we call this form — this mass of substance composed of astral atoms — the astral body, the body of one's desires, the body of one's emotions.

The astral body has its contact in the liver, causing it to be the seat of the most intense emotions and passions. The solar plexus chakra superimposes the liver, and the astral seed atom is located in the apex of the liver. The blood flowing into the liver is there charged with all the emotional impulses, which are then carried by the bloodstream out of the liver and throughout the entire body. Thus the bloodstream is not only a river of life but also can be a river of destruction carrying disease, decay and all varying qualities of emotion we cause to pass into and out of ourselves.

The Sea of Thoughts Around Us

One method, and there are several, by which we are victimized by our thoughts and emotions should be further explained. Proceeding outward from the brain are thought waves tinctured and colored by emotions we have expressed. These thought waves are filled with energy, since energy follows thought.

Thus we create around ourselves a forcefield filled with thoughtforms we project from our minds. Everything we think, every emotion we feel such as hatred, resentment, jealousy, despair, love, kindness, humility, radiate from our brain via thought waves and into the forcefield surrounding our particular physical form. Thus we mentally create our surrounding aura, which attracts particles of like nature from the ethers.

The atomic particles filling the aura are charged with energies conditioned by your feelings and thoughts. You in turn inhale these atomic particles. The breath carries them, tinctured as they are by your own mental and emotional characteristics, into the lungs and into the liver from whence they are carried throughout your body. This creates a perpetual and unending circle.

The vitality of the etheric body is affected by the bloodstream, and the bloodstream in turn is affected by your thoughts and emotions. Thus you may contribute to your own diseases, your happiness, your successes and your failures. You can think and feel success, radiate well-being and happiness and reap the harvest of the planted seed, or you can create havoc within.

Your emotions can have an unbelievable effect on the blood. To exemplify, let us analyze one of our greatest emotional impulses — fear. Fear is one of the most destructive and paralyzing emotions one can experience. Sudden fear can shock the body and lock the flow of nerve fluids and endocrine hormones in the blood. The intense reaction causes the blood to drain from the brain.

The blood and the nerve fluid rush to the seat of emotional reaction, the solar plexus brain; the temperature of the blood drops below normal and the individual freezes with fright. The brain becomes   partially paralyzed. So intense can fear be that if the blood is driven completely from the brain, the person may become temporarily unconscious in a faint.

The sudden emotional shock of fear can cause the glandular system to cease its function. The adrenals stop their perpetual supply of epinephrine, the hormone they ordinarily release into the nervous system and bloodstream. With the loss of epinephrine the heart slows its beat, the blood vessels become loose rather than tense, the blood ceases to flow normally, and because the brain is temporarily deprived of its blood supply, unconsciousness could follow.

If this condition persists and the brain is denied its needed supply of blood, and if the adrenals are not forced to secrete an emergency amount of their magical fluids, death could occur.

Fear, of course, is an extreme emotion but it has a tremendous effect upon the blood. The state of unconsciousness caused by a sudden shock of fear is often the means the body utilizes to overcome the shock reaction, freeing the body and the consciousness temporarily until the endocrine glands can start operating again to provide emergency supplies of hormones.

This one example testifies that the emotions are constantly exerting influence upon the body, especially the astral body. The blood, as it flows in enormous quantities through the liver and is there diffused with the emotional qualities of the individual, is the great field of expression for this astral body. Your blood reacts instantly to influences upon it, be they negative or positive.

Alcohol, for instance, if taken in excess, saturates the bloodstream with a destructive poison. Spiritual alchemy is impossible to one who is a slave to alcohol. The blood will continue to mix with oxygen, it is true, but it will not mix with prana or any of the higher ethers which help to regenerate and prepare a person to live in the coming new age. Those who drink intoxicants to excess will find it impossible to incarnate in our particular lifewave of humanity destined for the coming Aquarian Age, for their blood chemistry will not allow them to breathe comfortably in its rarefied atmosphere.

When one's desires are selfish and negative, the blood itself takes on undesirable qualities. Carnal living causes a thickening of the blood. Outbursts of violence, uncontrolled fits of temper, severe emotional reactions to disturbing events, all have their destructive effects upon the bloodstream, as do wrong foods, tobacco, excessive expenditure of sexual energies, and the abuse of alcohol, as well as habitual employment of sedatives, narcotics and all drugs.

If you would develop a dynamic, magnetic personality, you must learn healthy emotional expression and behavior so as to diminish to a minimum the lower quality in your blood, replacing it with the higher electromagnetic qualities of the soul breath.

Love is the most vital of all emotions. The expression of love has a paramount influence upon the etheric body and its power to assimilate and distribute into the physical form all the ethers from the atmosphere surrounding us. The presence of these ethers in the blood helps to determine the spiritual status of the individual. A person can absorb only the amount of these spiritualized ethers that his or her evolved state will allow. According to your evolution, you attract into and sustain in your bloodstream increasing amounts of these ethers.

As your bloodstream becomes increasingly purified it automatically attracts greater and more dynamic qualities of the mysterious physical ethers, creating an etherealization of the blood. Such purification changes the heat of the blood and makes it possible for Azoth, the Divine Substance, to attain some degree of regenerative influence. We shall teach extensively concerning this in coming Lessons.

THE EVOLUTIONARY TREND TOWARD INTERMARRIAGE

In the days of antiquity when the Masters and the more-highly-evolved teachers walked the earth plane to guide humanity, they found it the course of wisdom to encourage tribal marriages and to discourage marriage outside the tribe or clan. They were well acquainted with the mystery of the blood and the ancestral karmic picture images which were carried in it.

The guides were aware that in humankind's early stage of evolution it was necessary to keep the blood stabilized insofar as tribal blood karma was concerned, because they found it easier to impress the subconscious minds of those they were assisting and guide them, through these impressions, to higher states of development.

It would have been undesirable at that time to disturb the individual bloodstream with mixed karmic picture patterns through marriage outside the tribes. Humankind needed to become more in control of desires and thinking and more completely individualized before the guides could encourage intertribal marriage. By discouraging marriage outside the tribe, the ancestral blood pictures were kept in harmony and flowed unprohibited and uninhibited through many generations.

Among many orthodox religious and cultural groups, even today, intramarriage is honored, and marriage with other groups and religions is in disfavor. Intramarriage is also advocated among the Scots. They are renowned for their "second sight," and this is due largely to their continuance of the custom of clan marriages.

However, the former extrasensory faculty of involuntary clairvoyance, once prominent among those who persevered in the custom of tribal marriage, is now generally being replaced by voluntary clairvoyance as humankind is evolving individual inner faculties through mixing of the bloodstream. The greater the freedom one is able to acquire as ancestral pictures are erased from the bloodstream, the more one can develop these higher powers within him or herself, uninfluenced and uncolored by the past.

The custom of intramarriage within tribes and families prevailed until fairly recent times as history is measured. Only in the last two thousand years or so has the consciousness risen above family, tribe and nation. Since that time all nationalities have become international in outlook as nation has intermarried with nation, thus wiping out the ancestral blood record in individuals, and mixing the blood of all nations so that each incarnating ego may advance from the influence of tribal gods and seek to know, to understand and to unite with the Universal Parent.

It is extremely important that the individual personality align with their own High Self and make the Infinite Being in heaven prominent in his or her life.

When humankind became aware that all human beings are connected one with the other, this was more important than tribal connections, and laws eventually were passed preventing and prohibiting endogamy, or marriages in a family group. In course of time incestuous marriages, or marriages in the immediate family, came to be regarded as most improper and damaging in many ways to those involved. Also, intrafamily marriages were discovered to be the cause of hereditary problems in the offspring because of the unwise mixture of hereditary blood weaknesses.

Intermarriage between groups and tribes has gradually broken up the ancestral picture images carried in the individual bloodstream. It has caused the individual to abandon tribal traits and to personalize thinking and actions. It has caused each person to act more as an individual than as a member of a tribe or group.

America stands today as the great melting pot of the world. The "melting pot" implies, of course, the mixed bloodstream. The blood of many races, clans and tribes intermingle in the blood of most Americans. It is hoped that this creates more harmony and understanding between all of us as well as a celebration of our differences.

The one who bears a mixed bloodstream tends to express individual thinking and worship of a universal God. The bloodstream will carry picture images that each person has created. This "individualized" thinking thus makes the person with mixed universal blood solely responsible for the picture images in his or her own bloodstream.

INITIATION AND THE SAVING BLOOD

Preceding Lessons have taught that many of the dogmas and precepts of the Christian faith as well as other faiths are based upon the dramas of the ancient sacred Mysteries which had their origin in the dawn of time. We have also stated that the exoteric dogmas of the Christian faith have been presented with little understanding of the inner deeper meaning.

The dramas of the Mystery Schools had one purpose: to reveal truth to the candidates seeking initiation into the Mysteries.

Many of the Christian dogmas are based upon these dramas without a full and complete understanding of the inner spiritual significance of the teachings.

In future writings we shall present the teachings as they were taught in the Mysteries, as opposed to that which is accepted dogmatically in today's Christian faith.

It is our earnest prayer that those Astarians who still hold to the orthodox concepts of their faith will not be offended by these writings. In presenting some of the New Testament teachings in a more mystical concept we only hope to approach a better understanding of Jesus' true mission in coming to walk among us as we perceive it to be. His life paralleled the drama of the Mystery Schools and in presenting the teachings of the Mysteries, we in no way would diminish any of the light of this Master Teacher.

Since the subject of these particular Lessons is the blood, we are concerned with teaching of the saving blood as it is presented in orthodox Christianity, as opposed to the original teaching as presented in the ancient Mysteries.

Let us first understand the purpose of the Mystery Dramas. It was to portray the journey of a soul from personhood to godhood. The dramas allegorically told the dramatic story of a person who, through the travail and problems of life, through and by personal efforts, became an initiated divine leader. The dramas differed in their presentations, but the message taught was ultimately the same: to lead the individual into union with God, to show the way to salvation and to light the path to individual godhood.

We have said that the Mysteries were divided into two categories: the Greater and the Lesser. That which was reserved for the temple initiates was called the *Gnosis* or the *Esoteria*. That which was given in the Lesser consisted of myths, legends, ceremonial rites, allegories and moral precepts. The Lesser Mysteries attempted to reflect the Greater without actually revealing the inner esoteric teachings.

It was the documents and manuscripts of the Lesser Mysteries to which the Christian church fathers fell heir. These documents contained the outer, more exoteric teachings. The inner mystic tenets of the Greater Mysteries have never been revealed to the masses. The masses have been given the allegorical teachings based upon, but not completely revealing, the inner, deeper, profound teachings of the sacred Greater Mysteries.

Some of the secret ceremonies were based upon the mysteries of the Solar God and the drama of the heavens, which encompassed the science of the zodiac, the purpose being to instruct the initiate in the knowledge that the inner nature of human beings reflected this mystic science. Outer space of the world was mirrored in the inner space of the human being. The human being, the miniature universe, reflected God's outer universe in that the mysteries of the zodiac of the heavens were reproduced in the inner being of each person.

The candidate of the Mysteries was carried through four degrees of learning:

First Degree: S/he was taught the entire field of physical sciences concerning the heavens as related to the human being.

Second Degree: S/he was taught the esoteric interpretation of these scientific truths and how to understand the difference.

Third Degree: The next step carried the candidate into philosophy, through which he or she attempted to gain a better understanding of truth by the process of reasoning and logic.

Fourth Degree: In this last Degree s/he experienced revelations through initiation, which revealed the exact truth of the human being and God, and how humans may become more divine. Thus was the candidate given true wisdom.

This last Degree carried the initiate beyond the realms of mind into the realm of God consciousness. Through a mystical process he or she was enabled to step outside the limits of the waking conscious mind and dwell momentarily in tune with

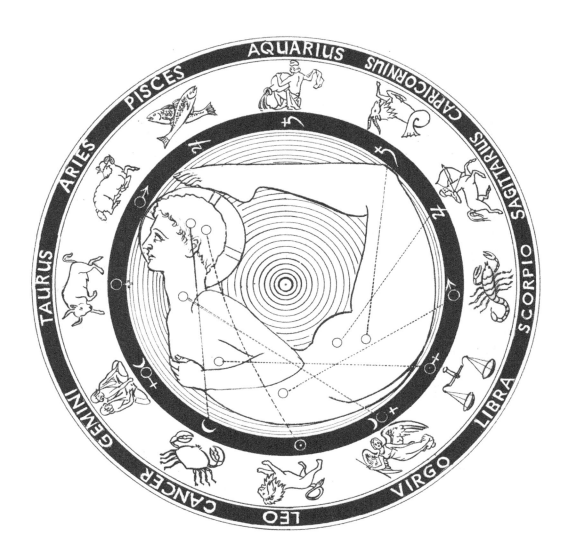

THE APOCALYPTIC ZODIAC

Some of the secret ceremonies were based upon the mysteries of the Solar God and the drama of the heavens, which encompassed the science of the zodiac, the purpose being to instruct the initiate in the knowledge that the inner nature of humans reflected this mystic science. Outer space of the world was mirrored in the inner space in humankind. The human, the miniature universe, reflected God's outer universe in that the mysteries of the zodiac of the heavens were reproduced in the inner being of each person.

the Universal Mind and become one with God. In this state, all the Mysteries were revealed. All questions concerning oneself and God and the universe were answered, and the initiate stood temporarily on the threshold of the Godhead.

S/he was taught how to discriminate between the lesser psychic senses and the greater spiritual attributes; how to elevate one's thinking above the intellectual level into the intuitional level. Having traveled the way of the sacred Mysteries, the candidate became the initiated esotericist — that is, one who understood the inner teachings of dogmas, precepts and creeds, and could live outside the confines of the five senses and dwell, at least occasionally, in the realm of the higher senses.

The purpose of the initiate in traveling the pathway of the Mysteries was not to gain knowledge and to know, but to become. *Initiation is the path of becoming.*

There is a marked difference between knowing and becoming. One can know how to become a Master, but one does not become a Master by knowing how. One becomes a Master simply by becoming, by practicing this "knowing how" and growing into Mastership.

The path of initiation shortens the journey between personhood and godhood. Humanity as a mass traverses the pathway slowly and painfully, marking almost imperceptible progress, while the initiate travels the pathway of becoming through the process of initiation, thus speeding the journey and arriving more surely and swiftly at the ultimate destination: godhood. Regardless of how much a person knows, he or she cannot know the ultimate wisdom of God until he or she has become more divine. This is the purpose of initiation through the sacred Mysteries. There can be no higher goal or nobler achievement.

INITIATION AND HOLY COMMUNION

The rite of Holy Communion had its birth in the days of antiquity in the temples of the Mysteries long preceding those of ancient Egypt. The Communion ceremonies differed considerably from the religious Communion rites witnessed in today's traditional Christian churches. The rite of Holy Communion was open only to the disciple who was ready to become an initiate, and performance of the rite was a part of the initiation. The rite was called the "Blood Initiation" and it was one of the most serious steps taken by the initiates.

At this ancient ceremony wheat cakes and the juice of the grape were consumed. They were not simply "cakes" and "juice." The Master of the Temple — the Hierophant or the High Priestess — through powerful, magical processes and ceremonies, endowed the wine and cake with his or her own powers. The Master Hierophant or High Priestess, through these alchemical processes, could actually draw the Divine

This engraving from a Sicilian painted vase shows a transparent scene from an ancient Mystery Drama such as was performed at Samothrace and Eleusis.

The scene depicts the representatives, or Cafirs, of the primary Great Cause in the workshop of Creation. In the dramas of the Lesser Mysteries they were known as gods or goddesses but the initiate understood them to be representative of powers or attributes rather than deities.

From left to right appear the Hierophant as a workman bearing a sledge hammer at his forge; the High Priestess bringing direction and creativity; the sacred Herald; and the Torchbearer with his torch across his knee.

The torch is about to be ignited at the command of Mercury, the spiritual agent in the workshop of creation. The primary Great Cause is not shown but His representatives, the elements, are present.

Varro, the Roman scholar, designates these figures to be representative of the elementary principles: Hephaestus, fire, Isis, water; Mercury, air; and Pan, matter. The sun associated with the last figure is represented by his torch.

It may interest the Astarian that we find these same primary deities in Egypt under the names of Osiris, Isis and Typhon, denoting the creating, preserving and destroying powers; and Horus, depicting the sun principle. In India, again, we find Brahma, Vishnu, and Siva as the primary powers; and Boud, a lesser known figure, personifying spirit. In Greece, Zeus, Hera and Hades.

Substance from the ethers into him or herself and impart it to the cakes and the wine. Thus they were transformed into substance containing Azoth, even though the outward appearance remained the same. As we progress with our contemplations concerning the human blood, in the Lessons following this one, we shall have much to say about Azoth, the mysterious Divine Substance which permeates our atmosphere.

The liquid consumed in these blood ceremonies was a highly magnetized fluid containing many other properties in addition to the juice of the grape. Through alchemical processes it was changed, both actually and symbolically, before it became a potion worthy to be consumed in the rites of Holy Communion. The bread cakes were always made of wheat and symbolized the life power found in the kernel. Wheat itself was considered to be "the staff of life" to the physical form, in that it increased power in the generative organs. These wheat cakes, too, were transformed.

The initiates participating in the ceremony understood that in eating the cake and drinking the wine they were partaking of the Deity's divine life. The wine symbolized the "blood" of the Deity, and the cake symbolized the "body." By partaking of the cakes and wine, the initiate absorbed the attributes and powers of the Deity, placed there through the powers of the Hierophant or High Priestess.

To partake of this magnetized potion and bread was to charge the entire bloodstream and nervous system with a tremendous power. The initiate, through this initiation, thus prepared his or her own bloodstream to receive the Divine Substance. The ancients were aware that this power filled the atmosphere but could not be held in the ordinary bloodstream...that it could only be active in a purified and regenerated bloodstream, and it was this purified state the initiates sought in drinking the symbolic blood and breaking the symbolic bread in their Holy Communion ceremonies.

Consuming the "blood" of the Deity, charged with powerful Azoth, helped the initiates draw unto themselves more powerful downpourings of the Divine Substance. The juice of the grape represented the cosmic vitality and divine life of the Deity, and it was this potent substance and power infused in the juice which the initiates sought to place in their own blood. A disciple must have arrived at an estate of complete purity in every way before he or she could partake of this powerful Blood Initiation, the Holy Communion of the Mysteries.

The true meaning of Holy Communion has been lost in ritual and ceremony. Who in the Christian faith today understands more than that one is eating bread and drinking grape juice which symbolize the blood of Christ? Who understands the mysteries of the blood? Who understands the mysteries of the Divine or Christ Substance? Who understands the true meaning of the wheat cakes as the "body" and the juice as the "blood" of Christ? Too many Christians enter into this occasion believing only that in some mysterious way it helps to promote their salvation. Many do it only because it was done in the church of their childhood, and understand no meaning behind it whatever.

BLOOD INITIATIONS AMONG THE ANCIENTS

The most celebrated of the Egyptian Mysteries were the Mysteries of Isis, which included the Blood Initiation, the ceremony which bound the initiates together in a true divine connection.

In the Egyptian Mysteries, Holy Communion was not the only process through which the initiates observed the Blood Initiation. The candidates of the Egyptian Mystery Schools actually made a small incision in the wrists with the point of a compass. During the ceremony the wrists of the candidates, initiates and the Master Teacher were bound together in such a way as to actually permit their blood to mingle.

They engaged in mystic rites which were to bring the divine Isis into their midst. The candidates understood it was far more than the mixing of the blood. They believed that each person taking part in the ceremony had indeed partaken of a portion of the blood of the divine Isis, the livegiver, the goddess of their order.

This portion of the Blood Initiation was one of the most important dramas of their Mysteries and was given only to initiates attaining a certain spiritual status. It was not an easy thing to take the Blood Initiation, for one assumed grave responsibilities. It was believed that the mixing of blood was the highest expression of "soul connection," and one whose blood had diffused with the others was a part of the "blood soul" of the spiritual community.

The ties of the mystic community in the days of the Mystery Schools were far more significant and binding than even family ties, for the blood of the mystic initiates — the soul blood — was considered to transcend all others.

The Egyptian Tet-Tie was a symbol of the blood of the goddess Isis. The Masonic Mysteries of modern times still employ some of the symbols of the Mysteries of Isis. And they understand the Tet-Tie to represent the ancient symbol for the blood of the goddess, and not a buckle, as is popularly believed.

The blood ceremony in the Mysteries of Mithra is described in the account of the initiation of the Emperor Julian by Maxime, the Ephesian Hierophant. As he bound his palm to that of Julian, Maxime pronounced the mystic formula: *"By this blood I wash thee free from thy sins. The word of the Highest has entered into thee and His Spirit henceforth will rest upon the newly born, the now begotten of the Highest God. Behold, thou art the son of Mithra."*

Eliphas Levi, in his account of magic, says:

"Blood is the first incarnation of the universal fluid. It is the materialized vital light. Its birth is the most marvelous of all nature's marvels. It lives only by perpetually transforming itself, for it is the universal Proteus. The blood issues from principles

where there was none of it before, and it becomes flesh, bones, hair, nails. It can be allied neither to corruption nor death. When life is gone it begins decomposing. If you know how to reanimate it, how to infuse life into it by a new magnetization of its globules, life will return to it again. The universal substance with its double motion is the great arcanum of being. Blood is the great arcanum of life."

THE BLOOD COVENANT

The blood covenant was of utmost importance in ancient times and is even now considered of supreme importance among the indigenous tribes of many countries, among them, Africa and Australia. They practice a particular rite that is of singular interest. It is called "the Kasendi." It involves two participants — the chief of the tribe and an outsider who seeks to become a member of the tribe.

A small instrument similar to our needle is used to pierce the pit of the stomach of the two participating. The right cheeks and the foreheads are also pierced. A larger incision is made in the palms of the hands and during the actual ceremony the hands are clasped together.

A stalk of grass is used to take small quantities of the participants' blood from each of the points mentioned. Two glasses of liquid similar to beer are used in the blood ceremony, the blood from one person being deposited in one glass and the blood from the second person in the other. The glasses are exchanged, the blood is mixed thoroughly into the beer and then is drunk by the two principals involved, thus making them blood relatives.

As the beer is being drunk, other members of the tribe form a circle and beat the ground with stubby clubs and chant an incantation, the better to seal the blood tie being established. After partaking of the blood ceremony the incoming member is considered to be a blood relation to all the tribe and not just the chief.

During earlier days in Scandinavia, the ancient blood rite was performed by allowing blood of the principals to flow together in a footprint. Warring tribes arriving at a time of peace dipped their hands in pans of blood, then joined hands in a chanting ceremony, thus making themselves blood allies and swearing to avenge each other as though they were actually family. This practice was the means of stopping many uprisings between tribes. Some peace treaties were established by dipping spear points in a pan of blood while oaths of peace were taken. The points of the spears were then held together so that the blood from the two tribes could merge.

Syrians, in earlier days, practiced an interesting form of blood ceremony. The principals involved publicly announce their intentions of entering into a pact. Their intentions are written down in duplicate statements. The copies are exchanged and each of them touches one copy with the other's blood while calling upon God to deceive him if he should deceive his new ally. The documents are then folded and bound to an arm of each of them or worn suspended for a time around their necks. These rites are of a very special kind and do not concern other members of a tribe. They concern only the two involved and each swears to remain an ally to the other as long as life lasts.

Blood ceremonies and blood covenants performed throughout the world are too numerous to be described. We have mentioned enough to establish the importance of blood in the minds of both industrialized and indigenous peoples and that they made the blood ceremony an important custom in their lives.

BECOMING A BLUEBLOOD

The four physical plane ethers have a tremendous impact upon the bloodstream. They enter the body via the breath and the chakras. At our present state of evolution their greatest influence is felt in the root chakra at the base of the spine, the solar plexus chakra in the liver, and the navel-splenic chakra.

In these lower "brains," the ethers become colored by our temperament, mood, food, thought, action, emotion and spiritual evolution. Since the blood is the principal carrier of these ethers, the blood reflects the spiritual status of a person. When these ethers are diffused into the spinal column as spinal gases, they color the spinal fluid according to our own individual spiritual and emotional status.

The color of the liquid fire in the spine fluctuates according to our momentary reactions and emotions. In the average person its usual color is a dominant red interspersed with streaks of blue and yellow. To get a fair idea of the description, turn on a gas heater to its full intensity and watch the yellows, reds and blues flare together in the gas flame.

During the process of meditation the spinal fire, rising out of the root chakra a bright red color, gradually becomes a brilliant blue, and toward the upper part of the spine near the medulla oblongata turns into a glorious yellow gold. During meditation when the chakras are accelerated, the spinal column with its etheric gases resembles a miniature blowtorch in action. Etheric "sparks" fly from the spinal fires, stirring the spinal nerves and activating the nervous fluid throughout the cerebrospinal system.

If the meditation is carried into increasingly spiritualized states, the Chrism Oil of the generative glands is released into the nerve fluid and the spinal fire becomes transmuted in the medulla oblongata. The medulla oblongata will not accept the spinal fire except in its transformed state. This transformation implies the purification of the spinal gases by combining with portions of the resurrected Chrism, raised out of the generative centers. The surest path of regenerating the bloodstream and the nerve fluid, and changing it from a thick, stagnant stream into a river of "light," is through practicing regeneration as we will teach it in forthcoming Lessons.

When the disciple, through meditation, arrives at the state of Samadhi, or cosmic consciousness, the transmuted spinal fire — kundalini, combined with Chrism — is allowed to pass upward out of the medulla into the brain ventricles and reacts upon the pituitary and pineal glands, causing the pineal to rise, and allowing the kundalini to flow into the third ventricle of the brain. There, mixing with the fluids, ethers and brain dews of the third ventricle, it explodes in a "spontaneous combustion" which momentarily opens the Third Eye and brings a tremendous charge of intuitive power.

As already stated, the ordinary individual exhibits a spinal fluid the color of red which in turn influences the color of the bloodstream. Under the influence of discipleship and yogic disciplines, the disciple will begin to exhibit the transformed spinal ethers, the color of brilliant blue. Over an extended period of time the bloodstream of the advanced disciple begins to take on a blue tinge and eventually the red of the blood will be overcome by the brilliant blue of the transformed spinal ethers and nerve fluids.

It will require millenniums before the human race as a whole exhibits the blue bloodstream. A "blueblood" in this sense, does not refer to the highborn as is the popular concept. In this implication it refers to those born into spiritual birth...a spiritual awakening... thus becoming a part of the royal family of initiates and Masters. These are the true "blue bloods" of the human race.

The blue blood is later transmuted to a still higher vibration, changing the color to gold. This is the river of light in the Master. The blood is then no longer a stream of crystallized "sins," but a stream of divine life.

The Mystic Lamp

Each lesson learned, each step taken on your path, brings you closer to spiritual enlightenment. Just as an ancient oil lamp burns away the darkness and the light reveals all obstacles, so do the *Book of Life* Lessons help light your way to self-fulfillment. And just as the lamp must constantly be refilled, so must you continue your journey for the mystic truths that await you in each Lesson.

Lesson 14, **Healing and the Blood** — Contains arcane information concerning the invisible ethers and their place in healing, how they influence the bloodstream and the subconscious mind, how we react to influences from "outer" space, the cause of hereditary influences and the real meaning of blood kinship. Explains the new age, the new person and the new God. Learn of the two "great delights" toward which we are evolving.

Lesson 15, **The Science of Salvation** — Beginning, God, Christ — the words contain much that we cannot comprehend, yet there is much which could be understood if it were not for the sands which time, misunderstanding, error and deliberate falsehood have deposited upon them, dulling their glory and hiding their wisdom. The pages of this Lesson brush away the sand that you might see for yourself what lies beneath. For instance, learn of the five celestial rivers that flow from the plane of Divine Substance — spiritual energies which you can perceive or absorb.

True Worth

True worth is in being, not seeming, —
    In doing, each day that goes by,
Some little good — not in dreaming
    Of great things to do by and by.

For whatever men say in their blindness,
    And spite of the fancies of youth,
There's nothing so kingly as kindness,
    And nothing so royal as truth.

We get back our mete as we measure —
    We cannot do wrong and feel right,
Nor can we give pain and gain pleasure,
    For justice avenges each slight.

The air for the wing of the sparrow,
    The bush for the robin and wren,
But always the path that is narrow
    And straight, for the children of men.

'Tis not in the pages of story
    The hearts of its ills to beguile,
Though he who makes courtship to glory
    Gives all that he hath for her smile.

For when from her heights he has won her,
    Alas! It is only to prove
That nothing's so sacred as honor,
    And nothing so loyal as love!

We cannot make bargains for blisses,
    Nor catch them like fishes in nets;
And sometimes the thing our life misses
    Helps more than the thing which it gets.

For good lieth not in pursuing,
    Nor gaining of great nor of small
But just in the doing, and doing
    As we would be done by, is all.

—Alice Cary (1820-1871)

The Lonely Brook

Up in a wild, where few men come to look,
There lives and sings a little lonely brook —
Liveth and singeth in the dreary pines,
Yet creepeth on to where the daylight shines.

Pure from their heaven, in mountain chalice caught,
It drinks the rains, as drinks the soul her thought;
And down dim hollows where it winds along,
Pours its life-burden of unlistened song.

I catch the murmur of its undertone
That sigheth ceaselessly, "Alone! Alone!"
And hear afar the rivers gloriously
Shout on their paths towards the shining sea.

The voiceful rivers, chanting to the sun,
And wearing names of honor, every one;
Outreaching wide, and joining hand with hand,
To pour great gifts along the asking land.

Ah, lonely brook! Creep onward through the pines ...
Press through the gloom to where the daylight shines!
Sing on among the stones, and secretly
Feel how the floods are all akin to thee!

Drink the sweet rain the gentle heaven sendeth ...
Hold thine own path, however-ward it tendeth ...
For somewhere, underneath the eternal sky,
Thou, too, shalt find the rivers by and by ...

— Author Unknown

Astara

Healing and the Blood

Second Degree — Lesson Fourteen

THE PRANIC ETHER AND HEALING

It seems there would be empty spaces between the electronic particles composing the cells of your body. But it is not so. These seemingly vacant spaces are filled with substance! Permeating every atom and cell of the physical form is the body or sheath called the *etheric double*. This body is composed of the four physical ethers: light, pranic, electric, mental reflecting ether.

Unlike the astral body, this etheric body possesses no consciousness apart from the physical form. It is the agency through which life and vitality are diffused into the cells of the physical form and without which the form cannot sustain "life." In any discussion concerning healing, we must recognize the presence of the pranic ether and the part it plays in both healing and psychic unfoldment.

Pranic ether, or prana, is both a healing force and a psychic force. It can operate effectively only to the degree that the etheric double is able to assimilate and distribute it according to the *love* expressed by the individual. Prana is one form of what Astarians call the White Light, and it enters the physical form principally through the navel chakra and the Third Eye, manifesting in the bloodstream as a healing force, and in the nervous system as a psychic force.

At our present stage of evolution the psychic force generated by the pranic ether passes through the nervous system undirected and unguided. The average personality is not even aware of the presence of this psychic force. When one ultimately gains a recognition and understanding of it, one can consciously begin to develop its power and use its influence in daily life.

When we come to understand that prana also is a healing force, we will begin to direct it properly to bring about healing via the nervous system and bloodstream. At present, the subconscious mind-sympathetic nervous system captures the pranic forces as they enter the physical form. The psychic and healing power in them passes through and out of the human being, unused and undirected. As we become increasingly aware of this prana and its tremendous potential, we will begin to control it with our conscious mind. The person who has gained complete domination of the pranic ether is worthy to be called "Master."

PRANIC ETHER AND THE SUBCONSCIOUS MIND

It seems expedient to speak now of Astarian healings in connection with pranic ether, karma, and the subconscious mind.

To accomplish a healing, the Astarian healer attempts to reach the subconscious mind of the one requesting spiritual treatment. Often it is the subconscious mind, reacting to guilt or to the influence of karmic picture images, which blocks the free flow of pranic ether and thus causes illness. If we are able to persuade the subconscious mind of the petitioner that he or she has suffered sufficiently for any misdeed in the past, and that s/he is deserving and worthy of a healing, the subconscious mind then opens the inner barriers to receive the inflow of vital pranic energies. The physical form positively cannot be ill if the pranic ether is permitted a free, harmonious flow throughout the cells and bloodstream.

The power of the mind over the flow of ethers throughout the system is so amazing as to be almost unbelievable. Expression of sudden fear, for instance, can absolutely paralyze the functioning of the sympathetic nervous system.

If a petitioner has buried in the subconscious a feeling of guilt, the bloodstream will be filled with toxins. If the Astarian healer can convince the subconscious that the guilt is unnecessary, that s/he is now deserving of greater peace of mind, then a healing manifests.

In some instances the one who seeks healing will work a remarkable change in his or her own subconscious which releases the energies of healing. S/he banishes guilt or fear complexes by some deed of service or penance. In any event, the subconscious receives the evidence that the person is worthy of a healing.

Followers of the Catholic faith, in praying for a certain blessing, a healing, protection or guidance, will often engage in some kind of self-denial designed to convince the subconscious that the healing or blessing is deserved. Some will, for instance, pray consistently for a certain number of hours before the statue of a saint. Or, for a number of days, they give up something that means much to them. They will find some way, at sacrifice to themselves, to cause the subconscious to respond and bring about that which they wish to manifest.

Those of other faiths will often donate their time and energy to some worthy organization, or will tithe to their church or synagogue far beyond their means, thus giving up or sacrificing something from their own lives.

Although none of these persons may be aware of it, this action is designed to convince the subconscious that they are worthy of a blessing, whether in the form of a healing, better employment, greater happiness ... whatever be the need. Whatever the method, it most certainly is important that the subconscious be convinced that a healing or blessing is deserved.

When we are able to reach the subconscious mind of the person needing healing with supreme conviction, it is only then that the subconscious will give the pranic ethers free reign and s/he frequently experiences an instantaneous healing. Until then the bloodstream is constricted, blocking their flow, and the psychic force in the nervous system is inoperative.

Some Astarians, puzzled that we are able to bring about incredible healings in others when they are seemingly left without help, should realize that it is not because we have given less effort to their cause. It may be because we have not been able to convince their subconscious that they are yet worthy of healing. There may be feelings of guilt or barriers buried deep within, preventing the healing from manifesting.

Pursuing the subject still further, let us say that you are an Astarian in need of healing. Ask yourself these questions:

"In my subconscious mind do I feel guilty about something that I should be doing and am not?"

"Have I hurt someone and neglected to ask forgiveness? If so, perhaps confined in my subconscious is a deep feeling of resentment toward the other, making me feel guilty and thus blocking the flow of White Light.

"Have I neglected to do all that I could toward helping some friend reach a goal when he has gone out of his way to help me reach mine?"

"Should I have given a tithe or performed a service for someone or some organization that has served me well? If so, could it be that I subconsciously feel guilty about it?"

" Do I carry a deep resentment toward others who have attained a higher place in life than I, when I feel that I am their equal in every way?"

"Do I go right on eating foods to which I know I am allergic, or drinking beverages which I know are harmful, simply because I do not use the proper will power?"

If you answer "yes" to any of these or similar questions, analyze the situation well for it could be that buried deep in your subconscious are the seeds of your illness, and thereby its cause. If any of these categories describes you, then this could be the reason you have not realized a healing when someone with perhaps a similar illness has. It is difficult to analyze your own particular case and find the deeper answer to it all. Only you can truly answer these questions.

These ideas should not be interpreted to suggest that if you are ill or have not achieved a healing it is your fault. These ideas are not meant to assess blame, but simply to remind you of the spiritually-based tools which are yours and which often can assist you in supporting your own healing process. They include forgiveness of self and others, praying for healing and that any negative karma be erased, serving others, tithing, nurturing and loving yourself. You may also use techniques such as Reiki, yoga, spiritual study, visualization, affirmations, massage, energy work, chiropractic, homeopathy, herbal remedies, acupressure and acupuncture, psychotherapy, and many more, combined with the best that traditional Western medicine has to offer.

MENTAL REFLECTING ETHER AND HEALING

It is involved, however, with the flow throughout your being of the White Light aspect of the pranic ether. Once this powerful White Light is given entrance into your bloodstream by the release of all feelings of guilt, as well as the other techniques mentioned, then a healing is more likely to manifest, for the pranic ether is one of the prime sources of healing in the physical form.

The priest-healers understood not only the circulation of the blood but the circulation of nerve fluid throughout the nervous system. They understood well that both these fluids were influenced by the power of the mind — not only of the patient but of the healer. They understood how to draw decomposing and toxic force from the blood, and infuse new magnetism into it through mentally directed prana.

To the Egyptian healers, blood symbolized the Universal Fluid in its densest form. The birth of blood in the bone marrow represented to them, as well as to medical science today, one of the greatest mysteries we have ever attempted to unravel, for out of the blood are truly the "issues of life."

Medical science shares much today with the Egyptian priests in their healing temples of old. Many physicians concur that the condition of the blood changes according to the mental attitude of a patient. They do not share with the ancients, however, an understanding of the presence and activity of the physical ethers in the blood, which has a bearing upon this mystery. They only know that it is so ... as the patient thinketh, so will the bloodstream react.

That is why the holistic physician strives to instill healing and calming thoughts in the patient. He or she knows that if the mind can be influenced to hold positive thoughts, the condition of the blood will react accordingly, and usually bring about a healing.

Although the physician is not aware of it, s/he is employing the use of the mental reflecting ether. If s/he can instill thoughts of serenity, perfection and healing in the consciousness of the patient, the bloodstream will pick up these minute picture images and carry them throughout the body.

Medical science constantly engages in extended research into the mind and its influence upon the human form with its myriad illnesses. During these investigations a physician might administer a placebo to a patient, saying that it is a powerful medicine. A placebo is something which contains no pharmacological value whatever — such as a sugar pill or an injection of distilled water — but which the patient believes to be medically active.

When such a placebo is administered, the physician suggests its healing action to the patient, and frequently healing is experienced. The waking conscious mind passes these suggestions into the subconscious and the subconscious, reacting accordingly, passes new thought pictures of health into the bloodstream through which they are carried to all areas where healing is needed. The glandular system, reacting under the influence of the subconscious, operating through the sympathetic nervous system, begins to pour important hormones into the bloodstream which also bring about the healing.

The placebo, then, acts only as a catalyst to begin the flow of pranic ether, under the active force of the mind, using the mental reflecting ether. The mind creates a powerful flow of picture images which carry the "picture" of health and healing throughout the physical form.

It is the flow of karmic picture images in the bloodstream that ultimately makes us what we are, or keep us from being that which we would like to be — or which, transmuted, can bring us into closer alignment with the Divine Source.

INFLUENCES FROM "OUTER" SPACE

The atmosphere around us is charged with the four physical ethers. (There are ethers from the astral plane, the mental plane, and all the celestial realms which also descend into our atmosphere, but speaking of them at present might add confusion. We shall discuss them in future Lessons.) We are presently concerned with continuing our thoughts regarding the mental reflecting ether of the physical plane and its effect on the bloodstream.

Many atoms of our atmosphere are charged with this mental reflecting ether which contains pictures of all the thoughts of humanity en masse. Since ether is energy, and since energy follows thought, and since the mental reflecting ether is a recording ether, it must then follow that this ether records every single thought expressed by anyone anywhere, and carries it in a perpetual procession of   activities throughout the atmosphere surrounding us. These mental ethers enter the brain, record the thoughts, and pass out and away from the brain in the form of brain waves, or thoughtforms.

We live in an ocean of these various drifting mental ethers — ethers which have photographed good thoughts and evil thoughts, inspired thoughts, prayerful thoughts, ideas for inventions, for war, for peace, for construction, for destruction.

This reflecting ether with its perpetual stream of images is like a tape recorder, running a magnetic tape constantly through your brain and bloodstream. What is recorded upon the ether need make no impression whatever upon your consciousness or upon your bodily system, and may pass out and away from you as do other waste substances if they find no affinity which would cause them to remain.

However, should any of the thought pictures impressed upon the reflecting ether encounter anything of harmony within you, they instantly will add to the magnitude of that particular thought. *Wherever fertile ground is found, seed thoughts find an anchor and take root.*

Your superconscious mind, or Oversoul, employs the blood as the vehicle in your physical form to carry on its impressional functions. Finding its seat of contact in the brain, the impressional impulses extend into the spinal cord, out of which they become infused into the bloodstream to influence your body and your life. These higher impulses from the Oversoul radiate throughout your bloodstream just as the mental reflecting ether carries impressions into your bloodstream from the sea of ethers around us.

Your life and its success greatly depends upon which of these two influences carries the greater impact. You can be perpetually influenced by the Oversoul, or you can be passively swayed by the influence of the mental reflecting ethers passing the homogenized thoughts of the mass consciousness into your being.

The incoming impulses of the mental reflecting ether are met either by picture images created by your own thoughts and actions, and find attraction there, or they find nothing with which to blend and therefore pass away completely. You are, indeed, through the action of your own karmic activities and your own individual picture images, contributing greatly to your own success or failure.

You are not governed by the presence of the mental reflecting ether in your blood except as it can harmonize with your self-created picture images. Having attained an understanding of the influence of the mental reflecting ether you can recognize it and control it.

Finding yourself thinking thoughts which seem to be foreign to your nature, you will learn to discard them at once. This is a "get thee behind me, Satan," approach. The wise disciple, recognizing them for what they are — foreign objects in the being — will immediately cast undesirable thoughts away, discarding them completely and denying them further power. If they do not find lifeforce in some mind, the undesirable thoughtforms floating in the atmosphere will eventually disintegrate.

It must be recognized that *the mental reflecting ethers also possess and pass into one's consciousness inspired thoughtforms released from the minds and hearts of great thinkers all over the world.* These can be a blessing to any individual according to the mental attunement with them.

YOUR ANCESTRAL BLOOD

The indigenous person in the past lived daily life instinctively according to the combined experiences of the tribe as dictated by the ancestral picture images flowing through the bloodstream. Life was lived according to tribal custom, and not as much as an individual, self-conscious being.

Later, through intermarriage, the mixed blood of many tribes caused the breaking up of crystallized picture images of the single clan, which reflected tribal customs and mass thinking of that clan. The newly mixed bloodstream began to reflect more of the thinking of the individual as gradually he or she gained release from the tribal pattern.

The blood of many ancient tribes flows in the bloodstream of every person today, but life now is dominated by the record of individual experience. Most of the ancestral picture images have long since passed into the seed atoms as emotional and mental qualities or deficiencies.

Every thought you think, the food you eat, every emotion you feel, is recorded in the three seed atoms — the physical seed atom in the heart, the astral atom in the solar plexus, and the mental atom in your brain. Picture images constantly pour out of these atoms into your bloodstream to be brought into manifestation in your physical form. Some ancestral picture images are still active but only from the level of the subconscious.

If these ancestral picture images contain records of violence and are powerful enough in their vibrations, they could bring about subconscious reactions even in your life today. However, you can erase much of their power as they rise through the subconscious. According to the extent of your control over their influence, they become dissipated.

On the other hand, any ancestral picture images which contain records of harmony with others, honoring and connecting with the Earth, knowledge of ancient healing practices, and so on, can contribute to your daily modern life and can be integrated through your mental and emotional skills.

You overpower and dissipate the residue of undesirable picture images in your bloodstream and you give power to desirable ones through:

1. spiritual study and activities including meditation, prayer, affirmations, etc.;

2. developing positive attitudes toward life;

3. intelligent thinking balanced with emotional awareness and health;

4. interest in cultural pursuits;

5. service to others through a worthy cause;

6. developing self-esteem and respect.

By these practices persistent undesirable picture images are rendered lifeless and soon disintegrate. It may very well be that this is precisely what Christ's overpowering influence accomplished in the life of the man possessed by spirits whose name, he said, was "Legion." Innumerable ancestral picture images in the bloodstream may have overpowered the man and driven him berserk. But their effect was disintegrated by the spiritual power of the Christ.

At the present time in our evolution the sympathetic nervous system, under the supervision of the subconscious mind, shares with the heart the function of automatically circulating the blood. As humankind's cerebrospinal system further develops, it will gradually assume conscious control of the circulatory system whenever the individual so wills it.

At present, the person who is unaware of the presence and influence of the picture images is greatly affected by the subconscious which houses all ancestral memories of past lives and experiences, and which causes the release of karmic picture images out of the heart seed atom into the bloodstream. Thus humankind as a whole is a victim of past actions through the *uncontrolled automatic operation* of the subconscious mind, functioning under the control of the sympathetic nervous system.

It is each person's subconscious nature to attempt to fulfill karmic obligations in each life, and each person is reminded of these obligations through these ever-present picture images. As our cerebrospinal nervous system develops, we will be able to *consciously control* the release of the picture images from the heart atom into the bloodstream. We will not be as prone to their automatic release, as we are at present. We will also be able to neutralize the effect of germs passing into the bloodstream from the ethers.

Thus the evolution of our consciousness will be extremely   accelerated because, as the cerebrospinal system assumes influence over the blood and its contents, it will simultaneously be able to consciously purify it.

Eventually every person is destined to learn that he or she   contributes to his or her own suffering, that every effect s/he experiences is brought about by a self-instigated cause. When we thoroughly learn this lesson we will begin to exercise caution in writing our karmic records so that the seed atom in our hearts gradually empties itself of past karma, recording only the karma of the present. Eventually the good of the present will outweigh the bad of the past which will be dissolved gradually and replaced by the good we are doing day by day in our present life.

It requires more energy for a person to be bad than to be good. We simply will not find the time to be bad and, having learned that we ourselves hold the key to positive change and having begun to exercise caution in our actions, our bloodstreams will begin to become karmically pure. Much of the disease and decay of the body will disappear. In our upward climb we will begin to etherealize the bony structure which will cause the blood to pass through a process of transmutation.

To repeat: the blood cells rise from the marrow in the bones. As the bones themselves become more etherealized in the eternal process of evolution, there must take place a certain alchemy in the blood as the red blood cells eventually fade away into a radiant river of blue-white light, and the river of death becomes the river of eternal life.

BLOOD TRANSFUSIONS

In earlier days when medical science first began experimenting with blood transfusions, it employed the use of animal blood, particularly that of sheep. The results proved fatal. We cannot survive the inoculation of blood of other life species. It is also true that the animal kingdom cannot survive inoculation with the blood of humans. The animal kingdom and the human kingdom share much in common, but not the bloodstream.

The blood remains one of the confounding mysteries to medical science. Indeed great caution must be used even in transfusing blood among humans. Medical science recognizes four blood types, namely: A, O, B, and AB. Meticulous care must be taken that a donor possess the same type as the donee or recipient. A patient possessing type A must not be inoculated with type B. The cells of such foreign types clump together instead of diffusing into the bloodstream. This is known as agglutination which results in almost immediate death to the recipient.

In the Canadian Medical Association Journal, December 1957, Dr. Bruce Chown wrote: " Blood has always had a mystical quality. Its use in the operating room is often more mystical than scientific." He states that at least half of all blood transfusions given today are unnecessary and carry a "hidden threat" of death when given to a woman of childbearing age. Most transfusions are given to women in relation to pregnancy and, according to his report, not 1% of them could be classed as lifesaving. They could create considerable damage years later, however.

He describes the case of a woman given a routine transfusion following a miscarriage. Five years later she gave birth to a baby with erythroblastosis, a blood condition in which the cells are not fully matured. The baby died before it could be transfused. The condition was not due to RH or similar factors, but to an entirely unrelated blood group system.

Dr. Chown stated, "The most careful selection of the donor blood under our present methods of selection would not have prevented the sensitization of the mother and the subsequent death of the baby." The woman had changed doctors since her transfusion, so the first one never knew about the bad results of his "good" treatment.

Blood and Brotherhood

There is much ado about "brotherhood" these days. We use this term here to refer to the connection and unity of each person, men and women, one to another. We use this terminology here to discuss the concept of blood brotherhood or connection through the blood. We witness proclamations and declarations on every hand that there will be no peace until we know and practice true brotherly love. Such words become empty platitudes without the spirit of understanding behind them. Loud commentaries concerning brotherhood and brotherly love are underscored by the muted phrase, "Blood is thicker than water." The implication is obvious — blood brothers are indeed brothers. Others are the "water" type and need not be dealt with as true brothers.

This is the subconscious reaction existing in the mass consciousness today despite numerous discourses concerning brotherhood and brotherly love. An esoteric implication obviously is involved with the secret of the blood. What is it in the blood that ties a brother to a brother? The only answer we can obtain from most would-be prophets and teachers is that blood brothers are "kin." No explanation is offered as to what establishes that kinship.

As long as true brotherhood cannot come into being except through the blood, there must be some Great Plan evolved to mix the blood of humankind so that even though we may be unaware of how it came about, we each feel a closer kinship to all people everywhere.

As the decades roll, the blood of humanity will become increasingly mixed so that eventually there will no longer be "water" brothers; all people will become blood brothers and sisters. God seems to have designed this massive achievement through the process of intermarriage and blood transfusions. Ironically, both of these factors are accelerated during times of war. Tragic as is war, God seems to find a way to bring some manner of good even out of our inhumanity to one another.

In the midst of the holocaust of war, soldiers pour out their blood upon the land, while those at home pour out their blood into the vials of life and healing which are transported to the wounded and infused into their veins. Coming out of the catastrophe is a universal blood mixture and thus a closer realization of true brother and sisterhood.

Blood transfusions, even in peaceful times, help to break down the blood barriers existing between races and religions of the world. It is extremely significant to note that in the exchange of blood whether in time of battle or time of peace, the purpose behind it is healing — sacrificing one's life essence in order that another may receive it — a restoration of life — the giving from one who is stronger to one who is weaker.

This is a most important note to remember. One does not usually sell one's blood; one donates it. One gives it to help another be healed. This is indeed altruistic brother or sisterhood in action, and it is probably the *only activity* in the world today which is done for the sole purpose of helping one less fortunate. It is the height of selflessness and love to give of one's very life essence to aid another, and this sharing of the healing blood is the first true step toward peace on Earth, heaven on Earth, and lasting and eternal unity among all people.

A person needing a transfusion to save his or her life would be little impressed by a wealthy person's offer of riches. The patient can only be helped if the person gives, instead, life-restoring blood. This, then, is one person "laying down one's life for another," and this action which costs neither of them anything materially, speaks of self-sacrifice and love for humanity.

Emerging from the catastrophe of war is also an upsurge of intermarriages. Soldiers from faraway lands are suddenly transported into the midst of strangers, and in the course of human events unions occur which bind the nations ever more closely together in blood ties. In the fever and heat of war a person becomes far more interested in marrying the person of his or her choice than a person of one's own race or religion.

The religious and racial gods crumble before the impact of the universal God. Catholics marry Jews — Jews marry Protestants — Protestants marry Hindus — Hindus marry the English — English marry the Germans — Germans marry the Italians — and so it goes. Americans, already carrying "mixed blood" in their veins, go into far lands, marry and mix blood with the people of the lands, either to remain in their midst or to return with their beloved to their homeland. Apart from war, of course, bloods of different cultures are mixed from the immigration of people from one country or culture to another.

As the blood of humanity becomes increasingly mixed, the masses will come to a greater understanding of each other. Gradually the negative ancestral picture images in the individual bloodstream will be obliterated. There will be no "foreigners" anywhere in the world. The mixing of blood is the answer. The Divine Source in wisdom has seen fit gradually to bring about one blood, one unity among all.

Astarians and Blood Transfusions

It is wise to plant a word of caution concerning blood transfusions. It is important for you to keep in mind that the blood is the channel of karma. An Astarian usually is an advanced soul and will have purified the personal bloodstream to a considerable degree. If, in the course of your life's events, you are forced to be the recipient of a transfusion, be aware that in accepting the life-giving blood from another, you are also accepting into your bloodstream the karmic picture images of the donor.

However, remember that you are the ruler of your personal domain and you can, in a brief course of time, completely destroy any negative influence of foreign karmic picture images. Since through these Degree studies you are aware of the mysteries of the blood, you will be able to discern that behavior which is not a part of your normal pattern might manifest temporarily in your personality.

In this event you will understand how to master it rather than to become victim of this "outside" influence. From this standpoint, *you need have no qualms about accepting a blood transfusion.* Remembering this Lesson, you simply would set about to overcome the influence of any undesirable karmic picture images, thereby creating a rapid dissolution. It is not difficult to destroy foreign blood picture images, *if* one is aware of their existence.

Alien picture images automatically and gradually lose their potency and disintegrate in time unless they find some attraction in the bloodstream of the recipient. Understanding this, you will have no difficulty in destroying the foreign particles by overcoming their influence, and utilizing only the beneficent attributes and lifeforce received from the blood of a generous donor.

The inflow of unfavorable blood picture images could present a problem to someone who is unfamiliar with this teaching, and it is important for you to speak of this Lesson to any friend who might be a prospective recipient of a blood transfusion. If strange behavior patterns begin, either work to release them, or ask for a family member to give more blood.

Astarians should accept any opportunity to be a donor, thereby helping to carry out the divine scheme of mixing the blood of humankind. Fortunate indeed is the one who receives the blood of an Astarian. It can lift him or her into a whole new cycle of life and living, adding power, vitality and spirituality to the bloodstream.

The "Power" in the Blood

Indigenous tribes in ancient times possessed innate instinctive knowledge of the "power" in the blood. When the death of a leader occurred, blood ceremonies were conducted. The blood of the departed chief was distributed among the important leaders of the tribe, particularly to the newly-crowned chief. The tribe firmly believed that in partaking of the blood of the departed king or queen, the newly-crowned ruler was endowed with those powers. At least to some degree, these people were aware of the presence of karmic picture images in the blood and it was the power in these atomic particles which they sought to capture.

It is most certainly true that the infusion of blood of some great person places his or her picture images in the bloodstream, thereby giving the recipient access to the qualities the great one possessed. It is this ancient belief in the blood's mysterious power which causes us to realize that indigenous people had a great grasp of the truth concerning the presence of picture images and their influence.

The same is true of blood and blood transfusions today. Whereas it is true that it is possible to quickly overcome any undesirable influences, it is also true that a recipient is able to make a permanent part of him or herself any greatness, any power, which may have been given from the blood of the donor.

* * * * *

Supplementary Monograph

A NEW AGE, A NEW PERSON, AND A NEW DIVINE BEING

With the dawning of the new day, humanity is struggling against the bondage of mental tyranny. Humanity, stirring against the darkness, is reacting to the tide of knowledge which has swept down upon it ... is awakening from the spell cast upon it by dogmatic creeds and rituals. Enlightened minds, lifted on the crest of that buoyant wave, are dashing old traditions and timeworn concepts from their course across the sea of wisdom.

In the light of their newfound "science" they find the shining of a greater God. Like the mountain stream which, swollen with the melting snows of spring, sweeps the collected rubbish out of its way to the sea ... so does the tide of newfound knowledge sweep aside creeds and dogmas that will not harmonize with the new age current.

The trend to mysticism is gathering might and momentum. The minds of the mystics will not remain frozen in the grip of bleak religious doctrines. They are sweeping into oblivion the mental obstacles which have blocked humanity's progress toward God. These obstacles, projected like ghostly shadows upon the screen of the human mind, once lulled us into a hypnotic, hazy persuasion which left us enslaved to religious tyranny.

But in the unfolding, revealing radiance of knowledge shadows fade and vanish, carrying with them the panoply of doctrines which lent an illusion to splendor in the midst of their oppression. In the course of such onrushing destruction of timeworn creeds, will truth also fall? Will humankind, loosed from the shackles of religious tyranny, find our onrushing headed downward into deeper darkness, or will we perceive truth ... and, following it, find a greater light?

Truth will stand unveiled for those who seek it. For truth can never dissolve under the blinding glare of scientific discoveries. Truth unveiled will only yield a greater light.

Science is opening the eyes of humankind to witness a universe which transcends anything that the boldest intellect could ever conceive. Incredible science beholds a universe boundless in its immensity, without beginning or end in any direction, extending itself throughout infinity and eternity, manifesting itself in countless arrays of solar systems and celestial bodies.

Researchers witness a balanced scheme of action ... every atom　and every solar system moving in its proper place, following its appointed course ... distances beyond the comprehension of the human mind; a universe so vast, so colossal that it baffles the power of mathematics to express it; yet so superbly synchronized from atom　to solar system that science could base its system of timing on a centuries-long orbit of a comet.

This universe, expanding itself in every direction, unfolds perpetual new vistas of grandeur — each more revealing and stupendous than the old. Immovable as a fundamental fact, yet moving without a pause in its expressed activities, it reveals in its rolling rhythm, laws which upset the ideas and faith of yesterdays. The groping eye of the scientist and the grasping mind of the mystic unite to create a formidable power against outworn concepts.

The unceasing quality of motion in all things negates the concept of death. Everything from an atom to a celestial body swirls with energy, moving in a given direction. And floating in the depths of space they move in unceasing, dynamic motion which speaks of lifeforce. Ponderous planets, hurtling on their course, manifest that perpetual motion on a gigantic scale, while electrons, darting about in their atomic boundaries, manifest that motion at a speed beyond our comprehension.

Inertia is nowhere to be discovered. The combination of eternal life and perpetual motion is the basis of all existence. Life-motion is the very essence of that universal substance from which all forms of matter are created throughout infinity.

There is no such thing as death — there is only perpetual change, continual transition from one form of life to another. In that endless cycle of life and motion there are indestructible forces of which not one iota can ever be lost. It is only human imperceptibility which admits to the false concepts of death.

Because of that irresistible energy of life-motion, new worlds are forever coming into birth. Colossal nebulae gather the dust of old worlds into the "vacancies" of interstellar space to become the nucleus of future planetary systems — celestial bodies which hold unerringly to their respective orbits through infinite space.

Electrons, the foundation of matter, eddy and whirl in the precincts of their atoms, making even so-called inanimate matter a living, moving substance. Seeds germinate, plants grow, animals prey and humans progress through the mounting cycles of their evolution. Solar systems are molded into suns, planets, moons and stars ... and breathing throughout the midst of all is the glow of the Creator's palpitating presence.

The human being, given dominion over all this immensity by the presence of the creative Spark within, becomes a creator, governing his or her own personal solar system. The infinitesimal cells throughout our bodies contribute their individual activities to the general activities of the whole, and form that unified life which is but the aggregate, the totality, of all the millions of separate lives which compose it ... organs, cells, tissues and their myriads of electrons.

Every form of life, reduced to its original constituents, splits into incalculable units of life, unceasing in activity. All these unnumbered units, taken together throughout eternity and infinity, comprise the sum total of all lives ... the one, eternal Boundless Life of the Creator from which everything flows.

The pattern of the human being came from the outer cosmos at the beginning of the formation of this system, and became an integral part of the body of the Solar Logos. Humankind, beholding such an incredible miracle, can find no name for the action except *lifeforce.*

Nature has made various forms through which lifeforce might express. But she has provided for a free contact with the original life current on which its existence depends. This principle, being an integral part of nature, is built into the very structure of every individual member in the entire scale of being, equipping it with the means by which contact is created. Thus we carry within ourselves a wireless television equipment, its antenna attuned to life vibrations which provide motion, power and vision to this little god-person who is learning the art of sending and receiving and struggling with the code of the Divine Message.

Such a struggle marks the progress toward which humanity has been groping blindly through a million years of slow and painful endeavor on Earth. Although we are evolved from eternal and universal life itself, humankind has until recently subsisted only on the outer margin of that power, unaware of its vitalizing presence, ignorant of its properties to bring out the wonderful latent forces and qualities of body, soul and spirit.

When, in the course of evolution, we rise above the concept of time in our lives, we will have left no empty margins in our beings for calendars to record. To us dead pasts and unborn futures will be dissolved in a living present.

One of our reasons for being is to live to our highest and best in the *now*. When we begin to fully believe that the Divine Being has given us eternity as well as the gift of life, even though we put the most we can into it and get the most we can out of it, still we will be pervaded by abiding peace and tranquility.

GOD VERSUS THE STUPENDOUS ACCIDENT

Faced with the appalling immensities of the universe, atheism is incredible. To deny the existence of a Creator presumes a stupendous accident. This little ball of transitory dust and water and inner flame managed somehow to become a peopled planet out of the nothingness of space. And by some preposterous accident appointed itself to swing into a certain rhythmic path among the stars, circling in an accidental yet precise pathway through the heavens. How this little ball of earth came to be a part of such a procession of planets in the solar system is unanswerable by the atheist. It should by all rights and purposes have gone hurtling into nothingness — into flaming obscurity.

To the atheist, life, living and Earth itself and all of the vast creation is an accident. Having no order behind it, all must ultimately end in chaos and nothingness.

The mystic sees a different view. The stars indeed are mute. But how they speak of God!

The atheist declares us to be only a higher animal. The mystic declares us to be a lesser god. The animal kingdom is content to exist in its round of self-preservation experiences. The human being is never content with anything. We express a perpetual desperation to escape our limitations and to capture, and make ours, that which we cannot find. We pace back and forth between the boundaries of our being, pressing always against the bars of our limitations, seeking to escape into that Something which we have not yet discovered.

If the mystic must concede to the presence of animalistic qualities in the human, we do so only if it is equally realized that the human also possesses the superior qualities of God.

In between dwells the thinking, the feeling, the plodding, the discontented and searching soul, the qualities of which set us apart from the animal kingdom and which confess our inability as yet to dwell on the level of the angels.

The adversities, which might on the surface seem to be a punishment to humankind for having fallen, are to the mystic the conditions we have woven about ourselves in order to evolve into a higher state of existence ... the price of our upward going.

The materialist views the universe about us, concluding that the only miracle observed is that the colossal accident did not somehow end in absolute chaos. He beholds no pattern behind the process of creation, observes no divine plan in action. The stars and planets and suns and galaxies simply hang poised in space, avoiding cosmic explosions by mere coincidence.

The scientist, viewing the universe, sees a boiling, boundless energy, turning inward upon itself or outward from itself ... judging the power of the energy by the substances of the planet Earth.

The mystic, viewing the infinite, sees only THAT — the infinite — the sidereal kingdom, the tremendous panorama of solar systems, galaxies, infinite time and eternal space beyond the limits of comprehension. To the mystic, first out of the void came vibration, the action of the positive and negative forces moving upon and against each other. Out of this field of vibration poured forth the air or ethers — the child of the first vibration. But the child-ether had to be clothed in other substance in order for form to manifest.

The ether extended from itself the principles of fire, light, electricity. And this, moving upon and diffusing itself with the great sea of etheric waters, brought forth the field of earth or matter in its solid, liquid and gaseous state. Thus forms came into being — not only the form of the human being but the whole of the sidereal kingdom which consists of all our planets, stars and suns.

And the mystic senses behind it all the Eternal Silence — the incomprehensible Law of Being that has formed the realm of becoming.

The mystic senses beyond the sidereal kingdom the grandiose Currents of the Godhead. And the Earth becomes only a momentary mite of dust moving in cosmic rhythm in the eddying Stream of Divine Life, the boundless boundaries of creation. And under the pressures of this formidable immensity, it is difficult to indulge humankind's appalling pettiness.

But the mystic simultaneously does not regard our transitory ball of earth as insignificant in the vastness which is God! Not by any means!

The mystic knows that though the Earth may be "one of the least of these," nevertheless it fills well its place in the cosmic scheme which may, even in the rolling tides of time, find opportunities to smile at those whose perception embraces the stupendous accident.

The mystic conceives the majestic movement of creation to be the Dance of God, sweeping in rhythm to the music of the spheres.

THE ANCIENT QUESTION, WHY?

If we accept the Divine, Supreme Being ... God ... as being omnipotent, omnipresent, encompassing all, then throughout every spiral of our investigations into a deeper knowing and understanding of this God, we come abruptly but always face to face with the ancient question: *Why? Why* has this Being infused out of Itself the forces which, uniting, create the bubbles in Its heart that become our suns and planets and solar systems. Not to gain more wisdom, for our Father-Mother God is all wise ... not to gain perfection, for the Divine is already perfect ... not to gain further glory, for Divine glory already transcends our comprehension.

THE COSMIC BLUEPRINT

Pondering the mystery, we can possibly conclude that the sole purpose of the created — the manifestations of the world of form — must be that creating gives joy to the Creator.

Having attained some measure of satisfaction in assuming this answer to be correct, we are confounded with seemingly obvious contradictions. If the Supreme Being is enjoying eternal bliss in the expression of creation, how is it that the offspring — humankind — dwells in the mire of misery? For if God expresses His unending delight in creation, we absorb very little of it. We seem compassed about with problems, with evil, with pain, with suffering.

The second *why:* How can the two extremes be reconciled? Logic and reason suggest that if the Great Parent desires children ultimately to become co-creators, they must learn how to be creators simply by becoming.

Life in form, then, is life in the laboratory of human experience, teaching us how to manipulate the elements and substances of the Creator. No scientist ever enters the laboratory, tosses ingredients into various vials without purpose and design, and gains a victory. Neither does a Creator create without purpose and design and knowledge of the work.

Thus the Father-Mother God, having given children free will, pours out the treasures of the vast storehouse and waits for us to find and unveil them, making them our own.

The question then reverses itself. We cease to ask why God established evil in the world if God is all good, and we begin to ask how is it that God tolerates within the Divine Self the evils which the offspring, through manipulation of free will, have created and continue to create. We arrive then at a better understanding of the all-pervading love of God falling about us like manna from heaven ... not creating a world of duality for us to live in but enduring in Him/Herself the dualities created by humankind.

The ancient Upanishads describe the expression of the Creator as the Immutable Delight. And we have only to attune ourselves to our Parent to partake of that delight. There is only one sure way of this attainment: to be delight or to *feel* delight one must *cause* delight.

Human beings live by two different laws: one, to find delight for ourselves; two, to give delight to others. God, the Parent, expresses both of these delights. Humanity as yet expresses primarily one.

In our mad frenzy to experience delight and to bring it to ourselves we forget that it is an impossibility in cosmic law to experience it completely without also causing it in the lives of others.

It is this action that creates the limitations of humankind. And it is in the boundaries of these limitations that we experience our world of duality: pleasure versus pain, evil versus good, hatred versus love, greed versus altruism.

Human beings, through the slow process of experience, must learn that we cannot bring persistent delight unto ourselves until we, from within ourselves, are the cause of delight for others. For seeking pleasure without thinking of the pain it may cause to others, creates a backwash of that same pain. Until we include the "others" of the universe in the expression of our own delight, we cannot experience the infinite currents of complete delight.

The pain we create by attempting to gain our own pleasures, reacts upon us as our own pain. When we cease to be the cause of it we will cease to be the receiver of it. When we become the cause of delight we will reap only delight. And we must each learn this of and for ourselves.

The toleration of the dualities created by humankind in the great Heart of God, and the answer to the reason why God tolerates it, lies simply in the understanding that it is the Great Parent expressing the ultimate of parental love, as any mother and father would do for their fallen but struggling children, their confused mass of humanity. The confusion arises because God's children are each expressing a search for the Great Delight within themselves and ways to share it with one another.

* * * * *

The Science of Salvation

Second Degree — Lesson Fifteen

GOD THE MACROCOSM — AND THE UNIVERSE

The mystery of creation — incessant enigma to people of all ages — was explained in the teachings of all the ancient Secret Societies. Although each school differed in its phraseology, the basic concept was the same. Kabbalist, Hermeticist, Rosicrucian, Mason, Dionysian ... each clothed this teaching in different raiment, but the body of truth thus hidden from the profane was always the same. Today in Astara the same ancient concept is offered in modern dress suited to the enlightened society of this remarkable age.

Like the ancients we have referred to the human being as the *microcosm* and God as the *Macrocosm* ... God, the infinite dimension of Being, and each human being a miniature replica made in divine likeness. We have said that all that is contained in God's universe is contained in us — in the periphery of our own individual universe, our auric forcefield.

To obtain a more definite understanding of the human being, it is important for us to attempt a better understanding of God, the divine Universe, and our relationship to both. It seems fitting that we study God the Macrocosm and the Universe first and then turn our attention to the human being, a miniature universe, made in God's likeness.

In this quest it may seem that we have lost sight of the subject of our present studies, which is the anatomy of the human blood. But it is extremely difficult to teach the mysteries of the blood without some understanding of the mysteries of creation, for there is a distinct connection.

A word of caution seems advisable. Some disciples of esoteric philosophy, finding the study of creation perplexing, become discouraged. We shall pass quickly over these mysteries — the concepts of universal creation — and return once again to concentrate upon the study of the individual person.

In any writing relating to the Deity, we must deal with concepts which belong in the realm of pure reason and which require profound abstract thinking. The disciple should approach these particular teachings with this in mind. They may not all seem clear at the first or even the second reading. Consider studing them again and again, meditating upon each step of the way. If you persist, you will find that gradually these seemingly abstruse concepts will open up to you and out of your subliminal Self will come the light of illumination to make all things clear. To your surprise and delight, the entire philosophy will suddenly burst upon you and afford a key to life which will open the door to a new understanding.

"IN THE BEGINNING"

The Judaic-Christian Scriptures open with a magnificent statement, the majestic sweep of which is awe inspiring: *"In the beginning God created the heavens and the earth."*

To go back to THE BEGINNING is impossible, for there never was a beginning. There can be no beginning, just as there can be no ending. And with that statement we must cease our feeble endeavor to comprehend so fearful a mystery if we would remain rational. The life of God has always been symbolized by a circle which is forever continuous, having neither starting nor concluding point.

But in the life of God, as in the life of humankind, there must be Days and Nights: periods of activity and periods of rest. We must say, therefore, that this verse quoted from the Book of Genesis does not refer to the *Primal Beginning.*

Although we cannot conceive of a beginning nor an ending in the existence of God, we *can* understand the beginning and the ending of *each period of activity* in the Great Life — the One, Only Life — the Alpha and the Omega. To such a lesser beginning the reference in Genesis must surely have been made. How to understand it otherwise? — since finite mind cannot pierce backward into the Mystery that WAS and IS and SHALL BE evermore.

In seeking out the origin of humankind and our relationship to the Parent of our being — in seeking out the mystery of the One and the mystery of the many — let us go back before the Day that now *is* into the Night that was. The Day is the period of manifestation that is and is called a *Manvantara.* The Night is the period which preceded this present Day of activity and is called a *Pralaya,* or period of rest.

What do we find?

Silence and Darkness!

Nothing perceptible!

Only THAT!

The word THAT is used to designate that which is inexpressible in English or any other language. There is no word which can adequate-ly describe that which designates God or that mysterious substance or part of the Divine which we can only term THAT.

THAT becomes the outer circle, the plane of the Absolute Divinity, paradoxically apart from, yet in and permeating every atom of existence. This plane becomes the divine Godhead ... the Unknown ... the Ocean of Spirit. In this sphere of the divine Godhead is the Essence of God, undifferentiated positive-negative forces — or masculine-feminine forces. It is not masculine-feminine combined. In this Godhead these forces are separate.

In the Silence and Darkness, and veiled in the profound mystery, THAT reposes as the Unknown — Unknown because there is nothing to know, save only Itself. *And that which is known only to itself is secret, unknown. For knowledge to exist there must be not only something to be known, but also someone to know the something to be known.* When we have the Known and the knower is aware of the Known, then we have awareness, consciousness. But in this supreme state of Absolute Divinity there is only the Unknown.

The Astarian postulates this Unknown as the fundamental principle behind everything in the manifested cosmos. Upon this fundamental principle it is useless to speculate. In fact, speculation upon THAT the Unknown is impossible, for it is beyond the range and reach of human thought since it is devoid of all attributes which the human mind can understand.

It is symbolized by three aspects or attributes:

1. Absolute Abstract Space

2. Absolute Abstract Motion

3. Absolute Abstract Duration

Abstract Space represents complete subjectivity, of which no human mind can conceive by itself. *Abstract Motion* represents unconditioned consciousness, which the human mind cannot understand except as perpetual change.

Let us comprehend THAT the Unknown, then, as Abstract Space and Abstract Motion. These two, space and motion, endure forever; that is, they never come into being and they never cease to be. They simply *are*, as God *is*. We may say, consequently, that THAT the Unknown is possessed of Eternal Being-ness — encompassing the three attributes of Abstract Space, Abstract Motion and Abstract Duration.

Abstract Space

Before proceeding further, we must state that we are attempting to describe abstract concepts in terms of our physical plane senses and finite consciousness. What we have to say must therefore be taken as an earnest attempt to clothe objectively an inner profound mystery in word symbols ... which words will, in some measure it is hoped, aid the disciple's intuition in grasping the teaching through persistent meditation.

We particularly stress meditation upon these words, for we recognize that no Ultimates can be understood from the physical plane consciousness alone. The physical plane is the plane of effects, not of causes, and the effects must remain a mystery unless the cause can be comprehended. The physical plane is many times removed from the Plane of Primal Cause, and only as the mind transcends the mental plane through meditation can the Ultimate or Primal Cause be understood. With this stated, we proceed.

All space is filled with Substance. This Substance is the power that is diffused through all atoms and all molecules, without which there would be no life, no motion, no being. If atoms are reduced to their fundamental particles, nothing remains except units of the power we presently term the Divine Essence.

The Astarian comprehends two types of space: *abstract space* and *concrete space.* By concrete space we mean the space upon which the scientist looks and upon which are based scientific discoveries. This concrete space, nevertheless, is contained in abstract space, which the scientist has not yet perceived, for it is occult, elusive, hidden behind the veil of concrete space-matter.

Even though we have drawn a circle to designate THAT the Unknown, it must be understood that the circle is only a symbol. THAT is boundless and limitless — of incomprehensible magnitude. The outer circle, symbolizing the Godhead, is necessary in our illustrations in order for our finite minds to grasp a teaching concerning the Infinite.

Further study of this space-matter must be left for future Lessons. For the present, suffice to say that the Astarian conceives of THAT the Unknown as being, first of all, only boundless space in a purely abstract sense — centerless and without circumference, turning ever both outward from and inward upon itself, and identical with the base of all Substance which is the indestructible "Matter" of Eternity.

This abstract space is Light, but it is dark Light. The Divine Substance — the Divine Child which shines forth in the heart of THAT the Unknown — is light Light, or *White Light.*

Abstract Motion

This Primordial Matter — this One Reality — is ever in motion.

By the Eastern schools, particularly the Hindu spiritual tradition, this motion is called the *Breath of Brahm.*

The One Reality — THAT — breathes; inhales and exhales. Just what is implied here we cannot pause to explain fully now. That, too, must be left for a future time. At the present moment we say only that there is perpetual motion in the plane of the Godhead. Just as there is with all substance, there is a rising and falling even of the bosom of THAT. Can you visualize the solar systems expanding and contracting both within themselves and in relation to each other? This pulsating process might be called "cosmic breathing," the universe breathing in the same way you breathe.

As the One Life inhales, we perceive THAT the Unknown in pralaya, a Sanskrit term from the ancient scriptures suggesting — dissolution, non-manifestation, rest,

GOD, THE ABSOLUTE DIVINITY

This is THAT the Unknown, the Godhead, the Primordial Dot ... God ... pure, unmanifested Substance, containing both positive-negative forces. This is the Great Ring, the Auric Egg of God's Macrocosmic Universe.

hidden mystery, darkness, the Night of rest or non-activity. As the One Life exhales, we perceive THAT in Manvantara, the period or Day of manifestation, the Day of activity described in Judaic-Christian Scripture as ... *the breath of God moved upon the face of the waters* ... and in the Hindu spiritual writings as *That One Thing breathed without air, by its own strength; apart from it, nothing existed.*

Pralaya and Manvantara are the Nights and Days of Brahm, Brahm being the One Life. In Manvantara, Primordial Matter glows with the electromagnetic Breath of the One, or Brahm.

Abstract Duration

THAT the Unknown can never come into existence, nor can It ever cease to be. It *is*. The process of divine Breathing, therefore, continues forever, eternally. This eternal continuation of THAT the Unknown is duration. Duration *is*. Time is, was and shall be. Our manifested universe is limited by time, being a Day in the life of Brahm — a Manvantara — but THAT, Brahm, simply *is*, eternal and everlasting without beginning or end.

THE SHINING FORTH OF THE DIVINE

On the plane of the divine Godhead, we have already said that the forces remain positive and negative. These two forces unite in a Divine Marriage to send forth their creation, their Child — the Divine Substance — which becomes the Child of God. How is this mystery consummated?

Within Itself, on the plane of the Godhead, THAT the Unknown sets apart a definite area to be devoted to the evolution of Its new creation. Manifesting in this circumscribed tract, if we may so designate it, the Unknown becomes the Known. It becomes the Monadic plane, the second plane down from the Godhead. It becomes the world of the Logos. The Logos is the manifested realm of being wherein are found the unnumbered Logoi or Great Beings whose plane of life becomes, by differentiation, apart from the Godhead and knowable, in an abstract sense, by humankind.

This Known, shining forth in and from THAT the Unknown, glows like a great field of light. To use more descriptive, understandable language let us say that there is a great prairie lying in darkness. Let us say that a certain area is set aside in the great prairie and that it is flooded with electric light. Now the electric power is drawn from hidden sources concealed in the great prairie, such as an underground river, for instance, providing power to illuminate the circumscribed area. The great prairie lies in darkness ... except for the lighted portion which shines forth in its bosom, and which draws the power for its light from the prairie's hidden resources.

The great prairie would thus be the Unknown.

The lighted area would thus become the Known ... the Monadic plane ... the plane of the Divine Substance.

THE CHRIST SUBSTANCE

In the Mysteries this Divine Substance was variously termed the Waters of Everlasting Life and the Bread of Salvation, the blood of Divine Substance and the body of Divine Substance. Here again, this reference to Christ refers not to the man Jesus, but to the metaphysical symbol his life represents in the mystical Christian tradition — that divine consciousness merging with human life to uplift it. The reference to Christ or to the Christ spirit in these Lessons means the divine spirit or spark of life present in every person of every religion, tradition or background. This Divine Substance, the Child of God, contains both the masculine and the feminine aspects of its Parent — the Supreme Being — THAT the Unknown, which sent it forth.

Each atom of the Divine Substance is infused at the core with the divine Seed of the Supreme Being. When THAT the Unknown breathes out the atoms which will compose the field of light called the Known or the Plane of the Divine Substance, THAT sees to it that these atoms are heavier than those in the Great Prairie. These heavier atoms congregate together to form the Known or Monadic plane, or, in our example, the lighted area.

The heavier atoms composing the area of the Monadic plane cannot then rise above a certain level of being. In other words, they cannot rise into and penetrate the realm of the Godhead, being heavier than the atoms of that Unknown Country. But, at the same time, each atom of the Divine Substance, as we have already said, is infused at its core with the divine Seed of the pure Light of Absolute Divinity, the Godhead.

FIVE CELESTIAL RIVERS

Five celestial rivers flow out of the Monadic plane, sometimes called the plane of the Divine Mouth. These rivers are called *Fire, Air, Water and Earth,* each tinctured by the divine ether, *Azoth* — Azoth being the fifth river, the Divine Substance. Out of these five substances are formed all the other planes of life: the Nirvanic plane, the Buddhic plane, the causal plane, the mental plane, the astral plane and finally the sidereal kingdom which comprises the suns and their numerous planets and stars ... all things that are manifesting on the lower dense plane of matter.

Therefore we depict God as a Supreme Being consisting of visible and invisible essences ... this Invisible Sphere bringing forth from within Itself manifested visible creations.

Thus we have our sidereal kingdom — the realm of stars, planets and heavenly bodies — manifesting and pulsating in the heart of the unmanifested Celestial Spheres. The sidereal kingdom is visible to the physical eye. The unmanifested Celestial Spheres are invisible. Nevertheless, the Celestial Universe has brought forth from in itself the crystallized manifestations we know as the visible realms. The visible sidereal kingdom proclaims the presence of the Celestial Universe around, within and outside of it.

The five celestial rivers of Azoth, Fire, Air, Water and Earth symbolize the great waves of essence and substance which continuously pour down from the Monadic plane to create the ethers or "waters" of space which surround us and the planets on which lifewaves of humanity dwell.

The planets are the gateways through which the Divine Substance makes its entrance into our solar system. Indeed, the planets could well be compared to magnifying glasses which diffuse through themselves rays from the higher spiritual planes, thus concentrating and distributing the essences of divinity into the worlds of matter.

Eventually there will be twelve such rays, projected through twelve planets. The sun will become the thirteenth. At present there are only seven known rays and nine known planets. In future Lessons we shall teach more fully concerning these rays and their effect and influence upon individual human beings.

The principal gateway for the entrance of the Divine Substance or Azoth into the world of matter is the sun of our solar system. But it is directed into our sun by the Great Central Spiritual Sun, found on the invisible causal spheres.

THE GREAT CENTRAL SUN

Paracelsus, mystic and scholar of the Mysteries, wrote: *There is an earthly sun which is the cause of all heat, and all those who are able to see may see the sun. And those who are blind and cannot see him, may feel his heat. There is an eternal Sun which is the source of all Wisdom, and those whose spiritual senses have awakened to life have seen that Sun and are conscious of His existence. But those who have not attained spiritual consciousness may yet feel His power by an inner faculty which is called "intuition."*

All the Mystery Schools clearly taught the existence of three suns:

1. *a spiritual Sun* unseen by mortal eyes. This they called the Great Central Sun of the universe. This Sun is the agent of the Divine Substance which radiates from the Monadic plane. Through this spiritual Sun the Divine Substance is beamed forth to reach:

2. *our terrestrial sun* whose daily rising and setting marks the diurnal rotation of the Earth on its axis;

3. *the head center, the Third Eye* in the human being, reflecting the rays of the sun of our solar system.

When the heart seed atom becomes cleansed of its crystallized "sins" or errors, only then can the head center begin truly to absorb and reflect the rays of the Divine Substance sent into our ethers from the highest Monadic plane. This Divine Substance

THE SHINING FORTH OF THE DIVINE

In the Unknown, the positive-masculine forces unite with the negative-feminine forces in a Divine Marriage to bring forth their creation, the Child of God. The Divine Substance combines the masculine-feminine attributes of the Parent Plane. Each atom of the Divine Substance is infused at its core with the divine Seed of the Supreme Being, the Unknown. It is the field of light shining in the heart of the Unknown.

cannot be absorbed or reflected by or within us until we have so purified our hearts that we can receive it.

The unseen Great Central Sun is the true source of divine power and light streaming down from the Monadic plane and, like a mirror, our terrestrial sun reflects those radiating beams. Like a spiritual magnifying glass, our solar orb catches and magnifies the Divine Substance. The Great Central Sun directs the principal river of Light into our sun and its rays, pouring down on our earth planet, bring with them great portions of the Divine Substance.

It is this mystic Azoth which brings "life" to the planet and its humanity. In its higher aspect it is the essence of pure and incomparable LOVE — Divine Love, God Love — a Substance measurable by us if we had instruments sensitive enough to detect it and amplify its radiations into visible and audible waves.

Those who have achieved an elevated spiritual awareness and consciousness can be transformed through this divine substance. For example, Jesus the man becomes Jesus the Christ when, at the time of his baptism, he opens and purifies himself to receive the downpouring grace from his Parent in heaven — the baptism and anointing of the Holy Ghost — the Divine Substance from God.

Although the Substance swirls all about us, we do not comprehend it, nor will we until such time as we are regenerated and purified. And then we, too, will become a Christ, a Buddha, a Mary, a god or goddess of the divine.

THE HUMAN BEING, THE MICROCOSM — THE IMAGE OF GOD

We have described the Great Universe — God the Macrocosm. Now we turn our attention to the little universe — the human being, the microcosm.

Since we are made in the image and likeness of our Maker, we depict the divine as a small god and miniature universe. Thus, traditionally we, like God, consist of two constituents: a visible realm and an invisible realm.

We have spoken of the Godhead as THAT the Unknown. In the microcosm, THAT becomes what we call the auric egg of the human being. In the Macrocosm, THAT condenses Its greatest power in the outer rim of Its Being and becomes the Godhead. In the human being, the microcosm, THAT condenses Its greatest power in the outer rim of the auric egg and indwells the divine Monad.

In the Great Universe, the Godhead projects the plane of the Divine Substance in the heart of Its Being. In the little universe of the individual person, the divine Monad projects the Divine Substance which finds its greatest concentration in the Oversoul.

Thus the Monad pours down through the silver cord the supreme essences of being to its Child, the Oversoul, the Christos within and above humankind. Again the Monad

THE FIVE CELESTIAL RIVERS

Five celestial rivers pour out of the plane of the Divine Substance — Fire, Air, Earth, Water, and Azoth, the Divine Substance. All of these substances create a sea of ethers around us, but we have not yet evolved so that we can perceive and absorb them. The Divine Substance swirls all about us. We only need to " breathe" it in, in order to be "saved." Our corrupt bloodstream obstructs its absorption. Future humankind, through a purified bloodstream, will be able to make the Divine Substance a part of the physical being, thus immortalizing the physical form.

extends its influence farther down the sutratma into "matter," the physical form, and finds its home in the heart center.

The Oversoul compares to the Great Central Sun of God's unseen universe and pours its power, via the silver cord, into the human being through the head center.

Pulsating in the heart of this auric egg is found the material form. Contrary to traditional belief, then, the spirit of the human being is *not* encased within the physical form. Being at the opposite extreme from the commonly accepted teaching, this concept bears repeating for emphasis:

> *The spirit of each person is not encased in the physical form. The physical form is encased in the spirit being, the auric egg.*

The physical form, the transient vesture of the soul, hangs suspended in the auric egg of spirit as an embryo hangs suspended by its umbilical cord within the bag of waters enclosed in the physical form of a mother. Portions of the Monad and portions of the Oversoul manifest within the physical form through the silver cord which carries their essences into the brain and heart centers.

The auric egg pulsates now with the Divine Substance. Several factors prevent our use of it:

1. the antahkarana, the spiritual umbilical cord, is undeveloped. This is the communication cord extending between the personality and the Oversoul which we must build by and through our individual spiritual efforts;

2. the bloodstream is corrupted with karmic picture images which reflect our past and present misdeeds;

3. the chakras are not yet vibrating on a wavelength high enough to receive it.

When we, through spiritual discipline and regeneration, develop the antahkarana into full power; when we cease to create more undesirable picture images in the heart atom, and when we create vortices of power at the chakric centers, then we will be delivered from our human bondage. We will have arrived at the beginning of the dramatic process of evolvement into a wider dimension of life.

The chick in its embryonic state in the egg is limited to the capacity of the shell. Reaching its time of birth, the chick breaks through the shell and emerges into the world to express a greater life.

The babe in the womb is limited to the capacity of the womb, cradled in the waters of gestation. Arriving at its time of birth it, too, emerges into the world to express as an individual being.

The human being, standing mature and upright, has filled the pattern of destiny so far as the form is concerned, but the physical organism is, in turn, surrounded by the

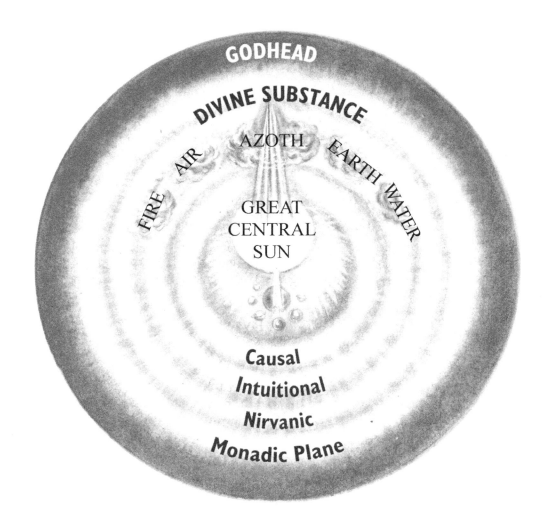

THE GREAT CENTRAL SUN

The Great Central Sun exists on the causal plane, the higher mental plane. Azoth, the Divine Substance, pours out of the Monadic plane into the Great Central Sun, which beams the divine Substance into the sun of our solar system which, in turn, pours it upon Earth and its inhabitants.

THE THREE SUNS — VISIBLE AND INVISIBLE

From its place on the causal plane the Great Central Sun projects the Divine Substance into our sun. It, In turn, pours the Substance down into the atmosphere and ethers of our world. The "sun" in the head cannot yet absorb this spiritual Essence. When our hearts become cleared of corrupt picture images, the head-sun will then absorb these waters of everlasting life, and humankind will live forever.

auric egg — the forcefield of that which each is to become — a greater pattern, the pattern of the god-Self toward which each is building. To attain this spiritual stature we must, by the power of our minds, break through, or transmute, the shell of the physical and emerge into the higher ethers of our ultimate Self.

We do not refer to the death process. We refer to the transformation of the cells of the physical form through which it assumes immortality — through which *this corruptible must put on incorruption, and this mortal must put on immortality.* (I Corinthians 15:53)

Birth into the higher organism requires tremendous struggle. But as the chick and the babe break their limiting confines, so we, in the fullness of time, will break the shell of our mortal self and merge with the greater dimensions of our true spiritual estate. There, having broken our human bondage, we will dwell in the fullness of our immortal Self. We will have outgrown our cocoon and become the butterfly.

We will have achieved immortality — not through death — but here and now, a transformation of the mortal flesh. The human being becomes the Master ... the Master becomes the god.

THE HUMAN BEING, THE MAGNET

The human being, like the planet, is subject to the law of gravity. All substances and elements of earth are obedient to the command of gravitation. It calls the waters of brooks and rivers down from snow peaks to flow into the sea. All the substances of the physical realm are drawn toward the center of Mother Earth by the power of the great magnet in her heart which attracts and holds to herself the elements of her being.

The human being possesses two such magnets:

1. *Kundalini,* the feminine creative fire. When the form still resided in ethereal realms, Eve, the pituitary gland — feminine portion of the cerebrospinal nervous system — took unto herself the "fruit" of the Tree of the Knowledge of Good and Evil, or the mental substance which was building the cerebrospinal nervous system, and gave of the fruit to Adam, the pineal gland. Thus the substance which was needed to build a better mental forcefield around the brain, in order for humankind to attain a higher state of consciousness fell to the lower chakras.

    But the fall of the creative substance also gave us the power to become a creator ourselves and, by that power, to evolve our own godhood. This feminine mental substance became kundalini — the creative fire coiled in the root chakra superimposing and diffusing through the generative center. We shall have more to say concerning this "fall" of humankind in later Lessons.

2. *Brahmarandra,* the magnet in the crown chakra which houses the Third Eye. One of its functions is to magnetize or draw the higher substances in the

blood upward to the brain. We shall enlarge upon our teachings of this head center when we enter our Lessons concerning the brain.

The substances in a person's bloodstream answer to the law of gravity so long as the bloodstream is filled with the iron, lead and chemicals of earth. The blood elements are drawn downward in the body to the creative centers in the generative organs by the magnetic power of kundalini, just as the law of gravity draws earth elements downward to the heart of the planet.

The Divine Substance, entering the bloodstream through the breath, is not of *itself* subject to the law of gravity nor the downward attraction of kundalini. But once it enters the bloodstream, it becomes clothed in the properties and corruption of the blood, muddied by our lower emotional qualities. And since no mental power is exerted to direct it upward, it is drawn into the eddying currents of desire and carried to the lower kingdom of kundalini.

The Brahmarandra is not yet powerful enough to break the downward pull of gravity and cause the higher substances in the blood to be drawn automatically upward to the brain.

Each person's bloodstream is filled with crystallized errors and the chakras are stagnant with carnal desires. The mysterious magnetism necessary to attract more Divine Substance out of the ethers and hold it in the bloodstream is lacking. Increased magnetic power in the blood is required. The present corrupt bloodstream can attract only those chemical properties which, obeying the law of gravity, are drawn downward by the magnet of kundalini, robbing the magnet in the brain, the Brahmarandra, of life's greatest treasures.

At present we walk through life not unlike a deep sea diver groping our way in the watery deeps. As the diver explores the waters, the substances and the life of the underwater world, s/he is protected from its pressures, its currents and its forces by the cumbersome diving suit in which the form is encased. Helpers on the deck of the ship above pump lifegiving air through a life line. Without it the diver could not live beneath the waves.

The human being, in the physical form, gropes through an ocean of ethers swirling all about the soul enmeshed with a cumbersome body of flesh, bones and blood. We inbreathe the air of our world, without which we could not live. But on a higher plane the Oversoul is constantly projecting down to the personality a force of tremendous voltage. Yet we, immersed in a sea of it, cannot make use of it. The antahkarana, the spiritual life line, is as yet too weak to absorb great portions of it, and the bloodstream is too corrupt. This force is the Divine Substance.

Walking through the ethers of our world like the deep sea diver, we see only with our physical eyes — poor lamps indeed for beholding the true universe. Our eyes beam forth their finite rays, beholding only a three dimensional world. Like the diver peering through the distortions of a watery world, our perception is dim and limited and inaccurate.

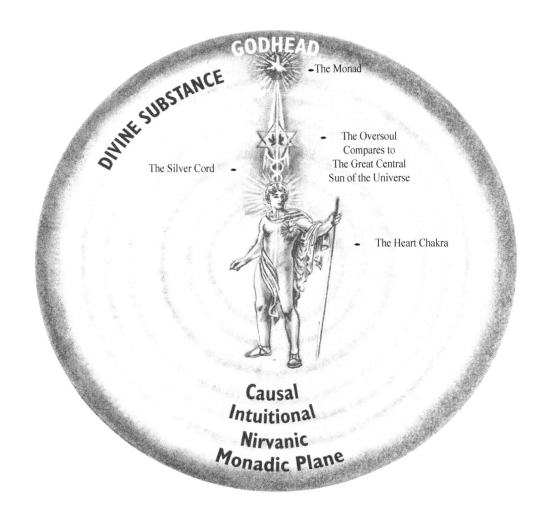

THE AURIC EGG OF THE HUMAN BEING

The divine Monad contains the concentrated essences of our divine spirit. The Oversoul contains the Divine Substance and compares to the Great Central Sun of God's Macrocosmic Universe. The heart chakra is the home of the physical seed atom, which controls the entrance of the divine substance into our being. Until the seed atom is purified of karma, the bloodstream is corrupted and cannot attract and "hold" the Divine Substance. We will attain "salvation" only when the bloodstream becomes filled with the "blood of the Divine" — pure enough to absorb and contain the radiant Divine Substance.

ABSORBING THE DIVINE SUBSTANCE

The Divine Substance is as real a force as is electricity. It operates on an entirely different voltage and wavelength than anything yet discovered by humankind. It is an eternal ocean flowing about us, waiting to be absorbed into the bloodstream. We call the great ocean of eternal Substance the *Holy Word*. We call it the great Cosmic Current, the Holy Nahd, the divine Sound — that great cosmic ocean of Substance living, throbbing, pulsating with a singular energy — the sum of which is God's *LOVE*. In the depths of this eternal ocean can be found the shining Drops of the Source of everything — the Shining Essence of God.

The Divine Substance indwells every person and is an innate part of each being. So densely are we involved in material substance, however, the divine Substance and its influence cannot be felt. Its impulses are largely ignored.   Truly Christ stands at the door and knocks — but the resident of the physical house seldom bids him enter.

The magnetic properties of the blood required to attract and hold the essences of the Divine Substance could be compared to a common lodestone. The lodestone contains a peculiar property which draws certain minerals to itself and holds them by the law of magnetic attraction. The lodestone of itself is only slightly charged with this mysterious magnetism. However, wrapping an electric copper wire about a piece of lodestone (or any magnet), and introducing an electric current into it, increases its power tremendously and enables it to attract and hold minerals many times its own size and weight.

Electricity cannot travel along a wooden rail or a post. It can travel along a copper wire — the proper conductor for its forces — a substance suited to its purpose. So must the Divine Substance have the proper conductor along which to travel — the proper conductor to attract it into the physical form.

The "copper wire" in the human being is the pure bloodstream, plus a powerfully developed spiritual thread, the antahkarana. The Divine Substance cannot be attracted in major quantities into the ordinary dense physical form any more than electricity could travel through a wooden post. Nor can the quantity that does enter through the breath be drawn upward toward the magnet in the brain, the Brahmarandra, unless we use some mental force to direct it there. The major portion of the Divine Substance is thus pulled downward into the lower chakras by the magnetic power of kundalini.

However, whereas the law of gravitation pulls all things downward, the Life Stream of the Divine Substance rises, like heat, and pulls everything *in harmony with it* upward. And our soul harmonizes, through the law of magnetism, with the divine Current *once the bloodstream is purified*. The elements of the blood must be so purified as to harmonize with the upward pull of Divine Substance.

This transmutation in the bloodstream occurs through lifting the Chrism out of the generative organs and into the spinal cord. When mentally directed, it is carried upward through sushumna to the medulla oblongata where it is again transmuted into a yet higher substance and released into the brain ventricles to mix with the brain dews.

There this divine water of everlasting life is utilized by the pituitary, which distributes it as "gold" into the bloodstream.

This "gold," or this transmuted Chrism, mixed with the Divine Substance in the bloodstream, is not subject to the downward pull of gravity. It rises upward to the brain if the mind, exerting enough mental energy, causes it to be diverted from its usual downward flow toward the reproductive organs.

Any measure of attainment brings untold rewards. One cannot open oneself to receive this Divine Essence without absorbing some portion of it any more than one could stand under a waterfall without getting wet.

When the brain is stimulated through meditation, and especially when it is attuned to the divine Sound of the Holy Nahd, then the activated magnet of the Brahmarandra temporarily pulls the spiritual currents upward. Tuning in to the divine Current not only floods the spiritual being with light but it causes a tremendous mental stimulation and development in the brain cells.

THE KARMIC BLOOD

It is the blood that carries the picture images of the past out of the heart seed atom. The blood also distributes picture images released by the mental seed atom in the pineal gland, making the body subject to the immediate effect of causes set in action by thought.

Thus, after being created in the heart and brain, both present and past karma mingle in the blood and either build or destroy the physical structure according to their picture images.

Love builds the physical structure. Hate and all its attributes destroys it. The brain which releases picture images of high ideals, aspirations, power and love, is the brain which is building a better body in this particular incarnation, and most certainly is preparing the mental power with which to build a better body for the next. One's higher aspirations give power to the soul, just as food gives power to the body.

The power of the soul is what builds the next body. The soul can be built only by the forces of love which are attracted into it by the higher mind. The person who does not express love does not build power into the soul. And after the death of the physical form the soul discovers it experienced in this particular incarnation in vain.

The bloodstream at its present voltage attracts iron, oxygen and other necessary substances out of the ethers, but only in minute quantities, only enough to sustain life. But with the regeneration of the physical body, the purification of the bloodstream, and the increased voltages of the psychic chakras, the body, like the lodestone, can bear the increased power of the higher voltage of the higher planes. We call this voltage the Bread of Life and the Living Waters of Eternal Life.

Mystical Christians see in this Divine Substance and the way it interacts with the human blood stream the symbolic meaning of divine communion — the body and the blood of Christ, the blood and the bread of salvation and eternal life.

Under the unrelenting process of time, our crystallized physical forms are being refined into a more radiant structure, into what the mystics call the *Living Philosopher's Stone*. This future human body, this Living Stone, is gradually becoming radiant with the light that shines from within.

When we ultimately realize ourselves to be immortal spirits with immortality as our only real goal, we will have taken the first step in attaining the status of the spiritual alchemist. We will have begun the arduous task of transmuting the lead, or iron, in the bloodstream into the pure gold of the Divine Body within, built of the shining, pure essence of Divine Substance. This is indeed finding the Philosopher's Stone. This is indeed transmuting lead into gold — the highest science of the ancient alchemist. Anyone who would be a conductor for and receiver of salvation ... of liberation ... must be able to transmute the iron of the blood into the pure gold of spiritual essence.

The mark of this attainment will be measured by the purified physical form. The chakras, representing the glands, will have become vortices of shimmering, swirling White Light, radiating pure Divine Substance throughout the physical form. Each chakra will be a dynamo of power constantly consuming, through the breath — manna from heaven — the Substances emanating from God's pure realms.

The bloodstream will have become a scintillating river of divine light, purified at last of the karmic picture images, of all the crystallized "sins" or errors contaminating the present bloodstream. Then the body will be constantly "washed in the blood of the Christ," immersed in the stream of White Prana emanating from the heavenly realm. It will pour into the purified blood with every breath and with every thought ... the breath inbreathed through the mortal form and the Divine Substance inbreathed through the Divine Being within.

As the bloodstream becomes purified, little by little the Divine Substance in the auric egg will begin to penetrate, adhere to and activate the atoms of the material being, transforming us gradually into the divine beings which we are to become. We shall no longer "see through a glass darkly," but we shall see with the unfolded Third Eye whose beam of light will encompass the true seven-   dimensional world around us.

The Lord (or powers of regeneration), rising up the spinal cord and passing through the land of darkness (the lower chakras), will find the pure blood of the lamb (the blood free from karmic sins) staining the doorway and the lintel (the medulla) and will "pass over" into the Promised Land (the head).

The Bull, the Ram, the Fish and the Human Being

Passing ages have their symbols, abundantly overflowing with meaning and inspiration to the perceptive consciousness.

The bull was sacred in the Taurian Age; in the Arian Age it was the ram; the fish symbolized the Piscean Age; and in the present Aquarian Age it is the human being — not the physical, but the person in the heavens, or the one who functions in the Aquarian Age consciousness.

You are in the process of becoming the Aquarian Age person. As you grow in understanding and enlightenment, you approach nearer and nearer the divine state which the symbol signifies. Your studies thus far entitle you to the next two Lessons which further your transition from the being of Earth to the Heavenly Being. Gain more insight to the Council Halls of Eternal Truth.

Lesson 16, **Salvation and Mystic Christianity,** opens the Book of Mysteries and its dramas which reveal life's significance. Learn what it really means to participate in the Passover, to partake of the Last Supper, to be crucified on the heavenly cross, to find the inner New Testament.

Lesson 17, **Immortality and the Second Birth,** reveals further Mysteries, the hidden meaning of the second birth, the bread and waters of eternal life, true immortality, developing the Divine Spirit within, transmutation through regeneration, the New Person.

THE DETAILS OF THE
INFINITE PLAN ARE LEARNED
IN THE COUNCIL HALLS
OF ETERNAL TRUTH.

THEY ARE NOT LOST

The look of sympathy ... the gentle word
Spoken so low that only angels heard ...
The secret act of pure self-sacrifice,
Unseen by men, but marked by angels' eyes ...
    These are not lost.

The sacred music of a tender strain,
Wrung from a poet's heart by grief and pain,
And chanted timidly with doubt and fear,
To busy crowds who scarcely pause to hear ...
    These are not lost.

The silent tears that fall at dead of night
O'er soiled robes that once were pure and white;
The prayers that rise like incense from the soul,
Longing for Christ to make it clean and whole ...
    These are not lost.

The happy dreams that gladdened all our youth
When dreams had less of self and more of truth,
The childhood's faith, so tranquil and so sweet,
Which sat like Mary at the Master's feet ...
    These are not lost.

The kindly plans devised for others' good,
So seldom guessed, so little understood;
The quiet, steadfast love that strove to win
Some wanderer from the ways of sin ...
    These are not lost.

Not lost, O God! For in Thy City bright,
Our eyes shall see the past by clearer light,
And things long hidden from us here below,
Thou wilt reveal, and we shall surely know ...
    They were not lost.

        — Selected from "Between the Lights"

SOMETIMES

Sometimes — a radiant way,

Sometimes — adrift;

Sometimes — a happy day,

Sometimes — bereft;

    But always — Your nearness.

Sometimes — the lonely call,

Sometimes — the hoping;

Sometimes — fulfillment,

Sometimes — the groping;

    But always — Your here-ness.

Sometimes — the quest is long,

Sometimes — the night;

Sometimes — the Wisdom's song,

Sometimes — the Light;

    But always — Your dearness.

        — Earlyne

Salvation and Mystic Christianity

Second Degree — Lesson Sixteen

THE BATTLE OF THE BLESSED BOOK

Midst the bitter battle of controversy, chaos, confusion and consternation, shines the much beloved Scriptures — the Holy Bible. Placed in a vast "no man's land," it stands between two embittered foes.

Planted on one side is materialistic science, flanked by its laboratories, microscopes, telescopes, stethoscopes, reactors, and its innumerable instruments measuring time and space in humanity's finite world.

On the other side, entrenched in dogmas, crystallized creeds and narrow precepts, are the staunch fundamental religionists.

The war is the Battle of the Blessed Book. Beholding its sacred pages, the battle begins even with the opening line of Chapter One:

> *In the beginning God created the heavens and the earth. And the earth was without form and void; and darkness was upon the face of the deep. And the spirit of God moved upon the face of the waters. And God said, Let there be light ...*

"Ah," says the materialistic scientist, "but there is no God. All of creation is one stupendous accident. Man is a quirk of chemistry. And earth is a fragment of a cosmic explosion. Man comes forth, lives and dies, and is heard from no more."

"Not so!" defies the fundamentalist. "There is indeed a God, and creation is His divine plan. He created the Earth in six days and on the seventh He rested. The Earth is six thousand years old, because the Good Book says so."

From there the interminable quarrel expands in myriad directions, covering every aspect of human existence: the past, the present, the future ... every state of humankind's being and not being.

It must be remembered that most scientists are not atheists. Many hold firm convictions about a Supreme Creator and their scientific research causes not a denial but a desire for perpetual seeking for the awesome Unknown. Neither are all believers fundamentalists, ultraconservative and anti-scientific. Many realize that religion, in order to be of practical use to humankind, must find a scientific basis upon which to build its more metaphysical precepts.

But regardless of how the soul and creation are viewed, there is controversy between some factions of scientists and religionists. Scientists themselves are divided on many of the subjects concerning the Bible. And the religionists are divided into so many denominations they are beyond number, all due to individual interpretation of the Great Book of the Secret Seals.

It is not our purpose to delve into this interminable controversy. Rather it is to plumb with you the depths of the pool of wisdom as taught in *mystic* Christianity. These esoteric and ancient teachings are now but wan reflections of their past glory as they ripple, unrecognized or misunderstood, across the surface of today's theology. If one will search the depths, if one will seek the inner meaning of the Scriptures, one will find the teachings there.

It is easily realized that the subject with which we are concerned is vast and comprehensive. In this one Lesson we can only lift fragments of the cosmic veil. Though the teachings here are fragmentary and our ultimate goal is an understanding of the mystery of the blood and its involvement in the soul's evolution and salvation, this Lesson will, nevertheless, help you discover hidden wisdom in the Holy Book.

As the future Lessons unfold, these fragments will become threads of a pattern of understanding which, woven into a whole, becomes a tapestry of wisdom.

In future Lessons we shall refer again to the "fall" of humankind, to the study of evolution, involution and epigenesis ... to the study of the Solar Drama and the sacrifice of the Solar God for the humanity of our solar system and its ultimate salvation. For this particular Lesson — a "digest" of the Christian Mysteries — we can touch only briefly the teachings involved in humankind's redemption.

THE SUN GOD AND THE ZODIAC

Let your imagination take you back in time some 2,500 years. It is high noon. You are in the spacious tiled courtyard of a magnificent temple. You are a candidate for the Mysteries, ready to be initiated as a custodian of the secrets of the soul's regeneration through the Sun God.

In a circle around you are priests whose robes are decorated with the signs of the zodiac. Moving slowly toward you is a tall figure whose head and face are covered with a mask depicting the head of a ram. You are about to learn the meaning of the Solar

Drama ... and how to become the Lamb of God. As the priests enact the movement of the planets through the heavens — and the path of the sun through the zodiac — you are presented teachings similar to the following:

The sun, traveling the zodiacal pathway through the heavens and the constellations, marks the production and the measurements of the seasons of the year based upon the equinoxes and the solstices: the vernal equinox, the summer solstice, the autumnal equinox and the winter solstice.

Solstice — the two times during the year when the sun is farthest away from the earth's equator. In the Northern Hemisphere the summer solstice is around June 21. The winter solstice falls on or near December 22. In the Southern Hemisphere, the solstices are reversed.

Equinox — the two times during the year when the sun crosses earth's equator, traveling from one hemisphere to the other. March 21 is known as the vernal equinox when the sun enters the Northern Hemisphere from the Southern. September 23, approximately (the dates of the solstices and equinoxes vary according to our calendar), is the autumnal equinox, marked by the passage of the sun across the equator as it enters the Southern Hemisphere from the Northern.

Ecliptic — the apparent path of the sun through the skies. The sun actually occupies a fixed position in the heavens: our earth planet — and the other planets in our solar system — revolves around it. For simplification in ascribing the seasons, however, astronomers "created" an orbit for the sun as if it revolved around Earth. This theoretical orbit is called *ecliptic* (path).

When the Greek astronomer, Ptolemy, delineated the constellations around 150 A.D., the vernal equinox, he discovered, had been located in the constellation, or sign, of Aries. The equinox has moved backward along the ecliptic, however, and is now located in the constellation, or sign, of Pisces. This movement backward through the celestial zodiac is called "the precession of the equinoxes."

The solstice north of the celestial equator is the summer solstice, falling around June 21. The sun is then at its greatest point away from Earth in the Northern Hemisphere. This marks the beginning of summer in the Northern Hemisphere and the beginning of winter in the Southern. The sun then travels toward the Southern Hemisphere, crossing the equator on the autumnal equinox around September 23, and the seasons of the Northern Hemisphere and the Southern are reversed.

The winter solstice, when the sun is at its greatest point away from the Earth in the Southern Hemisphere, is around December 22. From its position on this date the sun then begins its journey along the ecliptic back into the Northern Hemisphere, entering it as it crosses the equator around March 21 — the vernal equinox.

Thus the sun starts on its way along the ecliptic toward the Northern Hemisphere at the time of the winter solstice, although it doesn't actually enter it until it crosses the

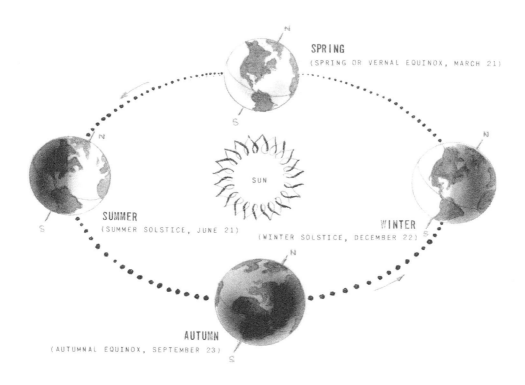

equator in March, marking the vernal equinox. This movement of the sun toward the Northern Hemisphere and away from the Southern explains the Christmas celebration, and the Easter festival celebrates the crossing of the sun over the equator into the Northern Hemisphere.

These festivals sometimes coincide with Christmas and Easter of Christianity, the Hanukkah and Passover of Judaism, as well as the myriad so-called pagan rites of other peoples and civilizations who recognized the Birth and Death of the Sun God, as Earth's sun was born and resurrected year after year, marked by the solstices and equinoxes.

THE NATIVITY IN THE SKY

At the time of the autumnal equinox our sun is moving slowly out of the Northern Hemisphere toward the Southern. If it continued its journey on southward, away from the Northern Hemisphere, it would leave the northern half of Earth destitute of light and life.

But at the time of the winter solstice, on the evening of December 21, the sun turns again toward the Northern Hemisphere bringing light, heat and life with it. Thus residents of the Northern Hemisphere celebrate the birth of the sun back into their half of the Earth at Christmas time, as well as the birth of the Christ.

The sun does not actually cross the equator to re-enter the Northern Hemisphere until the vernal equinox in March. But the winter solstice celebrates the "birth" of the Sun God as He begins His journey along the ecliptic toward the Northern Hemisphere, while the vernal equinox celebrates the maturity or fruition of the power of the Solar Deity as He enters it in His fullness.

On the night of December 24 the constellation Virgo — the Holy Virgin — stands on the eastern horizon to light the way of birth for the newborn Sun God. Opposite the point occupied by Virgo the Virgin in the eastern sky, over in the western sky in the belt of Orion, three stars called the Three Magi shine in splendid tidings to worship and bring their gifts to the newborn Sun God.

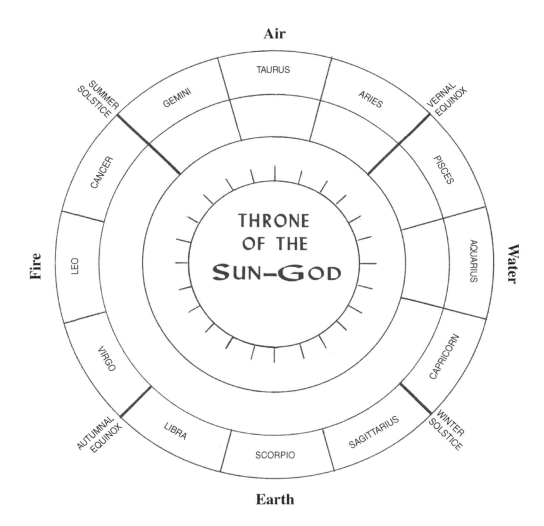

During this holy nativity the essence of the Christ Substance or Divine Substance pours down its effulgent light to bathe the humanity of the earth plane, washing it in Holy Dew and diffusing every atom and every substance of Earth. The hearts of humans, unconsciously witnessing this outpouring of Love from the higher planes, respond accordingly. Individual souls feel the magnetic pull of the upward current of Love at Christmas time, feel the rekindling of the Light in their hearts during the celebration of Hanukkah, feel the return of divine Light into their lives as they honor the Winter Solstice, or simply feel a resurgence of light, energy and divine connection in their lives at this time of year.

THE MAGIC CUP

The zodiac in the heavenly spheres forms a magic circle around our planet. In the Mysteries this circle of light, or of essences, was called a Cup. In that Cup are held all the forces and substances required for the evolution of this planet and its lifewave of souls.

As our planet passes from the influence of one celestial zodiacal house to another, each house pours into the ethers of our Cup, our planes, its own substance. And the mixture of substances from all the houses constitutes the magical formula of spiritual essences, prepared by God Him/Herself, that pour down upon humanity and our Earth, renewing and resurrecting humans, animals and vegetables alike.

THE LAMB OF GOD

In tabulating their zodiacal sciences the ancients always symbolized the sun by the animal representing the constellation through which it passed at the vernal equinox. For the last two thousand years the sun has passed the vernal equinox in Pisces, the sign of the Fish. For the two thousand years before that it passed the vernal equinox in the constellation of Aries the Ram, and it was during that time that the ram was placed at the head of the zodiac and became sacred as the zodiacal "Lamb of God."

In the Mysteries "the Lamb of God" had several different references. In the age of the Ram, the hierophants in the temples were given the name of "Shepherds." The initiates were called "Lambs," and each became a "Lamb of God" upon completing his or her initiations.

On certain occasions "the Lamb of God" referred to the symbol and title given the sun during the centuries that the vernal equinox occurred in the constellation of Aries. Rams and goats were sacrificed as blood offerings to this zodiacal Lamb of God. This period was called the Arian Age, during which the lamb became a sacred symbol in the religious rites and ceremonies of the time.

The Lamb of God was also a phrase which signified the sun who, born every year back into the Northern Hemisphere in the sign of the Ram, saves the people. The sun

CRUCIFIXION OF THE SUN UPON THE HEAVENLY CROSS

The "saving blood of the Lamb" was the powerful "saving" Divine Substance — an ether containing a "life" force just as the human blood — pouring down upon Earth through the sun, as it hung upon the Heavenly Cross in the sign of Aries the Ram. The sun was crucified upon the Cross and from this crucifixion poured forth the mysterious Christ Substance — the "blood" of the Lamb — which, breathed into the human form, "saves" and regenerates the soul.

re-enters the Northern Hemisphere in the sign of Pisces at the present time, hence this age is called the Piscean Age. Previous to the Arian Age was the Taurian Age, in which the sign of the Bull was prominent. During that age the bull became sacred in the religious rites and ceremonies because the sun crossed the equator at the vernal equinox in the constellation of Taurus the Bull.

The *bull* was sacred in the Taurian Age, the *lamb* in the Arian Age, the *fish* in the Piscean Age, and the *human being* becomes sacred as we are entering the Aquarian Age, which, although it is an air age, has as its sign that of the Water Bearer — the man with the urn on his shoulder pouring water upon the peoples of the planet. This "water" is not water as we know it but is "heavenly" dew. It symbolizes the Divine Substance which the Heavenly Human, during the Aquarian Age, will pour down in increased quantities upon the children of Earth.

In the Mystical Christian tradition, the Christ becomes "the Lamb of God" in that, during the Arian Age or the Age of the Ram, the Christ Substance or Divine Substance entered the ethers of the Earth's atmosphere with increased power during the time of the vernal equinox, when the Sign of the Ram was prominent each year. Thus the Lamb of God, as the Christ Substance, "taketh away the sins of the earth" and "saves" through the purified bloodstream. In this instance the "blood of the Lamb" refers to the Christ Substance emanating through our sun and pouring into the world through the constellation Aries.

Since the lamb was the symbol of sacrifice for sins in all the ceremonies and rites of ancient paganism, it quickly became the symbol of the Savior of the world, dying for the sins of the world. Thus, Jesus the Christ is often depicted as the Lamb of God.

The blood of the lamb, in the ancient ceremonies, was supposed to cleanse the participants of their karmic transgressions and sins. Thus, applying this mystic symbolism to the Christ — he, in saving humanity, does so through spilling his blood on the cross, as the lamb's blood was spilled on the altar of sacrifice.

To the enlightened initiate, however, the blood of the sacrificed lamb on the altar only symbolized the Divine Substance, the "blood" of the crucified lamb of Aries in the zodiacal heavens. The blood of Jesus, spilled at Calvary, was so powerfully impregnated with Christ Substance that it was used by the Solar Deity Himself in gaining entrance to the Earth's astral vibrations. This Mystery will be discussed in later Degrees.

The "saving blood of the Lamb" was the powerful "saving" Divine Substance — an ether containing a "life" force just as does the human blood — pouring down upon Earth through the sun, as it hung on the Heavenly Cross in the sign of Aries the Ram. The sun was crucified upon the Cross and from this crucifixion poured forth the mysterious Christ Substance — the "blood" of the Lamb — which, breathed into the human form, "saves" and regenerates the soul.

THE PASCHAL LAMB

The sacrifice of the Paschal Lamb was the purification ceremony practiced by the Jews. A lamb was offered as a sacrifice on the eve of Passover (which is celebrated around the time of the vernal equinox, approximately March 21). The sacrifice occurred in the court of the temple and great care was taken in selecting the ones who could participate.

Although a layman might be permitted to perform the actual sacrifice, the blood had to be caught by priests, each holding a silver or gold cup. The priests formed a line extending from the court outside the temple to the altar inside.

In the temple court the priest who caught the blood from the sacrificed lamb passed his cup to the next priest in line who, in exchange, gave him his empty cup. This priest, in turn, passed the cup of blood to the next who, again, gave him an empty one in exchange. Thus the cup containing the blood of the lamb was passed along the line until it reached the priest before the altar inside the temple, who then sprinkled its contents upon the altar.

THE MYSTERY OF THE PASSOVER

The Biblical account of the Passover concerns the exodus of the Jews from Egypt. It has become a religious festival celebrated by Jews commemorating their flight and their deliverance from slavery. Those observing this important Jewish tradition conduct a family feast in the home on the first evening of Passover and for the following seven days they abstain from leaven.

According to tradition, God commanded Moses to pass certain instructions to the Jews. Each household was to select a male lamb in its first year and on the 14th day of the month of Nisan the lambs were to be slaughtered. The flesh was to be roasted and eaten that same night with unleavened bread and bitter herbs. The Jews were to consume the lamb with their loins girded, their shoes on and their staffs in hand in order to be prepared for the exodus. They were to use the blood drained from the slaughtered lamb to mark the two doorposts and lintel of their homes.

When the Lord began to execute judgment upon the Egyptians for enslaving and oppressing the Jews, the blood upon the houses of the Jews was to be a sign that the angel of judgment should "pass over" those living within.

Can this Biblical account be related in any way to a ceremony of the Mysteries?

In the Mysteries the candidate-initiate symbolically became the Israelite fleeing from the bondage of the lower self. In the mystical tradition, the word "Israelite" refers not only to Jews but to the initiates of certain Mystery Schools. *Is* refers to the negative or Mother aspect of the Deity, *Ra* to the positive or Father aspect, and *El* to the Son of

Is-Ra — the Son of the Father-Mother God. Thus Is-ra-el-ite means *"one who has united with his Father-Mother God."*

The bloodstream and the spinal column become the Red Sea. The carnality in the Red Sea must be separated from the fluids and spinal gases of regeneration, freeing the latter to travel out of the land of darkness — the root chakra — toward the Promised Land — the head chakra.

The pure blood, represented by the blood of the slain, unblemished lamb, can then mark the door of the temple — the medulla oblongata. The medulla is the gateway to the Holy of Holies. The blood marking the doorposts and lintel signifies the pure blood of the lamb or the pure blood of regeneration.

The regenerated fluids, rising upward from the lower chakras, finding the blood on the doorpost and the lintel pure and unblemished, can then "pass over" into the head chakras.

In the Mysteries, the ceremony of the Passover signified that the candidates had acquired that spiritual status and ability required to transmute the creative energies of the reproductive area into the White Light of the Divine — the oils of initiation.

Every initiate understood the true meaning of the "blood of the lamb." Every initiate was aware of the true science of soul salvation and what it meant to be "saved by the blood." The blood of struggling souls had to be transmuted to the status of the pure "blood of the lamb" in order for the initiate to be "saved" from mortality into immortality.

THE LAST SUPPER AND THE PASSOVER

The esoteric idea of the Passover — that which was understood in the Mysteries — denoted the passing from one state of consciousness to another, of being delivered out of darkness into light, of being set free from bondage, a personal victory in self-mastery.

We have described the spinal gases to you. We have told you that they, bearing the qualities of the average person, rise up the spine and are blocked from entering the Garden of Eden, the brain, by the medulla oblongata. The medulla is the gateway to the Holy Mount, and the unpurified spinal gases cannot pass through the etheric web which guards the entrance to this higher estate of the soul.

The "Cherubims with the flaming sword" stand guard at the gateway, the medulla, to prevent the unpurified spinal gases from entering the brain ventricles. The soul is thus barred from re-entering its "Garden of Eden" — its mental paradise — until it has become purified.

The "Passover" in the Mysteries signified that the disciple had overcome his or her carnality and had thus purified the spinal gases which now could enter the medulla

TEMPLE BLOOD CEREMONY

oblongata, become transformed and "pass over" into the fourth ventricle of the brain — which ultimately led to union with God.

And this is the esoteric meaning of the Holy Supper. Consuming the magnetized bread and wine, symbolic of the body and blood of the deity can, under certain circumstances, transmute the spinal gases into a river of light which, passing into the brain, momentarily unite the disciple with the divine Mother/Father in heaven.

The firstborn — the struggling human born of the earth plane, engulfed in earth's passions, materiality, lust, greed, worldly ambitions and selfish desire — must be released and transformed so that the second-born — the divine spark of Light — may be given life.

The laws of nature decree that something must die before it can be born again. The soul coming down into incarnation must die to the heavenly realms to be born in the earth realms. The soul departing earth must die to the earth realms to be reborn into heaven. The lower self must die for the spiritual Self to be born. The firstborn must be overcome in order for the inner divinity to be born in the Third Eye.

The *second birth* is designated by the transmutation in the medulla oblongata of the spinal gases bearing the Golden Chrism and the "pass over" into the Third Eye. The pass over of the fluids and gases out of the medulla and into the brain cannot occur until the disciple has "girded up the loins," thereby conserving the regenerative forces.

In the Mystery Schools, candidates consumed cakes and wine which had been blest by the supreme hierophant-Ptah. This blessing transformed the food into the direct agency of the deity. When consumed by the disciple this special power became inwardly centered and helped the candidate transmute the spinal gases. As the disciple progressed spiritually the purified gases rose to the fourth ventricle — then the third — and finally brought illumination to the initiate.

The Red Sea of the spinal column must be parted. That which is lower must be left behind and that which is pure, fleeing from bondage, must be liberated in order that it may enter the Promised Land, the Third Eye. The passions of the lower blood must be transmuted so that, purified, they may "pass over" into new life.

When we drink the wine of life — the material waters surging with our unsatisfied desires and passions — we thirst again and again and never find a quenching draught. But when we drink the wine of the true sacrament — the blood of the Divine — we drink the living waters of eternal life.

This fountain of regenerative power, flowing up the spinal cord, enters the medulla where it becomes transmuted, thus enabling it to enter the fourth ventricle. There it stimulates the pineal into resurrection, which allows it to generate a flow of Chrism into the third ventricle where it combines with the brain dew to open the Third Eye. The one who drinks of *these* waters will never "thirst" again.

Such a resurrection brings new life or "new testament" into the blood. The "living waters" — or released brain dews, combined with the Chrism — exude from the brain into the bloodstream, carrying eternal life throughout the physical form.

If you ascertain from this that we are implying that the physical form, under certain conditions, can become immortal and know eternal life, that is exactly what we do mean.

There is no true reason for the physical body to grow old and die. The physical form's natural evolution is toward transmutation to an etheric form. By this transmutation process — not of death — the soul will gradually uplift this mortal form. Death will be overcome and humans will "live" forever. We shall have much more to say about this in a later Lesson.

THE NEW TESTAMENT

Let us see if we can arrive at an understanding of what Jesus meant at the Last Supper when he said: *"This is the new testament in my blood, which is shed for you."* (Luke 22:20)

What is the meaning of the word "testament?" It means bequeathing one's personal property to another. It differs from a will. A will includes the bequeathing of *all* things, but a testament refers only to one's personal property.

In this sense it must be understood that Jesus was saying that he was passing on to his disciples something which to him was very personal ... something belonging only to him as his personal property. What, then, could be more intimate than his blood? In giving it he was sharing his powers with his disciples, for he well knew that his bloodstream contained mysterious powers not yet possessed by other humans. This is the greatest gift a Master could have given to followers, the gift of the blood containing his "new testament" — his "new life" — his most valued "personal property."

We have attempted to describe the presence of actual power in the blood of great initiates, placed there by and through their own actions, deeds and spiritual evolvement. In the blood of any great initiate, few picture images will be found related to past karma. The blood has become a river of light. Purified, it reflects only the power and attributes characteristic of a Master.

The Master Jesus was well aware of this when he said to his disciples: *"Take this ... this is my blood."* When he blessed the wine, he imparted to it a portion of his own power, his own attributes.

He and his disciples well understood the blood covenant, which is to bestow upon the recipient, through the blood, the power of a Master. To mix the blood of a Master with that of a lesser evolved soul was to bestow upon the latter some of the qualities and powers of Mastership. And this is what Jesus was doing with his disciples. He was bequeathing this power of his — imparted to the wine — to his disciples.

In the ceremony of the Last Supper, Jesus gave his disciples the Blood Initiation when he passed the chalice among them and said: *"This is the new testament in my blood, which is shed for you."*

In blessing the wine he also caused it to be diffused with Christ or Divine Substance from the higher planes, making it doubly powerful for the disciples. Passing the chalice among them symbolized the diffusion of Christ's blood in the blood of the twelve.

The sacrament of Communion in the Christian faith symbolizes the blood ceremony of the ancient Mysteries, when the "body" and the "blood" of the Christ or the Divine was distributed among the initiated.

At the time of the Last Supper the "new testament" was "new life," or regenerated life, which the Master offered to every soul who would receive it. This "new life" in the blood symbolized the regenerated blood and the ultimate immortality of the mortal form.

THE NEW COVENANT

Jesus told the disciples that he was giving them a *new testament* in his blood. After the crucifixion, the law of fear was superseded by the law of love.

Jesus said: *"I bring you a new commandment, that ye love one another ... that ye love your neighbor as yourself, and that ye love God. Thou shalt love the Lord thy God with all thy heart and with all thy soul, with all thy mind, and with all thy strength. Thou shalt love thy neighbor as thyself."*

This was the new testament, the new covenant, that Christ was to leave with humanity. Henceforth, through giving his blood at the time of the crucifixion, humankind was to evolve toward God through love of God, and not to be held in bondage through fear of God.

SAVED BY "GRACE"

The sacrifice of the Master Jesus at Golgotha has become so inextricably interwoven with the doctrine of the remission of sin that it is almost useless to attempt a separation.

Jesus submitted to the crucifixion to show humankind the way to immortality. Immortalizing the physical form is not possible until the errors of the body have been remitted. Carnality must be crucified "upon the cross" of matter for the remission of the "sins" — the karmic picture images in the bloodstream. When this debt has been negated, the Divine or Christ Body can be born in the brain. There it will grow and develop like a vine through the nervous system and the bloodstream, transforming a lower human into a Christ.

The one who yearns for union with the Divine Spirit with all their soul can open their spiritual centers to receive a sudden inpouring of the transcending Divine Substance — and, through the "grace of God," or the purifying force of this power, erase their karmic "sins" and be "resurrected." This is called being "saved by grace."

You cannot force this downpouring of the Christ or Divine Substance into yourself. You can only open yourself to receive it by purifying your being to the best of your ability, and then wait upon an act of grace from God. Its sweeping entrance into your being washes away your "sins." Thus you are indeed "redeemed" by the blood of the Divine, or the bloodstream which is permeated by the Christ Substance.

This blood becomes filled with "the new testament" that the Master Jesus said was in his own bloodstream — the "new life" — the grace that he, as an evolved spiritual being, gave to all people. Jesus said, "None can come unto the Father except through me." He did not mean that everyone must become a Christian or follow rigid dogma. He did mean that we are all, like him, children of God, and that to truly become one with the Divine Source, anyone of any spiritual tradition can follow his example: to love, to heal or serve others, to believe that the divine spark of Light is within each person, and to purify the blood through erasing negative karma and through creating only positive karma.

ENVIRONMENT AND THE BLOOD

Today the bloodstream is beginning to purify itself of any negative ancestral picture images which were placed in the heart seed atom in past lives. When humanity as a whole eventually arrives at that time when its collective bloodstream has finally been cleansed, then humanity's spiritual evolution will be tremendously accelerated.

Individual souls are assuming more control of their destiny — their own subconscious thinking. You are developing mastery over your own personal experiences.

You stand, as a consequence, on the threshold of an increasing awareness of your own god-Self. To gain your individual godhood you must cease to surrender to past karma and break past karmic ties, which will enable you to evolve a purified bloodstream. You will then automatically absorb greater and more powerful quantities of the mysterious physical ethers.

The chakras, as you know, superimpose the endocrine glands. They, in turn, emit their hormones into the bloodstream, filling it with lifeforce and spiritual essences.

The spiritual essences pass out of your being unless you have spiritualized the bloodstream. The essences find no empathy there.

Your early environment can have a direct influence on your life. Childhood experiences, both positive and negative, give each person an opportunity to learn, to heal, to grow, to transform. Some of these experiences can be joyful and happy, and some very traumatic. In an effort to heal from traumatic experiences, remember your tools include spiritual study and practice, connection with nature, the support and love of friends and the help of an experienced therapist. Strong is the one who can heal any negative influences impressed in one's bloodstream from the experiences of childhood. Environment, of course, cannot supersede karma, but neither can it make too permanent an impression upon one who is faced with disagreeable surroundings *if* one resolves to "rise above it."

Keep in mind the mystical truth of the saving bloodstream. In dealing with any experience, the mental reflecting ethers must find something within you with which to harmonize, or the images upon the ethers cannot attach themselves to you or have any lasting influence upon you.

The Nazarene said: *"Resist not evil."*

To attack evil is to enter into direct combat with it. The better method is to direct light toward the evil and avoid conflict with it. For the power of the light will destroy dark forces far more rapidly and permanently than if you enter into attack against it. Attacking evil only adds to its resistance, increasing its influence upon you and adding to its destructive force. It also creates or prolongs a karmic debt with and against your combatant.

The forces of light, on the other hand, have no need to engage in conflict or battle. Light dispels darkness without any struggle on your part.

So, in the midst of evil do not attack it but hold steadily to the light, directing it toward the source of darkness — and leave the rest to God and natural law.

Thus, though it may well be difficult, in an effort to heal from a traumatic event it is important to move toward your own healing, toward building self-esteem and respect, in any positive ways you can. This may mean experiencing feelings of anger, revenge, hatred, and victimization, without becoming too attached to any of them as a part of who you are. Move through these feelings as a process on the way to ultimate forgiveness, resolution and thus freedom from the negative event. This is true healing.

THE FUTURE OF HUMANKIND THROUGH ITS BLOODSTREAM

The history of human evolution can be read in the blood. We have previously described the process of evolution in the embryo forming in the mother's womb — how its developmental growth reflects the entire evolutionary progress of humanity through the stages of mineral, vegetable, animal, and then into human form.

During this development the formation of the arterial system appears very late, which leads embryologists to believe that the blood system as it exists today is a comparatively recent evolutionary development in modern humankind — and this is true.

We have already described the process involved when the blood first began to attract the solar iron of the universe, which caused it to become heated and red as it is today. At present the bloodstream operates under the influence of the sympathetic system and receives its commands from pituitary, who also reigns over the subconscious mind. Thus the responsive blood usually carries negative commands throughout the physical form.

You, by your will power which operates through the cerebrospinal system, can counteract all the negative commands received through the sympathetic system. By affirmation, by spiritual study and practice, and by powerful positive thinking, you can set up in your body the proper, positive alchemical processes which will nullify the automatic negative operations of the sympathetic. The blood is the carrier of both, and you have already been taught how to charge your blood with positive power, if you will to do so.

The blood carries picture images from the past in conjunction with the subconscious mind. Simultaneously it carries pictures of the future. As you develop more and more of your will power, these pictures are increasingly released through the cerebrospinal system under the influence of the superconscious mind. Thus the bloodstream prophesies your future. Your present mental qualities are reflected as image patterns of the future you, and they will determine what the soul of today will be tomorrow.

In the coming Space Age the oxygen in our atmosphere will be imperceptibly transmuted to a higher type of solar cosmic substance ... imperceptible because the change will be so gradual and subtle. Even the scientists who are closely observing the cosmic rays may be unable to detect the change until many years following its inception. What, then, must humankind do to survive? The lifewave must transmute its bloodstream. The labor is not ours alone. It will happen automatically as an evolutionary process.

To recapitulate — the red blood cells act as magnets to attract and absorb oxygen from space. Without oxygen we die. The body can live but a scant few moments if denied its precious supply of oxygen. The oxygen is the fire of the blood — a life-giving essence. Therefore, the following remarks may seem startling:

Unless each soul conforms to the demands of the elements about it, the soul will be unable to proceed with the present planetary wave of humanity into the ethers of the new age. Instead that soul must reincarnate upon some planet now entering a Piscean magnetic field of expression. If we are to progress, the bloodstream must be transmuted and regenerated to attract and absorb the new type of "oxygen" which will pour into our atmosphere.

The new solar substance will be comparable to that of our present oxygen except that it will have an increased vibratory rate. The soul who refuses to purify its bloodstream by spiritual thinking, spiritual living and more pure physical habits will find it quite impossible to live under the impact of the new solar substance — just as it now finds it impossible to live without oxygen.

Spiritualizing and etherealizing the bloodstream not only will be a spiritual requisite but a physical necessity. As our scientists begin to discover the peculiar new cosmic emanations beginning to permeate our atmosphere, just so will they begin to notice its effect upon the human body. In some it may produce strange and puzzling human diseases of the blood and may react upon the system much as excessive radiation reacts now.

The new age thinker, such as the Astarian, will express vibrant qualities of radiant spiritual attainment. You will absorb and benefit by the solar emanations now beginning to enter our atmosphere. This new "fiery" element will penetrate, magnetize and regenerate the blood, gradually transforming it. Humankind will have gained considerably in its Godward climb — and God, lying all about and within each soul, will hold the struggling child nearer the Divine Heart.

Supplementary Monograph

BREATH CONTROL

We offer here a most important exercise, the purpose of which is to aid in achieving:

1. mental poise and serenity;

2. breath control;

3. development of the inner breath;

4. improved health.

This exercise requires a candle and a candleholder, a stand on which to place the candle and a straight chair or cushion. None of these need be expensive. For instance a candleholder from your local variety store will suffice.

Seat yourself either on a chair or on a cushion on the floor, depending upon the method you choose in practicing your daily yoga or prayers or meditation.

Place the candle on the stand directly in front of you so that the flame of the candle is on a line straight out from your lips.

Sit erect, but relaxed. Let your hands rest in your lap, with palms either down or up. Wait until you are perfectly composed and at peace, then:

Begin *slow,* easy breathing. Inhale through the nostrils. Exhale through the mouth. Ignore the flicker of the flame of the candle.

As you inhale, expand the abdomen.

As you exhale, be sure you pull the abdomen in.

Watch this closely, as it is very important.

As you exhale, open the lips *slightly* so that you are emitting a quiet, slow steady stream of breath. You must concentrate closely on this for it is one of the important factors in gaining the utmost value from the exercise.

You will be unable to breathe many of these slow breaths in the beginning, which is to be expected. The flame before your lips will waver as your slow, quiet breath reaches it. And this is all right in the beginning. Pay no attention and make no attempt to avoid movement of the flame. Center your attention upon the slow, even breath.

As you continue your practice, you will discover that little by little you are able to attain a wonderful degree of slow breathing. Gradually begin to watch your candle flame and attempt to *breathe so evenly that the flame does not flicker.*

This will require much practice, but when you are able to accomplish this you will have won a tremendous victory over body, breath and mind, as well as slowly rebuilding the cells of your physical form.

The prana which you have absorbed during these slow and quiet breaths will have penetrated into every cell, every nerve, every muscle, and into the bloodstream, transforming your body completely. Under such conditions it is most difficult for a disease to withstand the purifying energies which are aroused and remain in the body. Thus the exercise contributes to a most excellent physical condition.

You will also have attained a tremendous mental poise. Try the exercise whenever you are under mental stress. The quietness of the breathing can settle the turmoil of the mind and a sublime serenity will steal over your entire being, bringing you peace, peace, peace. After achieving this peace your problems will then be much more easily solved, or at least you will not be completely upset by them. You will be using a spiritual tool, or spiritual practice to enhance your daily life on this earth plane and to move you forward on your path.

Immortality and the Second Birth

Second Degree — Lesson Seventeen

THE CHRISTIAN MYSTERIES

Approximately two thousand years have elapsed since the great soul known as Jesus of Nazareth incarnated on Earth to bring his message to humankind. It is my belief that he came with two arcane spiritual missions in addition to his obvious desire to elevate the moral and ethical level of humanity:

1. to teach the *immortality of the soul;*

2. to teach the birth of the Christ Body or Divine Body within, followed by *the immortalization of the physical form.*

Both of these missions and all his majestic teachings have become so disguised by traditional church dogmas and precepts as to be almost imperceptible. Only those who are initiates or disciples can find the hidden threads of truth concealed in the present day remnant of the record of his coming and his ministry.

Tracing the thread throughout the four Gospels we find the teaching of the immortality of the soul, or life after death, taught usually to the masses, sometimes in parables, sometimes directly. But to his disciples, and those worthy to bear it, we discover that he gave the deeper, secret teaching of the birth of the Christ within which results in the immortalization of the mortal form, thus enabling us to triumph over our last great enemy, death ... as he did.

The secret which the ancient Mysteries revealed to their candidates was the same that Jesus, the great World Teacher, attempted to impart to his disciples: *the birth of the Christ Body within mortal form can resurrect the atoms of that form and immortalize it here and now, while the soul yet abides in it.*

The secret was never meant to be revealed to the masses. Mass consciousness was not yet ready, as Jesus stated, to "bear" it. Nor is humanity ready to accept it today. We are not ready to sacrifice earthly pleasures to give birth to the Christ within. The lifewave is not ready to walk the path of perfection. It is not ready to re-enter its true estate, the kingdom of God, which dwells dormantly in the human form.

After the birth of the Christ Body, the soul's destiny is to unite consciously with the Oversoul, the union of which resurrects the flesh of the mortal form. The soul then eats of "the flesh" of divinity and drinks of "the blood" of divinity and itself becomes immortal.

The method of this attainment was a secret science taught in the Mysteries ... the secret science revealed by the Master Jesus as well as other great spiritual teachers ... and the secret science taught in Astara today.

The Master talked to his leading disciples of spiritualizing and resurrecting the mortal body. He taught the birth of the Christ within, and of the spiritual body which is formed in and of the Divine Substance or Christ Substance. And he taught that this Christ Body — this I AM — was the only means of salvation.

I am (the body of Divine Substance) *the way, the truth, and the life and no man cometh unto the Father but by me.*

This Christ Body, built by your own spiritual efforts, could save you from the effects of your own "sins," the effects of disease and death.

The wages of sin is death, said Paul. (Romans 6:23)

It is true that Jesus taught the resurrection of the spiritual form after death, but he also taught that the human body could be "raised from the dead" — that the soul could raise its mortal form from its state of perpetual decay, from being subject to death — and resurrect it to a state of immortality.

When the Master taught the resurrection of the body he clearly referred to "raising" the physical living body here and now — not the resurrection of it at some future time of Judgment after it had long been dead. The dogma that "those who accept Christ as their personal Savior will be saved from their sins and be bodily resurrected at the day of Judgment," takes on a different meaning when understood in the true esoteric sense. According to the teachings of Mystical Christianity, those who "accept" Christ are those who can "absorb him" — the Christ Substance — into their blood. They are thus saved from their "sins" — the karmic picture images in the blood. Being so saved, the atoms of their physical forms are subject to transmutation into an immortal state. This is the *true* resurrection of the body.

Again, we are not at all suggesting that this path is available only to Christians. We do not believe Jesus meant this either. The term "Christ" means Divine or the Messiah — the Savior and was a term in use long before the man Jesus reincarnated on this earth plane to become one of the highest spiritual teachers and avatars ever known. Thus, absorbing the Christ Substance means absorbing the Divine or Saving Substance, and this path is open to everyone by erasing past negative karma, through spiritual study and spiritual practice such as meditation or Lama Yoga. These paths are open to seekers of all religions. Jesus was a Master Teacher who brought these teachings from the Mystery Schools to the seekers of 2000 years ago — teachings which still live today.

To the Master, our real "death" was reincarnation into the physical planes — when the soul "died" to the higher realms. The real "tomb" was the mortal form in its state of corruption. His principal teaching was how to avoid constant rebirth in the corrupted mortal form; how the soul could save itself from the "sins" which perpetually destroy its form, and how to resurrect it to a state of immortality.

He taught that once the Christ Body was born and formed in a human being, and raised to unite with the Oversoul, the mortal form could no longer be destroyed by disease or death. The ravages of time would have no influence upon it. In this immortal-mortal form we could live indefinitely, dwelling in the higher etheric planes or, lowering its atomic vibration, on the planes of matter. It would not be subject to the laws of the physical plane.

Such a body was possessed by the Master himself.

CHRIST AND THE CRUCIFIXION

Any teaching that the Master faced the crucifixion cowering and terrified is without foundation. Before he came to Earth he knew his primary mission was to so spiritualize his mortal form as to be beyond destruction, and his purpose was to demonstrate to his disciples that he could raise it again after it had been crucified, thus proving that *his body was not subject to physical death.*

And that is exactly what he did.

He entered the crucifixion not with resignation but with willingness. He endured the crucifixion because he knew it was necessary in order to demonstrate the resurrection. He did not "die" upon the cross. He only entered a state of "sleep" — a state of suspended animation — until such time as his body could be entombed, symbolizing usual death.

Although his spirit departed from the body, the silver cord did not break. Thus after his entombment he was able to animate it again and "raise" the atoms of his physical form, composed of the solids, liquids and gases of the physical plane. He transmuted the physical atoms into etheric atoms. He "raised" his dense physical form to the vibration of his etheric form, causing it to disappear in a physical sense. This he had done on numerous occasions during his teaching mission — when he disappeared "from the midst" of his tormentors because he knew the time of his crucifixion had not yet arrived.

He remained in the tomb only long enough to impress upon his followers and the populace the fact that he had been entombed.

The majority of esoteric students today believe that his crucifixion was a teaching of life after death; that there is no death of the soul, even though the physical form is destroyed. While true, this was not the *ultimate* purpose of the crucifixion.

Since the secret teaching behind his symbolic death was that of immortality here and now and the creation of a body that would not be subject to death, why then should Jesus have been afraid when the moment approached for which he came to Earth? The crucifixion was his ultimate great victory. Why should he have cowed before it?

The entire Biblical story of the time spent in the Garden of Gethsemane is so full of contradictions as to be almost without merit. According to St. Matthew, Jesus went apart and pleaded twice with his Father in heaven that "the cup" might pass from him. What cup could he mean? It implies, of course, that he is asking to be delivered from the cross. Does it not seem strange that Jesus would pray to be saved from the crucifixion, only to say a few moments later:

> *"Thinkest thou that I cannot now pray to my Father, and He shall presently give me more than twelve legions of angels? But how then shall the Scriptures be fulfilled, that thus it must be?"*
>
> (St. Matthew 26:53-54)

The two recorded statements are direct contradictions. The "cup" to which Jesus referred was the *cup of salvation* or the *cup of immortality* in his purified blood, cleansed of sins and filled with power. He prayed that *this cup of immortality* might pass from him to all humanity, and that his crucifixion would not be in vain. His fervent prayer was that humankind would capture the meaning of his sacrifice and the true purpose of his mission, his coming, his teachings and his "death."

The immortalized human form with its perfected auric forcefield becomes the cup of immortality — the cup of eternal youth — the cup of everlasting life. It was the transmuted blood held in this cup, filled with the presence of the immortal Christ Substance, which Jesus prayed would pass to all humankind — the cup of the "saving" blood, the blood of salvation, the "waters of everlasting life."

How puerile it would have been to pray that he be delivered from the crucifixion if it were true that, by calling, his Father would send him more than twelve legions of angels. Obviously he did not desire such deliverance because in his own words he says: *"But how then shall the Scriptures be fulfilled, that thus it must be?"*

He certainly knew that the moment of his fulfillment had arrived. He did not look upon it as a time of agony, but as a time of victory. It was for this moment that he had prepared through many lives, and for which he had been chosen.

" But how then shall the Scriptures be fulfilled, that thus it must be?"

Strange that the Book of John relates nothing about a prayerful entreaty for deliverance. Jesus and his disciples, according to John, entered the Garden of Gethsemane. The Master watched Judas arrive with the chief priests and Pharisees.

> *Jesus, therefore, knowing all things that should come upon him, went forth and said unto them: "Whom seek ye?"*

> *They answered him: "Jesus of Nazareth."*

> *Jesus saith unto them: "I am he."*

> *The soldiers retreated and fell to the ground, whereupon Jesus approached them again saying: "Whom seek ye?"*

> *And again they answered: "Jesus of Nazareth."*

> *Jesus then said to them: "I have told you that I am he. If therefore ye seek me, let these go their way."* (St. John 18:4-8)

Then Simon Peter drew a sword and cut off the ear of the high priest's servant. Jesus healed the ear and admonished Peter to put his sword away, saying: *"The cup which my Father hath given me, shall I not drink of it?"* (St. John 18:11)

Then Jesus was led away to the crucifixion ... an entirely different account. It speaks no word of inner agony, but presents him as standing forth, anticipating the arrival of the soldiers since *he knew what was to come* — stepping forward when they approached and identifying himself as the one whom they sought, admonishing Peter to put away his sword, saying that he was ready to drink the cup his Father had given him.

John does not portray him as a cowering, weeping, fearful individual, but as a prophet, knowing every detail of the approaching event, looking forward to it with determination, even anticipation. Certainly in every Gospel account it is recorded that he knew what was about to happen. And it is also obvious, according to the Scriptures, that he could have escaped had he so desired.

Either Jesus was a great Master and prophet who came to serve a divine mission, who knew when it was at hand and who performed the mission admirably — or he died one of the most timorous men in all history. A great many martyrs throughout time have died dramatic and agonizing deaths, yet have not displayed the fear which some attribute to the immortal Nazarene.

Joan of Arc was burned at the stake and a more horrible death could hardly be imagined. Yet, refusing to recant her statement that she heard the voices of saints directing her, she died bravely and honorably, holding to her faith and her knowledge that she symbolized truth. History's recorded pages are full of similar accounts of martyrs who died bravely and well.

Would Jesus do less?

Some verses in the Bible describe him to be in such a state of agonized fear that great drops of blood fell from his forehead. Yet, concerning his life, this same Jesus declares: *"No man taketh it from me, but I lay it down of myself. I have power to lay it down and I have power to take it up again."*

Then, referring to his physical form, he said: *"Destroy this temple and in three days I WILL BUILD IT AGAIN."*

Hanging on the cross of Calvary Jesus is pictured as cringing before his tormentors who taunt him by saying: *"If thou art the Son of God, prove it. Come down now from the cross. Let your Father save you. If you are a king, save yourself."*

To which Jesus, according to certain translated Scriptures, replied: *"My God, my God, why hast Thou forsaken me?"* This implies that the tormentors were right: he was *not* the Son of God — he was *not* the Master — he was *not* the king. He was only a fearful, suffering human being more afraid of pain and death than the two thieves who hung on either side of him.

In the Mystical Christian philosophy, these traditional translations of his agonized fear are illogical and considered to be inaccurate. His words have been misinterpreted. According to more ancient Scriptures, especially translations from the original Aramaic which was the language Jesus actually spoke, his true words were: *"My God, my God, for this Thou hast exalted me!"* Or: *"For this was I sent!"* Or: *"For this was I spared!"*

He gave himself over willingly to those who came for him. He did not go to the Garden of Gethsemane to hide. He went there because he had revealed to Judas where he might be found. And, knowing Judas would betray his whereabouts, his presence in the Garden was simply his way of making himself available when his prospective captors came for him. Knowing what was approaching, he could have escaped if such had been his desire. *"Think you not that I could not now call upon a legion of angels?"*

He stood silent before his enemies and accusers when he was questioned at the time of his trial. If he had sought freedom from the crucifixion, could he not have defended himself in some way? And yet, question after question was hurled at him, only to be met with silence. Pilate, possibly seeking some excuse to free him, begged him to offer even some meager defense, but he did not.

Pilate said to him: *"Whence art thou?"* But the Master gave him no answer. Then Pilate said unto him: *"Speaketh thou not unto me? Knowest thou not that I have power to crucify thee and have power to release thee?"* Jesus answered: *"Thou couldst have no power at all against me except it were given thee from above."*

Jesus obviously knew that Pilate would be the one before whom he would stand in his hour of decision, and he also knew that Pilate could do nothing but play his part in fulfilling the scriptures, as did everyone else involved, so that the mystical teachings might be revealed.

Jesus was assuring Pilate that, in the drama of these mysterious events, Pilate did not have the power to crucify him unless *he* submitted to it because it was thus decreed from above, and Pilate was not to be held karmically responsible.

He made no effort to defend anything he had ever said or done, waiting patiently to face his great victory. He recognized his unparalleled opportunity, knowing that his mission on Earth was approaching its glorious fulfillment.

The crucifixion was *not* a time of pain and sacrifice for him. Do you not think he was Master enough to control the operation of the nervous system so that he would experience no suffering? Most surely — if the yogis of India can do this, if the dervishes of Arabia can do this, if the fire walkers of the South Pacific can do this — could not he, one of the greatest Masters who ever lived, do the same?

Medical science is now blazing a trail toward an entirely new concept of anesthesia. They call it *audio-analgesia*. It is also known to electronics engineers as *white sound*. The method employed is to place earphones on the patient who, while listening to certain musical selections, undergoes dental operations and other surgery painlessly without any form of anesthesia.

Medical science cannot as yet explain *how* this therapy works, they only know that it *does* work; that the sensation created in the individual by listening to and concentrating upon certain music, when other sounds are closed out, has the capacity to override pain. There is also a blockage of the nerve fluids which lead to the brain and which telegraph the sensation of pain to the brain cells.

If an ordinary human, by being tuned in to certain vibratory sounds of music, can have pain sensation blocked from his/her brain, could not a divine one such as Jesus, with brain waves under his complete domination, attune his superior consciousness to a vibratory Sound of a higher cosmic nature — the Music of the Spheres — and block the pain sensation from *his* brain cells? It must be obvious that the answer can only be yes.

To be a Master most certainly implies that one has mastered and is able to control one's own emotional and thought currents, else one would not *be* a Master.

Jesus knew that for him there would be no "agony" such as some Biblical writers and contemporary preachers are wont to dramatize. The crucifixion was to him his greatest triumph, not his time of sorrow.

We can only come to a full realization of what Jesus the Christ actually "sacrificed" for us when we ourselves arrive at that estate when we are able to control, even to a slight degree, the sensation of pain in our own physical form. Only then can we begin to understand that the Master "gave his life" not only to "die for our sins," but to demonstrate the ultimate immortality of the human form — its final glorification.

The Master Jesus sought always to teach the secret of overcoming the world, of overcoming the material body, of overcoming the last enemy — death. He wanted so much for us to understand that death of the physical body is not necessary. The body in which the Master was to ascend was his mortal form, transmuted to a state of immortality. It was this he attempted to explain to his disciples. Even they failed to grasp the full implication of his teachings until after his crucifixion, when he miraculously appeared among them.

The mystery is revealed in the Christian Scriptures in the Book of Luke, Chapter 24, verses 34-48:

> *And they rose up the same hour, and returned to Jerusalem, and found the eleven gathered together, and them who were with them, saying: "The Lord has risen indeed, and hath appeared to Simon."*

> *And they told what things were done in the way, and how he was known of them in breaking of bread. And as they thus spake, Jesus himself stood in the midst of them, and saith unto them: "Peace be unto you." But they were terrified and frightened, and supposed they had seen a spirit.*

> *Jesus said to them, "Why are ye troubled? And why do thoughts arise in your hearts? Behold my hands and my feet, that it is I myself: handle me, and see, for a spirit hath not flesh and bones, as ye see me have."*

> *And when he had thus spoken, he showed them his hands and his feet. And while they yet believed not, because of their joy, and wondered, he said to them, "Have ye here any meat?" And they gave him a piece of a broiled fish, and of an honeycomb. And he took it, and did eat before them.*

> *And he said to them: "These are the words which I spake unto you while I was yet with you, that all things must be fulfilled which were written in the law of Moses and in the prophets and in the Psalms, concerning me."*

> *Then opened he their understanding, that they might understand the Scriptures. And said unto them: "Thus it is written and thus it behooves Christ to suffer, and rise from the dead on the third day: and that repentance and remission of sins should be preached in his name among all nations; beginning at Jerusalem. And ye are witnesses of these things."*

The significant teaching here is that the Master sought valiantly to *prove* he was *not* a spirit, but that his form was the mortal form of flesh and bones which could eat of meat, but which could appear and disappear as he willed it — a form not subject to the laws of the physical plane — an immortal-mortal form.

Said the Christ: *"Destroy this temple and I will raise it again after three days."*

He did not refer to the resurrection of the soul after death; he referred actually and literally to the dense physical form which, though "destroyed," would be raised out of corruption into incorruption, out of mortality into immortality, through the process of spiritual transmutation of its atoms.

THE BREAD AND WATERS OF ETERNAL LIFE

Jesus was born of Mary. *The Christ* or Christ Substance was born of the divine Spirit.

Jesus *the man* was the son of man. Jesus *the Christ,* after he became Christed with the Christ Substance of the Divine Parent in heaven, became the son of God.

Jesus, immortal initiate, came to Earth with a body equipped to absorb and employ the use of the divine Christ Substance, universal throughout God's great systems.

The Christ becomes not only a person as personalized in the Master Jesus, but is also recognized to be a Substance ... a Substance containing great portions of the divine Root Substance from the divine Godhead ... a Substance subtle and filled with splendor, waiting to be absorbed by the individual ... waiting to baptize each soul with its power ... waiting to be taken into the bloodstream to cleanse it, to purify it and to "save" the soul from its sins.

This divine Essence is truly the "saving blood." Any bloodstream filled and radiant with it is the "blood of Christ." Any flesh nourished and influenced by such a bloodstream becomes the "bread of life" and the "body of Christ," or the body filled with and immersed in Christ Substance.

The Christ or Christ Substance, descending from the higher divine spheres to penetrate our denser atmosphere, is forever "laying down its life" that we might be redeemed. The Christ "dies" for us, in that the divine Essence is perpetually penetrating the bloodstream, there to perish, unfelt, unrecognized, unused. The divine Christ Substance is crucified upon the cross of matter — the cross which is our physical body — waiting the time of its ascension, when it will raise or resurrect that body from the "dead" mortal form to a state of immortality.

And so it is that, in this sense, Christ becomes one's "personal Savior," indeed. Jesus the man, initiated to the truth of the Christ Substance and having been an initiate in the divine Hierarchy for many lives before he came to Earth as Jesus, was well aware that few would understand the true meaning of his teachings. His "death" upon the cross became a human-made dogma of the organized church and was called "the vicarious atonement."

The Master knew how hordes of humanity, following after him, would be peopled with minds which could be influenced only through the belief that someone died suffering for their misdeeds. He knew that his true mission would be little understood by these minds, but he also knew that they could grow and evolve only by holding to the doctrine and belief that someone gave up his life to save them. And such a teaching is not without merit. It has helped many a struggling soul to live a better life, or at least to abstain to some degree from making even greater mistakes.

The Great One knew the time would come when the world must become enlightened to his true mission — that he gave himself to the cross not only to "save us from sin," but that he "died" to teach us how to save ourselves ... to teach of the Christ Substance and how to use it to bring to birth the Christ Body within all people.

Flesh and blood, in its present state of corruption, cannot inherit the kingdom of heaven. But it can become incorruptible. The mortal body *can* put on immortality.

IMMORTALITY

We have turned our minds back to the distant days when the Master's feet walked the ways of the earth plane. We have examined his valiant efforts to lead humanity to an understanding of human immortality when he realized their current level of understanding could only encompass the seasons and the sword.

How to explain engineering to a child? A child cannot understand how to build a bridge. How, then, explain immortality to mortals? They cannot understand how to build an immortal form — the engineering of the soul. Even the Master's legion of angels could not help him plant in the human mind what that mind could not conceive. Truth is always the hardest of all things to bring to birth — for truth is born from the womb of the mind and the mental womb is often barren of the necessary seeds.

Many a moment the Master must have stood, straining against the tedious turning of time — knowing well it was not meant that humankind should grasp the fullness of truth while yet he tarried with them — knowing well that although he had much to teach, they could not "bear" it yet.

He was a Supreme Teacher yearning to share his wisdom with other initiates. He taught about the immortality of the mortal form as only a sage could instruct the simple. Some of the seeds of his wisdom fell on fertile soil. The mind of Paul, for instance, caught a glimmer of the light.

Paul, initiated by the Master Jesus himself, taught of immortalizing the mortal form:

As is the earthy, such are they also that are earthy: and as is the heavenly, such are they also that are heavenly. And as we have borne the image of the earthy, we shall also bear the image of the heavenly.

Now this I say, brethren, that flesh and blood cannot inherit the kingdom of God; neither does corruption inherit incorruption.

"Behold my hands and my feet, that it is I myself: handle me, and see; for a spirit hath not flesh and bones, as ye see me have."

Behold, I shew you a mystery: We shall not all sleep, but we shall all be changed. In a moment, in the twinkling of an eye, at the last trump: for the trumpet shall sound, and the dead shall be raised incorruptible, and we shall be changed.

For this corruptible must put on incorruption and this mortal must put on immortality. So when this corruptible shall have put on immortality, then shall be brought to pass the saying that is written, Death is swallowed up in victory. (I Corinthians 15:48-54)

Paul was teaching his followers what this Lesson teaches Astarians: that death of the physical form can be overcome; that humankind can see salvation through the Christ Substance in each mortal form and change this corruptible "in the twinkling of an eye." Paul teaches that flesh and blood cannot inherit the kingdom of God. But flesh and blood can be transmuted into substance that *can.*

Paul referred to the mortal body when he said "dead." *The mortal body shall be raised and we shall be changed,* he said. The corruptible must put on incorruption and the mortal must put on immortality. Then shall death be swallowed up in victory. When mortal human beings learn how to put on immortality we will not undergo the process of death. We shall *not sleep,* says Paul, but *we shall be changed.* We will be able to transmute flesh and blood into flesh divine and will no longer taste death.

John, the beloved, also speaks of immortality through the Christ: *And this is the record, that God hath given to us eternal life, and this life is in His Son.* (I John 5:11)

John is teaching the truth of immortality in the physical form. This is the record that God has indeed willed to us — the gift of eternal life in the physical form. But that goal can be attained only through the process of the Christ formed within — which makes the human being "God's Son or Daughter."

The birth of the Christ within can be accomplished only through the process of transmutation, and transmutation can be accomplished only through the blood. The blood, reddened at present by our errors, mistakes and missteps, must be transmuted first into the royal purple of Mastership, and again into the White Light so that it eventually will shine with the whiteness and brightness of the Christ light, of the Divine Light, and the body will radiate the inner purity of the blood.

Immortalizing the physical body is a science which humans must learn through a slow and tedious process. The slow-turning wheels of evolution will bring it in time. But humans can speed the operation if we so desire.

Each incarnation sees the seed atoms cleansed of more and more accumulated karma of the past and a purer record of attainment written so that in each new life, finer material is attracted to build a more spiritualized physical form. As the Christ Body is born in greater numbers of individuals, so will they begin to manifest bodies of transcendent spiritual natures, with minds turning more and more to the light, seeking and demanding more of truth, reaching for an understanding of the mysteries of life.

THE HOLY GHOST

The true Immaculate Conception occurs in the brain. From that conception of the pituitary by the pineal gland the Christ Child is born in the "manger" of the third ventricle. Its nourishment is the Chrism of regeneration and the Christ Substance.

This Christ Body becomes the Holy Ghost. This Ghost Body — this Holy Ghost, this wedding garment — is sustained by the Christ Substance which permeates the physical form through the cerebrospinal nervous system. After birth it either matures or remains latent according to the amount of Divine or Christ Substance the nervous system continues to absorb. As it matures it extends outward to form a luminous, auric light. This ghostly celestial form is indeed "Holy" because it is built only through processes of holiness, and it is through this Body that humans commune with the Infinite Being in heaven — our Divine Parent.

This Holy Ghost, this Christ Body, is masculine-feminine in nature. It is androgynous, in that it is the result of raising kundalini from the root chakra to the head, there to unite with the downpouring divine Monad. This androgynous Being will be the means of giving birth to forms in the new being of the new age. The "new being" will be androgynous, containing both masculine and feminine properties within itself and bringing forth its creation through the masculine powers of the Monad and the feminine powers of the Holy Ghost.

Paul refers often to "the new man, the new earth, and the new age," and speaks of the body that humanity must prepare to be able to dwell upon that new Earth in its new conditions. He calls this body the *soma psuchicon,* the Greek words for "soul body," or the vehicle of the soul. *It is this subtle body,* says Paul, *that, with the second coming of Christ, will be caught up* "*in the clouds, to meet the Lord in the air,*" (or in the ethers of the new Earth). (I Thess. 4:17)

Paul speaks much of this mystic body. There is a physical body, he says, and a celestial body.

> *What? know ye not that your body is the inner temple of the Holy Ghost*
> *which is in you, which ye have of God, and ye are not your own?*
>   (I Corinthians 6:19)

Paul thus refers to the soul body, the Christ Body, as the Holy Ghost.

This Christ Body, born and formed in humans, is the Temple of Solomon. And the soul who builds it well is called the Master Mason because it requires every ingenuity of spiritual engineering to construct such a form — such a temple not made with hands, eternal in the heavens and in Earth.

THE SECOND BIRTH

According to St. John: *He that hath the Son hath life; and he that hath not the Son of God hath not life. For there are three that bear record in heaven: the Father, the Word, and the Holy Ghost; and these three are one. And there are three that bear witness in earth: the spirit, and the water, and the blood; and these three agree in one.* (I John 5:7-8)

He that "hath the Son" or the Christ born within him or herself, hath life, or has gained the potential of developing the Christ Body, which will result in eventual immortality on Earth in the transmuted physical form.

The Father, the Word and the Holy Ghost are indeed one — in heavenly substance. First there is the Godhead, the Divine Father-Mother, from which proceeds the Christ Substance, or the Word. The Word is that divine stream of life which is composed of Christ Substance. Attunement with the Christ Substance produces the birth of the Holy Ghost, or the Christ Body, or the power which develops in the individual as s/he absorbs into him/herself the Word, or Christ Substance. This accumulated power becomes the Christ Body — the Holy Ghost — which comes into being by the process of the second birth.

John names the three that bear witness to the presence of the Christ Body within: the spirit, the water and the blood. *The spirit* is the essence of the Monad in the physical form. *The water* is the impregnated brain dews, and *the blood* is the transmuted stream of light flowing through the physical form.

Jesus taught of the second birth to Nicodemus:

Jesus answered, "Verily, verily, I say unto thee, except a man be born again he cannot see the kingdom of God." Nicodemus saith unto him, "How can a man be born when he is old? Can he enter the second time into his mother's womb, and be born?"

Jesus answered, "Verily, verily, I say unto thee, except a man be born of water and of the spirit, he cannot enter into the kingdom of God. That which is born of the flesh is flesh; and that which is born of the Spirit is spirit.

"Marvel not that I said unto thee, Ye must be born again.

"The wind bloweth where it listeth, and thou hearest the sound thereof, but canst not tell whence it cometh, and whither it goeth: so is every one that is born of the Spirit." (John 3:3-8)

Birth by water is the physical birth through generation. The second birth is the birth through the waters of the transmuted blood and the fire of Divine Life. To be born of Spirit is the birth which combines fire and water, and is the second birth brought about through regeneration. The waters are the transmuted blood and brain dews. The fire is the downpouring light from the Monad. These two, charged with the upsurging power from the generative organs through the spinal cord, unite to give birth to the Christ Child in the head. *This is the second birth.*

The wind which "bloweth where it listeth" refers to the Sound Current of the Holy Nahd, the Holy Word. Everyone who is born of the Spirit or has given birth to the Christ, *heareth the Sound thereof* even though s/he may not be able to tell *from whence it cometh and whither it goeth.* In other words, one is able to tune in with the Holy Nahd though one may not be able to enter its divine Current to be carried to the higher planes of consciousness. We shall have much to say about entering the divine Stream of Life, the Holy Nahd, in future Lessons.

The growing Christ Body in the brain of the illuminated initiate becomes "a well of water springing up into everlasting life." It becomes the mystic "meat" of the initiate, of which others know not.

DEVELOPING THE CHRIST WITHIN

Those who consistently practice the steps of the Penetralia cannot fail to change the keynote of their physical form to the higher vibratory levels that indraw great portions of the Christ or Divine Substance. They will change the entire vibratory structure of their form, raising it closer and closer toward the ultimate state of incorruption.

True meditation also "sounds another trump" as your bloodstream indraws greater portions of the Christ Substance. As you gradually refine your physical form, so do you, through initiation, approach the time when the atoms of your form will be fit to assume immortality. Your corruption will be taking on incorruption. The record of your past negative karma will be fading away to be rewritten and replaced by a purer record, until you at last gain physical immortality.

Such a victory over death cannot come until the initiate understands the science of regeneration which will bring about this immortalization of the mortal atoms. Generation breeds death — regeneration breeds immortal life:

> *For since by man came death, by man came also the resurrection from the dead. For as in Adam all die, even so in Christ shall all be made alive.* (I Corinthians 15:21-22)

Generation, or the process of reproduction through the sexual act, came into being through a human being — "Adam." Through such generation came death. "*For in the day that thou eatest thereof thou shalt surely die.*"

By human beings also must come a release from death through regeneration. To rephrase: through Adam — or generation — all die. Through Christ — or regeneration — all become immortal. Thus are you "saved" by the Christ, and thus, in the esoteric or mystical sense, does the Christ become your personal Savior.

The Christ within is as personal as the breath you breathe and the surest source of salvation which could possibly be held out to the soul — this personal, powerful, divine, immortal Christ-God within and above every human being, waiting to be known — a voice crying in the wilderness of the confused, chaotic mind, waiting to be heard in the deep silences of the soul.

TRANSMUTATION THROUGH REGENERATION

Once the Christ is born within, it begins to grow and mature, extending throughout the body like a spreading vine with many tendrils. This Christ Essence has been called by many names: (a) the Christ within; (b) the I AM; (c) the Soul-Body; (d) the Vine; (e) the Christos; (f) the Wedding Garment; (g) the Holy Ghost.

In his writings the Rosicrucian philosopher, Robert Fludd, declared "Christ" to be:

1. the cornerstone of the Alchemical Temple which the human being represents;

2. the mysterious substance which transmutes any other substance it happens to contact;

3. the "Magnum Opus" in every soul which transforms a philosopher into a Knight of the Golden Stone.

Fludd believed the Christ within to be born through the release of the Chrism Oil of regeneration which, released into the bloodstream, transmutes the river of life into a river of light.

The Christos, or Christ Body, is the hidden splendor imprisoned in every human, housed in the Oversoul and awaiting its time of birth. In the Mystery Schools the hierophant taught the initiate to resurrect the precious Chrism, the regenerative substance. It was through this inner resurrection that the Christ Child within came into birth. Once the inner Christ attained maturity, the initiate became "the Christed One," just as Jesus the Master became Jesus the Christ, or one in whom the Christ within was made manifest.

Although it requires a purified bloodstream for the birth of the inner Christ, once this Body is conceived, much more than the blood is involved. The Power permeates the blood, nerve fluid, generative fluids, hormones, and brain dews. Indeed every atom of the physical form is impregnated. The light fills the body like a drop of ink permeates an entire glass of water.

The birth of the Christ is not perceptible immediately from a physical standpoint. After the inner Christ is born, the Body must be brought to maturity by continued effort. Only as it begins to attain some degree of maturity, through prayerful attention and perpetual sustenance, can its divine presence be perceived.

It becomes the sole purpose of the initiate to nourish it and bring it to full maturity. Thus you are also building the antahkarana or "vine" between yourself and the Oversoul. When this vine becomes completely matured, the Oversoul merges with the individual personality, and only then can that individual truly say, to paraphrase Jesus: "I and my Father/Mother are one."

PROPHECY AND SALVATION

In his writings, Peter refers to the "new heavens and a new Earth wherein dwelleth righteousness." He alludes to the heaven and Earth which will exist in a coming new age.

In time, the atomic structure of the Earth and its inhabitants, passing through the ethers of magnetic fields of a succession of ages (the most imminent being the Aquarian Age), will have changed completely. The nature of the atoms of which matter is composed will have been so heightened in vibration that matter as we now know it, composed of gases, liquids and solids, will have "died" and in its place will be matter composed of the four higher ethers.

> *Whereby the world that then was, being overflowed with water, perished: But the heavens and the earth, which are now, by the same Word are kept in store, reserved unto fire against the day of Judgment and perdition of ungodly men.*

> *But the day of the Lord will come as a thief in the night; in which the heavens shall pass away with a great noise, and the elements shall melt with fervent heat, the earth also and the works that are therein shall be burned up.*

> *Seeing then that all these things shall be dissolved, what manner of persons ought ye to be in all holy conversation and godliness, looking for and hasting unto the coming of the day of God, wherein the heavens being on fire shall be dissolved, and the elements shall melt with fervent heat? Nevertheless we, according to his promise, look for new heavens and a new earth, wherein dwelleth righteousness.* (II Peter 3:6-7;10-13)

Peter is prophesying and warning initiates of things to come. The first great continent, Lemuria, and all its advanced civilization was destroyed by fire. Floods and tidal waves submerged Atlantis, jewel of the seas. The next great upheaval facing Earth will be a "dissolution" through the element of air. The "fire" referred to by Peter will be fiery ethers — or air — which will dissolve the lower physical elements within itself as the planet passes through the ethers of an age yet to come.

The elements shall indeed melt with fervent heat. That is to say, the elements now constituting our Earth and atmosphere will be transmuted into higher elements. They will "pass away" and a new Earth whose substance is etherealized and rarefied will remain. The conditions even of the heaven realms surrounding the Earth planet will become more rarefied as the lesser elements are "dissolved" in the mystic heat of future ethers.

Although it is possible that the passage of the earth planet into the higher ethers may be accomplished through the blistering, fiery process of war, we believe it is much more likely and true to the process of spiritual evolution that it will be a gradual process of transmutation. According to our use of the unfolding powers which are being given to us, shall it be done unto us.

The elements — fire, air, water and earth, and all the other elements familiar to scientists — will be transmuted. Matter, or material substance as we know it, will be no more. It will be dissolved into etheric substance.

THE NEW HUMAN BEING

"Foursquare" refers to your future immortal, transmuted, etheric body — composed of the four higher ethers. And "the new city" will be the new Earth.

The three dense physical principles — solids, liquids and gases — will "pass away" or be transmuted. Both the Earth and the human form will be "foursquare," composed of the four higher ethers. Our mortal forms will be etheric ... as will the new Earth in the new day of Brahm.

Just as our second birth is the birth of the Christ within, so Earth's second birth is the transmutation of matter into ether. Humanity and Earth shall indeed "pass away" and there shall be a new heaven and a new Earth, "wherein righteousness dwells." There shall also be a new human being — a new you — resurrected and glorified.

The Christ within lies like a mustard seed planted in the darkness of earth. The divine Seed lies buried in the darkness of the brain, the waking consciousness, unseen, unborn, in passive repose. When the disciple, through spiritual struggle, attains the birth of the Christ in the Third Eye, then the Christ Body, like the mustard seed, breaks open the confines of its prison and extends magnificent branches through the physical form.

Indeed, the birth of the inner Christ can well be likened to the grain of mustard which, when first planted in the "earth," or the brain, is the least of all the seeds but which, when cultivated, manifests an incredible harvest. In the words of Christ:

It groweth up and beareth greater than all herbs, and shooteth out great branches so that the fowls of the air may lodge under the shadow of it.

Given birth and sustenance, the Christ Body branches out to encompass the complete cerebrospinal nervous system so that "the fowls of the air," or your everyday thoughts, subconscious fears and complexes, may "lodge under the shadow of it" or be overshadowed by the power of the superconscious mind as it operates under the dominion of the Christ.

THE TRUE RESURRECTION

Every Easter, Christendom celebrates Christ's resurrection — his message of eternal life. If human beings thus far have understood Christ's message to teach of eternal life beyond the grave, this is indeed a blessed assurance. But even more glorious will the resurrection become when the lifewave comes to a full understanding of the ultimate eternality not only of the human spirit but also the mortal house of the divine Spirit — the human form.

Eons may elapse in attaining this high goal — but the corruptible *shall* put on incorruption. The body is sown with dishonor — it is raised in glory. It is sown in weakness — it is raised in power. It is sown in a natural mortal body — it shall be raised into a radiant spiritual body.

And so it *is* written.

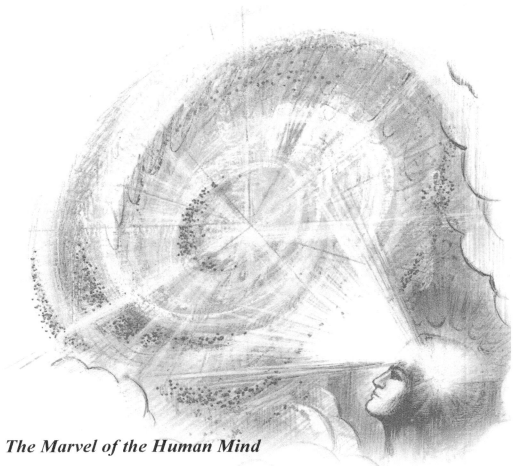

The Marvel of the Human Mind

Your mysterious mind is capable of the wildest imaginable range of expression...from cruelty to philanthrophy, from hate to love, from conformity to creativity.

It is an aspect of your Self that, more than any other, needs to be understood, controlled and directed. It is the richest field for exploration, the most abundant source of satisfaction, the most productive tool in your life.

It is the link between personality and soul...the receiver and transmitter of communications from your High Self...the organizer and director that makes your efforts productive or meaningless.

Is there any doubt about the importance of your learning its hidden secrets and vast potentials? If there is, consider the subjects discussed in the next two Second Degree Lessons.

Lesson 18, **The Brain — Humankind's Built-in Computer:** The brain in evolution, the seed of mind, your divine potential, the kingdom of God within, center of coordination, seat of instincts, matrix of inner magic, the mystic fire of the medula soul note, seven caves of the brain, the superior brain, solar plexus brain, root brain, God in matter vs. God in Mind.

Lesson 19, **Mind — The Human Maker:** Gateway to the inner kingdom, the mental forcefield, invisible nervous system, talent centers, "truth" center, genius and karma, the inner Trinity, the Tree of Knowledge, the Tree of Life, creator or corruptor.

LITTLE MINDS ARE POOR — LOFTY MINDS ARE RICH.

TOMORROW

He was going to be all that a mortal could be —
      Tomorrow;
No one should be kinder nor braver than he —
      Tomorrow;
A friend who was troubled and weary he knew
Who'd be glad of a lift and who needed it, too;
On him he would call and see what he could do —
      Tomorrow.

Each morning he stacked up the letters he'd write —
      Tomorrow;
And he thought of the folks he would fill with delight —
      Tomorrow;
It was too bad, indeed, he was busy today,
And hadn't a minute to stop on his way;
"More time I'll have to give others," he'd say —
      "Tomorrow."

The greatest of workers this man would have been —
      Tomorrow;
The world would have known him had he ever seen —
      Tomorrow;
But the fact is he died, and he faded from view,
And all that is left here when living was through
Was a mountain of things he intended to do —
      Tomorrow.

      — Anonymous

      To know the rose
      Is to know God,
      To know the faded rose will bud again
      Is to know Eternity...

Let God Be in Your Hands!

Let God be in your hands

    When you greet your neighbor;

Let God be in your eyes

    When you see the dawn;

Let God be in your heart

    When you daily labor;

Let God be in your feet

    When the way seems long.

Let God be there

    In the mists of the day's beginning;

Let God be there

    When fall the twilight's dew;

Let God be in your losses

    And your winnings —

Let God guide your life —

    He can do it better than you!

— Earlyne Chaney

The Brain -- Humankind's Built-in Computer

Second Degree — Lesson Eighteen

THE BRAIN AND EVOLUTION

The mystery of the beginning of life on Earth has never been solved. Protoplasmic cells simply multiplied and separated, broke apart and renewed themselves.

As the process of evolution continued, the forms of human beings became ever more complex. As the millenniums rolled, their brains began their perpetual development until, under the impact of the evolving soul, they arrived at their present development: an instrument radiating certain mental wavelengths, but capable of producing more spiritual wavelengths. A brain capable of abstract thought, of housing a greater mind. And a mind capable of absorbing the properties of the soul — a soul almost capable of union with the divine Spirit, the eternal part.

THE BIRTH OF THE SEED OF MIND

When the form of the human first came into existence on the Earth its state was almost as crude as that of the gorilla. The brains of the two forms were practically the same.

What is the mystery behind the evolution of the form of the human while the form of the gorilla has remained the same throughout the ages? What had the brain to do with it?

Perhaps those who declare that the mind is the brain would care to explain this enigma. If the form of the human could progress and become the instrument it is today, with originally the same type of brain structure as the gorilla, where then is the difference between human and gorilla?

The answer has to be the mind ... the consciousness ... the fact that humans are immortal souls inhabiting physical forms endowed with the potential of progression toward godhood. The gorilla remains a species of one of the higher animals, not blessed with an individual soul, not blessed with the immortality of humans.

If mind, operating in and through the crude forms in the beginning of time on Earth, caused those forms to evolve toward ever-increasing perfection, then there must have been an original pattern to which the evolving vehicles were meant to conform. This implies that our bodies, far from perfect now, are to evolve to complete perfection, according to the auric pattern invisible in the ethers surrounding it.

It is our opinion that the human being did not evolve from the monkey or the gorilla. Instead, all beings were created by the Divine Spirit, and the human being created as a separate and distinct being from all other, possessing from the beginning an individual soul and a mind. We do not endorse the Darwinian idea that the gorilla evolved into the human or that the human evolved from the gorilla. The gorilla has had eons in which to evolve into the human and he is still a gorilla. The human, beginning with a form comparable to, yet distinct from, that of a gorilla, has — through the powers of mind — evolved that form to its present state, thus separating it for eternity from the animal kingdom.

The answer is that God chose to give a conscious mind to certain of the creatures called human beings. And the forms of humans, through the powers of that mind, are evolving slowly toward perfection.

In its efforts to tie the evolution of humankind to the ape and to link the early human to the ape family, science becomes thwarted and perplexed. Although the physical construction of the brains may have been similar, the difference in the electrical waves was and is astounding.

Scientific tests should prove to the scientist the presence of not only the brain but also the mind in the human, and even the presence of the soul. Apes for the most part display a lack of human mental processes. They are, in short, animals — while every human is a being with an individualized mind.

The human is a being who, in the process of evolution, has become individualized — that is, you have departed from the group souls which encompass the animal kingdom and you operate as an individual soul. This individualization causes you to be responsible for your actions, whereas the animal is not. With individualization, humans become creators of karma, responsible for their actions, answerable to the akashic records for their rights and their wrongs. Not so the animal.

If science persists in attempting to find the missing link which separates the human from the ape, it must concede that link to be some level of mind. For there came a time in the early days when the gift of mind was given to the human form. And it was this great gift which, "breathed into the nostrils" or the brain of the human being, caused

us to develop; while the ape, lacking the gift, remains even now the ape. They do not evolve out of that state, having no individualized soul through which to progress.

The evolution of the human form gives testimony to the presence of the mind, and the fact that the form develops only through the impact of the mind.

HUMAN BEING'S DIVINE POTENTIAL

The human being is destined to evolve into godhood, and the womb of that spiritual growth is the physical body. Whereas the physical body is most often born with the capacity to see, hear, feel, taste and smell, the soul must use the physical form again and again as its womb of spiritual development. Thus the soul returns countless times to inhabit a physical form so that, through the process of spiritual evolution, it can continue its long journey of becoming.

Science proclaims you to be a composite of fluids, bones, muscles, nerves, and glands. The mystic declares you to be a spiritual being endowed with the capabilities of becoming a god or goddess.

Science invests you with the power to build a spaceship which will fly through star-clustered space. The mystic invests you with an individualized soul which will fly straight to the heart of the Divine.

Science declares you to be capable of controlling the destiny of the world. The mystic says that you have the potential to control the destiny of your own personal universe, a far greater attainment.

Science limits your life on Earth to a certain number of years, and strives to ever increase the number. The mystic declares that mortal you, may become immortal here and now, and you are endowed with the promise of eternal life.

Science and theologians declare that earthly existence is your last and irrevocable opportunity. The mystic declares that this present earthly existence, your birth into it and exit from it, is nothing more than an incident in your eternal destiny. It marks but a single milestone on your long spiritual journey from clod to god.

Science declares the brain to be the greatest instrument you possess, housing your entire thinking mechanism. The mystic declares the brain to be only a composite of certain cells, convolutions and neurons acting as an instrument for your mind which, in turn, acts as an agent for the invisible and individualized soul.

The mystic further adds that the soul is the property of the spirit, sent down into the world of matter to gain experience in the school of life — that the soul is becoming divine through these experiences and, upon graduation into its ultimate divinity, will unite again with the spirit, and will go no more out from the Father/Mother's House, having completed the purpose of its long day's journey into night.

INTEGRATED STUDIES

Neurological science, casting away the idea of a mind apart from the brain, believing that the brain encompasses our highest potential, loses its ultimate opportunity of discovery.

Discovering the mind to be a thing apart from the brain does not disqualify the brain from possessing unique and miraculous possibilities. The brain itself presents a laboratory of infinite investigation and it is only through persistence in this investigation that one enriches one's knowledge not only of the mind but also of the brain's unlimited powers.

Discovering the vast domains of God does not keep us from integrating our discoveries into the makeup of the whole person. Discovering the mind to be a thing apart from the brain does not release us from necessary research into the brain.

To integrate our full nature, we must encompass the physical, emotional, mental, psychic and spiritual aspects of our being. Although as mystics we are interested in the study of the mind, mind over matter and so on, it is important for us to become learned to some degree concerning the instrument of that mind, the brain.

THE KINGDOM OF GOD WITHIN

In the Stone Age humankind lived by a simple law ... survival of the fittest. The human with the strong back, with brawn and muscle was the hero of the times and the one most apt to survive the rigors besetting him. Presently, however, as humanity emerges into the dawn of the coming Golden Age, both men and women should fit themselves not only with a powerful and healthy body but — by far more importantly — with the power of enlightened mind.

Through the experiences humans are having on Earth today we are instinctively becoming increasingly aware that we must search for and find the world within ourselves. We must unfold mental capabilities and utilize to the utmost every innate gift of intellect and talent, not in a competitive sense but as a means of living to the highest and best that we can.

The race of competition has played its part in developing this inner urge to shine as brilliantly as possible in a world rapidly being peopled with exceptionally brilliant and creative women and men. This is the age of the brain-and-nerve person. The era of the muscle man is passing.

The brain is described as "— the enlarged portion of the cerebro-spinal nervous axis contained in the skull and extending down the spinal cord; the organ of consciousness, ideation and voluntary muscular control, receiving impressions from the organs of special senses."

It contains over ten billion cells. It weighs approximately three pounds, and resembles a pink-gray jelly. But medical science has long since discovered that it is not the size nor weight of the brain which determines the intellect of the individual.

You do not think *with* your brain. You think *through* your brain. You think with your mind as it operates through the glandular system — and then through the brain cells. The brain is but a passageway of memories arising from actions of the mind and glandular system.

The brain does not reason — it cannot love nor hate, nor experience sensational urges of any kind. The brain has no intellect of itself. It is the seat of the mind only insofar as the mind uses it as the principal focal point through which to function. The glandular structure and nervous systems have no power to operate by themselves. It is the force of mind which causes emotions to arise, and either creates a better person or utterly destroys one.

It is true that the power of one's mind is limited by one's brain capacity, which is to say that as the brain cells develop, one will be better able to progress mentally and intellectually, but the power to progress lies not within the brain itself. It lies in the indwelling soul of the personality who uses the glandular and nervous systems as avenues of manifestation.

However, the importance of the brain is accentuated when you realize that you can reach awareness of the world about you only through the mechanism of your brain. For within the cerebrum are found the sense motors of the body. That is, into the cerebrum, the seat of the cerebrospinal nervous system, flow impulses from the glands and nervous systems which make you aware that you can see, feel, taste, hear and smell.

Diseases of the brain which destroy one's ability to use these five senses indicate most clearly that within the brain is found the physical focal point of your consciousness and your ability to sense the world about you in every aspect. It is through the sense centers in the brain that you gather knowledge of the physical world.

The brain consists of involved and intricate nerve tissues, and may be divided into six parts:

1. the cerebrum, which lies in the upper areas of the skull, from front to back, and forms a "skull cap" over the top part of the brain. It is called the upper brain and is the seat of active intelligence. It is a vital part of "the Tree of the Knowledge of Good and Evil;"

2. the cerebellum, which occupies the back portion of the skull and is called the little brain. It controls the activities of the voluntary muscles. The fibers in its central lobe are arranged so that they form a tree-like mass of white matter called the arbor vitae — "Tree of Life;"

3. the medulla oblongata, which lies just in front of the cerebellum, and represents the beginning of the spinal cord in the neck region at the base of the skull;

4. the brainstem, which is located just above the medulla and is shaped like the knob of a walking stick;

5. the ventricles, which are the "hollow tubes" containing the brain fluids and dews;

6. the Third Eye, which includes the pituitary and pineal glands, discussed in previous Lessons.

THE CEREBRUM — HUMAN'S CROWN

The cerebral hemisphere of the human brain is a crown in more ways than one. Its functions set humankind apart from the animal kingdom and make you a co-creator with God. The circulatory, respiratory, digestive and the excretory systems are alike in human and animal. You differ from the animals a great deal in the cerebral hemisphere — the top part of your brain.

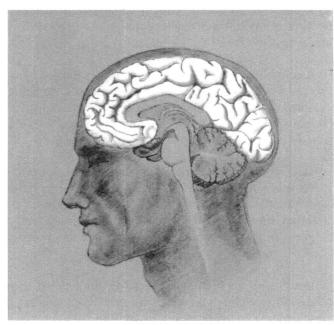

CEREBRUM

When we say that this development (which is a relatively recent part of our evolution) sets humans apart from the animals, we are stating principally that in this field of the brain lies our capacity to learn, to benefit by past experience, to change our behavior according to that which is most beneficial to us.

The cerebrum is constituted of a core of white matter completely surrounded by a layer of gray matter called the cortex. The cortex appears to be the seat of highest intelligence in the cerebral hemisphere. In the cortex gray matter is the mysterious factor which gives humans the ability to learn. It is also the sensory area of the brain.

Several trillion fibrils or wire-like connections finer than the web of a spider connect the billions of brain cells. This brain matter continues down the spinal cord itself. Although the whole of the brain mass is separated into individual cells, they operate as one magnificent unit. It is through this mechanism that conscious thought manifests on the physical plane.

The billions of brain cells are arranged in groupings very similar to the arrangement of the stars in the heavens. The force that operates this incomparable communication system is electricity. In the average brain it is equivalent to about twenty watts of electrical energy. The cells themselves are minute dynamos. They generate electrical charges from oxygen and body chemicals within themselves, discharging lower or higher levels of electrical energy according to the changing stimulus. In the sum total of the cortical cells is found the physical terminal of the personality — the thinker which you are.

The human being has been differentiated from the animal by the obvious capacity of the human brain to receive progressive impressions of mental illumination. The animal brain is not so capable and not so constituted. An obvious fact of nature, then, is that the human can become divine only by developing a brain power capable of receiving the downpourings of still higher illumination. Only by the expanding powers of your brain will you rise above that which you now are, attaining the heights of your ultimate becoming.

THE CEREBELLUM — CENTER OF COORDINATION

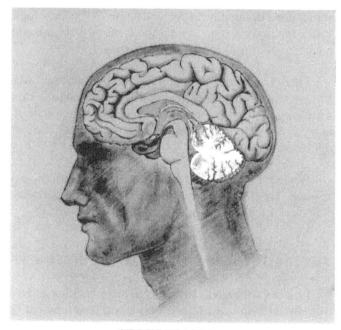

CEREBELLUM

The cerebellum, "the little brain," located in the rear part of the skull, compares in size and weight to a medium-sized orange. The cerebellum, a recent evolutionary acquisition, is not the seat of sensory perception as is the cerebrum. It can be diseased or destroyed without affecting the senses in any way, but the muscle tone of the physical form will be affected and so will muscle strength. The cerebellum is the organ which regulates equilibrium. It is the seat of coordination in the body.

There are many mysteries concerning this organ. One of these concerns its effect on the individual when, through disease or accident, some part of the cerebellum is injured. The removal of only a portion of the cerebellum results in inability to maintain equilibrium, to walk or to maintain a sense of balance or direction.

However, removal of the entire cerebellum corrects the situation ... and balance, direction and equilibrium are restored.

This fact understandably presented an enigma to medical science, which has only recently been solved by one of its most amazing discoveries: the human nervous system is in the midst of shifting its present position.

The cerebellum is gradually shifting toward the front of the head, and its functions are being transferred to the brain stem.

When we humans first adopted our erect position — that is, when the spinal column and skeleton had so crystallized as to enable humans to stand erect instead of assuming a partially bent animalistic posture — this new development liberated the arms. The jaws were relieved of a burdensome weight. As a result, the arms, freed for work, became shorter and more adaptable and the jaws became smaller.

The shifting of the spinal column made space available in the skull. The brain began developing new areas, and some of this development is still proceeding — the shift of the cerebellum toward the front of the head, and a change in the brain stem located just in front of the cerebellum.

There is now developing in this important brain stem what medical science terms a "new telephone exchange." In this new telephone exchange lie all the processes necessary to perform the functions of the cerebellum. It is this incredible network in the brain stem that assumes control and takes command when the cerebellum is removed completely.

What the shift of the entire nervous system indicates is not yet obvious to medical science. The Astarian, however, being familiar with the developing double spinal cord, is aware of the far-reaching implications.

THE BRAIN STEM — THE SEAT OF INSTINCTS

Lower vertebrates (animals having a backbone) possess the brain stem and actually, in many cases, their only brain development is found in the brain stem itself. Most animalistic instincts are housed in it. Here human and animal share a common ground for the brain stem is also the seat of our primitive instincts.

It was this portion of the brain that first developed in humans. Instincts arise from the sensory organs which end in the ganglia, or nerve cell clusters, of the brain stem. Animals primarily live their lives according to these brain stem perceptions and instincts. Humans, on the other hand, develop their individual personality in the cerebrum, as do the higher vertebrates, such as the dolphin, cat, dog, monkey, ape, and horse.

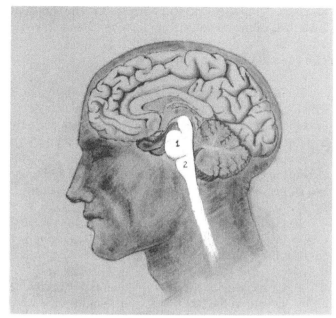

1. BRAIN STEM
2. MEDULLA OBLONGATA

The brain stem enables you to see, feel, hear, touch and smell, but without the developed cerebrum you would not be aware of these sensory abilities. With the brain stem only, you could see but you would not recognize that which you beheld. You could see your mother, for instance, but you would not recognize her as your mother unless the sense of sight was carried to the seat of perception, the occipital lobes in the back of the head. (See Lesson Eleven, Second Degree — Sight — the Soul Sense of the Human Being)

THE MEDULLA OBLONGATA — MATRIX OF YOUR INNER MAGIC

The medulla oblongata is the connecting link between the spinal cord and the brain. Where the spinal cord meets the brain it widens out, forming the medulla oblongata and the brain stem. The medulla actually could be said to be the upper end of the spinal cord although it is considerably larger in proportion.

The medulla connecting to the brain stem is located at almost a mid-point in your head. The medulla contains a mechanism so complex that scientists could never presume to duplicate its operations. It compares in weight to a boiled egg and could be held in the palm of a hand. God has seen fit to pack this tiny object with substances and mechanisms which stagger the imagination.

The medulla oblongata is shaped like an inverted pyramid. It comprises the central station of the nervous system. In this station lie the vital centers for respiration, blood pressure, muscle tension and numerous other functions. If a person's neck is broken and any of these vital centers are damaged, death can occur immediately.

The tracts of the spinal cord terminate in the medulla oblongata. However, they are joined by other tracts which lead upward into the brain and which transmit the spinal cord impulses into still other tracts. The spinal cord itself continues into the lower half of the medulla, from there to extend upward into the fourth ventricle.

The Medulla and the Holy Breath

The medulla holds in its body the fibers from a prodigious cluster of nerve cells which compose the vagus nerve trunk. Such a cluster is referred to as a nerve center. This medulla nerve center is one of the most supremely important in the entire body both biologically and physiologically. Also, the nerve plexuses extend downward into the spinal cord and connect with the breathing mechanism. An injury to the medulla affects the entire respiratory system. Thus we see again the importance of the medulla and its nerve plexuses as it relates to the breath of life.

Without breath there is no life, regardless of how perfect the body and its functions may be. It is the nerve impulses which, discharging in the medulla, move downward to connect functionally with the nerves which support breathing.

A clue to some of the reasoning behind the prominence of the medulla in the minds of the ancients is the fact that the channel for the Holy Breath — the vagus — reaches a terminal point in the heart of the medulla. It extends downward to terminate again in the right auricle of the heart so that the heart ethers are transmitted to the medulla by this supreme nerve.

The vagus, again, is the channel of the mysterious inner breath which the yogi frequently maintains during periods of meditation. We have previously mentioned this inner breath as that which sometimes automatically "takes over" following the breathing portion of Lama Yoga. (See First Degree, Lesson 17) This inner Holy Breath, as well as the breath of life, is mechanically controlled through the vagus nerve and medulla oblongata.

The Mystic Fire of the Medulla Soul Note

Every object of the universe emits a cosmic sound. The same is true of every soul according to the radiation of its particular aura, which is, in itself, a record pertaining to the past, and progression of the individual.

There is a soul note in the medulla oblongata of every individual — that is, the note on the cosmic keyboard which harmonizes with your own spiritual and personalized "music of the spheres."

When the incarnating entity enters the higher atmosphere of the earth plane at the time of your physical rebirth, the new body is constructed according to this mysterious sound and its vibrational quality. The note sounds begin not too long following conception. The vibrational quality of the soul note attracts into the matrix of the forming etheric body in the womb of the mother the type of atoms that will be harmonious — those necessary to build the best possible physical vehicle for the incoming soul according to one's "ripe" karma, and according to the missions to be accomplished during the approaching incarnation.

Standing in the open, near telephone wires, one frequently can detect a humming sound vibrating through the air. If the medulla sound were audible to the physical ear it would resemble the same muffled hum, faint and far away. The medulla sound is a reverberation of a more magnified sound — that which is emitted from the overshadowing Oversoul. It is in the Oversoul that the cosmic sound originates, the note in the medulla being only a faint echo of that higher "music."

In the temples of Mu and Atlantis, and again in ancient Egypt and Tibet, a flame was kept burning continually on an altar located on a very sacred site. These flames were housed in "perpetual lamps," which were so constructed as to burn interminably without refueling. A few of these lamps have been found in ancient tombs but the mystified archeologists have never unraveled the secret of their formula.

The perpetual flame of these lamps represented the divine fire which is God, and was also symbolic of the flame which burns upon the altar in the medulla oblongata.

The medulla is a supreme spiritual altar in the human form. Although the flame on the altar burns perpetually, still the power and potency of it can be influenced by the inner life of the individual. According to the way one "thinks in his or her heart," acts in daily life and reacts to emotional impacts, the medulla flame burns either more radiantly or fades to an ember and loses its light of life — in which case the sound of the soul note becomes almost imperceptible. When this happens the bodies of the individual — the physical, etheric, astral, mental and causal — often lose their alignment and become out of focus.

On the other hand, when one strives to live a spiritual life, the flame becomes increasingly luminous and the sound it emits rises higher on the cosmic musical keyboard to attract atoms of a higher vibration to the physical form. The spiritual bodies are given impetus to activate their powers. All the bodies fall into harmonious alignment, and the personality reveals remarkable spiritual progression during this particular incarnation.

There are several methods of fueling the fire, of raising the vibrational sound of the soul note:

1. the conscious intake of solar prana by the practice of Lama Yoga, meditation or other spiritual practice which also utilizes and involves the physical body and then consciously directing this prana to the brain. Also in this category would be found time spent in nature to deliberately take in her spiritual essences and ask that they enhance and heal your physical body and have a positive spiritual impact on all the levels of your being. Then, sending your own prayers of healing back to Mother Earth and nature would complete the cycle.

2. stimulating the mind by continuing to study Lessons or books which create a thought force of higher mental quality. Such study builds both mind and brain power and develops powers of concentration;

3. consuming as many uncooked foods and juices as seems practical for your individual need, for therein are found the vital fires of life which are transferred to our physical nature. To fill the diet exclusively with dead or overcooked foods is to deprive the body of the natural fire of the vegetable kingdom;

4. serving God, humankind and higher spiritual principles to the best of one's time, means and talents.

Ida, pingala and sushumna, the three lines of lifeforce proceeding up the spinal column, unite in the heart of the medulla forming a mystic cross. It is upon this cross, formed by the negative waters of ida, the positive fires of pingala, and the ethers and gases of sushumna — all combined with the dews of the brain — that the carnal soul is crucified and resurrected out of the tomb of matter. The medulla is the scene of that resurrection.

The word "medulla" signified "marrow" to the ancients and in their Mysteries the marrow of the bone was extremely significant. It is indirectly connected with the mystic Lost Word of Masonry, and the marrow or medulla itself signifies "the place of concealment of the murdered one." Thus the medulla oblongata plays an important part in the inner Mysteries.

THE BRAIN VENTRICLES — THE SEVEN CAVES

Medical science calls the brain a tubular structure, which is to say there are hollows, or tubes, in its interior. These hollows are called ventricles, and they are filled with mysterious fluids and gases about which medical science knows very little.

To gain a clearer perspective, let us picture the brain itself as a large tube which extends downward into the spinal column. This brain tube is filled with the brain parts such as the cerebrum, the cerebellum, the medulla, the glands, the thalamus and so forth. The cavities remaining in the brain are open tubes, which are called ventricles. These ventricles contain the mysterious fluid which mystics call the brain dew.

Medical science recognizes five ventricles. The first and second lie to the right and left of the brain. The third ventricle is placed in the center of the brain; the fourth lies to the rear of the head and below the third ventricle; the fifth becomes the lateral ventricle near the thalamus.

Mystics recognize the ultimate possibility of seven ventricles, the last two being composed of the four higher ethers of the physical plane. They extend down the tiny, microscopic tube of the spinal cord which we call sushumna. The mystics of antiquity called the seven brain cavities "the seven caves," and there were many dramas enacted in the Mystery Schools concerning these mysterious seven caves.

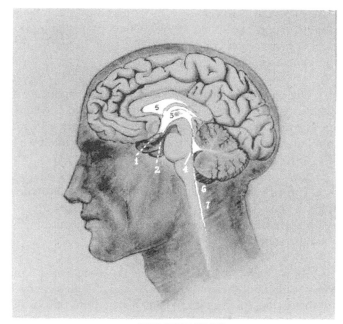

VENTRICLES

Brain fluids are formed in the ventricles and circulate slowly downward through the brain stem tube, some portion into the spinal cord itself.

There are other gases which also rise in the ventricles. These etheric brain dews penetrate the matter which fills the spinal cord more rapidly than does the recognized brain fluid. Medical science assumes that because the spinal canal contains matter, this matter acts as a deterrent to the flow of brain fluid. Whereas this is true concerning physical brain fluid, it is not true of the etheric gases which we term brain dews.

These gases penetrate the matter found in the spinal column in the same way ink is absorbed by a blotter. They flow almost imperceptibly through the matter to reach the root chakra and the reproductive centers.

In the convolutions of the brain are found other centers which will one day become vortices of power as the soul continues to unfold spiritually, until eventually the head area itself will represent a small universe — the sun being the pineal gland, the moon the pituitary. These two will be surrounded by tiny blazing centers of light — the planets in one's microcosmic universe.

BRAIN DEWS — BAPTISMAL WATERS OF THE INNER BEING

The sutratmic silver cord contains the stream of life which flows between the Monad and the brain. These lifeforces flow up and down the sutratma like a river of light, the "waters" of which are so vaporous they could be better described as ethers or essences.

As these essences impinge upon the brain they begin to condense into gases and dews. The precipitation begins in the crown chakra which permeates the cerebrum.

There they swirl in ceaseless motion as they are transmuted and condensed into a fluidic vapor. The sound of this chaotic perpetual motion is one of the first that the seeker hears when you tune in to the Life Stream — the Holy Nahd — mentioned in previous Lessons.

Out of the crown chakra the condensed vapors are absorbed into the brain cells. They converge upon and into the third ventricle, which is the reservoir of the brain dew. As you recall, the third ventricle is connected with the postlobe of the pituitary by a microscopic tube called the infundibulum, which we have also described in previous Lessons.

Through the infundibulum, or zu-tube, the brain dews pass from the third ventricle into the postlobe; from there into the anterior portion of pituitary where they are mixed with hormones of the body and carried downward into the spinal column and the bloodstream.

As we have previously written, it is the anterior lobe of pituitary which is the master gland of the entire endocrine glandular system. But pituitary is only the agent of the divine Spirit as it sends its waters of light down through the crown chakra to renew the bodily activities through pituitary, the feminine gland.

The brain dews remaining in the third ventricle evaporate or are lost in the bloodstream in the ordinary individual. The dews do not become spiritually potent until they can be mixed with the flow of Chrism Oil, which finds its way up the spinal cord through the medulla oblongata and into the fourth ventricle.

The pineal gland, in its state of dormancy, lies like a gateway blocking the passage of these two ventricles. The resurrected, awakened pineal of the spiritual seeker allows the Chrism of the fourth ventricle to flow into and mix with the brain dews in the third ventricle to bring about the opening of the Third Eye.

As you begin to unfold spiritually, the postlobe of pituitary will begin to release into the third ventricle the fluid we have already mentioned, called pituitrin, the love essence — which in highly evolved individuals penetrates the pineal barrier to enter the fourth ventricle and pass on through the medulla into the spinal cord, to be carried throughout the physical form via the nervous system.

As the spiritual essences of pituitrin filter into the nervous system, such an individual becomes highly spiritually evolved — for the soul which is influenced by this mystic hormone has already attained a portion of its godhood. As the brain centers become magnetized, the brain dews begin to flow more freely through the ventricles and the spinal cord. It is these brain dews which help make possible the action of the Christ Substance or Divine Substance in the bloodstream.

True baptism, as it was understood and taught in the Mysteries, referred to the flow of brain dews downward through the medulla into the spinal cord — there to bathe and purify the heart center — and on downward into the root chakra to meet the rising Chrism Oil from the generative organs in the process of regeneration. The flow of these brain waters was indeed the true baptism of the redeemed or regenerated spiritual seeker.

The sixth and seventh ventricles are involved with sushumna, the channel that rises up the spinal cord. They are most certainly elongated tubes — infinitesimal though they may be. These ventricles contain a very fine nerve, called Chitrini, along which the brain dews condense, active as "the nerve of wisdom" in the Spiritual Master. Along this mysterious nerve the brain dews must exude enough electrical magnetism to attract and pull upward the Chrism of the root chakra.

The power of this magnetic attraction is completely void until the human race itself arrives at a certain level of spiritual evolution, at which time the nerve fluid of sushumna begins to exude the dews containing this electrical magnetism which attracts the highest and finest essence from the atmosphere — the Divine Substance — to aid you in your regenerative processes. Thus the dews of the brain become of practical value to the individual only as you begin to evolve spiritually.

YOUR THREE BRAINS

Humans possess three brains:

1. the superior brain in the head;

2. the solar plexus brain in the abdomen;

3. the root brain in the reproductive organs.

It is of great importance that you understand the functions of the solar plexus and root brains which register their influence on the evolution of your mental forcefield. These are secondary centers, subject to control by centers in the superior brain, once these centers are developed.

Your Solar Plexus Brain

As you know, the solar plexus center is the dominating plexus of the sympathetic nervous system as well as the seat of the astral-emotional body. This emotional center can well be called a brain, since the thoughts of the majority dwell principally in the emotional plexus, and since energy follows thought, this becomes a center of tremendous thoughtforce.

This active nerve center in the pit of the stomach is the storehouse of electrical prana. It is appropriately called the solar plexus, for from it radiates pranic rays which flow to all parts of the body, much as the sun radiates energy to all its planets. It is a control station for operating the subconscious mind, under the dominion of the pituitary.

From this brain rise the more difficult emotions — hate, anger, envy, anx-iety, jealousy, grief, worry, fear. Understanding this, one can employ rhythmic breathing, directing prana to the solar plexus brain to quiet the nerves, soothe the mind, promote inner tranquility and an ability to experience these emotions in a flowing nonjudgmental way without becoming attached to any of them. Prana is the "medicine" of the ethers.

Surging currents of emotional energy pour from this solar brain under stress of grief and heartache. It is from this tremendously sensitive solar region that we feel our heartbreak, rather than from the heart itself. Its influence extends even into the region of the throat chakra, causing the "lump in the throat" experienced by all who have ever been under emotional duress — the "lump" being constricted, tensed muscles.

This solar brain is the "Delphic Oracle" of the heart. Out of it rises the "wee small voice" which frequently turns us from wrongdoing, and which we call the voice of conscience. This conscience is the most important inner directive of our lives so far as our instincts are concerned, if we would but heed it. Its guidance, however, does not stem from intuition, reason or logic; it wells up from within strictly through instinct — the voice of past training.

When the soul has erred in some previous incarnation and, as an entirely different personality, has suffered long in paying off some karmic debt, a glimmering memory of it is reflected from the superconscious into this tremendous solar network, and rises up to haunt — to warn — us as the voice of conscience if we are tempted to make the same error in this life. It is the voice of the soul bringing remembrances of the past.

The Root Brain

The root brain involves the reproductive organs — the testes of the male and the ovaries of the female.

The root brain is not to be confused with the root chakra, which is located in the prostate region in the male and the uterus in the female.

Under pituitary stimulation, the root brain produces the reproductive fluids, seed substances and hormones that combine to become the creative energies which rise up the spinal cord in rhythmic cycles. When the influence of this etheric force strikes the solar plexus brain, it produces the urge to create. These creative energies can be utilized toward building a more powerful brain or they can be dissipated in sexual activity, according to the interpretation the individual places upon the urge, and one's reaction to this driving force within.

The one who seeks spiritual unfoldment often exercises considerable restraint over one's habits of sexual activity. One usually does not seek to destroy the urge, recognizing it to be as natural as breathing. Rather, one attempts to transmute a portion of its etheric force out of the generative organs into the brain to be employed toward mental creative qualities and activities.

The controlled, normal individual, completely unaware of Ancient Wisdom mysticism and all it implies, also may exercise some measure of restraint over his or her sexual habits — not because it is deliberately planned, but because one's ambitions and worldly desires may frequently overshadow one's physical desires. They consume much of the energies otherwise employed in excessive sexual activities.

Responding to the creative force rising into and activating the solar plexus, the average individual frequently interprets it as a sexual urge and sends it downward to be lost through the generative organs. But if one is engaged in some creative enterprise, or motivated toward a driving ambition, one may raise the power out of the solar plexus center to infuse the brain cells as mental force.

Some people, on the other hand, care little for any worthwhile achievement. The etheric creative force, striking the solar plexus brain in rhythmic cycles, is usually interpreted as a sexual urge and the creative power is lost in excessive sexual activity. Any attainment of the world's goods or goals is purely secondary to his or her lustful habits.

The soul of these people, bent upon temporal satisfactions, cannot build the pure bloodstream necessary to capture the Divine Substance from the atmospheric ethers ... cannot conceive the seed of the Divine Body in the Third Eye ... cannot hold in one's physical atomic structure the atoms pouring down from the higher planes which would immortalize one's mortal form. This soul continually eats the forbidden fruit of the Tree of the Knowledge of Good and Evil.

YOUR ROOT CHAKRA

We must re-emphasize that the root chakra is not the same as the root brain. Whereas the root brain covers the reproductive area, the root chakra interpenetrates the prostate area in the male and the uterus in the female. This chakra houses the powerful kundalini.

The root chakra, with its mysterious kundalini, consists of primary forces which radiate in four directions: one up, one down and two horizontal, causing the chakra to appear as if a cross penetrated its center. A great portion of the kundalini force enters the root chakra from the spleen, drawn inward from the ethers around us — and through the soles of the feet, drawn upward from the earth. Much of the kundalini force flows downward to enter and stimulate the reproductive organs — the root brain.

Kundalini, composed of the electronic forces and energies of the root chakra, represents the dual "serpent" of the Mysteries. Mystics recognize that there is a serpent of carnality and a serpent of spiritual wisdom. Kundalini represents both. It is her fire, which helps stir the reproductive organs to their procreative activity. It is her fire, pouring into the root brain, that causes the production of the seed substance (sperm) and semen (fluid) in the gonads, and which activates the pressure which nature usually releases through sexual activity. In the female, kundalini vitalizes the ovum or egg released by the ovary.

The seeker, recognizing the influence of kundalini energy upon the procreative organs, attempts to turn the force upward through some yogic practice such as Lama Yoga. Or through prayer, meditation, or concentrated study of wisdom sources.

Denied some degree of its life essence from kundalini, the root brain fails to produce the usual quantity of seed substance in the reproductive organs, and the sexual pressures in these glands decrease so that the sexual urge becomes less frequent. This infrequency of the sex cycle in the seeker is not related in any way to any negative condition. It is only that sexual activities are desired less often, not that the force is weakened.

Thus the undirected, unchecked fire of kundalini, flowing down to stimulate the reproductive organs, becomes the serpent of carnality. When directed upward and aroused to her full power, kundalini, rising up sushumna like a brilliant river of light to the head centers, becomes the serpent of wisdom, to be utilized as brain power by the creative genius.

GOD-IN-MATTER VERSUS GOD-IN-MIND

The root brain in the reproductive organs represents God-in-matter. The superior brain in the head represents God-in-mind.

Until you transform the creative energies in the reproductive centers to the creative energies of the head centers, the generative organs will continue to consume a major portion of your creative powers. The root brain, one's God-in-matter, will dominate your earthly activities until the God-in-mind becomes supreme in your life.

At the present stage of humankind's spiritual evolution, the head centers are not fully awakened. Everything in one's daily life conspires to restrict the upward flow of kundalini. The etheric webs which interweave each chakra obstruct it. It is further blocked by the will of the average person who presently has no desire to conserve the creative force, and is unaware that he or she even should.

This soul does not recognize any connection between its spiritual apathy and its coming perfection. It knows of no connection between the reproductive center and its mental creative activities. This soul does not realize that conserving the creative energies would enhance its mental productivity. In fact, perhaps he or she pauses not to think of conservation at all, but may seek only to experience a well-rounded sensual expression. The only brake applied is the subconscious tendency to conserve energy for driving ambition toward earthly goals.

It is only as kundalini — the feminine power — is directed upward to the positive head chakras that the negative spinal chakras are stimulated to their full unfoldment.

And it is only as the spiritual creative energies of kundalini are shifted upward to the superior brain that the physical form is regenerated and the mind reaches for the level of the superconscious.

STIMULATING THE THIRD EYE

The following is a spiritual exercise designed to stimulate the Third Eye as a part of this positive, regenerative process. Sit in silent prayer or meditation for perhaps five minutes, attuning yourself to the White Light. Now place the forefinger of each hand on top of your ears, pointing toward the middle of the head and resting against the skull. Let your thumbs rest against your forefingers for added currents of spiritual energy. Now inhale deeply and fully through the nose, holding the breath as long as comfortable. Exhale very slowly through the mouth. Close your teeth and place your tongue against the back of them, making the sound of *th* as you exhale. Perform this yogic exercise only once in a 24-hour period.

Mind -- The Human Maker

Second Degree — Lesson Nineteen

GATEWAY TO THE INNER KINGDOM

Even though a new brain is born with each new incarnation, this is not true of the mind. The mind existed prior to conception and birth in the present incarnation.

Understanding the complexities of the mind is as difficult as understanding electricity. One can perform the simple act of turning on an electric light and, accustomed as we are today to such a phenomenon, it is an accepted common event. It is only when we think of the power, the forces and the activity behind the electric light that we begin to be aware of the mystery involved.

Scientists explain that the force is electricity but they do not tell us what electricity is. Thus it is with the mind and the brain. Scientists tell us that the brain is the seat of the cerebrospinal nervous system which, in turn, is the house of the mind. But they do not tell us what the mind is. They simply tell us what the brain is.

To speak learnedly of the brain does not explain the mechanism of the mind. Scientists believe the brain must encompass the entire workings of humankind's mentality. Yet a knowledge of the brain is far from a knowledge of the mind — that mysterious storehouse which uses the brain even as the power of electricity uses the light bulb for its center of manifestation.

The brain, like the light bulb, is dead without the power behind it to make it function. The light bulb lights at the flick of a switch. The brain lights at the flick of the mind.

THE MENTAL FORCEFIELD

To build a house, an architect first creates a blueprint. The mind, to function in the material world, first must build an instrument. That instrument is the human brain. But the architect of the brain — the mind — can build in the world of effect only that which the soul has evolved. The soul, in turn, is higher than the mind. In each personality it has inhabited, it has evolved different degrees of brain power so that the mind — the agent of the soul — must build the brain according to the exact blueprint dictated by the mental evolutionary status of the soul. That is to say, the individual personality, through many lives past, has built a certain mental forcefield surrounding his or her brain conditioned by one's experiences and mental evolution.

The brain, built into the physical form at each new incarnation, is simply the house constructed by the architect, which is the mind, according to the blueprint evolved. The mind can build no greater brain than that which the soul, through past experiences, has evolved or created.

The mental forcefield existed before the brain was, and was the pattern upon which the brain was constructed. Its forces built and are still building the brain through which the mindforces express. The mind permeates every cell of the brain *but is able to operate apart from it.*

Thus we establish humans as a trinity: a spirit, a soul and a personality. Humans no longer remain the enigma of the universe, once the operation of the trinity is understood. You are no longer considered a highly developed animal endowed with a superior intelligence. You are no longer a creature that begins and ends with the intelligence of mind. Nor are you even a creature with a soul. You are a spirit possessing a soul, a mind and a body, using all these composite parts to create a whole being — a being containing both matter and spirit, both evil and good, both animal and god.

The *spirit* sends down, or projects into the realms of ether, a representative of itself which we call the soul. The *soul* projects into the world of matter a representative of itself which we call the *physical body and the personality* and builds, through experience, a forcefield of mental substance surrounding the brain of that form. We call that forcefield the *mind,* an agency of the soul.

The soul is that part of you which is developing and unfolding. The spirit, on the other hand, is the divine Monad. The soul evolves according to the experiences of the personality in the body and takes to itself an increased degree of consciousness with each incarnation. Thus the soul, unfolding through the agency of the mind, or mental forcefield, eternally evolves from incarnation to incarnation.

COUNTERPARTS OF THE BRAIN

This mental forcefield surrounds your brain, and becomes a counterpart of the brain — a counterpart composed of etheric, astral, mental and causal substances.

These substances form themselves in the realms surrounding the brain, just as the unseen planes of life are formed around the Earth. The brain becomes a miniature

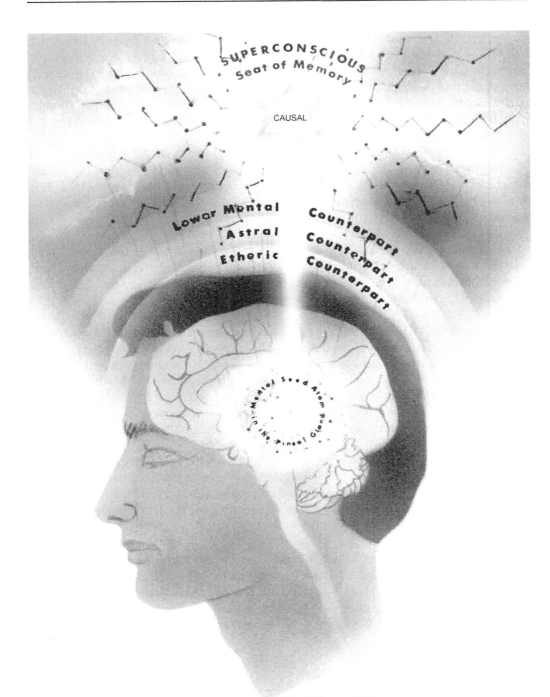

THE BRAIN AND THE MIND

The physical brain is only a channel for the human mind. The mind forms a forcefield surrounding the brain, and the mind substance permeates the cells of the brain.

planet, surrounded by its individual planes which, all together, compose one's mental forcefield.

Thus the brain possesses an etheric counterpart, an astral counterpart and a mental counterpart, above which lies the superconscious which houses the field of the causal body. Above these mental forcefields, or counterparts, we find the Monad — that part of you which is divine.

The storehouse of the mind is found in the forcefield of these combined brain counterparts. The brain cannot function unless it is connected to its powerhouse of mental substance. The brain without the mind is dead, a mass of substance without life or light.

Science tells us that we use only a small portion of our existing brain cells and that the others remain "undeveloped," meaning that although the brain cells are there in full physical development, they do not respond to mental impulses, either inside or out. They lie there in the brain fully developed physically but undeveloped mentally — that is, they are not used by the mind. They are like the unlit but perfectly constructed light bulb which is dark because the power of electricity is missing. There must be a connecting stream of force between the brain cell and the mind, just as there must be an electric wire between the light bulb and the powerhouse of electricity. If the brain cell is not connected to its source it lies in the brain unlit and unused.

The brain, then, filled with its countless brain cells, is only partially active. The cells which are lighted have connecting channels running into the mental forcefield. The mind lies like a great cosmic galaxy surrounding and penetrating the brain — a "universe" of swirling forces.

Thought energies stream into the brain, projected from the mind as light rays are projected from the sun. They travel down the etheric currents or cords established between the mind and the brain cells. We liken these connections to submicroscopic threads or wires, over which communication between the brains, or forcefields, are transferred. This connective system can best be described as an extension of the nadis.

THE INVISIBLE ETHERIC NERVOUS SYSTEM

As we have said, the nadis is an etheric counterpart of the entire nervous system in the physical form just as the chakras are etheric counterparts of the glands. This nadis is the invisible structure upon which all the nerves of the body are woven and without which they would be "dead" — a network of etheric "wires" along which the lifeforce flows as electricity runs through a network of cables.

This nadis, this etheric network, is not only interwoven through the nerve structure of the physical form but extends above the head as the carrier of mindforce between the physical brain and its counterparts.

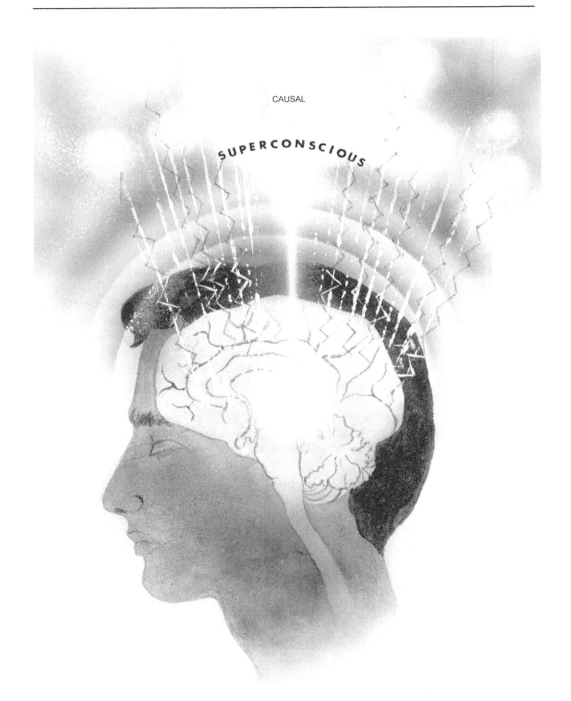

CAUSAL

SUPERCONSCIOUS

THE BRAIN, ITS COUNTERPARTS AND THE ETHERIC NADIS

The nadis, composed of mental reflecting ether, acts as the connecting threads between the brain and the mind. It is the channel of the "thought force" which flows from the mind into the brain cells.

There is this difference: whereas the nadis in the physical form, underlying the nervous system, is composed of the four physical ethers — the electric, pranic, light and mental reflecting — the nadis extending above the brain is not. It is composed only of the mental reflecting ether.

These streams of mental reflecting ether run through the cells of the brain recording every thought that one thinks, as the thought impulses strike the brain cells. They store the thought as a memory in the superconscious forcefield. These etheric mental channels must be developed by the soul itself.

Perhaps a more adequate description would be to say that the cells of the brain project aerials or antennas from themselves which extend into the mind or mental substance.

The individual antenna of a brain cell buries itself in the heart of a mental cell, and an interplay of consciousness proceeds between the two. The mental cell is comparable to a physical cell, but is composed of mental substance. Thus communication is established between the brain and the mind.

The picture is complete if you can conceive of the mental antennas as being of tenuous ether and not of physical, definable substance. But they are as real as the antennas which bring images to our television or computer screens and are composed of a force as dynamic and powerful as electricity itself. Like the television or computer, they bring "memory images" to the cells of the brain.

MARVEL OF THE HUMAN MIND

The motion picture industry spends uncountable dollars constructing soundproof stages, the better to record sounds on their sensitive recording instruments. Well do they know that every sound impresses its vibration upon their recording tape. Yet you go through life unaware that all about you in your auric egg is a recording medium a thousand times more impressionable than the most sensitive tape recorder: the mind recorder which records your thought vibrations.

Blindly the soul walks through its every day, recording its every impression upon these thought ethers. If you only realized how vividly you were writing your own book of life, how carefully you would guard your mind against thoughts that "play back" later in the form of complexes, guilt and shame. How carefully you would guard the doorway of your mind, for it is your most sensitive and creative instrument.

The power of evil thoughts, like the power of the x-ray, affects the human body destructively, whereas the power of love vibrations builds strength, health and healing into its cells and tissues.

Visualize an etheric forcefield overlaying and interpenetrating the cells of your brain. Add to that the superimposing forcefield of an astral counterpart, the surrounding forcefield of the mental counterpart, followed by the field of the superconscious. Within this superconscious is housed the forcefield of the causal body and the Oversoul. Visualize, also, the nadis — the threads composed of mental reflecting ether which run through the brain cells, recording the thought impulses, and which connect the mental forcefields, or brains, into a single unit of expression.

The nadis acts as a bridge between the forcefields and can only be built as one studies any particular subject and activates the thought impulses flowing along the etheric threads connecting the brains.

Each time a seeker takes up a new subject for study, forces are set into action which cause a molecular vibration. These vibrations stimulate brain cells which have not as yet been utilized. Therefore, with every subject studied, whatever its nature, dormant brain cells are activated and new tubes or channels of the nadis formed in the etheric, astral and mental counterparts of the brain.

Mental force, as well as electric force, seeks a line of least resistance. If one attempts to think in terms of a foreign subject, the vibrations and mental impulses must find their way down through already developed channels until such time as they develop channels for themselves in newly activated brain cells and brain centers.

If thought impulses concerning an unfamiliar subject such as science, for instance, have not been operating over established threads of the nadis, then new threads must be slowly built through the study of this particular subject. Once constructed, they will always remain. They can never be destroyed although they may deteriorate somewhat from disuse, as does a muscle when not exercised.

The study of any subject always adds to brain power not only in the present life but in lives to come. Let us say that in some life in the past you studied chemistry. If, in this life, you take up the study, you will find it easy to comprehend and assimilate. But if this is the first incarnation you have struggled with the subject, the study of chemistry might be arduous because you are forced to develop a new brain center.

Every thought of any intensity creates a molecular vibration in the brain. To master some subject, then, is to create what medical science calls a neuron or cell unit — a center which is "attuned" with that particular subject. And the knowledge gained concerning that subject is then filed away in the archives of the superconscious.

TALENT CENTERS

It is most important that we understand what is meant by a neuron or cell unit. Medical science describes a neuron as a nerve cell with all its processes and extensions, and declares that the nervous system is composed of units of neurons. Neurons form themselves into various brain centers, each of which carries out its particular task in response to the "messages" the brain receives from the nervous systems.

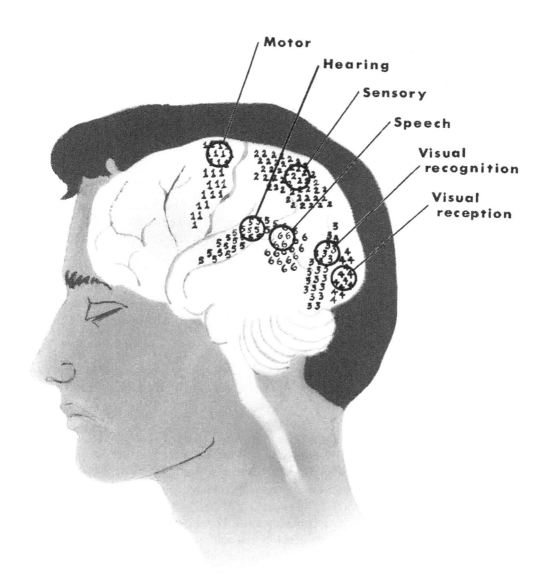

THE SENSE CENTERS

Medical science has established definite brain centers relating to the senses as well as talent and perception. The numbered areas in our illustration indicate the location of some of these functional centers: (1) motor; (2) sensory; (3) visual recognition; (4) visual reception; (5) hearing; (6) speech.

Physiology usually divides the nervous systems into two principal branches: the motor and the sensory. The motor mechanism is located just behind the frontal lobe of the brain and controls muscles, glands, etc., which act upon the body. The sensory mechanisms include a center of sight, a center of hearing, a center for sleep, etc. These centers are located in the cerebral cortex and extend down the spinal cord.

For our esoteric teachings let's call the groups of cells which compose the neurons "cell centers." In other words, millions of brain cells congregate to form a cell unit which performs as a certain center — for instance, a visual center, a memory center or an auditory center.

To be more explicit: let's say a group of cells form themselves into a unit to become a visual center. Impulses from the optic nerve strike these cells and you witness the outside world around you. Other cells congregate to form an auditory center which is receptive to sound stimuli.

We do not hear with our ears at all, but with the cells which have formed themselves into the auditory-sensory center. The sound stimulus passes through the medulla oblongata, over to the opposite side of the head, and upwards into the temporal lobe where the auditory center is located.

Another group of cells congregate to create a speech center. The speech center is located in front of the occipital lobe and is associated with the motor area of the cerebrum.

It is important to understand this grouping of cell units. To repeat: certain cells will form a speech center; a different group will form a hearing center; still another a visual center, and so forth. It follows, then, that certain cells must be developed in the individual brain to form a center for any developed talent.

Let's say that one wishes to become a pianist. Having no brain cells developed into a musical center, the beginner must develop that center. It is necessary to use the word "develop," although it must be understood that the cell itself is, in a physical sense, fully developed. It simply is not yet sensitive to impulses flowing through the nadis which relate to music. A group of cells must be developed into a center trained to receive impulses which create a talent in the individual.

Thus the beginner initiates the development of a music center in his or her brain. Practicing music lessons over and over begins to develop the cells necessary to form a music center. Once one becomes adept at music, this center becomes the seat of that particular talent.

Let's say that now you wish to become a scientist. Again, you must develop a cell center. The entire point is that the brain divides itself into small centers according to the knowledge given to it by the individual.

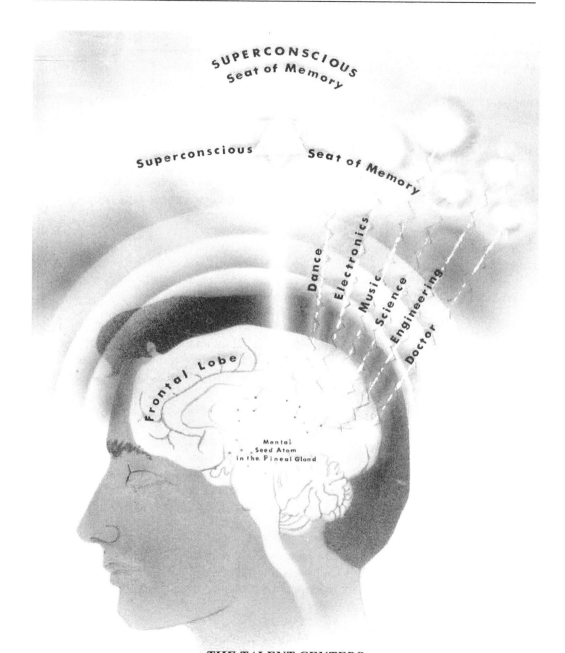

THE TALENT CENTERS

The seat of memory lies in the forcefield of the superconscious. The talents developed in any one life are never lost. They are stored in the superconscious. The "video recording tapes" which join the brains together contain a record of all you see, say or think. Together they compose your personal mental akashic record. At death the sum total of your mental development becomes an innate part of the mental seed atom in the pineal gland.

If the brain can be divided into sense centers — such as the hearing center, the sight center, the sleep center — it follows that it can also be divided into talent centers such as a dance center, a music center, a science center, a mathematics center, a writing center, a medical center: centers that have been developed, through training, for certain sought-after talents.

DEVELOPING A "TRUTH" CENTER

The brain has not been "trained" to comprehend the soul. Its thoughtforce has been outward to observe and conquer the outer world of the personality's daily life — your pleasures and your pains, your joys and sorrows, your problems and triumphs.

The brain must develop a "center" of awareness that will recognize there is a greater comprehension available. Since the constant repetition of a seed thought makes it grow into a living reality, each soul must be given a constant repetition of *truth* until the physical brain *en masse* automatically accepts it as a conclusion.

Being physical, the brain itself is the adytum*, the total of myriads of cell life. That atom of consciousness behind the cell, concerned only with the preservation of that cell, is, therefore, instinctive in action. Thus the brain en masse, instinctive in action, is incapable of accepting any condition or knowledge or action that lies outside its own experience.

It is an instrument which will do something automatically provided it has done that thing time after time after time. So, in order for a soul to accept truth automatically without the beginning and end of a logical process of thought and rejection — is to have truth constantly repeated. Each individual brain thus forges in itself a new avenue along which the consciousness of the Oversoul may travel. As each brain develops in awareness, there comes to that individual, in addition, the *full* experience of matter — the full experience of matter.

The best method of inducing this awareness is to bring to each soul the necessity of learning about the Greater Consciousness through the desire for the liberties of that Consciousness; through the desire to escape the demands of the flesh, the pangs of the flesh.

The constant repetition of this desire for liberation, the desire to overcome the limitations of the flesh, and prayers, decrees, affirmations — through these one finds a tremendous help in forging a brain center where truth is recorded. The soul with such a truth center established is well on its way to freeing itself from the demands of its master, the cell-life of the brain.

---

* adytum: the sanctum in an ancient temple.

GENIUS AND KARMA

A talent once learned by the individual can never be lost. It is not that the brain cells themselves remember, since a new brain is formed for each new incarnation. The talent is recorded and "remembered" in the forcefield of the superconscious and is brought into each new incarnation.

A child may exhibit scientific genius, musical aptitude, mastery of the dance or unbelievable knowledge of engineering without a great deal of study or effort. These youngsters are called prodigies. Here we see cases where it was not necessary to develop the cells of the new brain, since the power of the previously acquired talent in the superconscious was able to strike such an impact upon the new brain centers as to enable the child to perform "miraculous" feats without extensive training. In most people, of course, the centers of the new brain must be prepared by some degree of study.

However, there is never an individual coming into birth who does not have a certain amount of talent potential in the superconscious forcefield because of some interest, or interests, the personality has explored in past lives, the memory of which has been filed in the archives of the superconscious.

When the soul loses its physical brain in death you take with you all your developed talents. For you also take with you your auric egg which contains the superconscious forcefield which houses the "brain" of the Eternity Domain — your thought field — your brain of eternity — your mind. It is in this superconscious forcefield that all your past development resides. Thus the seat of memory lies not in the cells of the physical brain, but in the superconscious forcefield surrounding it.

If, in any life, you have become a skilled scientist, pianist, dancer, engineer, physician — or have developed interest in any area of endeavor — the skill acquired remains with you throughout eternity, and will come easily to you in any later incarnation.

On the other hand, if in a previous life you had little interest in these studies, no physical brain cells would have been developed to express them, nor would a talent center have been created in the superconscious forcefield, and it might be a slow and arduous process to master them. But in the learning and studying involved, a cell center is developed and the nadis communicates this information to the field of the superconscious where it becomes a "memory" for the future physical brain to draw upon.

OUR BUILT-IN COMPUTER

Medical science has given much thought to where the seat of talent is located in the brain. Its size and weight seem not to be involved in talent or genius. At first medical science believed the weight was indicative of unusual talent. Investigation of the brains of great geniuses proved otherwise. For instance, the brains of Raphael, Dante and

Bach proved to be smaller than average. On the other hand, the largest brain medical science has ever discovered belonged to an ordinary working man. Extensive research concluded that the weight and size did not indicate genius.

Next medical science hoped to find the answer in the convolutions of the brain. Research conducted with horses, dolphins, elephants and humans produced evidence that the brain of humans contained the simplest convolutions, and thus could not be indicative of intelligence.

The search for the seat of talent and genius has been unrewarding and confounding. Examination of the brain of Mommsen, the 19th century historian, revealed an abundance of convolutions. Investigation of the brain of Hans von Bulow, the Wagnerian director, revealed that the temporal lobe possessed an exceptional development of convolutions which proved that although the convolutions were not so important, the development of the temporal lobe was, in this case, apparently significant.

Where, then, does the seat of genius and talent lie? Not in the cells of the brain; not in the size; not in the fluid; not in the weight; not in the convolutions. It lies in the forcefield of the superconscious — the eternal brain — lying outside of and above one's head, but joined to the cells of one's brain by the nadis, or "threads" of etheric substance.

Two brain scientists once conducted their research based on the theory that our brain receives, stores, and uses information in the same way computers do. To them, the transistors and other electronic devices employed by the computer are paralleled by the molecules in the brain. Under stimulation of thought processes, say these scientists, the molecules change their shape by "flipping" or "flopping" from one or two basic shapes, and these changes represent the process by which the brain stores information. The eye, they say, is the source of the information, relaying in bursts environmental observations to the brain.

But the eye is only a camera-like device which knows nothing of or by itself, any more than does an ordinary camera. The eye must receive the message it relays to the brain from some source. Study of the eye does not reveal an answer any more than studying the words of a computer print out reveals how the words were transmitted to paper.

An investigator may trace the mechanisms which generate the power to transmit the words — but this doesn't explain the source of the words: *the thought which produced them.* Saying that the eye transmits messages to the brain does not explain the source of the message.

As taught in our Lesson concerning the eyes — a sheep surveys the same landscape as the shepherd. But the sheep sees without knowing, without perceiving. The shepherd possesses perception — a faculty of the soul. The shepherd possesses mind — and the power to use it as he or she wills. Many a blind person possesses wisdom, thereby proving it takes more than sight to operate a brain.

The brain is indeed our built-in computer, but one which operates under the mental force of a directing soul — just as human-made computers must be programmed under the direction of an outside source: the human. The computer without humans to operate it is a cold mass of steel and wires. The brain without soul to operate it is an inert mass of substance and cells. Both are quite dead without an operator.

THE TRINITY IN HUMAN BEINGS

You know that humans consist of three divisions: spirit, soul and personality. You know, too, that there is a silver cord called the sutratma which joins these three aspects together. You know that this silver cord drops from the heart of the spirit — the Monad — to reach the Oversoul and the soul, and from there continues on down into the physical being, the personality, terminating at the base of the spine.

In this sutratma we find the *life cord* which is associated with the spirit, the *consciousness cord* associated with the soul, and the *emotional cord* with the personality. Careful study of our illustration will reveal these important things:

1. The *spirit* is represented by the seven-pointed star above your head. Observe that the life cord extends directly from the Monad into the physical form and has its contact in the pulse point of the heart, where the physical seed atom vibrates. This cord has existed between human and spirit since the early days of your birth into the "human" family. It is in both an undeveloped mind and genius, criminal and saint. It is in infant or aged, mentally challenged or intellectual. This cord exists without any effort whatever on the part of the person, and through it pours the essence of LIFE itself. It is our contact with God. It is under complete Divine jurisdiction. It is divorced from our linear reasoning or petty emotions ... it simply supplies the force we call LIFEFORCE which flows from God to humans.

Once the heart seed atom is purified, the Third Eye will become the home of the spirit — not the heart where it is presently located.

2. The *soul* has its seat of inner contact in the pineal gland, the home of the mental seed atom, making the pineal the focal point of the conscious mind or intellect. The pineal is also one point of the superconscious contact, since it is part of the Third Eye. It is significant to note that the *consciousness cord* extends only between the seed atom in the pineal and the causal forcefield above the head, as represented by the lotus in the six-pointed star. This mind cord is built solely by the developing mental powers of the individual.

3. The *personality* has its principal point of contact in both lobes of the pituitary gland, and extends down to the solar plexus brain. The *emotional cord* extends from the

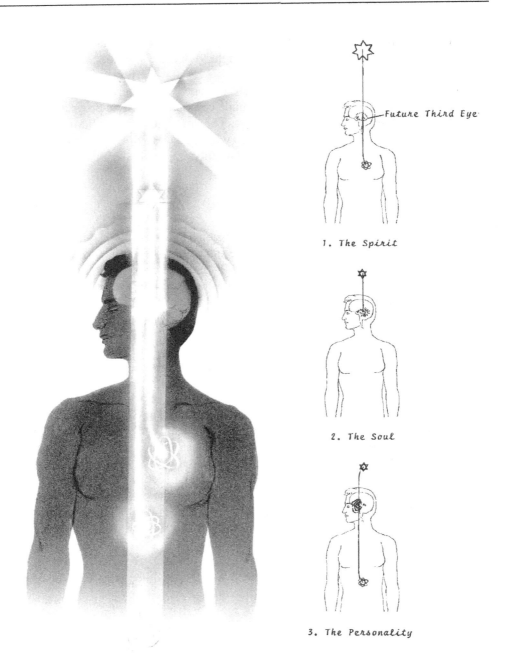

1. The Spirit

2. The Soul

3. The Personality

THE TRINITY IN THE HUMAN BEING

The spirit generates its kingdom of power in the region of the heart, the soul in the pineal, and the personality in the pituitary-solar plexus areas. The seat of spirit will transfer to the Third Eye later in human evolution.

superconscious forcefield to the solar plexus, terminating where the astral-emotional seed atom is located in the apex of the liver. The pituitary is the seat of the subconscious mind, and the mindforce it utilizes pours into it through one's five physical senses as derived from the surrounding etheric, astral and lower mental planes.

In brief:

1. The *seat of the spirit* is presently in the heart. Later, the Third Eye.

2. The *seat of the soul* is in the pineal and is connected to the superconscious as well as the conscious mind.

3. The *seat of the personality,* or lower self, is in the pituitary and is connected to the subconscious mind level.

Having taught generally concerning the Tree of Life and the Tree of the Knowledge of Good and Evil in past Lessons, it remains now for us to combine this information in outline form, so that your "mind's eye" can better assimilate the teaching.

THE TREE OF KNOWLEDGE

The Tree of the Knowledge of Good and Evil, as well as The Tree of Life, which is discussed hereafter, is referred to in the mystical Jewish tradition as The Kabalah. The mystical symbol of the tree within the human, depicting the knowledge of good and evil, as well as life and how the divine is connected to the human mind, body, and spirit is found in the mystical Mayan, as well as the Druid philosophies, consists of:

1. the *cerebrospinal nervous system,* which includes the five   senses: seeing, hearing, feeling, tasting and smelling;

2. the *pineal gland,* including the mental seed atom;

3. the *consciousness cord* extending between the mental seed atom and the causal forcefield;

4. the *waking conscious mind* as it develops through the cere-brospinal and as it operates through the three brains — the superior brain, the solar plexus brain and the root brain;

5. the *superconscious mind* as it sends its impulses and influence into the subconscious and waking conscious mind via:
   a.   the postlobe of the pituitary,
   b.   the consciousness cord which attaches to the mental
           seed atom in the pineal,
   c.   and the crown chakra;

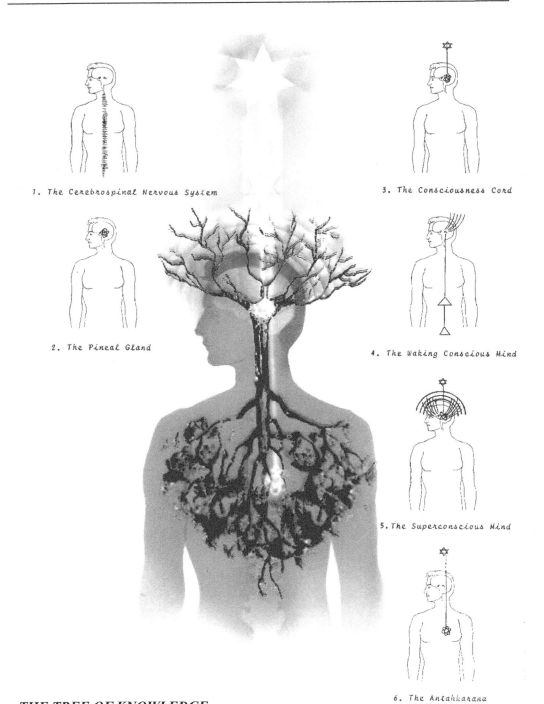

1. The Cerebrospinal Nervous System

3. The Consciousness Cord

2. The Pineal Gland

4. The Waking Conscious Mind

5. The Superconscious Mind

6. The Antahkarana

THE TREE OF KNOWLEDGE

This Tree has its roots in the forcefield above the human brain. Its roots are planted in the surrounding ethers and its life substance is drawn from the spiritual planes, the causal forces and the Monad.

6. the *antahkarana* — the "rainbow" bridge which one must build through one's own spiritual, altruistic endeavors. It is housed in the vagus nerve. However, the vagus extends only into the medulla oblongata while the antahkarana, the major thread of spiritual communication between the personality and the superconscious, eventually reaches the Oversoul. Its ultimate goal is union with the Monad and a chemical marriage with the sutratma, the fusing of which brings physical immortality to humans. We shall teach fully of this all-important bridge of consciousness in later Lessons.

THE TREE OF LIFE

The Tree of Life consists of:

1. the *sutratmic silver cord* extending between the Monad and the root chakra, including the etheric spinal cord, the sushumna, the pathway of the spinal fluids and fires;

2. the *bloodstream,* which carries the pranic life ethers over the entire physical system;

3. the *glandular system* — but not including the pineal gland which is associated with the cerebrospinal system;

4. the *sympathetic nervous system* as it operates under the influence of pituitary, carrying on all the automatic functions of the physical form;

5. the *subconscious mind* as it operates through:
   a. the glandular system, but principally through pituitary,
   b. the emotional impulses from the solar plexus region, and
   c. the generative urges of the root brain;

6. the *life cord* carrying the life essences to the heart as it downpours from the Monad above the head to the base of the spine, finding its seat of contact in the heart seed atom;

7. the *emotional cord,* extending from the solar plexus area to the superconscious forcefield and which is presently involved in the "life" process but which, through evolution, will eventually become transmuted to the "mind" process, fusing the Tree of Life with the Tree of Knowledge. When this occurs the emotional cord will have been absorbed by the antahkarana as one transmutes carnal lust into divine love;

8. the *vagus nerve* which presently belongs to the Tree of Life but which eventually will be transferred to the mind processes of the Tree of Wisdom as one builds the antahkarana in oneself. The vagus nerve is the "carrier" of this etheric bridge of mental substance.

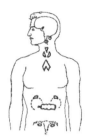

3. The Glandular System

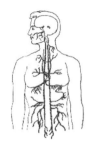

4. The Sympathetic Nervous System

2. The Blood Stream

5. The Subconscious Mind

1. The Sutratmic Silver Cord

6. The Life Cord

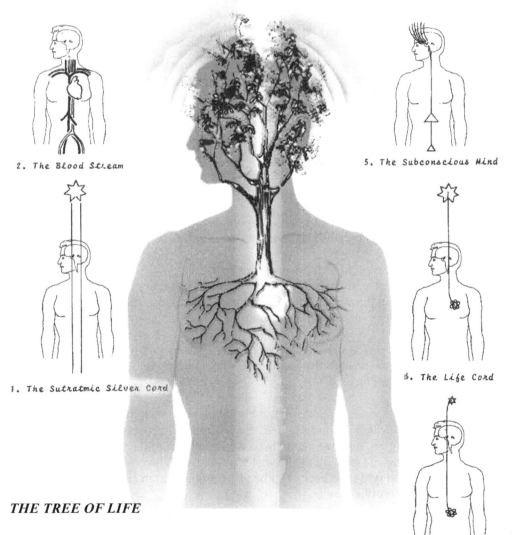

THE TREE OF LIFE

The roots of this Tree are planted in the human and its life substances are drawn from the four physical ethers and the solids, liquids and gases of the physical plane.

7. The Emotional Cord

A careful survey of our illustrations will reveal much to you concerning these "Trees." The Tree of the Knowledge of Good and Evil concerns itself strictly with the developing mind of humans and all things connected thereto. The Tree of Life concerns itself strictly with just that — lifeforce in humans. Its entire purpose is to see that lifeforce and all its essences reach and operate through one's physical form.

In the perfected person of the future, these two Trees are to merge — the Tree of Knowledge to become the Tree of Divine Wisdom and the Tree of Life to become the Tree of Immortality. When the Divine Light or Christ Consciousness is born in the Third Eye and begins to spread throughout the physical form like a great celestial vine, it will absorb the various branches of the Tree of Knowledge and the Tree of Life. They will become transmuted into the Golden Bough and you will have become a god.

HUMAN BEING — CREATOR OR CORRUPTER

When the lifeforce pours into the physical form through the life cord of the sutratma — directed by the divine spirit, the Monad — it separates itself into three streams:

1. one to supply the *sympathetic system* which is the Tree of Life;

2. one into the *cerebrospinal system* which is the Tree of Knowledge. This mental force is that which, properly directed, becomes the Tree of Wisdom;

3. one into the *solar plexus* to be used under the direction and will of the personality.

The lifeforce which permeates the sympathetic system is used to pump the blood through the heart; is directed into the reproductive organs to be transmuted into sperm or ovum; is directed by the sympathetic under the supervision of the pituitary to operate through the body and keep the lifeforce active.

The stream which goes into the cerebrospinal under the control of the mind produces thought power, also known as mind over matter.

That which is directed into the solar plexus is used for one's emotional processes. With it you can hate or love, create or destroy. From your abdominal brain you can produce all the emotional intensities of a Spiritual Master ... or of an undeveloped soul.

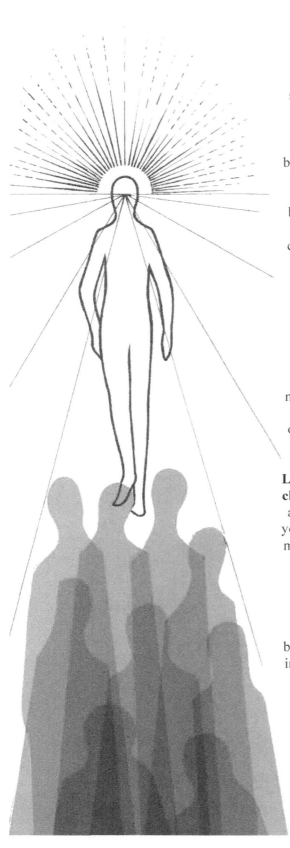

OUT OF THE MISTY SHADOWS...

... emerges the dawn of a new age. And striding in the forefront of humanity's journey to that golden dawn are those venturesome spirits who, even while the shadows lie about them, see the shining radiance of the new being ... the new being of a new and better age.

Lustrous visions of eternity's higher levels become visible to those who open their inner sight. The mechanism of spiritual optics, the channels of deeper perception, come to those whose knowledge differs from that of the ordinary person, whose wisdom transcends common knowledge.

The teachings in your next Lessons provide this kind of illumination. They are for those who aspire to lead the way ... those few who are becoming focal points of light for the many who follow...those who sense a personal destiny that places them in the vanguard of the transition to the next plateau of human understanding and accomplishment.

Lesson 20, The Human Being — The Miracle Maker: Levels of consciousness, memory and the superconscious, the mind and karma, your subconscious mind, your superconscious mind, your Third Eye — superconscious contact, the wisdom mind, mind mysteries and science, erasing karma in the subconscious.

Lesson 21, Antahkarana — The Tree of Immortality: Electronics and healing, the brain and mind power, remembering previous incarnations, the next step in humanity's evolution, building the antahkarana from heart center to Oversoul, the mystic mantrum, the ultimate goal — immortality.

THE STORY OF AGES PAST

MAY BE READ IN EVERY SOUL AND,

IN SOME, THE FUTURE AS WELL.

THE PRESENCE

Dawn; and a star; and the sea unfurled;
    And a miracle hush hanging over the world —
And I, standing lone by the side of the sea —
    When lo, God came and spoke to me.
He spoke to me and I hid my face,
    For a wide white glory illum'ed the place.
And I bowed me, trembling, "O God," I cried,
    "Is it here that Thy presence Thou dost hide?
Hast Thou always dwelt 'mid the sea and sky
    In the hush that quivers when day is nigh?
I have sought Thee long, but have sought in vain,
    Through years of trial, through nights of pain;
And all the while Thou wert waiting far
    In the wave, in the dawn, in the paling star!
Had I known, O God, of Thy dwelling place
    I might long ago have seen Thy face!"
But God made answer, "Not in the star,
    Or in the dawn, or the wave, did I wait afar.
O child of mine, I was close to thee —
    Thou wert always held in the arms of me.
By only now are thine eyes unsealed
    And my ever-presence to thee revealed.
Go, turn thee back to the world of men;
    Thou shalt never search in vain again.
On the darkest days thou shalt see my light,
    My eyes shall look from the eyes of night.
In the voices of children my voice shall ring,
    My splendor shine in the humblest thing.
Thy daily task — it shall thrill with me,
    For I shall be near to commune with thee.
O child, this moment thy breath is mine
    Hush — listen! My pulse beats with thine."
Dawn; and a star; and the sea unfurled;
    And a miracle hush hanging over the world.

—Author Unknown

A GREATER GOD

A boy was born 'mid little things,
    Between a little world and sky,
And dreamed not of the cosmic rings
    Round which the circling planets fly.

He lived in little works and thoughts,
    Where little ventures grow and plod,
And paced and ploughed his little plots,
    And prayed unto his little God.

But as the mighty system grew,
    His faith grew faint with many scars;
The cosmos widened in his view —
    But God was lost among his stars.

Another boy in lowly days,
    As he, to little things was born,
But gathered lore in woodland ways,
    And from the glory of the morn.

As wider skies broke on his view,
    God greatened in his growing mind;
Each year he dreamed his God anew,
    And left his older God behind.

He saw the boundless scheme dilate,
    In star and blossom, sky and clod;
And as the universe grew great
    He dreamed for it a greater God.

— Sam Foss

www.astara.org

The Human Being -- The Miracle Maker

Second Degree — Lesson Twenty

THE LEVELS OF CONSCIOUSNESS

It is important for us to establish a better understanding of consciousness, a clearer concept of the levels of the mind. We can easily grasp that which is obvious — the state of mind you exhibit in your waking hours — but such a shallow conception of consciousness becomes too superficial to consider.

That which once was metaphysical in terms of consciousness has now become fact. Materialist or scientist, whoever denies the operation of some level of consciousness whether one is asleep, dead, in a coma or in a hypnotic trance, is worse than the head-burying ostrich. Clearly, the mind is *always* conscious on some level, though we are not always consciously aware of it. We are usually only aware of the waking conscious portion.

The study of the mind's levels — the waking conscious, the subconscious, the superconscious and the Wisdom Mind — will require careful consideration. It will be of benefit to separate the information into segments so that the eye can more easily "see" what the conscious mind is attempting to comprehend.

1. *The waking conscious mind* is the mind we use in our daily living. It perceives the incidents of passing time as marked by our every day.

2. *The subconscious mind* is a portion of the superconscious. This subconscious substance is divided in its function:
   a. it automatically controls the functions of the physical form;
   b. it is the portion of the superconscious which stores memories of fears and phobias, and brings them into the waking conscious mind.

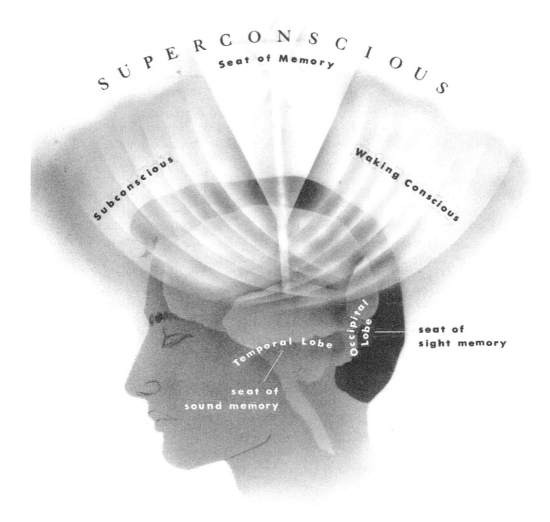

MEMORY AND THE SUPERCONSCIOUS

Memories are filed in the superconscious. Both the subconscious forcefield and the waking conscious forcefields are parts of the great storehouse of the superconscious. Mind streams flow from both the subconscious and the waking conscious to strike the various memory centers in the brain. This also explains the activity of the subconscious obsessions upon the waking conscious.

3. *The superconscious mind* holds life's entire library of experience. It is our book of life and judgment in one. It is divided into three principal aspects:
   a. the waking conscious mind,
   b. the subconscious mind,
   c. the causal forcefield.

4. *The Wisdom Mind,* sometimes called Adi-budha, the Supreme Wisdom, is the field of consciousness which, overshadowing each individual, is the home of the Monad, the seat of incomparable bliss where truth abides.

YOUR WAKING CONSCIOUS MIND

The seat of the waking conscious mind is the pineal gland which houses the mental seed atom. The pineal is also the terminal point of the consciousness cord which extends between the brain and the causal superconscious forcefield above the head.

The nadis, or etheric nerve threads which project into the mental field, flow into cells located in the posterior and central part of the cerebral cortex where we discover all the sense centers — the sight center in the occipital lobe, the hearing center in the temporal lobe, the speech center, the sleep center, etc.

The waking conscious mind operates through the cerebrospinal nervous system. This mind, experiencing some incident affecting the senses — those of seeing, hearing, tasting, feeling and smelling — registers a mental impulse which strikes a cell of the brain and travels into the superconscious forcefield via the nadis. There it is relegated to its proper file — the causal forcefield, the subconscious or the waking conscious forcefield, according to its emotional vibration.

To bring the memory of the incident again into the waking conscious mind from the memory storehouse in the superconscious, a mental impulse, triggered by physical sensations, strikes the mind substance in the superconscious forcefield setting up a responding vibration. The impulse travels down the etheric cord of the nadis to strike a specific brain cell or center to which the etheric cord is attached. The vibration in the superconscious sets up the same vibration in the brain center. The brain center responds to the vibration in the mental substance — *and you remember.* It is like tones on the musical scale. A tone is sounded in the mind substance which sends its vibratory impulse down through the etheric thread, connecting it to the brain center. The responsive neuron in turn vibrates to and echoes the tone.

The brain has no power in or of itself to think or to remember. Memories are not stored in the brain cells but these cells react to impulses reaching them from both the upper reaches of the superconscious mind and from the world around you. The brain is only a way station through which memories or impulses flow.

THE MIND AND KARMA

The question now arises: from where, then, come the dark phobias of the mind? — the unexplained complexes?

The answer itself is complex. We can explain better by using an example: Some people suffer, let us say, from an unexplainable and constantly returning fear, which reaction builds a brain center in a particular brain cell or neuron. These obsessions rise out of the subconscious forcefield and flow into the brain cells of the frontal lobe, but only as the heart seed atom sends impulses into the brain cells to activate the flow of these memories. Remember, the subconscious actually is a part of the superconscious forcefield — that portion where all the fears and phobias are stored.

The picture images flow out of the heart seed atom and, carried by the blood, strike the brain cells which contain the etheric thread upon which is recorded this particular fear. The impact stimulates this brain center to discharge electrical impulses, activating a flow of mental ether out of the subconscious where the fear is recorded as a memory. The "fear" image flows downward from the subconscious field to strike the brain center and the personality "remembers" the "fear" episode. If the fear is recalled often enough to create a permanent brain center, a phobia or an obsession results. It would seem that humans are sometimes caught in a self-created negative cycle. We shall pursue our method of escape later.

YOUR SUBCONSCIOUS MIND

The subconscious is divided in its operations:

1. that which operates through the sympathetic nervous system, automatically controlling the functions of the physical form — the heartbeat, breathing, etc.;

2. that which operates through the cerebrospinal, bringing the memories of fears and phobias into the waking conscious mind.

Superconscious mind substance flows through the subconscious forcefield into the frontal lobe of the cerebral cortex of the brain to converge in the pituitary gland. The pituitary, possessing two lobes, is also divided in its operation:

1. The frontal or anterior lobe is connected with the sympathetic nervous system. This anterior pituitary, operating *through* the sympathetic, automatically controls the functions of the physical form — but only as directed by the heart seed atom, releasing picture images of *past karma*.

2. The rear lobe, called the postlobe, is connected with the cerebrospinal system and the waking conscious mind, and also with the solar plexus atom

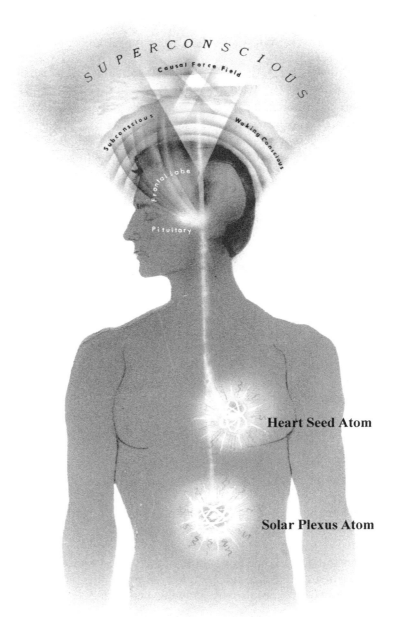

KARMA — PAST AND PRESENT

The subconscious mind substance flows out of the superconscious field into the frontal lobe to converge into the pituitary. The pituitary controls the subconscious operations but only as directed by the heart seed atom releasing picture images of past karma and the solar plexus atom releasing karmic images being presently created.

which constantly releases *karmic images being presently created* through our attachment to our desires.

Thus your subconscious activities are definitely controlled by your *past karma* and by the karma you *create daily.*

Let us consider first that portion of the subconscious which causes the functions of the physical form to operate automatically without any conscious thought — respiration, circulation, digestion, etc. This aspect of the subconscious is completely under the dominion of the life cord which extends from the Monad to the heart.

From the anterior lobe of pituitary, the subconscious mind substance travels downward through the sympathetic system which converges in the solar plexus brain, and again in the root brain.

Both lobes of pituitary and the root brain in the reproductive center are, at the present stage of evolution, subject to influence by the subconscious mind operating through the sympathetic nervous system. The pituitary releases the flow of chemical substances which cause the entire glandular system to release the proper hormones throughout the physical form.

Let us now consider the second aspect of the subconscious. We have already said that the subconscious mind substance flows out of the superconscious forcefield of which it is a part, into the frontal lobe of the brain to converge in the anterior lobe of the pituitary gland. We have said, too, that the subconscious is that portion of the superconscious which is the "filing cabinet" of all your fears and phobias.

Let us say that the heart seed atom releases picture images of a fear episode. The impulse travels to the frontal lobe of the brain. There the impulse strikes a brain cell through which passes a thread of mental reflecting ether upon which is "recorded" this same fear episode. The stimulated brain cell projects the picture of the episode into the forcefield of the subconscious via the nadis thread of ether and the memory of the episode pours into the consciousness.

It would seem, then, that you have two "files" of memories: that which is stored in the superconscious forcefield and that which is recorded in the heart seed atom. It is important to explain that they are duplicate records. That which is recorded in the heart seed atom simply reflects that which is recorded in the akashic record of the superconscious.

As we have said, it is out of this heart atom that the picture images of karma move into the bloodstream to be carried through your physical form. Thus it is through the seed atom that recorded karma is dissipated. "Erasing" the karmic record from the heart atom also erases it from the cells in the frontal lobe of the cerebral cortex of the brain, seat of the subconscious — or rather, from the nadis which contain a record of the memory and which is "coiled" in the cells of the frontal lobe.

It is essential to remember that as one's fears and phobias are gradually removed from these cells, more and more superconscious mind power can strike them until this frontal lobe, aligning with the Third Eye, *ultimately becomes the seat of the superconscious.* Also, with the dissolution of the etheric web which now divides the postlobe of pituitary from the anterior lobe, superconscious impulses and impressions can flow into the frontal lobe of the brain. With the dissolution of this web, the force of the superconscious will pour more of its power directly into the entire pituitary.

In the future, people will experience little influence from this aspect of the subconscious — the fears and the phobias — because we will have learned to accept and express all our emotions in positive and healing ways, as a part of our spiritual path, and this will assist with the purification of the heart seed atom.

YOUR SUPERCONSCIOUS MIND

The superconscious mind finds its seat of contact through the entire Third Eye area, including the optic thalamus, the third ventricle, the postlobe of pituitary and the pineal gland.

Although the superconscious embraces the subconscious and waking conscious mental fields, it also extends above and beyond these levels. This higher aspect of the superconscious contains the causal field. Over and above this superconscious field lies the mind we call the *Wisdom Mind.* It extends upward to embrace the Monad, your individual "share of God." We shall refer to it later.

The superconscious holds life's entire library of experiences in its imperishable substance. In it is recorded every desire and every act of the soul. It is indeed its book of life and book of judgment in one, for it has recorded everything that you have ever thought or done, said or heard. This record is reflected in the physical seed atom of the heart, and it is out of this heart atom that the picture images of karma move into the bloodstream.

The superconscious is divided into three principal aspects:

1. *The causal forcefield* is that aspect which lies in the heart of the superconscious. This causal field absorbs into its substance only the pure and altruistic experiences of the individual soul.

2. *The subconscious mind* is that portion of the superconscious which absorbs into its substance the phobias, fears, anxieties, depressions, obsessions, compulsions, neuroses, — all the mysterious enigmatical elements which can become mental blockages, things with which human beings often struggle.

3. *The waking conscious mind* is the mind we use in our daily living — the surface mind operating through the cerebrospinal nervous system which sees, hears, tastes, feels and smells the incidents of passing time.

As daily events are experienced they are noted by the waking conscious mind and pass from it into the superconscious. There events are filed as memories according to their vibrations. The memory of undesirable events is filed in the subconscious forcefield, the positive are absorbed into the causal, while the general events are filed in the waking conscious sensory area.

Some disciples may be confused that we place the superconscious as the seat of memories, which would cause it also to house our struggles as well as our nobility and wisdom. But it must be clearly understood that if a superconscious field is to contain the complete akashic record, it must file away a record of all of our actions and reactions, both positive and negative. Since the superconscious does contain the akashic record, then every thought, action, emotion and experience becomes a memory filed in its proper category according to the nature of the experience — whether it is positive, negative or general. Thus we have three different "memory files" in the superconscious mind:

1. *The causal forcefield* into which pass thoughts and emotions which are positive, pure, untinged with lower elements such as selfishness, hate, and greed, there become the "bricks" with which you build your "house not made with hands, eternal in the heavens" — your causal body. Only altruistic thoughts tinged with divine love will enter this causal field. Once you have completely built this celestial form by your own spiritual efforts, you need not again incarnate in the world of matter.

2. *The subconscious forcefield* into which your emotional and mental struggles are absorbed to become your fears, phobias, obsessions, and to create your *kama rupa* — the lower desire body.

3. *The waking conscious forcefield* into which flow thoughts neither pure nor evil — only those which are the fruit of "common knowledge." This field contains your general store of information and accumulated knowledge as experienced through everyday living, thus becoming your immediate finite memory reference.

YOUR THIRD EYE — SUPERCONSCIOUS CONTACT

It should be noted that the pineal gland is not only the seat of the conscious mind but also a part of the superconscious point of contact since it is a *part* of the Third Eye, and since the Third Eye in its entirety is the seat of the superconscious in the physical brain.

The superconscious also embraces the postlobe of pituitary which, when spiritualized to any degree, exerts its influence upon the anterior lobe — the seat of the subconscious mind. The superconscious does not extend downward into the physical form. However, it can be reached through the vagus nerve and the

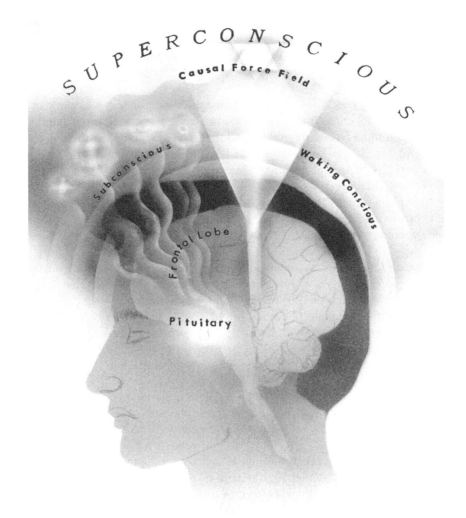

SUPERCONSCIOUS, SUBCONSCIOUS AND WAKING CONSCIOUS

The superconscious is the seat of the akashic records, which means it is the memory storehouse. In this capacity it holds a record of both good and evil. Only the pure essences enter the causal forcefield to build your eternal causal form. The undesirable sifts into the subconscious to become your blocked and unresolved fears, phobias, and complexes. The frontal lobe presently is victim of the subconscious flow but once the subconscious is cleared of its undesirable karma, this lobe will unite with the Third Eye to become a brain center for the superconscious.

spinal cord by the fires of kundalini so that, once your desires become tinged with aspirations, there is a constant upreaching toward the superconscious state. This, then, clarifies how both the conscious mind and the subconscious have a connection with the superconscious mind, although at your present level of consciousness the waking conscious connection is almost imperceptible.

With your future spiritual development, the anterior lobe of pituitary will be influenced by pituitrin — the "love" hormone released by the postlobe — and you will automatically begin to express good will in general through the subconscious.

The pineal gland, under future stimulation, will allow more definite and controlled contact between the conscious and superconscious minds. The tiny pineal antenna makes the pineal gland not only a receiving set for the superconscious, but a sending set as well, as it attempts to relay to the brain inspiration received from the Oversoul.

THE WISDOM MIND

There is a self that is of the essence of Matter. *There is another inner self of* Life *that fills the other. There is another inner self of* Mind. *There is another inner self of* Truth-knowledge. *There is another self of* Bliss. — Upanishads

The face of truth is hidden by a golden lid. That remove, O fostering Sun, for the law of the truth, for sight. High beyond the intelligence is the Great Self. Beyond the Great Self is the unmanifest. Beyond the unmanifest is the Conscious Being. There is nothing beyond the Being. THAT is the extreme ultimate. THAT, the supreme goal. — Katha Upanishad

We have spoken at length concerning the superconscious mind and have divided it in its trinity — the waking conscious mind, the subconscious and the causal forcefield. We must now teach of another aspect of mind to attain a clear understanding of some of the future teachings. We refer to the Wisdom Mind which is the heritage of every individual: the mind which is the godmind of the individual — your own portion of the universal Divine Mind of God.

The Wisdom Mind of each soul, called the Adi-budha, extends above your superconscious and embraces your divine Monad; it is that mind which becomes the seat of wisdom permeating your mental aura. It is the field of the supreme consciousness — an estate of rare quality of which you are almost completely unaware. It is the seat of supreme bliss, the realm of the Word, the field of the Divine Substance, the region of Divinity overshadowing each individual. Adi means *supreme;* budha interprets to mean *wisdom.*

Adi-budha is in possession of pure truth while all other aspects of the mind are hampered by their imprisonment in the obscurity of life in the physical form. Even the

THE WISDOM MIND

The Wisdom Mind, called the Adi-budha, extends above the superconscious and embraces the Monad. It is the field of supreme consciousness. It is the center of bliss; the realm of the Word; the region of the Divine Life Stream of the Holy Nahd; the home of the Divine Substance overshadowing each individual.

superconscious, an intermediate force operating between the waking conscious and the Wisdom Mind, is tinged with the *maya,* the illusion of physical life.

Since there exists what mystics call the universal Mind of God, or the Divine Mind, how then did the consciousness become separated from it?

Throughout the ethers of space we know that, pervading every atom, is a mental substance — a substance of the Mind of God, a quality of the Divine Mind. We know that pervading the aura is also a quality of mental substance. We know that the atomic particles of this substance permeate the cells of our brains, yet its quality does not seem to bear the stamp of divinity, which is contained in the Divine Substance. We know that the mental aura of the individual contains some portion of the Divine Mind and some quality of the Divine Spirit. Yet there seems to be a gulf between that innate Divinity and the manifesting consciousness of the individual. The soul seems only dimly aware of the presence of the Higher Quality. Even so, it perpetually strives to unite with it. Your life seems to be a constant chasing after shadows, which could equally be described as a search for light.

Your consciousness seems to be limited to a certain octave of sounds and colors. You are unable to distinguish that which is above that scale or that which is below it. The range of sound above and below it is inaudible to you, and the colors above and below your range of perception are invisible to you. So is your mind also tuned to a certain octave of awareness, and you seem unable to soar above your personal range of perception. Your only means of communicating with the animal kingdom is through vocal tone and the quality of your emotions. The animal thus feels your love or your hatred, not through words but through intuitive feeling. The same is true at the other end of the scale. You can only communicate with God through intuitive feeling.

One can no more deny the presence of the Higher Mind than one could deny the presence of animal devotion, even though the animal cannot say the words, "I love you." The qualities of the Higher Mind are there, but must be perceived by the normal consciousness through intuitive perceptions. The soul must *know* the love of God just as it must *know* the love of the animal. This *knowing* we call intuition. The rare flashes of communication between the normal mind and the Adi-budha result in our inspiration, our visions, our intuitive discernments, our moments of genius ... more rarely yet, the spiritual ecstasies the mystics experience when the veils of consciousness are momentarily parted.

Every mystic, every genius, every scientist, every inventor is aware of temporary penetrations of the consciousness by the Wisdom Mind. He or she is aware of the action of intuition which darts like a lightning flash piercing ignorance with knowledge, with understanding and with mental power.

The light of this superior consciousness must act within narrow limits; must subdue and adapt its force to the normal mind substance of the individual; must modify or diminish its dynamo until the original divine luminosity becomes the quality of inspiration rather than pure wisdom. Still the receiver, the mystic, is quite aware of the source of the revelatory vision or of intuitive perception.

One road to attainment of this superior estate for the Astarian lies through the practice of meditation in Lama Yoga — the inward movement of the mind in constant and ceaseless effort to pierce the web between your external and your super-Self. Breaking this consciousness barrier causes a double action of the cosmic forces of consciousness: an upward sweeping of the normal mind into the immutable status beyond and embracing the universe; and, at the same time, a descent of light and bliss which, pouring into the lower consciousness, illumines its mental energies.

Only the mystic who has experienced this union of consciousness can be truly aware of the existing gulf between one's potential wisdom and one's everyday mental level. And yet, the disciple also becomes aware that the higher mind seems to be a reservoir of truth, and that one need not go from one's present environment to find the whole of it. You need only unite consciously with your Oversoul to find the hidden secrets of the universe.

Receiving the downpour of Wisdom, you are aware of an automatic and spontaneous knowledge flowing in from the higher mind. You are aware of a difference in the process of thinking. There is no need for speculation or for attempting to find answers — the answers are simply there, for the Wisdom Mind is in possession of full truth, remitting vast degrees of knowledge in a single moment. The mystic is aware of the stream of knowledge-energy pouring in like a ray of sunshine, bringing with it true vision, true thinking and true feeling which, for want of a better word, we call *intuition*.

In this expanded state of awareness the mystic is conscious of the presence of the Adi-budha lying above his/her normal consciousness like great, outspread wings of light. You are aware that the veil of the superconscious, which usually hides the Wisdom from you, has parted.

The mystic is aware, then, of the presence of not only the superconscious but the Wisdom consciousness that lies above it — the seat of the supreme cosmic power of which the superconscious is only an ambassador. The mystic realizes that the superconscious is only an intermediate force between the waking conscious mind and the seat of the Wisdom Mind, acting as a protective screen to shield the waking conscious from an unbearable light; for indeed, the conscious mind is engulfed in a darkness which could not receive the direct impact of the supreme light, except as it pours down through the shield of the superconscious.

The difference between the Wisdom Mind and the superconsciousness is that in the field of the Wisdom there is supreme all-knowing truth existing without any method of thought or action. The superconscious, being subject to the world of maya, or illusion, is aware of the essential truth of things but must attempt to make this truth operable in the world of matter; must find some method of production, some means of taking the absolute truth and making it amenable to the narrow concepts of the conscious mind. It must find some process of transforming the dynamic power of the Wisdom light so that it will illumine and not destroy the limited field of the conscious mind. It must, in other words, convert the Wisdom into the ignorance, the light into the darkness, releasing only that portion of Wisdom that the conscious mind can contain.

In our normal consciousness, modern institutions of society create a false duality. For example, and for various reasons, an effort is made to make us believe that all religions, all philosophies, all political theories exist as opposites. Each of these opposites claims to possess that which is right, to be superior in all ways. Each taxes the other with falsehood. Each feels a destiny to destroy the other so that its own truth might survive. Each claims to be in exclusive possession of the true path.

The light of the superconscious, if permitted to pierce the ignorance, would refute this claim to exclusiveness and false dualism. Reflecting the light of the Wisdom Mind, it would permeate the conscious mind with the knowledge that *all* are necessary to the whole, and it would assign each to its field of endeavor in order to fulfill its rightful place and attain its own realization.

The superconscious, being in some possession of truth, would destroy the concept that all is false except one's own affirmations. But the superconscious, being only a delegate of the Wisdom, *cannot cause a change in the concepts of the conscious mind.* Only a downpouring of the bliss from the Wisdom Mind, only an attunement with the stream of the divine Word pouring down from Adi-budha, can bring an immediate dissolution of the ignorance and darkness, and a complete surrender to truth and understanding.

Thus we can say that the conscious mind is the mind of ignorance, of illusion. The superconscious is the possessor of *partial* truth, harmony and knowledge, the home of the waking conscious, the subconscious, and the causal forcefield. The Wisdom Mind is the possessor of *pure* wisdom, bliss, delight ... the Word not yet made manifest in the world of form ... the place of the hidden mysteries where the divinity of the individual resides, reposing in splendid patience awaiting the Becoming of the transient soul.

It is "the Father/Mother which art in heaven" of which the soul — groping its way through the depths of maya, the world of form and matter — is so completely unaware. When you attain the ultimate awareness, you will no longer be "a god in ruins." You will no longer beg alms from a universe of which you are master and ruler.

MIND MYSTERIES AND SCIENCE

A number of years ago, medical science reported a great discovery concerning impulses reaching brain cells under electrical pressures. Neurologists, probing with an electric needle, or electrode, discovered to their amazement that the brain cells themselves generate electronic currents. These neurosurgeons, first seeking to discover the cause of epilepsy, unearthed some of the most incredible mysteries of the human mind ever dreamed by scientists.

In their first experiments with the electrode, it was discovered that the patient would react differently as it touched various cells in the brain. First, touching a certain brain center would cause the hand to flex. Touching another would cause the lip to twitch. Still another would cause the eyelids to close, or the jaw to sag. The search continued until the electrode finally struck the brain center which would cause an epileptic seizure to engulf the patient. Having discovered the culprit, the neuron was removed and the patient was given every reason to hope for a future life with no further difficulties, epilepsy having been proved to be literally an electrical explosion in the brain itself caused by unbalanced pressures upon certain cells.

Of interest to us as mystics is that in their experiments these pioneering brain surgeons gathered considerable information concerning memory. The use of local anesthetics enabled the patients to remain conscious. As the electrode touched certain cells the patient would describe scenes from the past. One woman described the birth of her first child. Another recalled the exact music heard at a long-ago concert. A man "re-observed" a ball game he had in reality witnessed many years previously.

These scenes from the past — scenes that could be watched and heard like a motion picture unreeling before memory's eye — were described in full, the patients declaring they could see the scenes, hear the voices of the people involved, and even take part in the episodes themselves, while simultaneously lying fully conscious in the operating room. In other words, they could read the akashic record of the past and witness events in which they themselves participated, simply by having an electric needle applied to certain brain centers. Intrigued and perplexed by these discoveries, neurosurgeons stepped courageously into the field of esoteric science and opened the gateway to the superconscious mind of this curious being we call the human.

They have conceded that the human brain is like the video tape used in recording TV programs, with the "tape" which runs through the brain cells recording both the sights and sounds of every moment of time in the life of the individual. When the electrode strikes a certain center in the brain, it activates that portion of the "tape" upon which is recorded a certain scene, and the patient can then "see" and "hear" the episode all over again.

Having unintentionally but fortunately opened new vistas of the mind, neurosurgeons then turned their attention toward experiments with animals. It is certainly hoped that these experiments were conducted ethically and with the wellbeing of the animal protected at all times. Only the results of the experiments are discussed here because unfortunately, issues regarding the rights of the animals in question were not addressed when these results were reported to the public.

The process employed is called "ESB" — the abbreviation of Electrical Stimulation of the Brain — which is the insertion of an electrical conductor into various sections of the brain to control and observe the behavior of the animal under electrical stimulus.

An apparatus called a stimulator is attached to an animal — for instance, a monkey. It operates with a transistor and tiny battery. Microelectrodes are inserted in skull sockets without, we are told, the least sensation of pain, and the needle is directed to a certain center in the animal's brain, causing various reactions.

Electrical stimulation, or ESB, applied to a center called the amygdala causes the monkey to fly immediately into a rage, fighting and clawing at anything or anyone in his reach. Switching off the electric impulse causes the monkey to become immediately docile, peaceful and normal. Rage can thus be induced or turned off according to the electric stimulus striking a particular brain center.

It has also been observed that moving the electrode a mere fraction of an inch from the cells that bring on the destructive rage can transform the monkey into a most lovable and affectionate little being, thus establishing that the emotions of hate and love can be induced in almost the same center in the brain, being only very narrowly separated. Researchers have similarly discovered brain centers relating to fear, pain, pleasure, anxiety and even centers controlling the appetite. A monkey, by stimulation, can be made ravenously hungry, yet even in the midst of devouring a meal the flip of a switch can cause it to turn immediately away from food.

Although most of these experiments have been with animals, enough have been conducted with the human brain to convince researchers that human behavior can also be controlled very similarly to the manner in which animals respond. For example, neurosurgeons discovered what they term the bliss center. It is the stimulation of this center, they believe, which results in the mystical ecstasies of the saints. The medical researcher stimulates it synthetically with the electrode. The saint stimulates it by his or her dedicated life of service, spiritual discipline and spiritual practice. *The synthetic bliss, being artificial, does not become an integral part of the personality. The bliss of the saint speaks of a developed spiritual center in the brain which becomes their own personal "pearl of great price."*

THE DEVELOPING FRONTAL LOBE

Where in the brain is the physical focal point of your future and as yet unfolded spiritual nature? In the frontal lobe of the cerebral cortex. But at present this area is clouded with subconscious phobias, fears, and obsessions. Your superconscious finds it difficult to pierce or "work through" these obstructions. But the time will arrive when this superior mind will have an open channel from its level through to the physical. The heart seed atom gradually will be cleared of its karmic picture images

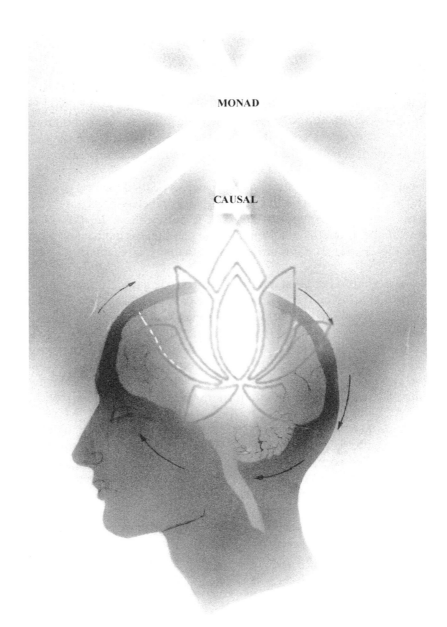

MONAD

CAUSAL

THE ROTATING FRONTAL LOBE

The frontal lobe is expanding toward the top of the head, while the cerebellum is shifting toward the front. The brain as a whole is "rotating." Millenniums from now, after the heart seed atom is cleared of undesirable karma, the frontal lobe will be the seat of the superconscious, aligned with the Third Eye and the causal forcefield.

which trigger your fears, phobias and obsessions. As they dissolve, the cells of the frontal lobe will become increasingly powerful until, with their ultimate elimination, the frontal lobe will become an unobstructed channel for the superconscious.

We have already told you that the brain is revolving: the cerebellum in the back of the head is rotating toward the front, which means that the frontal lobe is also in the process of shifting. Rather than actually rotating, it is *expanding* toward the center of the top of the head where it will ultimately become aligned with the crown chakra and the Third Eye. The lobe will by that time have been cleared of the subconscious fears and phobias, and will have become the center for the superconscious.

TRANSFORMING THE KARMA OF THE SUBCONSCIOUS

Although a neurosurgeon can remove a particular brain center which has been the seat of some emotional or physical disturbance such as epilepsy, there is another way to remove these unwanted visitors — non-surgically in the conventional sense — a kind of new age surgery using ultrasound.

When the extremely high frequency of ultrasonic waves strikes a particular brain cell, it releases or "erases" electromagnetically the neuroses, fears, phobias, anxieties and obsessions attached to that particular cell. It is no longer necessary to remove the brain cells. When ultrasonic waves are directed into the area the sonic bombardment "erases" the memory, or electromagnetic attachment, of the fear or phobia just as recorded sounds can be erased from a magnetic tape.

Magnetic recording tape consists of a thin ribbon of plastic to which has been attached a microscopic layer of iron particles. During the process of recording, sounds pass through the microphone into the recorder where they are changed into electronic impulses. These electronic impulses are then transmitted to the iron particles on the tape which, in turn, become infinitely tiny electromagnets.

When the tape is played for listening the electronic impulses in these infinitesimal electromagnets are amplified and directed to the speaker of the instrument which then magnifies the impulses so that the sound becomes audible. The tape is erased by an ultrasonic signal applied to an electromagnet called an "erase head." The magnetic field of the electromagnet rearranges the molecular magnets on the tape, relieving the infinitesimal magnetized iron particles of their electrical charge, and thus the record of sound is removed.

Much the same procedure happens in the human brain. Threads of mental reflecting ether wind through the brain cells, recording the sights and sounds of your every day. These events are deposited in the superconscious as memories. To "erase" these scenes from the "tape" of etheric thread, the brain section involved is bombarded by sonic waves. This clears the cells and the connecting threads of anything recorded in the past — making the cells available for recording new memories.

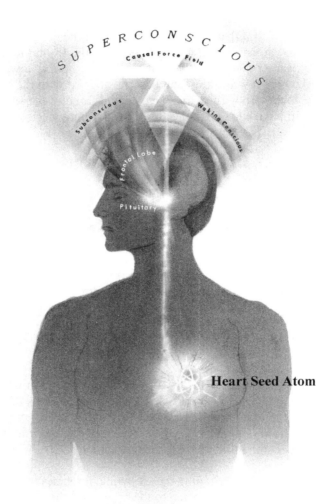

SUBCONSCIOUS MIND AND KARMA

The unprocessed or blocked fears and phobias, buried in the subconscious, are also recorded in the heart seed atom as karma. These karmic picture images, carried into the brain cells via the bloodstream, continually release electronic impulses which strike the "tape" of mental reflecting ether in the subconscious area. The subconscious mind force carries the fears into the waking conscious. The waking conscious drifts from "memory" to "memory." Thus one is victim of one's karma and the superconscious cannot gain prominence until the heart seed atom is cleared.

But we do not want to erase our memories. No matter how painful some of them may be, we need to use them to learn our soul lessons, and to transform ourselves. Can we use mental power the way the medical scientist uses ultrasonic waves? Not exactly. How then can humans escape from their self-created negative cycle?

1. By learning not to avoid your emotions. Through learning to accept your emotions, whether "positive" or "negative" and by working to develop the skill to express them in healthy ways, you conquer any negative aspects associated with them. Blocking one's feelings, denying them, rather than embracing them as a valuable and spiritual part of one's self is what creates the phobias and other mental and emotional troubles discussed in this lesson. For example, you can learn to express emotions such as anger, fear, hurt, and sadness in positive and healing ways both verbally and non-verbally. Learning to use your emotions as friends and guideposts to where your soul work lies, learning to work with them, accepting them and directing them to flow through you in positive ways then transforms emotions of every sort into a part of your spiritual path. Then the connective etheric thread is not erased but transformed in the subconscious and you are able to heal, forgive or transform any troubling, fearsome event or memory.

2. By attempting, through Lama Yoga, or other forms of meditation or spiritual practice, to merge with a downpouring river of light from above — grace from the Divine Source. Entering the current of this divine Stream cleanses the brain cells and the mental forcefield.

The disciple who can attune to the divine Sound of the Holy Nahd immediately attains a measure of the same effect the neurosurgeon achieves when sonic waves are directed to the frontal lobe in order to transform and unblock fears and phobias.

The disciple has washed the frontal lobe with a *Sound Current from God,* whereas the neurosurgeon has washed the cells and the recording thread with a *sonic wave or sound wave of magnetized mental reflecting ether.* Again, the memories in the cells are not erased, but transformed.

Either way, the cells and the nadis are purified and left free for the superconscious currents to flow into them. The threads of mental reflecting ether are transformed and the undesirable allowed to flow away, just as one transforms the material on a tape by running it through a recording machine or by placing it in a magnetic field. Although the "impression" is removed from the brain "tape," the event itself is not removed from the akashic record, and remains a part of this record of eternity. We shall enlarge upon this in our next Lesson.

Antahkarana
-- The Tree of Immortality

Second Degree — Lesson Twenty-One

ELECTRONICS AND HEALING

Medical science stands on the threshold of esoteric science and peers into the world of the unknown. Having glimpsed the astounding possibilities and adventures which lie ahead, science is about to cross the boundary from scientific wonder to esoteric splendor — from matter to miracle.

We spoke at length in our last Lesson concerning the ESB experiments which in some ways have opened such vistas of opportunity to the brain surgeon. Scientists may soon discover other uses for this technique. Many physical diseases may be able to be controlled by such a technique, especially if they are of a glandular nature. Let us say, for instance, that one is arthritic. Presently medical science frequently treats certain types of arthritis by injections of cortisone, a hormone released by the adrenal glands. The fact that an individual contracts arthritis is often indicative of an adrenal deficiency ... the adrenals are not depositing a proper flow of cortisone in the bloodstream. Thus, discovering oneself to be the victim of arthritis, the individual can have a certain brain center "wired." Pressing a control button at various intervals would activate an implanted electrode, causing the brain center involved to release the special impulse or chemicals necessary to stimulate the adrenals. Under such stimulation, the adrenals would, in turn, release a normal outflow of cortisone, thus possibly preventing the formation of arthritis or inflamed nerves.

At present the laboratory-produced synthetic cortisone used by medical science has proved unsatisfactory, often creating undesirable side effects. However, the cortisone produced by one's own adrenal glands would be more suited to, and chemically harmonious with, the atomic structure of the individual.

Now let us say that the individual is a victim of diabetes — a disease caused by pancreas deficiency. Insufficient or ineffective pancreas hormone, insulin, results in excessive sugar in the blood. Stimulation of a certain brain center would cause the pancreas to release a sufficient supply of insulin, and shots or tablets would no longer be necessary. The pancreas would distribute normal glandular releases into the bloodstream.

Thus by controlling particular brain centers with infinitesimal electrodes, some of our major illnesses might be brought under our control.

What then, asks the Astarian, becomes of karma?

It is important to explain that not all of our physical problems can be handled chemically by simply pressing a button controlling an electrode in the brain, nor would we even want them to be. The physical illnesses and mental or emotional challenges which have a karmic background will remain until a purified heart seed atom eliminates the record of one's past negative karma from one's bloodstream.

Ultrasonic waves directed toward certain cell clusters may remove the record upon the threads of mental reflecting ether embedded in those brain cells, but they cannot remove the record of a traumatic event from the akashic record in the superconscious, or from the heart seed atom. They still are a part of the akashic record of the individual and, as such, are there to be dealt with by the individual hopefully in a way which produces understanding, personal growth and healing.

By pressing an electronic button, you may be able to stimulate a necessary supply of cortisone to deal with something such as arthritis, but, on another level, in terms of creating negative karma during your life, if you continue to pour "negativity" into your blood it will find some means of manifestation. Those who have made others suffer *will* reap their "reward." You can never electronically clear from your memory field the record of the wrongs you have done to others. You will continue to suffer mentally until such time as you find some way of adjusting the karma and making the record clean.

This is one's *true* freedom. Being free from some measure of *physical* pain is only one freedom. One is not truly free who is held in *physical, mental, emotional or life circumstance* bondage to an old karmic debt. Only through "forgiveness" or a downpouring of the divine Current of the holy Nahd can full liberation come. Such an immersion in the divine Stream — a true baptism — will clear both the brain cells and the record in the superconscious, and only grace from God can perform this divine unction.

The supreme "chemical" is the Divine Substance permeating the ethers about us, and our bloodstream — regardless of how many electrodes may be implanted in our brains — cannot be caused to absorb this magical potion until we so spiritually attune ourselves as to be worthy of its reception.

All the electrodes in the world, stimulating the bliss center in all humans, cannot bring true and lasting bliss until that supreme ecstasy becomes an innate attribute of the individual soul. For, indeed, with all their miraculous discoveries, the most important of all is the discovery by medical scientists that they cannot control the human will. The neurosurgeon can *force* the patient to lift an arm by the pressure of an electrical impulse upon a brain neuron. But no amount of pressure can make the patient *want* to lift the arm unless *the patient* desires to do so.

The neurosurgeon can wire a patient to electronically stimulate a brain center by pressing a button. BUT the neurosurgeon can do nothing to cause the patient to *want* to push the button. The neurosurgeon has already discovered that outside the physical brain lies a higher aspect of the human mind — that which *makes one behave as an individual human being* with one's own individual will. No outside stimulus or influence can *force* the human will to *want* to do that which one does not want to do.

Lying somewhere outside the brain cells — obvious but as yet unrecognized — there is a higher intelligence at work which controls the thoughts and feelings of personality. The neurosurgeon, aware of the higher aspect of the mind, has not "named" it as an actuality. It must ultimately be recognized to be related to the superconscious mind which is the true storehouse of our memories — not the cells of the physical brain, although they act as conveyors for the mental impulses which carry specific recollections once again into the waking consciousness.

A significant point in present medical findings is that, although painful incidents can be recalled to the memory of the patient, a brain center itself does not register pain, thus proving that the center is not the filing cabinet of the memory. Rather *it is the "tape"* containing the picture images of the past scene which, penetrating the cells, carries the memory of emotional pain and distress into the center.

Science admits that the brain is like a tape recorder. Its quest now is to determine the substance and locate the fountainhead of the mysterious "tape" or "thread" which pervades the brain cells. From where does it come? Of what is it composed? How does it record the thoughts, scenes, feelings, and sounds of one's everyday life? What puts the "messages" on the tape?

The strict scientist may well ask, "Can it be that humans DO have a soul!"

BRAIN ALIGNMENT INFLUENCES MIND POWER

The *genius* is the soul who has mastered many things in previous lives and who has built many powerful nadis antennas that extend into the field of mind substance, bringing down thought impulses which activate and develop the power of the brain. This does not necessarily mean that the soul of every genius has cleared the heart seed atom of karmic records. Such a soul may demonstrate remarkable talents but be limited by physical problems.

The soul, having developed considerable mind power, may have accumulated undesirable karma which must first be erased before it can exhibit both mental *and* physical perfection and a life freed from numerous problems and frustrations. It must be said here again, we are not suggesting that if you struggle with physical, mental or emotional problems, this is somehow your fault. We do believe that these issues are sent to some degree to every human being to either give us the opportunity to clear away past negative karma, to assist us in learning important soul lessons, as well as to help us see that we can develop mastership of our physical plane existence through the power of the spirit. This learning about and using the connection between mind, body and spirit helps us realize that we are not just our bodies, that we do go on, and that our spiritual progress has an impact on every aspect of our physical lives. Thus, when you struggle with these issues, your spiritual knowledge and practice gives you many more tools with which to deal with them.

As compared to the genius previously referred to, the *Master*, on the other hand, is the soul in whom the etheric, astral, mental and causal brains are completely aligned with the physical brain ... in whom the nadis is operating without obstruction and in whom the heart seed atom is cleared of undesirable karma. In the Master, thoughts emanating from the aligned brain force-fields flow smoothly up and down the nadis without interference, like a complex intercommunication telephone system with all its wires "plugged in" and operating. Full charges of electricity flow through every perfected "tube," "wire," and cell.

The child born with a moderate to severe manifestation of Down's Syndrome is a clear example of the importance of the frontal lobe. With this small frontal lobe, the child dealing with this difficulty can experience subconscious influence but is not responsible for the creation of new karma. Much of the karma involved in this condition surely must be intertwined with the karma of the parents to whom this soul is born. It is quite probable that, in planning their own earth missions before incarnating, these two souls had deliberately chosen to give birth to one who is working out their karma or soul lessons in this manner. These parents and these children are often quite remarkable. Many times parents of a child with Down's Syndrome speak of learning a great deal from their child, about love, about acceptance, about belief in the spiritual aspects of life. And the parents themselves are great gifts in the life of this child.

The *amnesia victim* is reacting to a mental shock, the impact of which has temporarily damaged a certain brain center — a center containing scenes of an experience the personality usually does not wish to remember. The center, immediately reacting, no longer generates electrical impulses. Although the memory is still recorded on the thread of mental ether in the sub or superconscious mind, the memory cannot pierce the waking consciousness until the brain cells can recharge themselves, or until a new center can be created. Much depends upon the will of the person. Frequently the soul does not wish to remember and will check all efforts to cause a recurrence of what is a painful or unendurable memory.

REMEMBERING PREVIOUS INCARNATIONS

"Why do I not remember a previous life?" This question forms the stumbling block for many who would otherwise be greatly helped by the concept of rebirth. Every new incarnation institutes a new body and a new brain which is to be filled with new memories. It is not expected that the incarnating personality remember past lives, for no brain centers or nadis have been developed with specific attunement to that portion of the superconscious where the akashic memory of past lives resides.

As each brain is built in a new physical form, it acts as a filter through which all the new memories will flow, *but it is not necessarily an instrument receptive to the memories stored in the great mental reservoir of the superconscious.* Only as the brain cells in the newly built physical form evolve will they be able to receive impacts from the superconscious which would cause them to remember past training, past experiences, past lives and incarnations. The new brain must begin over again to be built into a filter for the recorded experiences of this particular life.

The brain can be compared to a highly efficient radio waiting to be turned on and tuned in to its source of receiving. The mind could be compared to the radio station ready to transmit along its specific wavelength. The brain can only receive wavelengths which it is properly prepared to receive. In the radio world this is called "balanced reception." The brain center cannot receive that which is transmitted from the mind unless the reception is balanced — unless the brain center is tuned to the proper wavelength of the mind. Thus the mind can be filled with considerable wisdom, but the brain can receive only that to which it is properly attuned.

Mind lies encompassed throughout the cerebrospinal nervous system, permeating every cell and atom of the brain, but is able to operate apart from it. Once scientists accept this they will stand on the threshold of their greatest discovery — the human soul. Recently, scientists have detected a measurable loss of weight when an individual dies, and are questioning whether this is due to the departure of the soul.

Once science places the waking consciousness in a state of simulated sleep and sends the mind soaring into time and space to observe, return and describe events seen and done, and records these events as a medical reality and not as a weird occult phenomenon, *then* perhaps humankind truly will be on its way in search of the soul.

THE SUTRATMA, THE SUSHUMNA AND THE ANTAHKARANA

Previous Degree Lessons considered in detail the sushumna and the sutratma. We must now speak of another cord, the antahkarana, the bridge of spiritual consciousness. It is important to bear in mind the difference between the sutratma, the sushumna and the antahkarana. They are the various threads that make one a human being — the threads which connect the personality to the God which sent it forth. We must find their relationship to each other and to the personality now in incarnation.

While both the sushumna and the sutratma come with the physical form at birth as "God-given" gifts, such is not true of the antahkarana. It is a spiritual cord which must be created and constructed by and through the spiritual efforts of the individual.

1.   The *SUSHUMNA* is the nerve thread which is housed in the spinal cord. It extends *from the root chakra to the crown chakra.* There it ends. The sushumna is the pathway of kundalini as she rises to reach the Third Eye.

2.   The *SUTRATMA* is a life line which extends from the Monad to the root chakra. *It is the silver cord over which forces of life and mind flow* into the cells of the physical form, and it operates as lifeforce, emotional force and consciousness force. The breaking of the sutratma brings death to the physical form, because no more energies can flow into it.

The difference between the sutratma and the sushumna is that sushumna ends at the top of the head and is the thread over which the kundalini power rises, while the sutratma extends on upward to the Monad, and contains within itself the three threads or cords called: (a) the life cord; (b) the emotional cord; (c) the consciousness cord. These cords lie inside of and are woven out of the essences of the sutratma.

3.   The *ANTAHKARANA* is entirely different from the sushumna and the sutratma. *It is the spiritual filament of light,* gossamer as a spider's thread, *spun by the disciple's own spiritual efforts* through life after life of experience in mortal flesh. It is housed in the vagus nerve, extending eventually from the heart chakra upward to the Monad. Like the causal forcefield, the antahkarana must be constructed solely as the soul creates it, and *only that which is of spiritual vibration can enter and vitalize it.*

The connection of the antahkarana to the heart chakra indicates that the thoughts and forces which permeate it and give it power must be pure, else they cannot find a place in this bridge of mind. The antahkarana must mainly be built through conscious efforts. It is not so much a process which will occur in the nature of things, as a child grows into an adult, although all the good, the pure and the beautiful *do* automatically become a part of it. It is rather a bridge which must be constructed through spiritual engineering. Becoming aware of its presence in our lives, and the fact that its status relies on and is related to our own endeavors, our own spiritual practice, the building of it assumes an aspect of sacrifice.

For some seekers, holding the pure thought energies, doing the good deed, visualizing through the meditative processes, practicing tai chi, and so on will all come as a natural consequence of daily life. But for other disciples, these activities represent some measure of sacrifice and effort. Building the antahkarana thus becomes a transcending project and, like building a house, requires its "blueprints," its patterns, its planning and its day by day effort as a deliberate spiritual undertaking.

In Lesson 14 of the First Degree, pages 4-7, we spoke of the consciousness cord as being the antahkarana. We must now qualify that teaching somewhat. At that particular

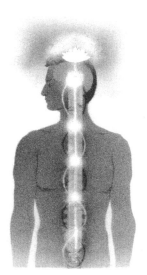

THE SUSHUMNA

The sushumna is a nerve thread in the spinal cord. It extends from the root chakra to the crown chakra.

THE ANTAHKARANA

THE SUTRATMA

The sutratma is the "silver cord" which descends from the Monad to the base of the spine. Out of its substance is spun the life cord, the emotional cord, and the consciousness cord.

The antahkarana is the spiritual thread woven only by spiritual efforts. It extends from the heart chakra upward, eventually to reach the Monad.

stage of your learning it was necessary to speak of the antahkarana simply as the bridge between the waking consciousness and the Oversoul, making it synonymous with the consciousness cord. However, there *is* a distinction between the consciousness cord and the antahkarana: the consciousness cord contains all the mental forces of a general nature, whereas the antahkarana is constructed only of spiritual-mental qualities.

It is true that you have been building both these cords since you came into birth in the human family, but the consciousness cord has long since been constructed between your waking conscious mind and the mental forcefield in the Oversoul. The antahkarana, on the other hand, has gained very little power, since in this cord can be found only the spiritual qualities of the individual. It goes forward minutely as a spider spins its silver thread and projects it from itself.

Thus the antahkarana becomes the Path itself. You create and build your own pathway back to God and pull yourself upward by it simultaneously through electromagnetic attraction. Each incarnation sees the antahkarana extended farther, for the soul never fails to make some degree of spiritual progress in any given incarnation.

The antahkarana inches upward by infinitesimal, tenuous threads spun through your own spiritual efforts. It is not that the entire bridge or any portion of it is created all at once. Little gossamer threads of light will edge upward so that at any given time, regardless of where the antahkarana ends in its upreach, from that extension can be found tiny individual threads extending on further toward the Oversoul. Each spiritual or creative accomplishment sees more threads stretching upward, until finally there are enough to cause a permanent extension of the bridge, as these gossamer cords weave themselves together creating a higher, permanent extension of the antahkarana.

Knowledge — and the mental force created in connection with attainment of knowledge — concerns the personality, the waking conscious mind and the world of materiality. Wisdom — and the mental energy and imagery involved in its attainment — directly concerns the soul, the Wisdom Mind and the antahkarana. Knowledge energy utilizes the consciousness cord. Wisdom energy utilizes the antahkarana.

Little by little, the bridge of spiritual mind substance spans the gap between the lower waking conscious mind of the personality and the Oversoul in the causal forcefield. It climbs steadily upward, finally and ultimately to unite with the Monad. With the completion of the antahkarana bridge — its union with the Monad — the soul has attained its ultimate resurrection or the power to immortalize the physical form and "live forever."

THE NEXT STEP IN HUMANITY'S EVOLUTION

The next step in human evolution involves the development of the individual antahkarana. Each soul must create its own. The gradual building of the antahkarana has progressed since humankind's early appearance on this planet.

In long ago Lemuria, the sutratma, housing the *life cord*, was the principal connection between the physical form and the spirit, the Monad.

In the days of Atlantis the *consciousness cord* had its beginning as the soul first recognized the law of action and reaction as it related to itself.

In the days of long ago Egypt and Africa, humanity brought the *emotional cord* to its fullest intensity.

Now, in this present Aquarian Age, it remains for each individual to stabilize the emotional cord, and consciously begin to build the spiritual cord of the antahkarana which eventually will be woven into both the consciousness cord and the life cord, bringing immortality, divine life and all-pervading wisdom.

The first aspect of the soul to be affected by building the antahkarana is the astral body and its emotional cord. This body and cord are built of the lower emotions — the emotions that pertain to the material realm of life, desire for possessions, the "things" which bind the mind to Earth. As the soul, through spiritual unfoldment, begins to develop into a conscious creator on the physical plane, the powers of the antahkarana will blend with those of the emotional cord. When the antahkarana develops an increased degree of dynamic power, it will gradually harmonize with and become one with the emotional cord. This is when the soul will be guided by the best of its mental and emotional powers, valuing them equally, and becoming thus whole, will live its life influenced by its creative spirituality. When it has attained some measure of contact with the Wisdom Mind the lower nature disappears.

At present a small portion of humanity expresses the antahkarana only in embryo. They represent the lowest octave of humanity on the evolutionary scale. The great mass of humanity, however, has built the antahkarana to extend into the lower mental plane. A few have extended it farther into the causal and are capable of meditation, visualization, projection, some degree of transmutation, abstract thinking and control of the will. Even fewer have extended the antahkarana to reach the Wisdom Mind. These are the adepts.

But those who have extended the antahkarana so that it has united with the Monad have become the immortal Masters. They possess all the spiritual attributes and are endowed with immortal life while yet in the physical form. These souls, these rare individuals who have attained this spiritual status, are the Masters of the divine hierarchy, operating through the spiritual kingdom of Shamballa.

BUILDING THE ANTAHKARANA

The impulses of one's thoughts influence and mold one's life. If the thought is undesirable and is repeated as a regular pattern — repeated thoughts of hatred, jealousy, greed, personal power, illness, disease — then the thoughtforce attracts substances of the lower astral plane. Clothed in these murky forces, the thought strikes the brain cell and the person reacts, infusing the aura with a lower astral substance which creates the *kama rupa*, the lower astral body, adding undesirable impetus to the emotional and consciousness cords.

If the thought is a desirable one — expressing love of God, devotion, holiness, aspiration, kindness or love to others, esteem or positive regard directed to oneself — then the thoughtforce, rising upward, will clothe itself with substance from the spiritual planes and embed itself in the brain cells, and the person reacts. Their aura has been infused with spiritual essence and has added to the dynamics of the spiritual cord, the antahkarana.

Thus it is that *whatever one dwells upon mentally one brings into manifestation.* The material of which one's physical form is constructed reacts to the impulses of the thoughtforce which the soul itself generates.

Any discernible progression toward building the antahkarana takes place only after the disciple arrives at a certain level of understanding and spiritual unfoldment. You must have your mind frequently focused upon the spirit and its place in your life. The soul not involved in spiritual pursuits usually slants its waking consciousness only toward material attainments. So does the disciple, but only in part. A great share of your mental energies will be directed toward spiritual purposes and, once becoming aware of the existence of the antahkarana, you will *consciously* begin to construct it.

The personality has made very little conscious effort to bridge the gap between the minds. The only effort has been on the part of the soul as it attempted to stimulate the personality toward increased creative and spiritual expansion. Now, becoming aware of the antahkarana, the personality begins a more rapid development of the threads, which automatically causes an integration and fusion with the energies of the soul.

What is the next procedure you, the seeker, must follow to develop the antahkarana to its ultimate? What must you do to extend it further upward? What must you do to bridge the gap between the waking conscious and the superconscious to reach the Oversoul, and ultimately to attain the Wisdom Mind?

1. You should pursue the study of the Degrees or other similar teachings in an attempt to transmute your knowledge into wisdom — studies which create intense mental activity.

2. Interpret your life in terms of spiritual progression rather than only personal desire.

3. Become aware of and believe in the existence of the antahkarana and realize its importance in your role as a spiritual disciple on the path.

4. Understand that while any appreciable development of the antahkarana comes by simply doing good, the infinitesimal threads of light which extend upward like etheric antennas attain their greatest impetus through conscious effort. It is not enough simply to think altruistically — though such action has its rewards and is a contributing factor. The substance of the antahkarana is the stuff that requires more than lip service, more than idle dreams, more than church going. It requires action to follow the positive thought.

5. Realize that building the antahkarana requires creative imagination to add dynamic power to it through the practice of visualization.

6. Possess a desire to light your own mental substance, and to make mental effort to project it upward.

7. Regularly engage in spiritual practice such as meditation, yoga, chanting, any particular practice which is meaningful to you.

8. Know that the goal to be attained is to merge the physical form with the Monad. This is quite a task. You should become a spiritual alchemist of the first magnitude.

Every act containing the magic potion of love causes a stimulation in the antahkarana and creates a tenuous thread of light, if only a minute extension. But it remains for the disciple to enter occasionally into meditative visualization, directing dynamic power upward to weave the vague strands of light into a stronger cord and endow it with power.

QUO VADIS?

When you arrive at this status it is only natural that you will inquire, within yourself, where you stand on the spiritual pathway. You realize that behind you extend many past incarnations, the accumulated experiences which have brought you to your present status and made you aware of your spiritual potential.

Spiritual labors toward building the antahkarana have no outward visible rewards. You must work on blind faith that you are making progress. There is nothing tangible to your physical senses that would verify either the existence of the antahkarana or denote any measure of success in your efforts. You can only watch and wait and listen within for any possible evidence of accomplishment. Such evidence comes only through flashes of intuition, occasional sudden insurges of understanding; a brief ability to speak with unbelievable wisdom; unusual sensations about the top of the head not necessarily of a physical nature — a sudden feeling of expansion from within as if the brain were a balloon and some invisible being had just blown vaporous ethers into it. Any or all of these speak a silent message of progression.

A display of psychic powers is not necessarily an indication of contact with the Oversoul. The development of psychic ability and the construction of the antahkarana are two completely different fields of endeavor. The psychic is not necessarily spiritual, but the intuitional disciple automatically demonstrates a sure contact with the Oversoul through the thread of the antahkarana.

You will begin to realize the presence of the antahkarana and its influence in your life in the way you respond to different environmental stimuli. You cannot be part of a plot or plan that is not coordinated with spirit. Every purpose of your life must be slanted toward spiritual progression. You find yourself serving others in the most unexpected ways. You find yourself, regardless of your outer circumstances, constantly in a state of silent prayer. You cannot take advantage of dubious opportunities, or accept a profit from any endeavor gained through hurting others.

This born-of-spirit attitude cannot help but make an impact upon your mind and the minds of your co-workers, friends and family. Such an attitude eventually becomes habitual, and as it does so you will find yourself increasingly aware of the spiritual influence in your daily life, radiating from your own antahkarana and its connecting link to your Oversoul.

Building the etheric antahkarana is somewhat comparable to laying a cable or a bridge to connect two great countries. The difference is that the material cable is constructed by collective human effort whereas the cable of the antahkarana is built by individual thought-power. It requires mental force rather than muscular strength. You must persevere, even though you think you are making no progress whatever. Each time you practice spiritual prayer you are building the mental cable higher and higher to carry your thoughts upward into the planes of divinity.

The Astarian who gives earnest attention to the Great Work of the Degrees and attempts to live the Astarian principles to the best of his or her ability is most assuredly proceeding in building the antahkarana. Even though you may not have a moment to give to planned and deliberate meditation, your studies, which stimulate spiritual brain centers, point the way toward sure progression.

Suddenly one day the cable you have so patiently constructed will pierce the web of the spiritual plane, and your consciousness will burst into the light. You will be bathed in its glory which, pouring down through the antahkarana, pervades the atoms of your brain. Although this light will withdraw, your mental substance — having been baptized in effulgent glory — will never again be the same.

THE FIRST GOAL: HEART TO CROWN CHAKRA

The first goal is to build the antahkarana between the heart and the crown chakra — between the personality and the soul. This first link of the bridge enables the personality to receive intuitive impressions from the soul — to become dimly aware of the soul's influence in your life, not only in your waking conscious mind, but in your dream state during sleep. A faint continuity of consciousness will become established, so that you may begin to have vague recollections of your journeys in the higher planes.

You live your daily life according to your response to two types of perception:

1. objective perception — that which concerns your conscious reaction to sensations experienced through your five senses as they come in contact with the world and the environment about you;

2. inner perception or soul perception — that which comes to you in fragments through visionary dreams, intuition, inspiration, and occasional flashes of genius and wisdom. These come only from the higher mind and their entrance into your waking consciousness is through the bridge of the antahkarana.

You progress spiritually according to the way you respond to intuitional perceptions, for it is only via the higher mind that you may contact the Oversoul. When the higher mind is able to establish continuous contact with the lower mind via the antahkarana, you will begin to become aware of increased mental energies, of occasional flashes of intuition and the attainment of knowledge without the process of investigation.

THE SECOND GOAL: CROWN CHAKRA TO OVERSOUL

The second goal is to extend the antahkarana from the crown chakra upward to reach the Oversoul.

At present, only a small portion of the superconscious mind is able to manifest through the brainpower of the average person. One is extremely limited by one's brain capacity. The thinking process is met on every hand by limitations and hindrances. But the Astarian who lives by Astara's principles, who develops brain cells through study, meditation, prayer and moments of spiritual attunement, whose brain cells have been touched by the power of the Word, will begin to receive downpouring impulses from the Oversoul.

Mental currents will flow through the antahkarana first into the causal field, then the mental, then the astral, and then into the physical brain itself. As your "brains" become aligned and in focus you will begin to experience flashes of intuition which arouse increasing desire for more light and expanded powers of perception. Many occurrences will begin to manifest:

1.   You may begin to dream visionary dreams and to bring memories of them back into wakeful consciousness. When your physical brain is entering its sleep state you will be aware of a gradual awakening of your superconscious mind, and of events occurring during these hours when your physical form lies sleeping. You will begin to realize that, with the construction of the antahkarana, you are building a bridge over which blessings from On High can flow more easily into you and upon you, influencing your outer life beyond your greatest expectations.

2.   You may begin to be aware of guidance from the Oversoul and, acting under such influence, your life will proceed without committing any undue errors, or creating more negative karma, which would cause distress or delay in the attainment of your goals. Working under such unimpeded illumination can only bring a life of serenity to the unfolding initiate. The spiritual radiance of the antahkarana will begin to blend with the emotional cord.

3.   You may begin to recall astral flights into heavenly realms, including studies embarked upon and lectures attended there. You will become completely responsive in your daily life to impressions that reach you from the higher mind, accepting that which obviously is your destiny with a vision and a purpose of accomplishment, no longer questioning: "Why did this happen to me?" Instead you will calmly approach your problems and meditate upon how best to handle them.

As the lower concrete mind gradually becomes subordinate to the downpouring of the higher consciousness, the personality automatically identifies itself with some kind of service, some kind of spiritual effort, some kind of program to help enlighten the world.

The existence of the higher planes will be no enigma to you. You will be acquainted with them and their functions, and they will be as real to you as your everyday existence on the physical plane. This incredible accomplishment will be realized with the development of the millions of brain cells which now lie unawakened, for they will have been "washed in the blood of the lamb," baptized with the waters of eternal life, the Divine Substance. Once you have constructed the bridge over which only this higher mind force can travel, it will not be so difficult for you to send the mind force upward again into the higher planes.

4.   With development of the antahkarana you become aware of the presence of a diffused light in your head, especially during meditation.   This is the radiance of the electromagnetic field of vibration which is beginning to operate in the Third Eye. It is intensification of this inner light which, rising like mercury in a thermometer, strengthens the power of the upbuilding antahkarana. It extends upward as a ray of light projects from the sun. The light diffused in the head is the beginning of the appearance of the famed halo which is witnessed around the heads of saints. It also indicates that

the mystical "Door of Brahm" is opening through the upper part of the skull, and the etheric webs which have imprisoned the crown chakra are breaking away. It is through this Brahmasutra that the soul, withdrawing during the hours of sleep, will begin to pour its impressions so that the mental reflecting ethers, registering in the cells of the brain, will bring remembrance of the soul's adventures to the waking conscious mind.

5.   As further finite streams of force begin to edge upward, you will gradually gain an unobstructed continuity of awareness of other planes of life around you. This will have a tremendous impact upon your daily life and your waking consciousness. First of all, fear of death will be removed for it will be completely obvious that death is but a doorway to a greater state of awareness. It will also negate other fears, particularly that of separation from those whom you love, for you will be able to establish contact with them, whether awake or asleep.

Having gained this power while yet in the physical form, you will understand its potential once you depart the physical plane. As you become more aware of an unobstructed universe, you will begin so completely to understand the process of death that, at the time it actually occurs, you will pass from physical consciousness into the higher state without a break in consciousness, for you will have developed the faculty of extended consciousness while yet in the physical.

6.   As you realize the existence of the antahkarana and attempt consciously to endow it with power, you will become aware of an increased capacity to contemplate and meditate. As you begin to make obvious progress in your Lama Yoga meditation, for example, and definite progress toward constructing the antahkarana, you become increasingly aware of a downpouring response from the realms of the Oversoul, as if some Silent Watcher waited to reward you for your upreaching toward the light.

The disciple who meditates cannot help but attain some measure of success, whether there is an awareness of this progress or not. No period of meditation is without reward. Practice of the yogic exercise, Lama Yoga — the act of holding the mind centered upon the word AUM and directing every ounce of energy toward that concentration — is a sure method of steadily building the antahkarana. It is this "steadfast steadiness" of attention and concentration that pours intensified light forces into the brain and all the forcefields surrounding it. The result can only be automatic upward projection of the antahkarana.

Since thoughtforce is an actual substance, it automatically follows that the spiritual practice of meditation, and spiritual study, both create an actual vortex of energy, and when directed to the innermost centers of the brain it becomes a stream of ascending power. The stream of force becomes enhanced because it is tinctured with the quality of love and aspiration.

7.   When you become accustomed to this expanded awareness, you will automatically subordinate your lower self to your superconscious, and to your

Oversoul, and even to your Wisdom Mind. The disciple who completes the construction of this bridge between the crown chakra and the Oversoul will no longer live in the consciousness of the limited personality but will express the powers of the Oversoul itself.

You will then dwell "in the secret place of the Most High," and will "abide under the shadow of the Almighty." You will walk under the constant protection, guidance and inspiration of the Oversoul, the "Father-Mother which art in Heaven." "Ten thousand may 'fall' at thy side but no harm shall come nigh thee; neither shall any plague come nigh thy dwelling, for God shall give the angels charge over thee to keep thee in all thy ways."

Blessed is the one who has built the antahkarana and established a bridge of light between oneself and one's Oversoul. For this one the travails of life are ended, and the joys of the Divine Spirit can be truly appreciated and experienced.

THE THIRD GOAL: FUSION WITH THE WISDOM MIND

The essence of love is real, a substance which would be tangible had scientists the instruments with which to capture it, measure it, perceive it. The same is true of wisdom, and this is the third goal: *building the antahkarana to fuse with the Wisdom Mind*. The substance of which the Wisdom Mind is created is as real as the wind. It is from the substance of love and wisdom that the antahkarana must be constructed. Those who understand Eastern philosophy refer to this spiritualized mental substance as *chitta.*

The expression of true love and wisdom on the part of the disciple results, as has been said, in the creation of infinitesimal threads of light. These threads, flowing upward and becoming strengthened by one's mental-meditative efforts, weave themselves into a bridge over which the personality consciousness must travel to attain union with the purest states of consciousness. These states of consciousness exist progressively in the causal forcefield, the Oversoul, the Wisdom Mind, and eventually the Monad.

Building the antahkarana is the way of liberation for the disciple. It is across this bridge that you eventually will escape from the prison of the three lower worlds — the world of the concrete mind, the realms of the astral and incarnation in the physical planes.

The Mystic Mantrum AUM

The magic of the mantrum is the Sound of liberation, the Sound symbolizing the vibration which, in action, brings regeneration and resurrection of the physical form, ultimately resulting in immortality. It is the Lost Word symbolizing the Divine or Christ Substance ... the Word which is lost in the three lower worlds.

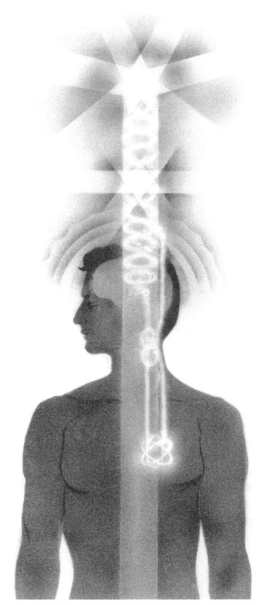

TRANSFUSING THE HIGHER ETHERS

Merging the antahkarana with the sutratmic life cord results in immortality for the physical form. The silver cord will no longer break, causing death, but instead will have become a bridge over which the Divine Substance, flowing into the physical, will transform the life forces of the physical atoms into the immortal forces of spiritual planes.

To come into possession of the Lost Word is to enter the divine Stream, a Current of Light which unites one with the Infinite. Having entered that Stream through the vibration of the Lost Word, one comes into communion with the divine arcanum of wisdom or the Wisdom Mind. The soul who lives the Word — who lives with the antahkarana so constructed that it penetrates the Wisdom Mind — is the incomparable healer whose entire form breathes an aura of magical healing, a teacher whose lips speak matchless wisdom, whose touch and whose presence perform miracles.

The Sound of the Word, the Holy Nahd, emanates from the great Central Spiritual Sun, the power of which penetrates the aura of our planet, permeating its atoms with divine Light. It is the Sound Current upon which our solar system revolves. The Sound Stream which the initiate hears and enters is the lowest octave of the Divine Sound, creating the ineffable Name of the Supreme Being.

When the disciple, through the practice of meditation or any type of spiritual practice, begins to hear the Sound of the divine Current, it indicates achievement of the first goal — that the personality is becoming integrated and infused with the soul, and that the soul is beginning to have more positive influence over the personality and its vehicles.

As the disciple achieves the second goal — becoming the initiate and undergoing higher initiations — so does this soul become even more influenced by the Oversoul and eventually, through further building of the antahkarana, begins to be influenced and assisted by the Wisdom Mind.

This is the third goal — uniting the antahkarana with the Wisdom Mind and thus coming into direct communication with the divine realms of life. One then need no longer live under the guidance of vague impressions, for the Great Ones will constantly downpour their blessings through the etheric substances of the higher planes. They may frequently speak to and communicate with the initiate directly.

Knowledge, and the force of knowledge, expresses through the consciousness cord, the waking consciousness and the superconscious mind; but the force of wisdom, operating through the antahkarana, is the force of the Divine Substance.

The surest source of wisdom is development of the antahkarana to reach the Wisdom Mind, the Adi-budha, which brings the Divine Substance pouring down into the brain and heart. These downpourings increase the strength of the antahkarana, the bridge which eventually leads to im-mortality of the mortal form. This is the ultimate goal.

THE ULTIMATE GOAL: IMMORTALITY

The supreme purpose of building the antahkarana is to integrate humans into perfected beings. This means that the grosser expressions of humankind — the astral emotions and even the personality-ego on its mental plane — must be absorbed into the Monad so that only a perfected being remains. This perfected being becomes at one with its Father-Mother in heaven, just as the man Jesus became the Christ. As the man Siddhartha became the Buddha. As the woman Mary became the Holy Mother. As the woman Brigit became a form of the Goddess worshiped in ancient Celtic days in the British Isles, Spain and France. And so many more.

As the soul evolves and perfects the construction of the antahkarana between the Oversoul and the Monad, the antahkarana begins to weave itself into the essences of the sutratma which, remember, contains *the life cord* extending from the Monad to the root chakra. As the sutratma and the antahkarana fuse, the sutratma, containing the LIFE FORCE, will absorb the spiritual qualities of the antahkarana.

It is this silver cord — the sutratma with its life cord — which *now* breaks at death. When it eventually becomes interwoven with the immortal-spiritual antahkarana it, too, becomes vicariously immortal, and its power so spiritualized that it no longer need withdraw from a worn-out physical form. Rather it will keep that form supplied with spiritual energies, which can only mean *immortalization of the atoms in the form.* The soul in whom such a transmutation has occurred has immortalized the flesh. It has become a divine being on Earth. Even though it dwells in a type of physical form, such a soul transcends the laws of the physical plane. It is controller of its destiny in every way. Even the elements obey its commands and the cells of its being remain constantly vibrant with living force.

It is through this transmutation that the soul will attain eternal life in the physical realm. Then the soul will truly be born again, or born in the spirit, a birth by fire — when it will truly have overcome death, for it will be able to live in all worlds at once. As such a soul, you will be able to enter the higher planes with no break in consciousness, raising at will the atomic structure of your form to such an etherealized state that it will temporarily disappear from the physical realms as you journey into and become compatible with the forcefields of those higher planes, as if you were a "resident" of them.

It must be understood that the "physical" aspect about which we teach is not the physical of today. By the time the soul has completely constructed the antahkarana the consciousness will have so evolved as to cause transmutation of the physical form into a causal, or soul form. This is the "body" you alone create by your altruistic actions, pure thoughts and expressions of divine love and spirituality. This, then, becomes the form through which your spiritualized soul will express, having absorbed into it the personality-ego so that you now become a dual being of soul and spirit. The "personality-physical" will have evolved into the soul body to express as an immortalized and individualized spark of God.

This future form will be so completely transformed as to be unrecognizable as physical in terms of our present scientific knowledge. This soul form will be composed of a substance so tenuous that it could hardly be called "matter." The physical aspects of both human beings and the planet will have been transmuted from "dross" to "gold." Your consciousness will then flourish in the sustained light of the downpouring divinity. It will have attained its own true power without having to be shielded from the light. The conscious mind will have achieved its immortality. You will have become one with your Parent in heaven.

Thus weaving the sutratma and antahkarana together results in "physical" immortality through union of that spiritualized form with the spirit which "sent it" into the planes of matter.

Once the antahkarana and sutratma have wedded, there is no more personality-ego. There is only divine being — soul united with spirit — the Prodigal Child returned home to his Father-Mother in heaven. A human being that is the divine, immortal, individualized god within God.

THE ATTAINMENT OF ILLUMINATION...is achieved in two ways.

One is through experience and studies — a process by which insight is gained gradually through analysis, comparison, and acquiring knowledge step by step.

The second is through a sudden burst of perception which may also be the consequence of experience and study, or may be the result of spontaneous intuition.

Astara's Degree Lessons lead to the attainment of illumination by both methods. The Lessons provide the foundation on which illuminative insights are gained ... they clear the inner channels that lead to sudden and often unexpected intuitive insights.

And illumination leads to initiation — to being accorded the privilege of entering a higher stage of wisdom and being, the opportunity for still greater awareness, graduation to a higher state of Self.

Your next two Lessons lead you through these higher portals of Light.

Lesson 22, Approaching Initiation is preparatory knowledge for a higher initiation. It describes a new view of your relationship to the Infinite, to the mystical association with God. It describes initiation, how you experience it on the higher planes and how you react to it on this. It accepts you as a Second Degree Astarian.

Lesson 1, Third Degree, The Sevenfold Person, rewards your achievement as a disciple of the Emerald Cross and outlines your journey to becoming a disciple of the Ruby Cross. It is the first step on your becoming a sevenfold cosmic person who discovers new worlds of aspiration and achievement awaiting the many but known only to the few.

WORRY NOT ABOUT THE PAST.
IMPROVE THE PRESENT.
GO FORTH TO MEET THE FUTURE.

HEAVEN IS NOT GAINED
IN A SINGLE BOUND

Heaven is not gained at a single bound;
But we build the ladder by which we rise
From the lowly earth to the vaulted skies,
And we mount to its summit round by round.

I count this thing to be grandly true,
That a noble deed is a step toward God —
Lifting the soul from the common sod
To a purer air and a broader view.

We rise by things that are 'neath our feet;
By what we have mastered of good and gain;
By the pride deposed and the passion slain,
And the vanquished ills that we hourly meet.

We hope, we aspire, we resolve, we trust,
When the morning calls us to life and light,
But our hearts grow weary, and 'ere the night
Our lives are trailing the sordid dust.

We hope, we resolve, we aspire, we pray,
And we think that we mount the air on wings
Beyond the recall of sensual things,
While our feet still cling to the heavy clay.

Wings for the angels, but feet for men!
We may borrow the wings to find the way...
We may hope, and resolve, and aspire, and pray,
But our feet must rise, or we fall again.

Only in dreams is a ladder thrown
From the weary earth to the sapphire walls;
But the dream departs, and the vision falls,
And the sleeper wakes on his pillow of stone.

Heaven is not reached at a single bound;
But we build the ladder by which we rise
From the lowly earth to the vaulted skies,
And we mount to its summit round by round.

— Josiah Gilbert Holland

LAND OF BEGINNING AGAIN

Oh, I wish that there were some wonderful place
Called the Land of Beginning Again,
Where all our mistakes and all our heartaches
And all of our poor, lonely grief
Could be dropped like a shabby old coat at the door
And never put on again.

I wish we could come on it all unaware,
Like a hunter who finds a lost trail;
And I wish that the one whom our blindness had done
The greatest injustice of all
Could be at the gates, like an old friend who waits
For the comrade he's gladdest to hail.

We would find all the things we intended to do
But forgot, and remembered — too late.
Little praises unspoken, little promises broken,
And all of the thousand and one
Little duties neglected that might have perfected
The day for one less fortunate.

It wouldn't be possible not to be kind
In the Land of Beginning Again;
And ones we misjudged and the ones whom we grudged
Their moments of victory here
Would find in the grasp of our loving handclasp
More than penitent lips could explain.

For what had been hardest we'd know had been best,
And what had seemed loss would be gain;
For there isn't a sting that will not take wing
When we've faced it and laughed it away;
And I think that the laughter is most what we're after
In the Land of Beginning Again.

Let Astara for you be that wonderful place
Called the Land of Beginning Again.
Where all your mistakes and all your heartaches
And all of your poor, lonely grief
Can be dropped like a shabby old coat, at our door
And never put on again.

— Selected and transposed

Approaching Initiation

Second Degree — Lesson Twenty-Two

THE INCOMPREHENSIBILITY OF THE INFINITE

It is well enough for us to declare our faith in Father-Mother God. But what mind is capable of interpreting divine glory, divine laws, divine worlds, divine manifestations? Who can say how the Infinite Being operates the combinations of innumerable atoms to produce different qualities and different powers? Who can say how this majestic chemistry combines a formula to create substance, either seen or unseen?

We can teach that a seed contains the mysterious power of developing into a tree, but we have yet to understand the "how" of it. Who can explain the "life" in the seed ... the energy in the seed ... the substance in the seed ... the formula in the seed ... which brings forth the tree?

We can declare that genes and chromosomes, DNA and RNA (deoxyribonucleic acid and ribonucleic acid) create hereditary transmissions but we cannot explain how varying characteristics can issue out of these substances. We cannot discover the formula of life or of mind. We see it operate but we see through a glass darkly. In fascination and incredulity we watch the cohesion of atoms as they create the molecular structure of cells which evolve into the glands, nerves, organs, bone, hair and tissue of a complete physical being. But we cannot duplicate the processes nor explain how they ultimately produce a genius or one of normal intellect.

When the genes and chromosomes are in their play — when the DNA and RNA, responding to the genetic code, are developing a human form — *who* is it or *what* is it that determines whether the mind which will operate in that form will exhibit knowledge, wisdom, genius? Who or what is the Cosmic Magician that decides the status quo of the perpetual coming forth of humankind? Is it an inconsequent force playing a game of chance, darting blindly throughout the void spilling the qualities of mind at random through the dusts of Earth? Such a fantasy is dispelled by a simple observation of the stars and planets.

A view of the quiet majesty of their procession through the heavens speaks silently but eloquently, testifying to the immutable plan of the Cosmic Magician we call God. Operating as the Infinite Being does in unchangeable Omniscience, God could not so produce a universe and leave humanity, the shining creation, to chance. Reviewing the orderly action of the universe, one may still be an atheist or an agnostic, but it is difficult to understand how one, observing God's humanity, can so be.

One day humans may be able to simulate the seed which begets the tree, even endowing it with some measure of life. We might, with arduous labor, create a being similar to humans. We might even endow this creature with some form of life. But the giving of mind — this only God can do. The fact that we might perhaps be able to create a creature similar to ourselves — but the stark realization that we could never endow it with the gift of mind — should point immediately to the existence of One who *can* perform this astonishing feat.

Mind is something that is not of this world. Its essence is not of Earth's essences. It comes from a different realm. A mind can never be created out of the substance of earth, yet it seems to be the only reality which science will not ultimately duplicate. Science may unveil the secret of producing lifeforce but it will never be able to produce mindforce.

What, then, is the substance of this mind ... this consciousness? It differs from the energy that composes the form it occupies. The energy that creates a form and gives it life differs drastically from the substance that produces consciousness.

Grasping the significance that consciousness exists apart from the energy and the form brings us abruptly face to face with the realization that some type of Consciousness created the world. That Consciousness is apparent in its creations, yet is veiled behind them, just as our minds are veiled behind our forms.

A planet in far-off space is not simply a globe of matter. It is a globe of matter moving in ordered sequence through the heavens, following an intelligent pattern of operation. Therefore, behind the existence of that planet there must be some Mind, some Consciousness at work. It is the *procession* of the planets which speaks of the presence of God, not simply the presence of the planets themselves.

Humans can create a miniature satellite and even send it soaring into orbit, but we cannot cause the flowers to grow on it ... nor the rivers to flow. We cannot create the swamps, the jungles and the crawling things. We cannot create a human form and breathe into it the quality of life and mind. We cannot create a solar system and set its planets moving in organized processions. This drama requires Omnipotence and Omniscience.

The fact that a universe endowed with lifeforce and operated in an orderly fashion surrounds us, signals the presence of Cosmic Intelligence even though It is undiscoverable by our physical senses. The acceptance of this truth posits at once a question: seeing so divine a plan in operation, how is it that the One who wrote the drama left it to be worked out in such a seemingly meaningless fashion?

If God "breathed" the world into being, what could have been the purpose in projecting this ultimate creation — humankind — into such an unhappy and sorrowful existence? In the midst of such an astonishing orderliness and wisdom, could not God have given us a greater share of divine Omniscience?

Possessing all-knowingness, the Great Spirit could have created children already expressing perfection in mind and body had it been divine desire to do so. He could have caused our forms to be immune from all disease and endowed us with a mind already developed in its highest state.

One glance at the human race reveals the obvious truth that its Parent — its Father-Mother God — did not wish it to come forth perfect. Rather the Divine Being gave man and woman everything here on Earth by which they, through their own endeavor and free will, could arrive at their own unfolded perfection.

Withholding nothing from us and giving us a mind to work with, our divine Parent released us in the world of matter to make our own way back to the higher realms as perfected beings.

THE AWAKENING

In previous Lessons we referred to the beginning, when the lifewaves of humanity first began to flood the earth plane. In those days there walked among the masses the Great Beings who incarnated on Earth to guide early humanity through its life on Earth. During those days these Great Ones established schools of initiation, and initiation was possible for any who progressed enough to become receptive to it.

There was nothing secret or mysterious about these schools of learning. All were free to enter and seek initiation in them. The Teachers and Masters of the schools were those who came to Earth for the sole purpose of helping humanity, as a due process of their soul evolution.

These Beings who arrived did so from choice — not from necessity — for they had long since passed through their evolutionary Rounds and gained a consciousness. Those who arrived were called gods and goddesses by the average person of their time.

The children of the gods intermarried with the children of Earth. The Revised Bible says:

> *When men began to multiply on the face of the ground, and daughters were born to them, the sons of God saw that the daughters of men were fair; and they took to wife such of them as they chose.* (Genesis 6:1-2)

The offspring of these unions were called children of the gods and goddesses, although exhibiting considerably less divinity than their parents. They were, however, exalted above the children of average people:

> *The Nephilim were on Earth in those days, and also afterward, when the sons of God came in to the daughters of men and they bore children to them. These were the mighty men that were of old, the men of renown.* (Genesis 6:4)

The Lamsa Bible says (Genesis 6:4): *There were giants on the Earth in those days; and also after that, for the sons of god came in unto the daughters of men and they bore children to them, and they became giants who in the olden days were mighty men of renown.*

As soon as some of the earth-born children of gods and goddesses gained a degree of wisdom through the processes of initiation, the spiritual teachers allowed them to assume control over their own lives and, in turn, to attempt to guide others. Gradually the Great Beings withdrew from the destinies of human beings, leaving the Mysteries and initiations under the guidance of their earth-born children.

Using the terms gods and goddesses here is not meant to suggest that in every case the mythological gods and goddesses we know of today were historically real individuals. It is meant to suggest that these were people, Initiates, who incarnated on this earth plane and possessed spiritual knowledge far in advance of the average person of that time. It is these teachers whom we are referring to as gods and goddesses, for they were looked on as such by the people of their time.

As the ages passed, the strain of divinity diminished until the record of its presence in the blood of humanity passed into myth and legend. The Mysteries were left to the children of human beings. But these children failed to measure to so great a challenge. Many who entered as candidates for initiation fell to the temptation of employing their meager wisdom for self-aggrandizement; for acquisition of wealth, for wielding power ... and ancient Lemuria and Atlantis fell.

But the Mysteries remained. Many reborn children of light established the Mysteries of early Egypt, of Greece, of Samothrace, of the Druids. But again, as in Lemuria and Atlantis, the secret documents and records of the Mystery dramas fell into the unscrupulous hands of those who interpreted the glorious truth teachings to suit their own purposes.

It became obvious to the Great Beings, observing the actions of the earth leaders from afar, that it would be necessary to seal away from human beings the inner, sacred process of initiation — making it unattainable until each individual soul had awakened within itself a sufficient degree of spiritual consciousness to receive an inflow of the power and become enlightened. Thus the Secret Wisdom came into being.

The rare soul among the millions who displayed some measure of spiritual discernment was taught on the astral dimension, usually during sleep when the higher consciousness was active, and was there initiated into the Mysteries. The Wisdom gained, however, did not completely diffuse itself into the conscious memory of these souls until they had attained a certain degree of spiritual unfoldment — until they became "awakened" spiritually in their conscious minds.

As soon as their spiritual consciousness had awakened, the Wisdom and the secrets of initiation which they had received on the astral planes began to enter their memories. From that time forward, these became selected souls to be overshadowed by a Great Being and led more swiftly toward Mastership and Self-realization.

This same process is true today. Those who become Degree Astarians are initiated on the astral planes. They are taught the secrets of the Mysteries. Their Astarian studies prepare their consciousness to receive more and more wisdom and greater unfoldment.

These Astarians are taught the processes of initiation on the astral but most do not retain a complete awareness of it in their waking memories. As they begin to unfold spiritually, however, they begin to be more and more receptive to the teachings they have received. The Masters refer to this process as "the awakening."

As the years go by, the awakened ones become more numerous. More and more Astarians are initiated on the astral. The seals of the secrets are broken as fast as their minds can bear the process. Astarian initiates are instructed in the manner best suited to their personality, their circumstances, their environment and their culture.

Each Astarian who has completed the Second Degree is worthy to be called an "awakened initiate." In addition to the knowledge gained in their Degree studies, they will begin to be increasingly receptive to the Secret Wisdom from the astral. They will become increasingly aware of the guidance of the Great Ones who overshadow them. They have become "Initiates of the Emerald Cross."

The Second Degree Astarian will probably recognize his/her awakening. As you study the Degrees, they will seem strangely familiar to you, even though you may be reading a Lesson for the first time. A certain paragraph may suddenly reveal an enormous amount of truth about something that may have baffled you in the past, and you will experience a tremendous expansion of comprehension concerning it.

The burst of understanding will come because you have received prior teachings concerning the Lesson on the astral. And your consciousness, receiving the teachings again in Lesson form, will respond to a downpouring of wisdom.

Any Astarian who experiences this thrilling sensation of sudden wisdom — a feeling of having grasped considerably more than the Lesson itself presents, a feeling of suddenly being able to understand what was previously strange and confusing — can know that s/he is indeed an awakened one, that s/he is so considered by the Order and that s/he is being taught the mysteries of initiation on the astral during his/her sleep.

To such an Astarian, the Degree Lessons assume tremendous importance, for they contain the key which unlocks the waking consciousness to that which is already germinating in your higher consciousness, waiting to be received into the lower, everyday mind. Regardless of how much wisdom and learning is planted in the sleeping consciousness, it usually cannot penetrate the waking memory until some key unlocks the door which lets it through. This key is the Astarian Degrees.

Those who have experienced what is being described will immediately recognize the process. It's the same sensation you experience when you walk into a room for the first time and feel that you have been there before ... or the curious feeling you receive listening to an unfolding conversation when you know that you have heard the same words being said on some previous occasion and know exactly what is going to be said next. The memory will be dim and far away but as the words are spoken they will be strangely familiar.

It is the same sensation that occurs in the Astarian who, during the study of a Degree Lesson, feels that s/he has previously read these same words or been taught this same teaching — some place, somewhere.

Some Astarians may even have attained sudden illumination — that instantaneous rising of the consciousness into the very heart of bliss — which usually occurs only a few times during any incarnation. Those who are experiencing these flights into cosmic consciousness can better understand that they mark the way to higher initiation.

WHAT INITIATION MEANS

Above and beyond the range of normal, intellectual comprehension lies a state known as Perfect Understanding and Wisdom. This incomparable state is attained through the process we call initiation. Initiation consists of steps or stages of evolutionary progress leading the soul from decadent generation into regeneration and perfection.

The steps may be described as a series of spectacular awakenings, or one grand downflowing of supreme enlightenment. There are seven major initiations faced by humanity en masse, with many minor initiations marking the way. Only the first two will be considered at present. The other five, being of cosmic nature, must wait for future Degrees.

The First Initiation is usually the time when the soul "enters the Stream." This will be the salient point in a long line of earthly existences, the culmination of many lives. Whether the salvation be through the path of mysticism or through the orthodox dogmas, the soul nevertheless turns toward the light. There is this difference, however:

The "saved" of several orthodox religions are usually experiencing a minor first initiation because they have found their salvation through the sacrifice of a savior or through the guidance of an avatar and not through a built-in innate quality of self-unfoldment and Self-realization. The mystics, on the other hand, will have entered their major First Initiation because salvation will be through their own upreaching toward wisdom, and not their reliance upon a savior. Whereas one is initiation by faith, the other is initiation by one's own innate soul progression.

Whereas the saved of the orthodox may remain turned toward the light, they still may build within themselves no substantial fortress of purity. The mystics, understanding that salvation lies completely within their own destinies, construct with their First Initiation a part of the "mansion not made with hands, eternal in the heavens" — the causal body. And they build a fragment of the antakharana.

Almost all those who gain the First Initiation, whether it be the orthodox or the mystic, will have experienced either some obscure vision or some astral experience, perhaps only vaguely remembered. The impression of that memory may stimulate the personality to turn completely away from one's previous life, or the contact may be so vague that the impression is too fleeting to make a lasting effect.

Many, relying upon the sacrifice of a savior, do not remain on the path. They neglect any powers which have been invested in them and they overlook any guidance which is at hand. The mystic, on the other hand, entering the major First Initiation, usually draws somewhat away from the life pattern hitherto established. The interests and activities which seemed so necessary for happiness now seem trivialities.

The Astarian Disciples of the Second Degree have certainly met and passed their First Initiation. Your continuing search for truth through Astarianry signals the fact that you have absorbed some measure of the light. If there is no conscious memory of an inner plane contact — the experience of an initiatory ceremony — it should not disturb you. Whether the conscious mind remembers or not, these events are all firmly implanted in the Oversoul.

Out of the study of the Degrees and meditation, the organs of functioning on the inner planes are developed. Inner sight is awakened, consciousness of higher levels of contact are unfolded, and gradually the Astarian is prepared for the Second Initiation.

For many seekers the First Initiation was taken when they first identified themselves with Astara. Seekers cannot become actively united with the light when they are halfheartedly drifting from book to book. Although they most certainly are seeking something that they cannot find, they cannot necessarily be said to be practicing mystics. However, when you identify yourself with a Mystery School you will have united yourself in spiritual fellowship with many traveling the same Path.

When you enter the study of the Degrees and persevere in your training, this in itself constitutes the passing of some elementary or minor degrees. You will be building the truth center in your brain, developing the powers of your soul, and increasing the purity of the physical form. You will be overcoming your hesitancy to speak of esoteric subjects. You will be developing the courage to stand in defense of principles you believe to be best and true. Whether you realize it or not, you will be unfolding the ability to carry spiritual responsibilities.

You may be aware of the slow expansion of your consciousness and the approach of your "new birth." You may be aware of a new sense of power and of upliftment as you witness its effect in your everyday life insofar as you yourself will permit it. You may be aware of a gradual transformation of your mental attitude and a reorganization of your daily program to include some form of spiritual practice.

You will most surely understand that the initiation ceremony itself is not one which transforms a disciple suddenly and miraculously into an adept. Discipleship is possible only through the efforts of the neophyte and adeptship is possible only through the efforts of the disciple. The powers of adeptship must be cultivated, and the ceremony itself is only recognition of the work previously performed.

The ceremony in itself does, however, crystallize the forces the disciple has developed. It further refines your intentions and matures your judgment. It is a finishing process, a graduation. Such a process is not possible unless there is innate material upon which to build the character of the initiate. The experiences of the disciple constitute a rich and stimulating background upon which the requisites of adeptship are built. Attainment of the initiation ceremony signifies that the highest qualities of leadership have been developed.

The initiate is certainly one who has passed through many sorts of experiences. It is no discredit if the neophyte stages have been difficult ... if the physical life has been a struggle.

The Second Degree Astarian realizes full well that initiation does not imply that the initiate direct the lives of his/her fellow beings, nor criticize their actions. You are aware that your course is to further the cause of spiritual unfoldment, and to act in such a way as to promote spiritual values in the world around you.

Initiation is the recognition received for having qualified for higher service. The formative years on the Path are like an apprenticeship which each neophyte serves in order to be given the privilege of Mastership when the novitiate has been completed.

It is natural for the neophyte to desire to improve and develop. Sometimes this desire is frivolous and fickle. It does not spring from the innermost depths and is not sufficiently compelling to withstand the steps of the upward journey.

On the other hand, when the desire is born of karmic influences and experiences and is fired by the divine aspiration for adeptship, then it stimulates, encourages and energizes until, governed by will power, it bodily lifts itself from mundane conditions to a higher plane. From that plane it progresses still further, ever onward and upward until it reaches the degree of spirituality equal to that of the Logos Itself.

The cycle is from materiality to spirituality; from the mundane to the abstract; from the physical body to the etheric, and on upward. Awareness is away from self-centeredness to God-centeredness. Initiation is that estate in which the individual consciousness is made to transcend its own boundaries to harmonize with and enhance universal consciousness.

Initiation and the development that leads thereto is never forced upon any soul. Such development only occurs as each soul indicates a willingness to receive enlightenment, to expend the energy and concentration necessary to develop it, and to utilize inner plane force efficiently and sympathetically when it is bestowed. To understand this divine force is to acknowledge it as supreme, and to respect and revere it.

Initiation breaks the shell of ignorance and darkness, of mistrust, suspicion, avarice and greed. Seeking outside the narrow objective consciousness, you find your source of inspiration. You find also a stimulated desire for the accumulation of knowledge. You find growing within you the divine impetus to reach for wisdom. You find you are often fed with the satisfying spiritual food of the inner planes, as it conditions your efforts and your actions.

Initiation leads ultimately to consecration, a seeking of forces which we know to be greater than ourselves. The Disciple of the Second Degree realizes that the higher initiations come only after the qualities, the character, the faithfulness of the seeker have been well proven, and you realize the veils of illusion must be removed by yourself, not by any other.

Initiation signals the unfoldment of many talents. Initiation, in identifying the personality with the Oversoul, releases a flood of hitherto restricted forces. Through their release the initiate realizes that his/her mental faculties are capable of divine action; that through the process of initiation the release of infinite power is made possible, and consciousness is more closely identified with Universal Mind.

In truth the Holy Spirit *does* descend upon the initiate!

THE SECOND INITIATION

The Second Initiation may be marked by actual physical experience — a sudden illumination — an expansion of consciousness which bathes the mind in light; which releases the power of the mental seed atom.

Such a spiritual baptism erases many carnal weaknesses and floods the entire being with spiritual dynamics. It may be a slow process, as a child gradually grows into adulthood, or it can be an apparently sudden process — the final leap into spiritual maturity being attained in this one lifetime after many previous lives of slower spiritual evolvement.

However, just as a child cannot become an adult overnight, neither can the spiritually immature become spiritually mature instantly, though a sudden flash of superconscious illumination may make it appear so. Astarians who attain sudden Realization must understand that, even though they do not remember them, they have spent previous lives growing into that spiritual maturity.

There is this difference: a child has no control over the length of time required to become an adult, whereas the soul always has under its own control its personal progress and spiritual evolvement. You can traverse the slow path of human evolution and eventually attain Divine Realization or you can, through your own spiritual efforts, gain your spiritual maturity more rapidly.

A seed planted in the ground pushes its shoots upward to find the light of the sun. The mental seed atom buried in the pineal does the same, once it is stimulated into a cosmic explosion by the power of the White Light. It begins to grow upward through the sutratma and the antahkarana, piercing each of the layers of the planes until it finds the sun of the Monadic Plane, the true plane of light. For its ultimate purpose is to grow to maturity just as the purpose of any other seed is its upward growth toward the sun.

The mental seed atom is the seed of the mind planted in the soil of the brain. And it breaks through the barriers of matter, just as a flower breaks through the earth, bringing illumination and spiritual maturity to the one whose mind is so unfolded.

RESULT OF THE SECOND INITIATION:
SPLITTING THE MENTAL ATOM

How science struggled to split the atom! — and with destruction the original intent! On the other hand, consider the staggering spiritual possibilities when the soul learns how to split the mental seed atom of its mind and use it for constructive purposes!

Splitting the mental atom is the goal of every individual soul and can be achieved only by itself with the help of no outsider. This is truly "walking the lonesome valley," for no one can "go there" with you ... no one else can help you accomplish this purpose, this mission. Splitting the mental atom brings to birth the Divine Spirit within, and each soul must struggle with this birth alone, utterly alone.

Consider the tremendous machinery necessary to split a single physical atom. Consider also what is involved for each soul to split its own mental atom in the pineal gland. What building it must accomplish also! Not tremendous structures designed to divide a physical atom, but "machinery" within itself which will equip it to handle the tremendous, soul-shaking "explosion" which occurs inwardly when the soul splits the seed atom of its mind.

Building this gigantic cosmic machinery requires what is called great sacrifice — giving up many physical pleasures and directing the soul's mental energies toward spiritual attainment.

Cyclotron

Splitting the mental atom

SPLITTING THE MENTAL ATOM

Tremendous machinery is involved in splitting a physical atom. You must build "machinery" within yourself which will equip you to handle the soul-shaking "explosion" which will occur when you split the seed atom of your mind. The "heat" needed for this explosion is a cosmic fire, released only through the spirit and the soul.

The tremendous heat necessary to split the mental atom is a cosmic fire, released only through the spirit and the soul. This fire can never burn before the idol of mammon. Each soul must forsake the lower path and tread the path of God-Realization. Lighting and nourishing the cosmic fire can be done only as one attains immersion in the stream of divine Sound, the Holy Nahd.

Merging with this Sound can set the soul aflame with cosmic fire which, burning in the brain, can bring the "explosion" that shatters the mental atom and releases the wisdom of the gods.

Splitting the mental atom, the attainment of divine illumination, cannot be achieved without a downpouring of the pure light from above. And it is this light, this grace, pouring down from the Father-Mother, that brings the supreme bliss. No soul attains it until some part of it dies ... until some part of its life in the carnal forcefields of physical substance bursts through the limitations set by the world of matter to explode in the realms of the infinite.

The one who attains the Father-Mother's grace does not simply suppress their carnality. He or she overcomes it.

Exploding the mental atom results in illumination, or union with the Father-Mother in heaven. We could well call the process a matter of divine-human chemistry. The atomic structure of the physical form must be raised in vibration. The atomic structure of the brain must speed up its vibratory rate through spiritual practice and unfoldment.

Vibratory increase in the atoms of the brain sets into motion the law of attraction. The magnetic quality of the attraction, which is created by an intense desire for God, brings down divine bliss, a definite matter of chemistry: a change in the atomic structure ... a change in the atoms ... a speeding up of the atoms ... an increased velocity. The bliss turns on a "light" inside the brain, flooding it as an electric light switched on suddenly illuminates a darkened room.

Simple? It can be. But it requires spiritualized mental power directed toward the mental atom. Directing mental energies toward this atom, and focusing the light ray of the mind upon it, can set it afire just as a sunbeam focused upon paper through a magnifying glass can set it ablaze.

Stimulation of the mental atom: this is the secret. The disciple must strive to bring down that "heat" — that light. No soul can do it without inner seeking.

The initiate must attempt to send his/her mindforce soaring inward and upward to pierce the eddying currents of consciousness to attain the core of the mental forcefield. Comparing the swirling, raging mental currents around the brain with a cyclone, the situation of the mental atom in the heart of the pineal could well be compared to the "eye" of a cyclone which lies in peaceful repose while all around it the turbulence rages.

It is this inner core of the mental cyclone that the disciple attempts to reach. If you can "fly your mental airplane" through the currents of the mind cyclone and reach this inner core of tranquility, you will find your consciousness falling away from self to be embraced by Self.

The heart of the mental cyclone is where Reality is found. So long as your conscious mind goes galloping after things and places, time and space, you cannot merge with the divine Life Stream. Only when you have stilled the outer consciousness and sent your mind currents plunging inward to the inner core can you attain God-Realization.

The Astarian may find the inward way of initiation to be the path of Lama Yoga. This is certainly one path which brings you to the accomplishment of this splitting of the mental atom. Centering all your mental powers in concentration upon the Third Eye, you drive your mental forces inward to the heart of the divine Stream. Practicing this intense concentration upon one point over and over must ultimately result in attainment. Certainly the path of meditation, other forms of yoga, and spiritual study can accomplish the same thing if it is accompanied by intense focus on spiritual advancement firing the divine spark of light within you.

This intense concentration automatically pulls upward the energies of the generative centers, which are usually stopped at the medulla oblongata. These energies so necessary for ultimate attainment are blocked from entering the brain until you, through intense mental effort, open the door of "the temple," allowing the transmuted spinal gases to flood the brain ventricles.

Mind must give way to Love, for only Love possesses the Lost Word which opens the doorway to the Holy of Holies. Mind must become humble. Mind must surrender to Love. Those who say, "mind is all," say this only because they have never attained Love. Love is God. And without Love nothing really is.

When mind has surrendered to Love, one must be still and wait for the downpouring grace to come. You must reach up, not with your arms but with your mind, your emotions, your heart and soul. You must reach up in a way that stimulates the mental atom to such a vigorous state of vibration that the grace of God — the light and essence of Love — downpours into your mind and penetrates the cells of your brain. It is this downpouring, responding to your upreaching, which splits the mental atom and sends its tremendous power exploding through the mind and the brain like an atomic bomb explodes when the physical atom is split.

THE ANTAHKARANA AND ILLUMINATION

Does this expansion of consciousness mean that the antahkarana suddenly projects upward to pierce the Oversoul or the Wisdom Mind in these rare moments of illumination only to drop again to a state of normalcy? Indeed it means just that — for how else explain these experiences in ecstasy?

When the disciple, pursuing spiritual studies, attains the Second Initiation, s/he may certainly experience a temporary extension of the antahkarana. It may only reach the Oversoul, which in itself brings an indescribable state of enlightenment. But the temporary expansion may even attain the realm of the Wisdom Mind. The initiate, experiencing a downpouring of the bliss, is baptized in the waters of Divine Substance as they carry him or her to the heights of spiritual ecstasy.

It is this spiritual baptism which "washes away" humanity's karmic debts. It is this baptism — not submerging the physical form in water — which is humankind's salvation from our "fall;" which places us "outside the stain of original sin" and assures us a place in heaven. Fundamentalist Christian theologians teach that we must accept Christ as our personal savior because he died to save us from our sins. One step of this "acceptance" is submission to baptism by the church which, they teach, purifies us and thereafter shifts all our karma to the Christ, placing the burden of our redemption upon him.

But this is not the baptism of the Second Initiation. After studying the Second Degree and attaining inner plane unfoldment, the Astarian understands that your salvation is indeed through baptism — but not by the water of Earth, which is only symbolic of the inner baptism. Rather it is one in which you must so purify yourself as to be worthy of the downpouring "saving blood" of the Divine Substance. After this rare moment of spiritual baptism subsides, the antahkarana — like mercury in a thermometer — recedes again to its normal position.

In the expanded state of the Second Initiation the disciple realizes what the Christ meant when he said, "I and my Father are one."

THE REWARDS OF THE SECOND INITIATION

Let us observe the initiate who, following his or her Second Initiation, experiences momentary luminous heights of consciousness. Let us consider the rewards of this self-transcendence, this mounting up to the summit of human consciousness. This is the initiate who can tune in to the divine Word, who can sit in indescribable moments of superhuman experience, listening to the divine Sound.

But of what practical purpose is such an achievement in your everyday affairs? There is a universal misconception about the accomplishments gained by the soul who attains Self-realization, and the good it spreads abroad in a needy world. Those who misunderstand, voice the complaint that it is of no earthly purpose to sit in meditation by the hour while the world languishes in woe.

If the trance produced only personal revelations this protest would be valid, but this is by no means true. The purpose is to develop a dynamic power, an unfoldment of wisdom that can make the initiate a bridge between the world in need and the world of light.

The one who attains union with divine Sound is well on one's way toward gaining knowledge which, distributed to the world, will make it a better place; who is developing a tremendous power that will flow like a river from him or her to all of life on Earth.

It must be remembered that the entire purpose of being is to dwell permanently on the highest summit of human consciousness. To reach it momentarily from time to time is enough at humanity's present stage of evolution. But the soul should be lifting itself toward this sublime level of consciousness as a permanent state.

The Second Initiation brings an understanding that the little "I" is the self of maya or illusion, while the Oversoul is the real Self; that the small self is veiled with matter, while the Oversoul is a repository of divine light.

Our present purpose is to unite with the Oversoul. It is enough that we realize that the Monad still exists beyond the Oversoul, but that attainment is beyond our present comprehension. Suffice for the moment to strive for union with the Oversoul. You are never the same after the Second Initiation, after splitting the mental atom. The resulting "fallout" of such an explosion is too much a part of you. It changes your life. The radiation, the power, seeps into your very being, like ink into a blotter. No solution can remove the ink. No power on Earth can dissolve the effects of the spiritual fallout. The soul is drenched in it and diffused with it. This is the Pentecostal Power which "saves." We, of course, realize that terms like "fallout" have a negative connotation. We are using them to extend our metaphor to help make this concept clearer and mean them here only in extremely positive ways.

This divine Substance contains all the gradations of lesser energies, just as White Light contains, undetected, all the gradations of lesser light. All colors are combined in white and only become discernible when separated by a prism. Permeating the aura, this White Light is breathed into and distributed through the bloodstream, purifying and transforming the heart and mind.

Although outwardly unchanged, the baptized has been inwardly reborn. You have experienced a second birth — "born again," orthodox Christianity calls it. But we mean it in its higher, mystical sense. The Divine Spirit is conceived in the head — a miraculous conception. And like a fetus growing in a mother's womb, the spiritual fetus of the Divine Child begins to grow. It spreads like a vine through the physical form, gradually penetrating the glandular system, the nervous system, the bloodstream — unseen, like spreading underground roots. Little by little the divinity within transforms the initiate, clothing the soul with its essence of divinity.

You who have awakened this Divine Spirit within yourself feel the difference. Your soul is at peace, cradled in the radiance of light. If you seem to react with outward emotions, in your heart you are divinely unattached to irritating frustrations. You are not like others, interested only in affairs of Earth. You do remain active in improving the situations of Earth however, bringing to your efforts a spiritual understanding.

You feel an aloneness that cannot be explained ... not necessarily a loneliness but an aloneness. You are not really lonely, except in a cosmic sense, because you are never alone again. The Divine Spirit is always with you, a part of you. You walk in quiet inner majesty, even though outwardly you may seem to remain the same. You eat, you laugh, you sleep, you work, but the days of your life have taken on a new meaning. You live in an aura of silent prayer that God will hold you patient with earthly limitations and frustrations. You face your problems as you know you must, but your days on Earth are never completely fulfilled because you are a stranger here. Your soul longs for "home," wherever that may be.

You love life, you love home, you love family ... but most of all you love God. You yearn for the time in the swing of eternal events when you and those you love will have passed beyond the limitations of Earth and the mists that blind us here, into the higher spheres. It is there that you know your higher destiny lies, even though you turn your hand to accomplish a worthy mission in the world of humankind. Although your soul strains sometimes against the waiting, outwardly you never rebel because you realize it is Divine will that your devotion be, in part, directed to those who have need of life's experiences on Earth.

You spend many a moment asking the Mother/Father to stay close, to send you inspiration, and above all to help you accomplish the work you came to do. Though your body is busy with the duties of the daily round, your soul is always in prayer, for divine grace for your own unfoldment and for the blessing of all of life. Though you are *on* the Earth you are not *of* it in the same way you once were.

Whether you are poor or whether you live in great wealth, you feel that you are in want because no matter how many "things" you acquire you never have enough of the inward treasures to completely satisfy your spiritual needs. There is always the inner hunger.

But the soul who never so hungers for God will be satisfied with life's spiritual "crumbs." Such a soul cannot know the joy the soul experiences once the Divine Spirit has been born within. It may gain the wealth of the world, but lose the treasures of the soul — the only lasting wealth of a life on Earth.

THE LIGHT AHEAD

Although the disciple of the Second Degree may not have attained the Second Initiation, you are certainly well on the Way. You have passed through the initial stages of development from the first step of curious interest to actual awakening. You have proven your endurance, your courage and your sincerity.

The question before the Second Degree Astarian is whether or not you wish to prepare yourself for initiations beyond the First.

The Third Degree will begin to cultivate the quality of the mind so that it begins to automatically reject superfluous ideas and thoughts. Enrolling in the Third Degree, you will realize you have taken a giant step forward.

Just as a child must maintain a certain average in school if s/he expects to pass to a higher grade, so does the Second Degree Astarian feel an inner compulsion to maintain his/her grasp of truth. The child realizes that in order to graduate, s/he must at least possess a rudimentary knowledge of the subjects under study. So it is with training for the Second Initiation. The initiate cannot expect to enter the higher initiations if s/he has not absorbed at least a partial degree of wisdom.

Possessing a deep desire for major initiations will not necessarily culminate in that attainment, any more than does the happy expectancy of the child in school necessarily assure its passing to the next grade. Coupled with his/her desire and anticipation, the child must prove its ability.

Although in attaining major initiations we are not assigned particular subjects, nevertheless we must meet general qualifications. Initiation is not open to the untrained and undisciplined. To enter higher initiations, actual, active, direct study and meditation is half the training. Practical observance of life and the application of our training is the other half.

Passing the grades of initiation differs, however, from our educational system. An entire class of graduating students will receive the same token diploma signifying their ability. Some of the members of that class will have been poor students, some average, and some will have marked a brilliant record.

Initiates also possess varied qualifications in soul development. But soul development does not depend upon book learning. Some of the most highly developed initiates are not necessarily trained intellectually, scholastically, and academically. One person with a seemingly mediocre educational background will display a brilliant capacity for spiritual perception or philosophical understanding. Possessing little educational training, one may unfold the qualities of a saint.

On the other hand, competent scholars who have distinguished themselves in academic training, who also have attained apparent qualifications for higher initiations, still may find themselves without that sublime experience. Initiation is a matter of soul training, and only the Masters of the hierarchy can present the "diplomas" which mark the stages of "graduation" from one "grade" to another.

Certainly there is born in each Second Degree Astarian a feeling of exaltation and the certainty that one is at last treading the path that leads to more happiness, understanding and wisdom. Often the subconscious mind recognizes the path before the conscious mind is aware that actual progression has occurred.

This inner awareness of the right direction may come from the memory of a past life responding to subconscious recognition of familiar landmarks, or from uniting oneself with the group consciousness of other Astarians who reach always upward for more light.

YOU AND INITIATION

Disciple of the Emerald Cross, do you remember that day long ago when you first began your Degree studies? When you were asked to contemplate your image in a mirror? Will you repeat it now? Will you observe intently what your reflection indicates? Try to pierce the physical image and behold a reflection of your deeper Self. Have you changed since your first observation many months ago? Has your First Initiation brought a better change? Has your world within become a shrine, a place of worship? Has the process of living become a ritual of joy, or a submission to ordeals?

Do you feel — at this moment — like an initiate of the Mysteries? You are. As you begin to absorb the deeper meaning of the teachings, you will begin to know yourself as such. Your personal darkness will be rent asunder and the fleeting light will stabilize. The wisdom which can only come from the recess of the Oversoul will open out the hidden petals of the inner lotus and you will understand what it means to say OM MANI PADME HUM — "I am the jewel in the Lotus." For you will comprehend the endless, unquenchable love of the One whose immeasurable boundaries enfold us all.

(Continued on Page 22)

LESSON 2
The natural dissolution of the etheric web protecting the third eye allows recall of astral visitations and activities.

LESSON 8
The many layered magnetosphere surrounding our earth is symbolic of the invisible House of Many Mansions not built with hands.

LESSON 4
Is another world interpenetrating our own world, lying all about us, filled with conscious beings?

LESSON 5
Twelve planets? Lesson Five explains this coming phenomena — the evolution of our own planet and our purpose upon it.

LESSON 7
The earth is the forming place of the essences which form its surrounding spiritual spheres.

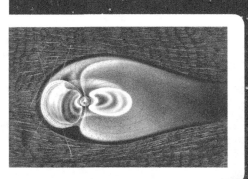

LESSON 10
In the initiate's
Otherworld, one
learns how to use
one's mind to
mold the tenuous
mental substance
to the betterment
of one's life.

LESSON 13
For the spiritually
enlightened, the Bardo
becomes the ultimate
Initiation into Light.

LESSON 12
The Clear Light
of Initiation at the
moment of death.

These illustrations are a sampling of
the wondrous teachings awaiting you in the
Third Degree

At this moment you stand on the summit
of achievement — completion of the Second
Degree — but before you are still grander
vistas of mysteries that lie ahead.

Truth never changes. Change happens only in the consciousness of humans as our minds unfold and are able to bear more light. Third Degree Astarians are very special people. They not only seek more light, but their understanding is considerably more profound — pointing toward wisdom.

The Third Degree will find us entering sacred studies indeed. We begin with searchings into the etheric form. We disclose how science has found a world of antimatter; how the spiritual planes are formed; how we build our future astral forms and future abodes. Then we enter the mysteries of death. We carry you into the death initiation completely, presenting Astara's *Book of the Dead,* a sacred rite to be performed at the moment of death. Then we begin our adventures into life in the higher realms.

It is my prayer that, in these writings, I have caught truth as God means it to be reflected into the minds of humanity in this, our day and time; that these teachings sustain those who seek wisdom through the Astarian Way until, some time hence, the Infinite Being sees fit to send another messenger who, carrying the torch still further, will reveal more of that which it is meant for us to know and understand.

Initiates: seek out other initiates. Seek your spiritual understanding, practice and unfoldment with the support of a community of like-minded seekers. Most of all: try to set an example of spiritual excellence in your daily life. Use what you know for the blessing and advancement of all of life, never for your own power and control over others.

You possess the formula for greatness. Use it well, initiate!

Hail! Disciple of the Second Degree!

Hail! Disciple of the Emerald Cross!

Selah!

Two universal symbols
have uplifted humankind
through the ages.

They've inspired and healed.

They've helped overcome ignorance
and strengthened the brokenhearted and weary.

The light — and the path.

On the path there is a magical power
that enables you to walk side by side,
hand in hand, with those who may at the same time
be ahead of or behind you.

The path is that mystical journey
each of us takes into the unknown —
passing alternately through momentary shadows
and divine rays of radiance.

It's the journey of your Self toward the goal
of spiritual wisdom and understanding.

The light is that flood of illumination
that appears unexpectedly in a dark hour,
or a puzzled moment.

Your consciousness suddenly possesses
ethereal buoyancy.

Enlightenment, either prosaic or spiritual,
lifts your entire being to a cosmic plane
where suddenly all is known,
healing energies are vitally potent,
and God is experienced.

You walk the path
and you seek the light in these Lessons.

To a greater or lesser degree
you've already experienced both.

The pages that follow take you
further upon that Grand Journey of the soul.

Follow the path.

Seek and keep the light.

An Astarian in need never walks alone.

This book is part of a series of eight books. Altogether they cover a large and comprehensive body of esoteric material gleaned from sacred texts, timeless philosophies and teachings of Great Masters as channeled through Astara's founders, Robert and Earlyne Chaney.

Each Degree book contains 22 Lessons covering some of the most important aspects of achieving spiritual understanding, oneness with self, raising self-awareness and initiating collective, universal and even cosmic consciousness.

For more information about the content of each Degree, about other books written by Robert and Earlyne Chaney, and about Astara as a metaphysical non-profit since its beginning in 1951, visit our website - www.astara.org

Made in United States
North Haven, CT
08 April 2023

35191928R00272